Praise for

Trading Commodities and Financial Futures, Third Edition

"Congratulations to George Kleinman for writing a comprehensive futures compendium that should be mandatory reading for anyone considering futures trading. Kleinman dispels the myth that the individual trader always loses against the Goliaths in the markets."

—Mary Cashman, Head of International Operations,
Global Commodity Intelligence

"Discipline and execution are the two most important and difficult aspects in trading. George Kleinman offers the solutions to the problems, and they are superb. Clear, crisp writing that will keep you reading and help you become a superior trader."

—Yiannis G. Mostrous, Editor, *Wall Street Winners*, Financial Advisory

"Without a doubt the best book I have read on the industry! Perfect for the novice speculator, yet comprehensive enough for the seasoned veteran to refer back to time and again. The trader who has been around awhile will enjoy reading the stories. Believe me, they are true!"

—Joseph M. Orlick, The Chicago Board of Trade

Trading Commodities and Financial Futures

Trading Commodities and Financial Futures

A Step-by-Step Guide to Mastering the Markets

George Kleinman

Vice President, Publisher: Tim Moore
Associate Publisher and Director of Marketing: Amy Neidlinger
Executive Editor: Jim Boyd
Editorial Assistant: Pamela Boland
Operations Specialist: Jodi Kemper
Marketing Manager: Megan Graue
Cover Designer: Alan Clements
Managing Editor: Kristy Hart
Project Editor: Jovana Shirley
Copy Editor: Kitty Wilson
Proofreader: Sheri Replin
Indexer: WordWise Publishing Services
Compositor: Gloria Schurick
Manufacturing Buyer: Dan Uhrig

Publishing as FT Press
Upper Saddle River, New Jersey 07458

Printed in the United States of America

First Printing: March 2013

ISBN-10: 0-13-336748-7
ISBN-13: 978-0-13-336748-5

Pearson Education LTD.
Pearson Education Australia PTY, Limited.
Pearson Education Singapore, Pte. Ltd.
Pearson Education Asia, Ltd.
Pearson Education Canada, Ltd.
Pearson Educación de Mexico, S.A. de C.V.
Pearson Education—Japan
Pearson Education Malaysia, Pte. Ltd.

The Library of Congress cataloging-in-publication data is on file.

To Sherri

Contents

Introduction 1

1 The Four Essentials 5

Do you have what it takes? / 7

Patience / 8

Knowledge / 8

Guts / 9

Health and rest / 9

2 How to Become a Successful Trader 11

3 A Diabolical Story 17

4 The Futures Primer 21

Futures markets and the futures contract / 22

It is as easy to sell "short" as to buy "long" / 26

Margin and leverage / 28

Delivery months 31

Brokers and commissions / 34

The players / 34

Basis risk / 36

The short hedge / 37

The long hedge / 38

The basis / 39

Speculators versus hedgers / 40

How is the price determined? / 40

Order placement / 41

Another true story / 44

5 The Options Course 45

An options primer / 45

An option for what? / 46

Advantages and disadvantages of options / 47

Types of options / 47

Strike prices / 48

Styles of options / 48

How are option prices quoted? / 48

Buy 'em and sell 'em / 49

Advantages and disadvantages of selling options / 49

How options work / 49

How are option prices determined? / 51

How changes in the price of the underlying commodity change an option's premium / 55

Exercising profitable options / 55

Should you ever exercise an option? / 56

If selling options puts the odds in my favor, why not do it? / 57

Options as a hedging tool / 59

Stock index options / 61

Advanced option strategies / 61

Straddles and strangles / 66

Ratios / 69

Eight winning option trading rules / 71

6 The Intermediate Trading Course (Or Just Enough Knowledge to Be Dangerous!) 75

Fundamental analysis / 76

Technical analysis / 76

Which is best: fundamental or technical analysis? / 77

The 4 futures groupings / 78

Financial futures / 78

Energies / 80

Agriculturals / 83

Metals / 102

Continuing your commodity trading education / 107

Contrary opinion theory / 109

Spreads / 110

7 Algorithms Eliminating People 115

Open outcry is dead / 117

Rogue algos / 118

Exploding volatility / 119

Speeds accelerating / 121

Melding the old with the new / 122

Panics, manias, and bubbles / 123

Explosive commodity demand / 124

8 The Advanced Trading Course 127

Fundamentals versus technicals / 127

Does technical analysis really work? / 128

The trend is your friend / 129

Basic chart analysis / 129

The trendline / 130

Trend channels / 134

Support and resistance / 136

Breakouts from consolidation / 137

Additional classic chart patterns / 144

Volume / 156

Open interest / 156

RSI / 159

Stochastics / 162

Elliot wave analysis / 163

Point and figure charts / 165

Japanese candlestick charts / 166

Spreads—a valuable forecasting tool / 167

Head and shoulders / 170

GK's significant news indicator / 177

Breaking par / 186

9 The Moving Averages Primer 193

Bottom pickers versus trend followers / 193

A moving picture / 195

The simple moving average / 197

How many days should you use in your moving average? / 199

Alternatives to the SMA / 199

Exponential and weighted moving averages / 200

Natural numbers / 203

10 GK's Pivot Indicator 205

Generating the buy signal / 206

Generating the sell signal / 208

The pivot indicator method in practice / 210

Diversification / 216

11 And Finally 219

Determining your motive / 219

Overcoming the six hurdles to trading success / 220

Developing the winning touch / 223

If you don't feel right, you won't trade right / 225

Jesse's secret / 225

Comments or questions? / 228

Appendix: 25 Trading Secrets of the Pros 229

Secret 1: The trend is your friend! / 229

Secret 2: When a market is cheap or a market is expensive, there probably is a good reason / 230

Secret 3: The best trades are the hardest to do / 231

Secret 4: Have a plan before you trade and then work it / 231

Secret 5: Be aggressive / 232

Secret 6: No regrets / 232

Secret 7: Money management is the key / 232

Secret 8: Success comes easier when you specialize / 232

Secret 9: Patience pays / 233

Secret 10: Guts are as important as patience and more important than money / 233

Secret 11: The "tape" (quotes) will trick you / 233

Secret 12: Be skeptical / 234

Secret 13: Be time cognizant / 234

Secret 14: Watch the reaction to "the news" / 235

Secret 15: Never trade when you're sick, worried, or tired / 236

Secret 16: Overtrading: your greatest enemy / 236

Secret 17: Keep a cool head during blow-offs / 236

Secret 18: Never let a good profit turn into a loss / 237

Secret 19: When in doubt, get out / 237

Secret 20: Spread your risks by diversification / 237

Secret 21: Pyramid the correct way / 237

Secret 22: Watch for breakouts from consolidation / 238

Secret 23: Go with the relative strength / 239

Secret 24: Limit moves are important indicators of support and resistance / 239

Secret 25: Never average a loss / 240

Index 241

Important Risk Disclosures

Before you trade with real money, familiarize yourself with the risks.

Commodity futures trading is speculative and involves substantial risks, and you should only invest risk capital.

You can lose a substantial amount or all your investment, and you should carefully consider whether such trading is suitable for you in light of your financial condition.

The high degree of leverage that is obtainable in commodity trading can work against you as well as for you, and the use of leverage can lead to large losses as well as large gains.

If the market moves against your position, to maintain your position, you may on short notice be called upon by your broker to deposit additional margin money. If funds are requested, and you do not provide them within the prescribed time, your position may be liquidated at a loss, and you will be liable for any resulting deficit in your account. Under certain market conditions, you may find it difficult or impossible to liquidate a position. This can occur, for example, when the market makes a "limit move." The placement of contingent orders, such as a "stop-loss" or "stop-limit" order, will not necessarily limit your losses to the intended amount.

There is no guarantee that the concepts presented in this book will generate profits or avoid losses.

Past results are not necessarily indicative of future results.

Acknowledgments

My sincere thanks to these former pit traders whose stories made for entertaining and informative contributions to this work: William G. Salatich, Jr., from the cattle pit, Joe Orlick from the corn pit, and Joseph Santagata and James Gallo from the copper pit. Thanks to my editors at Pearson—Jim Boyd, Jovana Shirley, and Kitty Wilson—for making my thoughts flow much better. Jim, thank you for persuading me to do this latest edition. I did the best I could, and the result is the best to date. Thanks to the people at CQG who made the charts possible. Thanks to my best clients, who choose to put up with me, and my beloved wife, Sherri, who has no choice.

About the Author

George Kleinman is the president of Commodity Resource Corp., a futures advisory and trading firm that assists individual traders and corporate hedgers. George has a track record of success in the commodity futures business that spans more than 30 years.

A graduate of Ohio State, with an MBA from Hofstra University, George entered the commodity trading business with Merrill Lynch Commodities in 1979. When he left Merrill to start his own trading firm, George was a member of "The Golden Circle" (the top 10 commodity brokers internationally).

From 1983 to 1995, Commodity Resource was located on the trading floor of the Minneapolis Grain Exchange, where George held multiple memberships and served on the MGE board of directors. George was also a member of the COMEX Exchange for over a decade.

George has been featured for his trading in national publications and has lectured at major financial conferences regarding his trading techniques. He is the author of four previous books on commodities and futures trading and is an active trader for clients as well as his own account. George has developed his own proprietary trading techniques, some of which are highlighted in this edition. He can be reached via email at gkleinman1@mac.com.

In 1995, George and his family moved to northern Nevada, and he now trades from an office overlooking beautiful Lake Tahoe.

Introduction

"It is not the strongest of the species that survives, nor the most intelligent. It is the one that is the most adaptable to change."
—Charles Darwin

New York's oldest commodity exchange, the New York Cotton Exchange, was established in 1870. For over a century, traders packed the cotton trading pit. They would discuss weather and crop reports, and they would make and lose fortunes. On a rainy Friday, October 19, 2012, the floor traders in cotton (as well as in coffee, cocoa, sugar, and orange juice) donned their trading jackets and yelled out their bids and offers for the last time. You see, this was the final day of "open-outcry" trading. The following Monday, for the first time since 1870, every trade in these markets was matched by computers.

I found this passing of an era sad. The best stories in this book emanate from the days of the floor traders. Human stories make for more entertaining reading than rogue computer algorithms (which is why I kept them in this edition).

Critics of electronic trading tell us that the old days of the pits added order to the markets. A professional market maker standing in the pit would observe the order flow in terms of the news, and he or she would take the other side of excessive speculative order flow. This made for a more orderly market environment. Many of the computer programs don't even look at the news but monitor the order book in milliseconds to hop on for a ride. Liquidation works in a similar manner, as the computers scramble to exit. Stops are hit, generating margin calls, causing more liquidation as it all feeds on itself. Having no professional market maker leads to vacuums and overextended moves because fewer players are available to take the other side of momentum. When the vacuum is finally filled, the move back in the opposite direction is just as frenzied.

I admit I'm sentimental for the days of the pit traders. I dealt with them most of my trading life, but we have no choice other than to move forward and adapt to change in order to survive. In the words of Ayn Rand, "You can ignore the reality but you cannot ignore the consequences of an ignored reality."

Today's electronic markets are like a battlefield. In the words of Napoleon Bonaparte, "The battlefield is a scene of constant chaos. The winner will be the one who controls that chaos, both his own and the enemy's."

Today, there is more chaos than ever before. Speed and volume have combined to make the markets more volatile than they've ever been in the past. This chaos is cleverly programmed—not by traders but by engineers. I've always been good in math, but introductory calculus was the extent of my academic math training. Today's programmers code formulas similar to the one shown in Figure I.1—only much more complicated. (The example shown in Figure I.1 is a relatively simple trading formula, now 10 years obsolete.)

$$E\left[S_i \mid t\right] = P_n(t)S_i^* + P_b(t)\underline{S_i} + P_g(t)\overline{S_i}$$

$$B(t) = E\left[S_i \mid t\right] - \frac{\mu P_b(t)}{\varepsilon + \mu P_b(t)}\left[E\left[S_i \mid t\right] - \underline{S_i}\right]$$

$$A(t) = E\left[S_i \mid t\right] + \frac{\mu P_g(t)}{\varepsilon + \mu P_g(t)}\left[\overline{S_i} - E\left[S_i \mid t\right]\right]$$

$$\Sigma(t) = \frac{\mu P_g(t)}{\varepsilon + \mu P_g(t)}\left[\overline{S_i} - E\left[S_i \mid t\right]\right] + \frac{\mu P_b(t)}{\varepsilon + \mu P_b(t)}\left[E\left[S_i \mid t\right] - \underline{S_i}\right]$$

Figure I.1 A "simple" trading formula

After the formulas are constructed and coded, they're fed into sophisticated trading computers that cost millions of dollars. Many of these computers are actually located in the Exchange building for a speed advantage proximity that you and I will never have. With technology evolving seemingly at the speed of light, how will we ever compete with these folks? The simple answer is that we won't (nor do I want to), nor do we have to. That's not to say adjustments from the days of the pits are unnecessary. As traders, we have all had to adjust our methods to the new market realities in stocks and commodity futures. In this book, I've used the KISS ("keep it simple, stupid") method. I know I'm nowhere near as smart as the computer wizards, but in the words of the great Homer Simpson: "Stupidity got us into this mess, and stupidity will get us out!"

I'm not going to blame today's heightened volatility totally on computerized trading. It also has to do with central banks, government policies, global uncertainty, and instant dissemination of information. The newest variable, however, is the computers replacing the pit traders. Previously, "news days" were volatile, but now we see volatility just about every day. We now receive instant fills, which is a good thing, but in the process, the Internet has created a dog-eat-dog trading world. We need to get used to this because it's not going away. The good news is that the more extreme the moves, the better it is for the trend-following methods I present to you in the following pages. In this book, one of my goals is to provide you with strategies designed to help you capture your share of the profit pool.

As an old-time trader once told me, the key to success in trading is "Slow and steady wins the race." This requires calmness at all times, which is not always easy to obtain, but a systematic approach will help. With that said, I can almost guarantee that you'll stray from your original plan at times because you're human.

So, the pit trader has gone the way of the dodo bird, the eight-track tape, and the VCR. Still, despite all the changes, much has remained the same. The markets have dramatically changed in certain respects, and I've addressed these changes in this revised edition. In my first 30 years in this business, there was nothing I can recall akin to "banging the beehive" (a strategy in which high-speed traders send a flood of orders just prior to the release of a major report, milliseconds before the data is released, in an effort to trigger huge price swings). Yet, the markets have remained the same in the respect that human beings, with their emotions (particularly fear and greed), are ultimately behind all the transactions. Today, there are what can be termed "synthetic" as opposed to "real" moves. While there may be chaos in the millisecond, in the longer run, the basic fundamentals of supply and demand affect commodity prices in the same ways they did for hundreds of years. And there are times that computers get stung "banging the beehive;" they whack each other. You and I don't have to participate right before major reports are released; we have the ability to wait for that fat pitch, that fastball into our sweet spot.

In 1951, the legendary trader W.D. Gann said, "The tape moves in mysterious ways, the multitude to deceive." And in 1923, Jesse Livermore said, "It is literally true millions come easier to a trader after he knows how to trade, than hundreds did in the days of his ignorance."

My primary goal in this new edition is to help you navigate the shark-infested trading waters to avoid the sharks.

George Kleinman
Lake Tahoe, Nevada

The Four Essentials

"It's tough to make predictions...especially about the future."
—Yogi Berra

A floor broker once told me the following story, and he swears it's true:

> In the 1960s, there was a corn speculator who traded in the pit at the Chicago Board of Trade. He was known for plunging: taking big positions.
>
> Early one summer, he put on a large *short* corn position for his own account. (Short positions make money if prices fall but lose if prices rise.)
>
> Within days, the weather began to heat up in the midwestern United States, where the corn is grown. The corn crop needed rain, and prices began to rise. Day after day, the sun shone, the temps rose, not a cloud in the sky—the corn crop was burning up. The market continued to rally against this guy, and he knew if this continued, he'd go broke.
>
> Late one trading session, the big trader started a rumor in the corn pit. His rumor was that it was going to start raining the next morning sometime around 10:30 a.m. The other traders laughed at this prediction.
>
> The following morning, the sun was shining without a cloud in the sky, and the market opened higher once again. Then, almost miraculously, at precisely 10:30 a.m., rain started pouring down the windows that surrounded the grain trading room. (The old grain room, located on the fourth floor of the Chicago Board of Trade Building, had tall windows that looked out over La Salle Street.) Inside, in the corn pit, a selling panic immediately developed, as the pit traders scrambled to sell out their corn futures. Traders around the world saw prices crashing and joined in the selling frenzy. The market quickly went down the limit! On this break, the speculator covered his entire short position and was saved from bankruptcy.
>
> How did the floor broker know it would rain at 10:30 that morning? It seems he was owed a favor from his drinking buddy, the chief of the Chicago Fire Department. The chief brought out the hook and ladders, and decided it was a good day to wash those tall windows that looked out on La Salle Street!

So you're thinking of trading, but you don't know the chief of the Chicago Fire Department? Actually, today, even if you do know him, it wouldn't matter much because computer traders from tens of thousands of locations globally have replaced the pit traders, and computers don't care about the weather.

So, let's assume you've just finished reading a private newsletter, a firsthand report of how the "witch's tail disease" is devastating the cocoa crop in Ghana. Cocoa sounds like a moneymaker, but you have no way of knowing for sure how true all this is. You do like chocolate, but you didn't even know it all starts with a bean called the cocoa bean. (You thought it came out of a can.) Hey, you don't even know where Ghana is, and you're thinking of trading cocoa against the likes of Hershey and Nestlé and whoever else really does know what's going on? Why would you do this? To make money, of course!

You do know one thing: You can observe that the cocoa market is moving higher, and it's moving fast. Although you aren't exactly losing money by doing nothing, it's starting to feel that way. Do you have the guts to act? Do you have the money? Is now the time?

You assume that the shorts (those betting on lower cocoa prices) are beginning to experience financial pain. The longs (those betting on higher cocoa prices) are experiencing the opposite emotions: elation and the satisfaction that comes from being right. The accounts of the longs are growing bigger—money from nothing. The shorts are watching their money evaporate.

Let's think about this for a moment, because it's time for your first lesson: Even though trades are now entered using computers, trading is a human game. As a result, emotions affect price as much as, or perhaps more than, the news. You will learn that price movements themselves affect future price movements. It's all a function of who is being hurt and who is benefiting. It's a function of which side of the market is being "sponsored" by the "strong hands." Shorts and longs act differently, based on price movements, and those movements affect their emotions as much as their pocketbooks.

Your job as a trader is to identify what happens next. To do that, I want you to start thinking about how others feel because feelings affect actions. People who are generally right tend to do certain things (on balance). People who are generally wrong tend to act differently. The majority acts a certain way, but be warned: The majority is usually wrong at major turning points (although they also can be right at times).

So, determine whether the majority is now long or short cocoa. The shorts are in pain, the longs are not; but then again, this can change just as fast as the market's tone changes.

Here's lesson number two: On balance, when talking about futures trading, the uninformed majority will lose. Because the profitable minority act in a completely different manner, you must learn what makes these people tick and how to act like them. One fact is certain: People make markets and, generally, people tend to act the way they did in the past. With certain stimuli, they could act opposite how they generally act, but you are playing the odds here. You need to identify what manner of move the market is in now. Is it a "normal" move, or is it extraordinary? (At times, the market acts in an extraordinary manner, and these can be the best times to play.) If you, as a trader, are able to accurately predict what the next pattern will be, your rewards will be substantial.

In this book, I present various methods designed to identify profitable market patterns. No method is foolproof, and the best I can do is try to put the odds in your favor. My goal is to teach you to approach commodity futures and options trading like a business. This is not a casino. In a casino, risk is artificially manufactured for risk's sake, and the odds are engineered in favor of the house. In the commodity futures and options markets, you are dealing with natural risks associated with the production and consumption of the materials that make life possible and worthwhile—food, metals, financial products, and energy. You cannot bend these risks to your will, but you do have tools to manage them. Unlike in a casino, in the market, I believe you can move the odds to your side of the table. To do this, you must be disciplined.

You will need patience, and you will need guts. I cannot force these qualities upon you, but I can describe how a successful trader acts. It will then be up to you to act the right way. To profit in the commodity futures and options markets, you will need a systematic approach, a well-thought-out strategy. I will present you with some good ideas, but it's up to you to implement them systematically. After all, a strategy is just a consistent approach to trading.

Do you have what it takes?

If you've decided to risk some of your hard-earned cash, go for the big bucks, and trade commodities, you need to know that this is a zero-sum game—that is, for every dollar someone makes, someone else loses it. Some of the money goes to your commodity broker in the form of commissions, and a small amount goes to the Exchanges for their fees. Then, if you are lucky or skillful enough to win, you owe the taxman some of your profits. When you lose on any particular trade, most of your loss is transferred electronically to someone else's account (and you still pay that commission). You will never see this person on the other side of your trade, but he (or she) is out there somewhere.

You will be pitted against some of the best financial minds in the world. Professional traders, hedge fund managers, commercial firms that use commodities, and other commercial firms that produce commodities. Then there are those other individuals with more experience than you have. Can you hope to compete? The answer is, emphatically, yes! But I didn't say it would be easy, did I? You will need to develop a sensible trading plan and a feel for the markets. This book will help you. You must develop certain human qualities, too, which nobody can give to you.

More than 50 years ago, the legendary speculator W.D. Gann discussed the four qualities essential for trading success: patience, knowledge, guts, and health and rest. Gann's observations are just as valid today as they were half a century ago, and trust me, you must have these qualities if you ever hope to compete and win. (If you don't have them now, then develop them!)

Patience

According to Gann, patience is the most important of the essential qualities for trading success. A good trader possesses the patience to wait for the right opportunity. If you are a good trader, you will not be over-anxious, because over-anxiousness consumes capital and, over time, will tap you out. When you are fortunate enough to catch a good trade, you need the patience to hold it when it starts to move your way. Perhaps the primary failing of the amateur is to close out a profitable position too soon. In other words, patience is required for both opening and closing a position. Hope and fear need to be eliminated. Gann tells us if you are in a profitable position, instead of fearing that the profit will turn into a loss, you should hope it becomes more profitable. You have a cushion to work with in this case. When you are in a losing position, instead of hoping it will turn around, you should fear that it will get worse. If you see no definitive change in trend, use your essential quality of patience and just wait.

Knowledge

The stakes are high, and the competition is intense. You need a well-thought-out and thoroughly researched trading plan before you begin, and you need to do your homework. Your plan should always have a mechanism to cut the losses on the bad trades and to maximize profits aggressively on the good ones. You must be organized and remain focused at all times. If your plan is a good one, you need the consistency to stick with it during down periods.

My personal goal is to make money daily, but that is not always possible, so I try not to lose too much on losing days. It is a constant trial to maintain the vigilance necessary to not to let good judgment lapse. If you are a novice, it makes sense to "paper trade" before you trade for real. If you are trading currently, you should keep a logbook. Log your triumphs and your failures. You want to avoid making the same mistakes again, but I must warn you, all traders repeat mistakes. At the very least, learn not to make the mistakes so often. By keeping a record of what you do right and what you do wrong, you can identify areas of weakness and areas of strength. If you are not totally prepared on any given day, don't trade. You can't "wing it" in this business because the competition will eat you up. Over time, you will develop what I call a "trader's sense." You will know when a trade doesn't feel right, and when this happens, the prudent thing to do is to step aside. You cannot ignore the danger signals, and when they occur, you must act without hesitation. You must have a game plan and stick to it, but the paradox here is that you also need to be flexible. At times, it is best to do nothing, and you need to fight the urge to play for every pot. And, as I said before, stay focused. At times, I've been distracted by day trades and missed the big move because I missed the big picture. By the time I finally saw the light, it was too late.

Jesse Livermore, the legendary trader of the 1920s, once shared one of his secrets: He attempted to buy as close to what he termed "the danger point" as he could, and then he placed his stop loss. In this way, his risk per trade was low. This makes sense, but how do you know where that 'danger point' is? In normal markets, you need to accept normal profits, but on those rare occasions when you have the chance to make a windfall, go for it. But, how can you tell when a market is normal as opposed to extraordinary? It takes experience, and it takes knowledge, an essential quality for success. Knowledge takes study and hard work. Reading this book is a good first step.

Guts

Call it nerve, courage, bravado, or heart; I call it guts, and this one quality is as essential as patience and knowledge. Some people have too much guts, and this isn't good because they're too hopeful and tend to overtrade. Some lack the guts to act (either to enter a position when the time is right or to cut a loss when it isn't). This is a catastrophic fault and must be overcome. You need guts to pyramid positions, which is not easy, but it's where the big money is made. In this book, I am going to teach you to trade without hope, without fear, and with the right amount of guts. I will instruct you to enter positions on the proper basis and then urge you to remember at all times that you could be wrong. You will need a defensive plan to cut your losses when you are wrong. I've been a student in the school of hard knocks many times, but I've never lost my guts. At times, I know I've had too much and have overtraded, but then there are some people I know who have an inability to pull the trigger, and that is just as deadly. Looking back only brings regrets, so you need to face the future with optimism, knowledge, patience, and guts.

Health and rest

Gann's fourth essential quality for trading success is health and rest. If you don't feel right, you won't trade right, and that is the time to remain on the sidelines. When you stick with something too long, your judgment becomes warped. Traders who are continually in the market without rest get too caught up in the day-to-day fluctuations and eventually get tapped out. At least twice a year, it makes sense to close out all your trades, get entirely out of the market, and go on a vacation. When you return, recharged, your trading will improve.

So, that wraps up Gann's four essential human qualities required for success. You'll need them. Shortly, this book delves into specifics that will help you travel the rocky road leading to trading success. Some of the most important lessons I've learned over the past 30 years are in the pages to come, and they should help you make money. However, if you don't have patience, guts, knowledge, and good health, all the rules in the world are just words.

So, with that said, let's get into the meat of the matter. I'm not trying to be all things to all people, but I do believe this book appeals, to novice and veteran traders alike. We'll begin at the beginning. If you are new to this game, you'll need to know how the game is played, what the rules are, and how the money works. I strive to be as complete as possible, and at times, it might actually appear simple. If it were really so simple, however, most people wouldn't lose, but the nature of the futures markets is to punish the majority. Let's begin our journey to join the minority, because it is the minority who reap the rewards!

2

How to Become a Successful Trader

"Let it be known that we're all just tumbling dice, and the outcome of this crap shoot's hard to see."
—John Mellencamp

So, you want to make money trading?

Looks easy, but if it truly is so easy, then why do the great majority lose money? What is it that the profitable traders do that most other traders don't?

Believe me, this game of trading is no piece of cake. I've studied successful traders and, as a result, refined my personal approach over the past 30 years. My studies have revealed that successful traders throughout history tend to share common traits, and I'll share them with you shortly. However, I'll start by mentioning that there are respected theorists (like Nassim Taleb, author of *Fooled by Randomness*) who argue that chance and luck play a much larger part in trading than most will admit. After all, nobody knows with certainty where the market's going.

Taleb's basic premise is that, with a large number of traders in the universe, there exists the probability that a minority at the end of the bell curve will dramatically outperform the market based on nothing other than chance. If you have thousands of monkeys in a room flipping coins, chances are good that at least one of 'em will flip heads 15 times in a row.

While I understand this logic, I don't agree. If Talib's premise is universally true, why is it then, that throughout history market crashes have occurred when the *fewest* number of people have been positioned for them? In boom markets, the great majority ("the public") make most of the money on paper—and that's where they leave it (on paper), never actually cashing in. When the crash takes place, the masses always lose most of what they made. This phenomena is far from random; only a small minority ever profit from market crashes.

In the longer term, commodity price moves of significance are driven by real-world supply/demand fundamentals, not chance. However, even if Taleb is right about randomness, I contend that profitable trading can still be achieved in a chance-driven environment. Consider the game of poker. Poker is a game of chance, with the distribution of the cards totally random. Yet, university studies analyzing more than 400 million poker hands have concluded that poker is a game of skill. Many of the same tournament players top the money winning lists year after year. The majority (the suckers) might make money at times, but not consistently.

Novice traders are constantly looking for that "holy grail," a program, system, technique, or strategy that's a consistent money maker. Traders use many methodologies and indicators to get an edge (and I'll provide you with some later). However, I will concede that markets are not *always* even-driven; at times, they're erratic and random. So we can rule out a "holy grail." Why is it then that in the trading game, as in poker, many of the same players achieve success over and over again? Why do the majority of novice poker players and the majority of novice traders lose money? Perhaps the winners have found a way to overcome randomness, luck and chance? While I agree that nobody can unerringly predict a market, there are certain processes winners employ that losers do not. Successful traders are able to work with chance. Instead of searching for the "holy grail," successful traders look for that fastball pitch directly into their sweet spot. How do they find it? Unless someone is trading on "inside information" (something we have no interest in doing, as it would land us in jail), winners know guaranteed outcomes are impossible. Instead, their processes involve *trading discipline*, which in turn involves *money management*.

Chance favors the well prepared.
—Louie Pasteur

If you've decided to trade futures, you've made the decision to accept risk. The basic problem develops when this becomes a willingness to hang onto losing positions for too long. Due to the nature of markets, many times losing positions revert back into winners. The dilemma is that they don't always.

Most traders (and remember most traders are losers) are far more skittish when dealing with gains. University studies have proven that the great majority of traders are willing to take a greater risk in an effort to not lose $500 than to gain $1,000.

Trading involves risk taking, but what I want you to understand is that the line between winning and losing basically depends on how you manage the risk.

The very nature of risk taking means you will be making decisions with incomplete information. The marketplace is composed of unpredictable swings. You will be functioning in this environment, and while you'll be right at times, you *will* also be wrong. The best traders are constantly wrong, this is inevitable. Both bad and good traders get lucky at times, and there will be situations when a "lucky" break bails out a bad trader. Based on statistical randomness, there are bad traders who will be profitable for extended periods, and they will believe they are good.

However, bad traders will inevitably face catastrophic losses that either wipe them out for good or require fund injections from capital sources not related to trading.

In reviewing my personal notes for this book, I see that over the years, I've compiled plenty of "rules." Rules that the winners strive to stick to and losers never consider. We are not machines; we're human and won't always stick to these rules. Still, to be a successful trader, you absolutely must understand and then apply what I'm about to share here. If you're a beginning trader, please keep an open mind. If you're experienced but to date not very successful, you will need to drop your bad habits and develop a new concept of what can be achieved in your trading account.

Here's what the losers do (train yourself *not* to do these things):

- They lose more in their losing positions than they make in their winning positions.
- They get aggressive with their losers (by adding to them, or "averaging down").
- They have few fears or reservations before a losing trade but plenty after.
- They get trapped by their own self-doubts, brought about by previous mistakes. They tend to overanalyze (particularly after a string of losers) to the point that they get trapped into inaction. As a result, they miss the best trades while watching from the sidelines. They price every trade (instead of entering "at the market"), and because of this, they miss some good ones but are filled on every bad one.
- They have a goal (and that's fine), but get obsessed about reaching that goal (which is not good). This allows losers to get out of control.
- They take on high-risk trades because they visualize only the profits and not what could go wrong. Then, if something does go wrong, the stress can put them on tilt. Some losers are compulsive, always needing to play, regardless of whether the odds favor their play.
- They're opinionated, argumentative, and great at placing blame (on the broker, the funds, the government—anything but what they're in control of).

Here's what the winners do (train yourself to do these things):

- They make more in their winning positions than they lose in their losing positions. How do they accomplish this? By (a) holding the winners longer and (b) by being *bold*—getting aggressive with winners by sizing up. They have the ability, on good days, to quickly make back the bad day's losses.
- They trade in the present, guided by what the market is doing (reality) and not their bias of what the market should be doing (hope). And they are totally prepared, ready to take the trades. They have a plan, and follow it. Once in a

trade, if the market is giving them what they expected, they play it out; however, if it isn't, they accept what the market is prepared to give them. Again, this is reality versus hope.

- They take on a high-risk trade only if there's an edge in that trade—a favorable risk-to-reward ratio. They have patience to wait for the best signals, and when signaled, they can act without reservations or anxiety. They have the ability to buy or sell "at the market," knowing they could miss some of the best trades by pricing. They realize that "bad price fills" can many times be a symptom of the very best trades.
- Because they have a plan and the discipline to follow it, they are relaxed, without stress or excuses. How do I avoid stress during trading hours? I do my market analysis before the market opens and write out a script with the plan of action for varying circumstances. . . While I don't always trade "at the market" (at times I try to price an entry better using a limit order), if I don't get the trade on fairly quickly, I will not hesitate to go "at the market" to get it on (even if I have to "pay up"). When the trade is completed, I review what I did right and what I did wrong. Did I get out too soon (profitable trades) or too late (losing trades)? Did I size up correctly to maximize my profit? Did I act in a disciplined, consistent manner, or did I panic or gamble?

When you trade correctly, you'll find that the great majority of your trading profits are the result of a very small percentage of your trades—typically less than 10%. This highlights the importance of maximizing profits when you are smart (or lucky enough) to catch a winner. How many times have you looked at a chart of a position you were in months ago and seen the proof of how much you left on the table?

So, how do you maximize profits? First of all, you need to take care of your losses. You have to physically place your stops: Move your stops favorably when the market moves your way, and (unless you have a very good reason to get out) let the market take you out. If you're in doubt when in a winning trade (or quiet, small winner or small loser) , it's usually better to stay put and just let your stop do the work for you. On the other hand, when in doubt in a losing trade, it's usually better to get out!

The small percentage of big winners also underscores the importance of trading bigger when you're winning and smaller when you're losing. The losing traders either take on too much risk or not enough; they don't size up when the odds favor their play, and they get out of positive trades way too soon.

When a trade has met or exceeded your risk point, or profit objective, you can't become complacent. Be ready to stop the bleeding and/or to turn paper profits into cash.

Bottom line: Winning traders and losing traders are consistent in their behavior—but in opposite ways. People are taught from childhood in sports and other endeavors to win, but you *have to lose to win* in the trading game. Remember, if you get out with a small loss, you've put out a fire. You can always get back in when the market is going your way, and with far less emotion and stress.

This isn't all you will need to know to achieve success. You still need to develop a trading methodology that you're comfortable with, which includes your own risk/reward parameters based on the size of your account, but these are merely tactics. The nuts and bolts of what you need to know to succeed in the trading business is contained in this book.

3

A Diabolical Story

"Still a man hears what he wants to hear and disregards the rest."
—Paul Simon, "The Boxer"

On a beautiful Iowa summer's day in 2012, Russell Wasendorf, Sr., the chief executive of a major futures brokerage firm, was found by an employee, unconscious in his car. Wasendorf had rigged a tube directly from his exhaust into the Chevy's cabin in an apparent suicide attempt. He was revived and subsequently confessed to stealing over $200 million from his customers' accounts over a 10-year period. He spent the money on a new corporate headquarters, real estate investments (primarily in Romania, of all places), a private jet, and travel and entertainment for family members and staff.

How did Wasendorf get away with this over such a long time period? Basically, the same way Bernie Madoff got away with his scheme. When the regulators and auditors came to verify the firm's customer account balances, Wasendorf handed them an envelope addressed to the local U.S. Bank branch. The regulators mailed their audit confirmations to the bank, but the address on the envelope was a post office box Wasendorf controlled. When the audit confirmation showed up, Wasendorf merely filled in a false customer account balance and mailed it back. It was that easy. What tripped him up was when, in 2012, the regulators changed their audit procedures. They finally joined the digital age and required direct electronic verification from the bank. Unlike MF Global executive John Corzine (who said he had no knowledge of his loss of nearly $2 billion in customer money), Wasendorf, like Madoff, will likely spend his remaining days behind bars.

It seems that these Ponzi-like schemes repeat themselves throughout history. Which brings me to this diabolical story. The same floor broker who told me the tale of the corn speculator and the fire chief also told me this story. He says he believes it's true because, once upon a time (many years ago now), he hired one of the main characters as his clerk, which is how he got to hear the story in the first place.

The clerk had an opportunity to join a college buddy of his in San Diego and become a commodity broker. He quickly packed, left Chicago, and moved to the West Coast.

The San Diego office the clerk joined produced some business, but nothing spectacular. Customers would come, many would lose and leave, and new ones would take their place. One afternoon, as these two characters were staring out their office window (which looked out over the Pacific Ocean), they spawned an idea. They discussed how just about all their customers would lose money; in fact, over 80% of the trades would ultimately be liquidated as losers. With this thought in mind, the two characters placed an ad in the paper to hire rookie commodity trainees. After interviewing a number of applicants, they hired 10 "average Joes." They told these new hires that they would perform the normal duties of a commodity broker, servicing customer accounts and the like, but in addition, they each were going to be given a rare opportunity. The 10 would each be given a no-strings-attached $50,000 account with the firm to "manage" a portfolio of commodity trades. If they could show profitable performance, they would share in the profits and receive a bonus.

The trainees were allowed to each trade the $50,000 accounts as they saw fit; there was just one procedure they had to follow. Unlike with trades for customers of the firm, if they were going to place a trade in their "managed" accounts, the order had to go through one of the two principals (either the owner or the guy from Chicago). You have to ask yourself why these two would trust 10 novices—we're talking 10 raw rookies here—with $500,000 of their money. Well, you see, this was all just a diabolical scheme the two hatched that one afternoon.

What would happen is that one rookie broker would call to buy 10 cattle contracts, another would want to sell 7 soybeans, and another would buy 3 copper or short 5 silver. The two guys behind the scheme would call the various trading floors and sell 10 cattle, buy 7 soybeans, and sell 3 copper or buy 5 silver. In other words, they would do exactly the opposite of what their "traders" wanted them to do. You see, the money in the traders' accounts was fictitious. The firm's money was, in reality, going the other way, with opposite positions. The next day, fictitious position sheets would be distributed to the "traders," showing them what the rookies believed to be true.

Over 80% of novices who trade lose money. Inevitably, the rookie who "bought" the cattle couldn't stand the market moving against him, so he would call one of the two principals to liquidate his "losing" position. This was the signal for one of the principals to call the floor, buy back their shorts, and actually take the profits! The next day, the cattle "trader" would show a losing trade on his sheet—his $50,000 would be something less—but in reality, the two were cashing in. This pattern continued with the guy in the bean trade, the guy in the copper trade, and so on.

In the very first week, one trader actually lost his entire $50,000. He was immediately summoned to the boss's office. Thinking he was about to be fired, before anything was said, he started to cry. He said he had been married for only a year, just had twins, and really needed this job. He promised he would do better and would learn from his mistakes, and he pleaded for another chance. Imagine his surprise when they gave him another chance. In fact, the boys couldn't wait to "recapitalize" his account with another fictitious $50,000. They also couldn't wait for him to leave the office because they could hardly contain their laughter. By this fellow losing $50,000, they actually made $50,000 in the real markets. It was better than printing money.

The scheme proceeded much the same way for a while. One trader would blow out, and then another. The only problem was that the two bosses were finding it increasingly difficult to supply the traders with the fictitious statements for all the transactions. They couldn't keep up with the paperwork and started falling behind. Nevertheless, they continued on with the plan as best they could—that is, until the silver trade.

Now I should mention that this was all happening during the early 1980s, the same time the Hunt brothers tried to corner the silver market. Silver ran up to about $50 per ounce, and one day, one of the traders in our story called to sell short five silver. Of course, our boys actually bought five silver. The silver market moved erratically sideways for a few days, and then it started to turn over.

During this time, the trader who sold the silver went to Kansas to visit his mom. While he was visiting, a tornado hit his town, a tree fell on the house, the roof collapsed, and he ended up unconscious in a hospital bed. He remained in a coma for two weeks.

Meanwhile, our masterminds back in San Diego were wondering where the hell he was and when he was going to take his "profit" so they could take their loss. In New York, they raised the margin requirements and declared that silver was for liquidation only, and the market started its famous collapse.

The masterminds went belly up. The guy in the coma awakened, and the first words out of his mouth were "Get me a newspaper." He immediately turned to the commodity section, and when he saw how far silver had broken, he screamed for joy. He quickly called San Diego, anticipating praise and looking forward to his big bonus. Instead, he heard two words: "You're fired!"

4

The Futures Primer

"There are known knowns; there are things we know that we know. There are known unknowns; that is to say there are things that we now know we don't know. But there are also unknown unknowns—there are things we do not know we don't know."
—Donald Rumsfeld, U.S. Secretary of Defense in the George W. Bush Administration

Performing a few mouse clicks and transmitting an order isn't all that hard. It's not all that difficult to understand how the money works, either. What is difficult is extracting profits from the markets (something we'll tackle later), but you have to start somewhere. This chapter is for those who need to understand the basics.

Commodities are not only essential to life, they are necessary for quality of life. Every person on the planet eats. Billions of dollars of agricultural products are traded daily on the world's commodity exchanges—everything from soybeans to rice, corn, wheat, beef, pork, cocoa, coffee, sugar, and orange juice. Food is where the commodity exchanges began.

In the middle of the nineteenth century, businessmen started organizing market forums to facilitate the buying and selling of agricultural commodities. Over time, farmers and grain merchants met in central marketplaces to set quality and quantity standards and to establish rules of business. Over the course of only a few decades, more than 1600 exchanges had sprung up at major railheads, inland water ports, and seaports. In the early twentieth century, as communications and transportation became more efficient, centralized warehouses were constructed in major urban centers like Chicago. Business became less regional, more national; many of the smaller Exchanges disappeared.

In today's global marketplace, approximately 30 major Exchanges remain, with 90% of the world's business conducted on about a half dozen of them. Nearly every major commodity vital to commerce, and therefore to life, is represented. Billions of dollars' worth of energy products—from heating oil to gasoline to natural gas—are traded every business day. How could we live without industrial metals (such as copper, aluminum, zinc, lead, palladium, nickel, and tin); precious metals like gold or platinum and silver (considered both industrial and precious metals)? How could we live without wood or textiles? It's hard to imagine life without them, and yet few people are aware of just how the prices for these vital components of life are set. Unlike 100 years ago, today the world's futures Exchanges also trade financial products essential to the global economic function. From currencies to interest rate futures to stock market indices, more money changes hands on the world's commodity exchanges every day than on all the world's stock markets combined.

Governments allow commodity exchanges to exist so that producers and users of commodities can hedge their price risks. However, without speculators, the system would not work. Anyone can be a speculator, and contrary to popular belief, I do not believe the odds need be stacked against an individual. In this book, I share with you techniques designed to help you make money trading commodities. Actually, you as an individual have one distinct advantage over the big players, and that's flexibility. You can move quickly, like a cat, something a giant corporation can't do. Many times, several of the big commercial operators that utilize the Exchange for hedging literally hand you your profits on a silver platter because they're in the market for a different reason. So, let's start by looking at how futures contracts work and the various participants in the marketplace. We'll also look at what those participants are attempting to accomplish and how they interact with each other.

Futures markets and the futures contract

Futures markets, in their most basic form, are markets in which commodities (or financial products) to be delivered or purchased at some time in the future are bought and sold.

A *futures contract* is the basic unit of exchange in the futures markets. Each contract is for a set quantity of some commodity or financial asset and can be traded only in multiples of that amount. A futures contract is a legally binding agreement that provides for the delivery of various commodities or financial assets at a specific time period in the future. (Prior to the time I was in this business, I envisioned the parties actually signing contracts. It's nothing like that.)

When you buy or sell a futures contract, you don't actually sign a contract drawn up by a lawyer. Instead, you enter into a contractual obligation that can be met in only one of two ways. The first method is by making or taking delivery of the actual commodity. This is by far the exception, not the rule. Fewer than 1% of all futures contracts are concluded with an actual delivery. The other way to meet this obligation, which is the method you will be using, is termed *offset*. Very simply, offset is making the opposite (or offsetting) sale or purchase of the same number of contracts bought or sold sometime prior to the expiration date of the contract. Because futures contracts are standardized, this is accomplished easily.

Every contract on a particular Exchange for a specific commodity is identical except for price. The specifications are different for each commodity, but the contract in each market is the same. In other words, every full-sized soybean contract is for 5,000 bushels. Every full-sized gold contract is for 100 troy ounces. (I say *full-sized* because many markets also trade *mini* contracts. For example, there are also active 50-, 33-, and 10-ounce gold contracts, but for most commodities, the full-sized contracts get the bulk of the volume and liquidity).

Each contract listed on an Exchange calls for a specific grade and quality. For example, a full-sized silver contract is for 5,000 troy ounces of 99.99% pure silver in ingot form. The rules state that the seller cannot deliver 99.95% pure silver. Therefore, the buyers and sellers know exactly what they are trading. Every contract is completely interchangeable. The only negotiable feature of a futures contract is price.

The size of a contract determines its value. To calculate how much money you could make or lose on a particular price movement of a specific commodity, you need to know the following:

- Contract size
- How the price is quoted
- Minimum price fluctuation
- Value of the minimum price fluctuation

The contract size is standardized. The minimum unit tradable is one contract. For example, a New York coffee contract is for 37,500 pounds, a Chicago corn contract is for 5,000 bushels, and a British pound contract calls for delivery of 62,500 pounds sterling. The contract size determines the value of a move in price.

You also need to know how prices are quoted. For example, grains are quoted in dollars and cents per bushel: $5.50 per bushel for corn, $9.50 per bushel for wheat, and so on. Copper is quoted in cents per pound in New York and dollars per metric ton in London. Cattle and hogs are quoted in cents per pound, whereas gold is quoted in dollars and cents per troy ounce. Currencies are quoted in the United States in cents per unit of currency. As you begin trading, you will quickly become familiar with how this works. Your brokerage firm can fill you in on how prices are quoted on any particular market where you decide to trade.

The minimum price fluctuation, also known as a "tick," is a function of how prices are quoted and is set by the Exchange.

For example, prices of corn are quoted in dollars and cents per bushel, but the minimum price fluctuation for corn is 1/4¢ per bushel. So, if the price of corn is $6.00/bushel, the next price tick can either be $6.00 1/4 (if up) or $5.99 3/4 (if down). Prices can trade more than a tick at a time, so in a fast market, the price could jump from $5.00 to $5.00 1/2, but it could not jump from $5.00 1/2 to $5.00 5/8 because the minimum price fluctuation for corn is a quarter penny. Therefore, the next minimum price tick for corn from $5.00 1/2 up would be $5.00 3/4, or down would be $5.00 1/4. The minimum price fluctuation for a gold contract is 10¢ per ounce, so if gold is trading for $1,525.50 per ounce, the minimum it can move in price would be $1,525.60 if up or $1,525.40 if down. Once again, in a fast market, or if the bids and offers are wide, it might jump from $1,525.50 to $1,526 even, but in liquid and quiet markets, many times the market moves from one minimum tick fluctuation to the next.

The value of a minimum fluctuation is the dollars and cents equivalent of the minimum price fluctuation multiplied by the contract size of the commodity. For example, the size of a copper contract traded in the United States is 25,000 pounds. The minimum price fluctuation of a copper contract is 5/100¢ per pound (or 1/20¢). By multiplying the minimum price fluctuation by the size of the contract, you obtain the value of the minimum price fluctuation, which in this case is $12.50 (1/20¢ per pound times 25,000 pounds). In the case of the grains and soybeans, a minimum price fluctuation is 1/4¢, and a contract is for 5,000 bushels, so the value of a minimum fluctuation is also $12.50 (1/4¢ per bushel times 5,000 bushels).

Except with grains, minimum fluctuations are generally quoted in points. For example, sugar prices are quoted in cents and hundredths of a cent per pound. The minimum fluctuation is 1/100¢, or one point. If the price is quoted at 25 1/2¢ per pound, you would say it is trading at 2550, and if it moves up by a quarter of a cent per pound to 25 3/4¢, this would be a move of 25 points, to 2575.

In certain cases, the value of a minimum move may be more than a point. In the copper example, the minimum move is 1/20¢ per pound. A penny move is 100 points (for example, if copper prices rise from $5 per pound to $5.02 per pound, the market has moved up 200 points), but because the minimum fluctuation is for 1/20¢, a minimum move is 5 points, or $12.50 per contract. A move of 1¢ is worth $250, which is 100 points. You must understand what the value of a move is for the commodity you are trading. For example, if you are trading soybeans, you should know that a move of 1¢ is worth $50 per contract (either up or down), and if you buy three contracts and the market closes up 10¢ that day, you would make $1,500, or $500 per contract. If the market closes down 10¢, you would lose the same amount. Although this all might seem confusing at first, you'll quickly understand the value of a minimum fluctuation and the value of a point at the time you pay your first margin call.

This reminds me of an amusing true story once told to me by Joey, my favorite copper pit broker, a guy who retired in Florida when copper went electronic.

When the pits were active, on the floor of the COMEX (the world's largest metals Exchange, now owned by the CME), where copper is traded, the pit brokers always talk in terms of points instead of dollar values. You would have heard a trader say, "I made 300 points today," or "I lost 150 points on that trade." A number of years ago, there was a big commission house broker (a floor broker who made his living filling buy and sell orders from customers who call in from off the floor) who was pressured by his wife to hire his brother-in-law. The brother- in-law wasn't all that bright, but the broker felt his brother-in-law couldn't do that much damage if he were on the phone as a clerk. After all, the clerks just used to take the buy and sell orders over the phone and run them into the pit to be filled.

Well, everything went reasonably well for a few weeks, and then the first inevitable error occurred. Apparently, the brother-in-law took an order to buy five contracts, and he wrote "sell" on the order ticket. By the time the error was discovered, it had resulted in a loss of 370 points ($925) that the commission house broker had to make good. After the market closed, the broker took the brother-in-law aside and carefully spoke to him. The broker said, "Look, mistakes happen and, fortunately, this error relatively small, only for 370 points. It could have been much worse, but you have to be more careful. We cannot afford to have any more errors like this one."

The brother-in-law replied, "What are you getting so hot under the collar for? Sure I made a mistake, but it's only points."

From that day on, whenever anyone in the copper pit made an error, the guys on the floor would say, "Hey, what's your problem? It's only points!"

Certain contracts have associated daily price limits, which measure the maximum amount that the market can move above or below the previous day's close in a single trading session. Each Exchange determines whether a particular commodity has a daily trading limit and for how much. The theory behind the limit-move rule is to allow markets to cool down during particularly dramatic, volatile, or violent price moves. For example, as this text is being written, the rules for the corn contract state that the market can move up or down 40¢ per bushel from the previous close if it did not close "limit" the previous day. (Limit moves result in expanded limits, and the rules on limits can change, so consult Exchange websites for current limits per market, if any.) So, if the corn market closes at $8.10 per bushel on Tuesday, then on Wednesday, it can trade as high as $8.50 or as low as $7.70. Contrary to popular belief, the market can trade at the limit price; it just cannot trade beyond it. At times of dramatic news or price movements, a market can move to the limit and "lock." A lock-limit move means that there is an overabundance of buyers (for "lock limit up") versus sellers at the limit-up price, or that there is an overabundance of sellers (for "lock limit down") at the limit-down price.

For example, suppose that in a drought market, the weather services are forecasting rain one weekend, thereby causing the market to trade lower on a Friday. However, the rain never materializes, and on Sunday evening, the forecast is back to drought, with record-high temperatures predicted for the week. Conceivably, the market could open "up the limit" as shorts scramble to buy back contracts previously sold, and buyers would be willing to "pay up" for what appears to be a dwindling future supply of corn. Let's say the market closed on Friday at $7.50 and that it opened at $7.90 on Sunday evening. Now it could trade at that price, or it could trade even lower that day. But suppose 30,000 contracts are wanted to buy at the limit-up price of $7.90, with only 3,000 contracts to sell. The first 3,000 would trade at $7.90, with the next 27,000 in the "pool" wanting and waiting to buy. If no additional sell orders surface, the market would remain limit up that trading session, with unsatisfied buying demand at the $7.90 level. However, nothing says the market has to open higher on the next session (it could unexpectedly rain Monday evening), but all other factors remaining equal, this unsatisfied buying interest would most likely "gap the market" higher when the following session began.

Most markets that use limits have what are called *variable limits*, which means limits raised if a market closes limit up or limit down during a trading session. Cattle is one of the markets with variable limits. Cotton is another. If one or more contract months close at, for example, the 3¢ (300-point) limit, the limit is raised to 6¢ the next business day. (You can consult the websites of the various Exchanges for the daily price-limit rules for each market.) Limit moves are rare, but they do occur during shocks to a market. Pork bellies used to be notorious for moving multiple limit days after an unexpectedly bullish or bearish "Hogs and Pigs Report." Alas, the "bellies," once a speculator's favorite, were delisted in 2012.

The best stories I have come from the pit days. It's just hard to tell a humorous story about a rogue computer algorithm. So here's another true story of how gutsy some of the floor traders at the Board used to be at times.

Bill, who once worked my soybean orders (when they were traded not in contracts, but in "bushels") told me about one summer day when the soybean market was down the limit. It wasn't just down the limit; it was "locked down the limit," with 5 million bushels offered to sell down the limit and no buyers in sight. It was very quiet. Then, out of nowhere, one large "local" wandered into the pit and uttered, "Take 'em." "How many?" they asked. "All of 'em!'"

The other brokers in the pit literally fell over themselves, selling the entire 5 million to this guy. What could he be thinking? But then, as soon as the 5 million were bought, and the quote machines around the world showed this, the telephones around the pit started to ring. Off the floor, traders around the world assumed that with such a big buyer at limit down, something was up, and they started to buy, too. The market immediately started to rally. When it moved 5¢ per bushel off the limit-down price, the large local stepped back in and sold his 5 million bushels right before it went back down the limit. It was a quick $250,000 profit, and it took only 20 seconds!

To review thus far, before you trade in any market, you need to know, at minimum, the Exchange the market is traded on, the trading hours, the contract size, and the delivery months traded. You need to know how prices are quoted, the minimum fluctuation, the dollar value of the minimum fluctuation, and whether there are any daily trading limits. You also need to know the types of orders accepted at that particular marketplace. Finally, you need to know what the margin requirement is for the market you are trading, as well as what commission your broker will be charging.

It is as easy to sell "short" as to buy "long"

The concept of selling short is confusing to novices, but after you begin to trade, selling short will become second nature.

Everyone knows that if you buy something at one price and sell it for a higher price, you make money. If you sell it at a lower price than what you paid for it, you lose money. When you trade futures, you can buy or sell in whatever order you like. You can buy and then sell, or sell and then buy. Whichever you choose, the idea is that the selling price should be higher than the buying price. One question I've often heard is, "How can you sell what you don't own?" Well, here's how: A buyer of a futures contract is obligated to take delivery of a particular commodity or—and this is what happens most of the time—sell back the contract prior to the delivery date. The process of selling back, which can be done anytime during normal market hours (assuming that the market is not "locked limit down" in a market that has limits, which is a rare occurrence), in effect, wipes the slate clean. If you buy at one price and sell at a higher price, you make money, and vice versa.

For example, if you buy soybeans at $12 per bushel and sell them at $12.20 per bushel, your profit is 20¢ per bushel, which is worth $1,000 for a soybean contract. (A penny move is a profit or loss of $50.) If you buy a contract of beans at $12 and sell them back at $11.80, you lose 20¢, or $1,000 per contract. If you buy 10 contracts of July soybeans, you could cancel your obligation to take delivery by selling back 10 contracts of July soybeans. You would then be out of the market, and the difference between the price at which you bought and sold would determine your profit or loss on the trade.

When trading futures, because you are trading for future delivery, it is just as easy to sell first and then buy back later. Selling first is referred to as *shorting* or *selling short*. To offset your obligation to deliver, all you need to do is to buy back your contract(s) prior to the expiration of the contract(s). This process of buying back is known as *covering*. You can "cover your short position" to wipe the slate clean. The purpose of shorting is to profit from a fall in prices. If you believe the price of a particular commodity is going down, due to an oversupply or poor demand, you want to go short. The objective is to cover at a lower price than you sold.

In the soybean example, if you believe prices at $12 are too high and are heading for a fall, you could go short at $12. If prices fall to $11.80, you might want to cover your position and take the 20¢ profit. A short sale at $12, covered at $11.80, is a profit of 20¢, or $1,000 per contract. Of course, if prices rise and you have to cover at $12.20, you would have a loss on the short sale of 20¢ per contract, or $1,000. "Sell high, buy back low" can be just as profitable as "buy low, sell high."

Kevin "Mac," who once leased my COMEX seat, told me this humorous (and true) story. Kevin traded in the copper pit, as did Al, a big commission house broker. Al was big in more ways than one, and his weight seemed to roller coaster, depending on which diet he was on at the time. Diet or not, Al was a big guy, and this was an advantage that would get him noticed in the pit. Al was also a colorful guy who liked to play the horses, but at heart he was a shy man. Still, you wouldn't know it when you saw him in the pit because he moved nimbly and possessed a gruff voice. He "filled paper" for a living, meaning he executed customer orders in the pit (a profession that became extinct after electronic trading).

This happened in the copper market of 1987–1988, a particularly wild time. The day of the stock market crash, the market spiked downward 10¢ per pound, a huge single-day move, to a copper price of less than 80¢ per pound. (Interestingly, just a few months later, it was more than $1.40 per pound.) The market was wild and noisy that day, and Al was summoned to the phone to take a large buy order from a New York client. Al was on one of his diets, and that day he had forgotten his belt. He rushed into the pit, raised his arms to bid for the copper, and his pants fell to his ankles. It was a wild day, but for a few seconds, no one could believe their eyes. Everyone stopped trading to stare at Al's boxer shorts. Al turned red as he put his hands over the hearts on his boxers. (He had gotten them for Valentine's Day.) Then Kevin broke the silence (as Kevin tells it, he didn't stop to think—it just came out), yelling, "Look at Al! He's covering his shorts!" Now there's a story only commodity traders find funny.

Margin and leverage

One of the big attractions—and what makes futures exciting—is leverage. Leverage is the ability to buy or sell $100,000 of a commodity with only a $5,000 security deposit so that small price changes can result in huge profits or losses. Leverage gives you the ability to either make a killing or get killed. You need to understand how this important concept works before you trade, and a thorough understanding of the powers and pitfalls of leverage is imperative to sound money management principals.

Each contract bought or sold on a futures Exchange must be backed by a good-faith deposit termed *margin*. This is not like buying on margin in the stock market. When a stock market investor buys on margin, she is, in effect, borrowing half of the purchase price of the stock from her broker. The investor is charged interest on the balance. This provides a degree of leverage, but nothing like with commodities.

To see how powerful leverage can be, let's compare a futures purchase with a stock purchase for cash. If a stock investor buys 200 shares of a stock trading at $10, his purchase cost is $2,000. If the stock moves up by 10%, to $11 per share, the investor has made $200 on his $2,000 investment, or 10%. Margin in commodity trading is like a good-faith deposit. It is a small percentage, generally in the neighborhood of 2% to 10%, of the value of the underlying commodity represented by the contract. Margin deposits are set by the Exchange, and they can change with price movements and market volatility. Because you are trading for future delivery and not borrowing anything, no interest is charged on the balance. Margin is not a partial payment or a down payment at all, and it's not even considered a cost. If you make money on the trade, upon liquidation, your total margin deposit is returned, along with your profits. Commissions are deducted, and they are a cost. Margin is money deposited in your brokerage account that serves to guarantee the performance of your side of the contract. Margin is a form of "earnest money" deposited by both the longs and the shorts, and it serves to ensure the integrity of every futures transaction. In effect, margin ensures that you are paid when you win and that whoever is on the other side of your transaction is paid if you don't.

When you enter a position, you have deposited (or will deposit) the margin money in your account, but your brokerage house is required to post the margin with a central Exchange arm called the clearinghouse. The clearinghouse, in effect, manages the daily process of debiting the accounts of the losers and redistributing the money to the accounts of the winners.

Now back to the leverage example. Assume that the margin requirement for a 5,000-ounce soybean contract is $2,000. At $6 per bushel, a contract is worth $30,000 ($6 per bushel times 5,000 bushels). If the price of soybeans rises by 10%, to $6.60, the same contract is worth $33,000. However, suppose that the same investor puts up his $2,000 and instead buys a soybean contract. If the price of soybeans rises by 10%, or 60¢, he makes $3,000 on his contract. This is 150% on margin, not 10%. It's powerful leverage, but it's also a double-edged sword. If prices fall by 10%, the investor's $2,000 is now worth a negative $1,000. When you trade futures, you are responsible for the total value of a move of any position you hold. In most cases, if a market moves against you, you have time to liquidate before the account shows a deficit; however, this is not always the case. If you don't use adequate risk-control measures, or if a market moves very quickly against you, your account could go into a deficit situation, and you are obligated by contract to pay the difference.

There are two types of margin: initial margin and maintenance margin.

Initial margin is the amount that must be in your account before you place a trade. If you do not have enough initial margin in your account, you incur a margin call. Most brokerage firms require the initial margin to be in the account before they allow a trade to be placed. Some might issue credit for good customers, but they generally require that the margin call be met within one or two business days. Any firm has the right to require same-day deposit by bank wire transfer at any time and might request this during volatile markets. Maintenance margin is the amount that must be maintained in your account as long as the position is active. If the equity balance in your account falls below the maintenance margin level, because of adverse market movements, you incur a margin call as well. After the margin call is issued, you are required to meet the call or liquidate the position. If you fail to meet a margin call in a timely manner, the broker has the right (and will use it) to liquidate the position for you automatically. This is done to protect the broker from additional adverse movements in the market because he is responsible for meeting your margin call, even if you're a deadbeat and don't.

If you fail to meet a margin call, and the position is ultimately liquidated at a loss that leaves a deficit in the account, the broker is immediately responsible for the deficit, but you are legally responsible. In other words, the initial margin is not the extent of your liability. You are responsible for all losses resulting from your trading activities. If you are in a coma and the market moves against you five, six, or seven days and you did not get out because you were unable to, if the market moves limit against you and eats up your margin, you are still responsible for any and all losses. Later in this book, you'll learn ways to manage the risk, but at this point, be aware that whenever you trade futures, your risk is not limited to the initial margin or your account balance. It can go further than that. (Options work differently.)

Assume that corn is trading at $6 per bushel, and the initial margin requirement is $2,000. A corn contract has a size of 5,000 bushels, so at $6 per bushel, the total value of the contract is $30,000. However, all that is required to purchase or sell a contract is $2,000 (in this example, about 6%). A rule of thumb for maintenance margin is that it will be at the 75% level of initial. If the initial is $2,000, for example, maintenance might be $1,500. If you have an account value of $20,000 with no other positions on, you could buy 10 contracts without a margin call; however, this is not recommended because you would be overtrading, or too highly leveraged, and a relatively minor price movement would move you into margin call territory.

For illustrative purposes, let's assume that your account balance is at $20,000 and that you buy 10 corn contracts. Your maintenance level is at $15,000. If the market starts to move your way immediately, you're okay. Because a corn contract is for 5,000 bushels, a 1¢ move results in a profit or loss per contract of $50. In this example, the 10 contracts give you a profit or loss of $500 per penny move. Suppose you buy the 10 contracts at $6, and the market closes that same day at $6.05. Your account balance is $22,500 at the close of business that day. You have an unrealized profit of $2,500. The profit is unrealized because the position is still open. The increase in equity value of $2,500 is the result of the 5¢ move in your favor (5¢ times $50 per contract times 10 contracts). Suppose that the next day the price falls 10¢, to close at $5.95. Your account value decreases by $5,000, to $17,500. You would not have a margin call because your value still would be above the maintenance level. If on the next day prices rose 5¢, back to $6, your equity value would move back to $20,000.

Basically, the futures involves a process of generating a credit or debit daily against your initial position until you close it out. If you make money on any particular day, the unrealized credit balance is credited immediately to your account and debited from the people on the other side of the transaction. (You will never know who they are because it's completely anonymous, but they are out there.) If the market closes against your position on any particular day, the loss would be immediately debited from your account.

Now, let's get back to the example. On the fourth day, the market drops 25¢, to close at $5.75. Your account is debited $12,500 (25¢ times $50 per contract times 10 contracts). Your equity balance is now down to $7,500, which is below the maintenance margin level, so it's margin call time. You now get a communication from your broker, who informs you about your $12,500 margin call. After your equity level falls below the maintenance margin level, you are required to bring your balance up to the initial margin level. You now have two choices: You can either liquidate the position in whole or in part, enough to move your equity back above the initial margin level, or you can meet the call. In this case, you could sell out 7 contracts, realize your loss on those 7, hold onto the 3, get your initial margin down to $6,000, and hope the market recovers. If you feel strongly about the position, you could opt to meet the call. Let's say you deposit the additional $12,500 in your account. Your account balance now shows $20,000, so you are "off call." You have deposited $32,500 into your account at this point, but if you close out the position at the current price of $5.75, you have a balance remaining of $20,000 minus any transaction costs. If your thinking is correct, and the corn market recovers to $6, your account balance would grow back to $32,500. You now have the right to request that the $12,500 (the amount over the initial margin) be sent back to you, even if you are still in the position. If the market falls again, however, you could certainly be issued another margin call.

It is important to leave a cash cushion in the account so that you have the ability to ride out normal market fluctuations without receiving a margin call. My general rule of thumb is to never margin higher than 50% maximum. In other words, if your account value is $25,000, I would not put on positions that, at most, would require more than $12,500 in initial margin. Each market has its own margin requirement, based on the volatility of the particular market and also the volatility of the markets as a whole. Greater volatility equals greater risk and higher requirements.

Here's another important point on margins: Although the Exchange sets a minimum margin requirement, individual brokerage houses have the right to charge higher than "Exchange minimum." This protects the brokerage house from overtraders who tend to *plunge* (trade in excess of prudent speculation, even in excess of their ability to pay), which would require the broker to make good on his commitment to the clearinghouse.

The entire point of this margining system is that all positions are "marked to the market" by the clearinghouse daily and revalued to the current market price. Profits and losses are paid daily.

One last point about margins: The Exchange allows initial margins to be posted either in cash or (in the United States) U.S. government obligations of less than 10 years to maturity and even, in some cases, gold. If an investor wishes to post T-Bills for margin, he can do so; the interest (when T-Bills are paying interest) passes back to the customer. So, in effect, the initial margin can earn interest.

Delivery months

Every futures contract has standardized months that are authorized by the Exchange for trading. For example, wheat is traded for delivery in March, May, July, September, and December. If you buy a March contract, you need to sell a March contract to offset your position and meet your contractual obligation. If you buy a March wheat contract, and you sell a May wheat contract, you have offset nothing. You are still "long" March and now "short" May. Some commodities are traded in every month, but by convention, some contract months are traded more actively than others. For example, gold trades in every month of the year, but the active months are February, April, June, August, October, and December. On the London Metal Exchange, or LME (where aluminum, copper, zinc, nickel, lead, and tin are traded), a different system, known as *prompt dates*, is used. At the LME, the active contract on any particular day is the 3-month. If you buy or sell a new 3-month on say, May 10th, you are in the August 10th contract (assuming that August 10th does not fall on a weekend or holiday). Then, to offset your position, you need to sell the August 10th contract. You can do that prior to August 10th, but your buy or sell price is based on an interpolation of the cash (or spot contract) to 3-month differential on the day you liquidate. The margining procedure is different for the LME as well, so if you are thinking of trading in these markets, talk to your commodity broker about how it works.

Which month should you trade? This is a general rule of thumb only, but unless you have a specific reason for trading a specific month, trade the active month. For example, say that it's May but you want to be short December corn because this is the first new crop month and, despite tight supplies, you think there's a big crop coming and predict that this month will fall faster. Otherwise, you would trade the active month. The active month is the one with the highest open interest, and you can obtain this information from the Exchange for any particular commodity at any point in time. This is because the active months have the greatest number of players and, therefore, the most liquidity. Because of this, you can get in and out with a smaller degree of slippage. *Slippage*, in effect, means having your order filled at a price unfavorably different from that which existed as the last trade.

For example, let's say you want to buy gold, and the last quoted price is $1,801.10, but the best bid is $1,801.10 and the best offer is $1,801.30. It is a fast-moving market, and you want in. You buy at the market, and even though the last trade is $1,801.10, your price fill comes back at $1,801.30. These 20 points represent $20 per contract, and they're likely to go into the pocket of a market maker. It is legal, and as long as there are no lower offers in the order book, it is the price you pay for the liquidity the market makers provide. The point is, for minimum slippage, it is best to trade in high-volume, active markets.

In most cases (and there are exceptions to this rule as well), it doesn't make sense to trade in a delivery month. Therefore, you want to avoid entering positions that are close to delivery because you'll need to "roll over" into the next contract sooner. The rules are different for each market, but in many cases, a contract enters actual delivery the last day of the month prior to the delivery month. For example, with March wheat, the first *notice day*—that is, the first possible day the shorts can make a delivery—is the last trading day in February. What happens if you fail to sell out and are still in the contract on first notice day? Well, there is a possibility you will get actual delivery of the wheat, but the shorts are not required to make delivery the first day or the next. A short is required to make delivery only if you have not covered your contract prior to the last trading day. The last trading day for March wheat is in the third week of March, so the delivery period lasts about three weeks. A long can receive delivery, at the discretion of the shorts, on any one of the days in the delivery period. If the cash price is above the futures on first notice day, the shorts may not find it lucrative to deliver and wait. If the cash price is below the futures, odds increase for deliveries. Now, just because deliveries are made on any particular day does not mean you will get delivery on any particular day. Early in the delivery period, the number of open contracts exceeds the deliverable supply. If open interest in the March wheat is, say, 100 million bushels, and the deliverable supply in the elevators licensed for delivery is 20 million bushels, the odds of delivery are high only if you purchased the contract months ago instead of days ago. This is because deliveries are assigned to the oldest date first. The oldest long is first in line for delivery. However, as the delivery period progresses, the odds for receiving a delivery increase as the number of outstanding contracts is liquidated downward and your date becomes "fresher."

So, what happens if you do get delivery? Contrary to popular belief, you do not get a load of wheat dumped on your doorstep—or, worse yet, a load of hogs. Instead, you receive a warehouse receipt that shows you now own 5,000 bushels of wheat in, for example, a Toledo elevator. Because you are now in a cash contract (the delivery offsets your futures), you're now required to post the full value of the contract. Your leverage is gone. If your margin deposit was $1,400 for the futures, you now need to pony up an additional $38,600 if you received delivery at $8 per bushel. If you don't have the money in your account, your broker will have to post this amount on your behalf, and she will charge you interest on the balance. Other fees include an additional commission, insurance, and storage costs. You can pass your delivery receipt on to someone else. Because only the shorts can make delivery (and you are long a warehouse receipt), you first need to sell a contract short and then instruct your broker to make your delivery on your short contract. This is the way to sell back your warehouse receipt. In most cases, there is no good reason to be trading in a delivery month unless, of course, you have a good reason to do so. A good reason might be a belief that there is not enough of the commodity available to deliver, which could cause a short squeeze, a panic situation for the shorts. However, be aware that this is generally a game for sophisticated traders. Of course, as a short, you have no chance of receiving a delivery (because it is at your discretion as to when to make it), but then your chance of being squeezed increases with each day you are in the contract during the delivery period. If you are in on the last day, and your broker hasn't forced you out, good luck in making the delivery. This is a game for the commercials.

Many years ago, when I was at Merrill Lynch, one of the commodity brokers had a client who refused to liquidate a long sugar position prior to the delivery period. The client thought there was no sugar but, alas, there was. (The sugar contract is written so that you can receive delivery at any one of 100 ports around the world.) He got his sugar on a barge off Bangkok, and it cost him plenty for Merrill Lynch to find a cash operator and dispose of this distress merchandise in the cash market. (The commercials knew he had no use for 112,000 pounds of sugar on a barge.)

One last point: Most financial futures (stock indices and currencies) and even some of the agricultural futures (feeder cattle and hogs) are cash settled. Any positions still open when a contract expires are closed at the settlement price. The amount paid or received is calculated for everyone who remained in at expiration, based on this common price.

Brokers and commissions

Although margin isn't a true cost (you get it back at the end of the trade, plus any profits or minus any losses), commissions are a true cost. Commissions are your broker's fees for his or her services, and they range across the board and by broker. The two major types of commission firms are discounters and full-service firms.

Commissions, while important, should not be your only consideration when choosing a broker. I run a full-service firm, and although our commissions are competitive for full service, they are higher than discounters. If you are a self-directed trader, are relatively sophisticated, know exactly what you want to do in the marketplace, do not require advice or additional services, and only need order execution, then you should certainly go for the cheapest rate. However, you need to evaluate what you're receiving. With some firms, discount commissions equal cheaper service, particularly when you have a problem. In addition, you need to evaluate how much help your broker is providing you versus how much help you require. A knowledgeable full-service broker who provides you with profitable recommendations is worth higher commissions charged. Just as importantly, is your broker helping you to control your risks properly on the bad trades? Is he or she helping you avoid classic mistakes such as overtrading? These are factors you'll need to evaluate when you begin. A brokerage relationship is extremely personal, and whom you trade with can mean the difference between profit and loss.

One last thought about commissions. When talking commodity futures, the fee per contract traded is low compared with many other types of investments. The fee can be less than a fraction of a percentage point of the total contract value. It is a higher percentage when compared to the margin deposit, but it's still small. The other side of the coin is that futures traders are much more active than more traditional investors, and total commission costs for an active trader can run up substantially over time.

The players

The two major classes of participants in the futures and options markets are hedgers and speculators.

Hedgers can account for 5% to 30% of the volume and open interest in the major futures markets and up to half or more in some of the smaller contracts. Hedgers use exchange-traded contracts to offset the risk of fluctuating prices when they buy or sell physical supplies of a commodity.

For example, a copper-mining company might sell copper futures to lock in a sale price today for its future production. In this way, the company protects its profit margins and revenue stream from a possible future drop in copper prices. If future copper prices rise, the company loses on its futures position; however, the value of its physical metal rises. The copper mine is a producer and is just trying to offset, or hedge, its price risk. A hedger can be a buyer or a seller.

A tube manufacturer that buys copper as a raw material in the production of copper tube used for plumbing might buy copper futures to lock in its copper cost for future purchase. If the price of copper rises, the manufacturer has a profit on its hedge, which can be used to offset the higher price of physical copper it needs to purchase in the marketplace. If copper prices fall, the manufacturer shows a loss on the futures side of the transaction, but it is able to buy the copper cheaper in the marketplace.

In either case, the copper mine or the tube manufacturer has the ability to hold its contracts into the delivery period. It then has the option to make or take copper delivery through the Exchange at an approved warehouse licensed to do business on the Exchange. This option is as important in theory as in practice because it is what allows physical commodity prices and the Exchange-traded contracts to come together in price. If the price of the commodity is too high in relation to the futures price, then the people involved in the use of a particular commodity buy the low-priced futures contracts and take delivery. Their buying, in effect, pushes futures prices up to meet the physical price. If the price of a futures contract is too high in relation to the actual commodity, then producers of that commodity sell the contract to make delivery because the higher-priced futures (in relation to the physical) just might be their best sale. Their selling pushes the price of the futures down to the cash price. This entire process is known as *convergence*. This potential process of convergence is what makes the system work; however, in practice, only 1% to 2% of all commodity contracts end in delivery. Odds are that you, as a speculator, will never get involved in a delivery, and there's no need to. In fact, even the majority of hedgers do not use the markets to actually make or take delivery; they use the futures as a pricing tool to help stabilize their revenues and their costs.

I once had a client, a major manufacturing firm that published a biannual catalog with prices it honored during the life of each catalog. This firm used copper and zinc in its manufacturing process, and it knew what its profit margin was based on today's price of copper and zinc. If it didn't hedge and lock in the six-month price of copper initially, and the price went up during the time the catalog was distributed, its entire profit margin could have been wiped out. The other side of the coin is that if copper prices fell and the published price remained based on the published higher prices of the raw materials, the firm could have reaped a windfall profit. However, the firm was not in the business of speculation; it was in the manufacturing business. It was more than willing to forgo the chance of a windfall to be assured of a profit margin that allowed them to keep the plant running and avoid layoffs.

A few times each year, I sat down with this firm to determine where to buy copper and zinc futures to lock in a price the firm could live with for the coming six months. After it knew this price, the firm published its catalog with peace of mind, knowing that its profit margin was secure. If the price of copper rose, the firm would have to pay the higher price in the cash copper market; however, its futures contracts rose in value as well, and the profits from the futures offset the higher price that had to be paid in the physical market. If the price of copper fell, the firm realized a loss on its futures, but this was offset by the lower price it enjoyed in the cash market when it bought copper.

Many of the products hedged on a futures Exchange are actually cross-hedges. For example, jet fuel is similar to heating oil, and they are often priced within a few cents of each other. A major airline might use the heating oil contract to hedge its jet fuel requirements, and a trucking company might use the same contract to hedge its diesel fuel needs.

Basis risk

Basis is the difference between the cash, or spot, price and the futures price. Every contract traded has *specifications*, which make the contracts fungible and standardized. For example, let's look at the contract specifications for heating oil:

Trading Unit = 42,000 U.S. gallons (1,000 barrels).

Price Quotation in U.S. dollars and cents per gallon.

Trading Months—Trading is conducted in 18 consecutive months, commencing with the next calendar month.

Minimum Price Fluctuation—$0.0001 (0.01¢) per gallon ($4.20 per contract).

Maximum Daily Price Fluctuation—$0.25 per gallon ($10,500 per contract) for all months. If any contract is traded, bid, or offered at the limit for five minutes, trading is halted for five minutes. When trading resumes, the limit is expanded by $0.25 per gallon in either direction. If another halt is triggered, the market will continue to be expanded by $0.25 per gallon in either direction after each successive five-minute trading halt. There will be no maximum price fluctuation limits during any one trading session.

Last Trading Day—Trading terminates at the close of business on the last business day of the month preceding the delivery month.

Settlement Type—Physical.

Delivery—F.O.B. seller's facility at New York harbor, ex-shore. All duties, entitlements, taxes, fees, and other charges have point paid. Requirements for seller's shore facility: capability to deliver into barges. Buyer may request delivery by truck, if available, at the seller's facility, and pays a surcharge for truck delivery. Delivery also may be completed by pipeline, tanker, book transfer, or inter- or intra-facility transfer. Delivery must be made in accordance with applicable federal, state, and local licensing and tax laws.

Delivery Period—Deliveries may be initiated only the day after the fifth business day and must be completed before the last business day of the delivery month.

Grade and Quality Specifications—These generally conform to industry standards for fungible No. 2 heating oil.

When you read this contract, you can see that it is standardized, in that all contracts created are the same. Contract specifications for all commodities traded on the Exchange are available from the Exchange website. As a speculator, you really are not concerned with the delivery specifications because you will not be involved in delivery—you'll be out long before it starts. What about a hedger? This particular contract calls for delivery of No. 2 heating oil in New York harbor. Of course, not all heating oil is used in the New York area, and prices in other cities will vary due to differences in transportation costs, storage costs, and local supply-and-demand considerations. A wave of Arctic air sweeping through Europe would no doubt raise the price of heating oil globally, but the price would rise faster in Rotterdam than in New York. These differentials are known as the basis. The basis can be stable and predictable at times. For example, if it costs 3¢ per gallon to transport heating oil from New York to Boston, the basis in Boston may predictably run at "plus 3¢ per gallon," all other factors remaining equal. However, if Boston is under a deep freeze and New York isn't, the basis might move up to "plus 4¢."

For the manufacturing firm I worked with, the price of scrap copper could, at times, be at the price of the virgin metal (when there is a scrap shortage). Other times, it could be as much as 4¢ or 5¢ per pound under. The point is that a hedger has what's called *basis risk*. Basis risk is almost always far less than the price risks involved without a hedge. A hedger who does not hedge is just like a speculator because she is assuming the natural risks of the marketplace. Once again, I want to point out that even most hedgers close out their futures positions long before their futures contracts expire, and the majority of them do so long before the delivery period even starts. Then, they take or make delivery of the physical commodity they are involved in through normal channels by using their standard suppliers. Knowing that each contract is actually keyed into a specific actual grade of the underlying commodity keeps the value true to life. No matter what the underlying commodity is, each Exchange ultimately guarantees the purchase and sale, as well as the delivery grades for quality and quantity. This is why quotations from the Exchanges for most of the commodities traded are used as pricing standards around the world.

Hedges come in two basic forms: short and long hedges.

The short hedge

A *short hedge* is entered into to protect the value of an inventory. Consider an example using crude oil. An inventory of 1,000 barrels of crude oil constantly changes in value from wellhead to consumer, even before it is processed into gasoline or heating oil. A short hedge is used by the owner of a commodity to essentially lock in the value of the inventory prior to the transferring of title to a buyer. A decline in prices generates profits in the futures market on the short hedge. These profits are offset by depreciation in the inventory value.

Let's say an oil producer is afraid of a future price decline. In August, he anticipates he will sell his August production in September. His production is 1,000 barrels a day for 25 days. The cash price in August is $120 per barrel, and October futures are quoted in August at $120.10 per barrel. Here's what the producer might do in the futures market: sell 25 October futures (each contract is for 1,000 barrels, so this represents his August production of 25,000 barrels) at $120.10, which locks in a value of his inventory equivalent to $3,002,500 ($120.10 per barrel times 25,000 barrels.) Suppose he is correct about the price falling. Along comes September 15, and the price of crude falls in the cash market by $20 per barrel. Because the futures mirror the cash fairly closely, the futures also fall in price. Let's say that the futures on that date are quoted at $100 per barrel. The cash price on September 15 is now $100, or $20 less than the $120 price at production time. He sells his product in the cash market to the refinery for a total of $2,500,000 ($100 times 25,000), or $500,000 less than what he could have received in August. However, the futures have also dropped, and he buys back his October futures contracts on September 15 for $100. (This offsets his position; he does not have to make delivery.) Remember, he sells for the equivalent of $3,002,500, he buys back at the equivalent of $2,500,000, and the difference of $502,500 is his gain in the futures. The futures gain of $502,500 offsets the cash market loss of $500,000, and the oil producer has, in effect, protected the value of his inventory at the August price.

What if the oil producer is wrong, and the cash price rises? Let's say that instead of falling to $100, the cash price rises to $130 by September 15, and the October futures rise to $130.10. His 25,000 barrels realize him $3,250,000 in the cash market, or $250,000 more than he could have received in August. However, his futures also rise, by a total value of $252,500 ($10.10 times 25,000). When he buys his contracts back, he realizes a futures loss of $252,500 Therefore, the futures loss of $252,500 must be taken into consideration with the extra cash profit of $250,000. He still comes back to approximately the August price. The short hedge has protected the value of his inventory at about $120 per barrel, which is the number he was targeting.

A Nebraska farmer who wants to lock in the price of his corn for harvest time in the fall, while it is still in the ground during the summer, would use a short hedge in much the same way that this oil producer uses a short hedge.

The long hedge

A commodity user (buyer) enters into a *long hedge* to fix acquisition costs and ensure a certain profit margin. For example, let's say that a producer of ethanol (a corn-based fuel additive) uses 1 million bushels of corn to meet the production for their major customer during the peak summer driving season. It is April, and July corn futures are quoted at $6.50 per bushel. By July, depending on weather, exports, and other unknowns, the price of corn could be much higher or lower. This big customer wishes to enter into a contract with the producer for delivery at today's price in August. (For ethanol, the producer will manufacture in July.) The producer can make a profit at today's ethanol prices if the price of corn remains at $6.50. He calculates his gross profit at $6.50 corn to be $50,000. The profit would be greater if corn prices fell. The break-even is at $6.70 corn, and if corn prices rise above this level, this would actually wipe out the profit margin (assuming today's ethanol prices, which also could fluctuate).

To keep their customer happy and loyal and to ensure that the plant continues to run at capacity, the ethanol producer enters into an agreement to deliver ethanol at today's price to the big customer in August. Rather than take the risk of the marketplace and run the risk of potentially selling the production at a loss in the summer if corn prices rise, they forgo the gamble of a windfall profit (in the event that corn prices fall) and enter a long hedge in the futures market. The producer buys 1 million bushels of July corn in the futures on April 15. This is the day they also enters into the cash contract for delivery of ethanol to the customer next August. The price of July corn on April 15 is $6.50. A drought develops, and in July, when the ethanol producer needs to go into the cash market to purchase the 1 million bushels, the price of corn has risen to $7.00 in both the cash and futures. It has gone up by 50¢ per bushel, which is an additional cost to the producer, over and above the April price, of $500,000 (1 million bushels, or 200 5,000-bushel contracts times 50¢ per bushel).

However, the futures have also risen by 50¢, and the ethanol producer sells the July futures contracts they purchased for $6.50 at the then-prevailing price of $7.00. They realize a futures gain of $500,000, exactly offsetting the additional cash loss of $500,000. In this way, a $50,000 gross profit was assured on the transaction. Without this long corn hedge they would have lost $450,000 on the cash contract instead of realizing a profit of $50,000.

Now if the weather had been good, and it looked as if a large crop were forthcoming, prices might have fallen to, say, $6.20 by July 15. The ethanol producer's cash corn cost in this case would be $300,000 less. If not hedged, and if they had entered into a cash contract for ethanol at the April price, they could have realized a windfall profit of $350,000 versus $50,000, all other factors remaining equal. If hedged, they lose $300,000 on the futures transaction (a fall of 30¢ per bushel times $50/penny times 200 contracts). However, the ethanol producer makes the decision to always enter into profitable contracts with their users, and they know they will remain in business. They are not in the casino business; their business is ethanol production).

This simple example demonstrates that the objectives of hedgers and speculators are not the same. A speculator is always looking to make money on transactions. However, a hedger is not always looking to profit on the futures side of the transactions. The hedger's goals are to lock in a price that will assure an overall profit or prevent a loss for his business—either the production or consumption of some product. A bread baker who wants to lock in his future wheat purchase prices would use a long hedge in much the same way.

The basis

In these examples, I have kept the basis fairly constant, but in reality, it can change. If a short hedger (one who sells futures) experiences a widening of the basis (where cash prices have fallen to a greater degree than futures—either cash has fallen faster or risen slower than futures), a basis loss may result. In other words, the short hedger's cash position loss may be greater than the gain realized on the futures side of the transaction. Or, in a rising market, the gain on the cash side of the transaction would not be as large as the loss on the futures side.

Conversely, a basis gain would occur with a widening basis on a long hedge. The futures would rise in price to a greater degree than the cash. A narrowing basis yields additional gains for a short hedger (the cash falls less, or rises more, in relation to the futures) and incremental losses for a long hedger (the cash falls less, or rises more, in relation to the futures). Basis gains or losses are a risk to a hedger, but they're not nearly as big a risk as what is called *flat price risk*. The price of heating oil may move 20¢ per gallon in a couple days, whereas the basis might move 1¢ either way. For example, the flat price move could be a result of a warmer-than–normal, winter whereas the basis change may be due to the fact it was colder in New Haven than New York that particular winter. A speculator might analyze basis changes to help determine the strength or weakness of a market, but this is really more of a hedger's concern.

Speculators versus hedgers

It doesn't matter whether the user needs copper or soybean oil or to purchase yen six months hence; any market in which prices fluctuate creates price risk for commercial participants, which in turn creates the need for a hedging tool. Remember, hedgers are not trying to make a killing in the market; they wish to offset price risks. A speculator, on the other hand, tries to make money by buying low and selling high (or vice versa). A speculator is a marketplace participant who is neither a producer nor a consumer of a commodity or financial instrument. By definition, he does not have or want the underlying commodity, and this participant could be you or me. Without speculators, the system would not work; they add liquidity. Speculators often take the other side of the bids and offers in the marketplace put out by hedgers. At times, they take the other side of a speculative bid and offer, and at times, different hedgers may be on both sides of a transaction. However, a trade cannot be completed unless someone is willing to take the other side, and if there were only hedgers and no speculators, the system would not operate smoothly. By assuming the risks the hedgers are trying to avoid, the speculators will make money when they are right and lose when wrong. In the earlier ethanol example, when the manufacturer made the $500,000 in the futures market, some person or persons lost that money. Those persons could have been speculators betting that the crop would be good and prices would fall. On the other hand, if prices did fall, this hedger's loss might have been made by speculators who were betting on lower prices.

How is the price determined?

Conspiracy theorists would tell you that price is determined by the big banks or the oil companies. A simpler explanation is supply and demand or, in other words, buyers and sellers. If the buyers are more aggressive than the sellers, prices go up. If the sellers are more eager, prices go down. In a free market, prices are determined by what the seller can get from the buyer. Prices are made by what someone is willing to pay for a given product. You might think any given price is too low or too high, but at any point in time, the market sets the price, and there's an old adage that says that the market is always right.

Order placement

Assume that you're ready to place your first trade. What's the procedure? Very simply, you need enter the symbol of commodity you want to trade, the quantity (in terms of numbers of contracts), the month, and whether you want to go long or short. You then need to determine how you want your order to be executed. There are various order types depending on your objectives on how and when you want to enter the market.

Market order

A *market order* is an order to buy or sell at the prevailing price. By definition, when a commodity is bought or sold "at the market," this is an order to fill immediately at "the next best price," but in reality, it is the "next offer" (if a buy) or the "next bid" (if a sale). I've seen advice in some trading manuals that states that you should never use a market order. The reasoning has to do with the bid/offer spread.

In an auction market, traders make bids and offers. The *bid* is the price put out for immediate acceptance. The *offer* (sometimes known as the "asked price") is the price at which the seller is "offering" for immediate sale. In most cases, you buy at the offer and sell at the bid. You potentially lose this difference—it may be small—but you can lose it by placing a market order.

I do not agree with the advice never to use market orders. For one thing, if you use a limit order at a specific price, there is no guarantee that it will be filled. The market may have to move away from the direction you think the market is moving to get filled. Most importantly, with a market order, you know you will be filled. This is important in a fast-moving market because these are the ones you most want to be in. By definition, you will be filled on every bad trade at a limit price (because it has to move opposite your bias first), but you could miss some good trades. If a market is moving at 50, 55, 60, 65, 60, 70, 80, to close at 120, and you place a market order to buy at the 60 level the first time you see 60, you might get 60—more likely 65 or even 70—but you know you are in a trade that is at least starting out right. If you limit your price to 55 or 60, you might never get in this good move. Who knows? The next day it could open at 150.

Limit order

When you place a *limit order*, you know what you will get in the worst-case scenario (you could get better), but there are strings attached. A limit order prevents you from paying more than the limit price on a buy order or receive less than the limit price on a sell order. However, unless the market is willing to meet your terms, you will not get in. The drawback of a limit order is that there is no guarantee you will get in. You could miss trades. You are not even assured that you will get in if your limit price is hit. In the preceding example, if you place a limit order to buy at "50 or better" and the market touches 50, this may be your trade, or it may be someone else's. You can be only reasonably assured that you are in if the market trades lower than 50. It is frustrating to place an order to buy at 50, see the market trade there once and find that you're not filled just as the market's crossing 75. That's not to say there isn't a place for limit orders. I like to use them in quiet, back-and-forth-type markets so as not to give up the slippage seen with a market order. I also use them to take profits on a good position. I try to let the market reach out to my limit price. After all, if the market doesn't reach my limit, I can always revert to a market order.

Stop orders

Stop orders, or *stops*, are used in two ways. The most common method is to cut a loss on a trade that is not working (also known as a *stop loss order*). A stop is an order that becomes a market order to buy or sell at the prevailing price only if and after the market touches the stop price. A sell stop is placed under the market, a buy stop above the market.

For example, say that you buy July sugar at 11¢ (1100). You buy it because your analysis suggests that the market is going to go higher. However, you do not want to risk more than approximately 50 points, so you place a sell stop, to "sell July Sugar at 1050 stop." As long as the market moves higher—fine and good—your stop will not be elected. However, if the market trades down to 1050, your stop loss automatically becomes a market order to sell. Depending on the speed and direction of the market, you will be out at the next best price. It most likely will be 1050 or slightly below, say, 1049. In a fast market, it could be lower, say 1048, or it even could be higher, say 1051, if the market upticks after the stop is hit.

A stop can also be used to lock in a profit and cut a loss. In the sugar example, let's say the market starts to move in your favor, up to 1150. You might decide to cancel your 1050 stop and move it up to 1104, thereby assuring a worst-case break even or a small loss after commissions. This is a *cancel/replace* order. The market continues to move up, reaching 1210. You decide to move your stop up to 1150, thereby assuring a profit on the trade, even if it trades back down. This is, at times, termed a *trailing stop*, which occurs when you move your stop with the market. A buy stop is placed above the market to liquidate a losing short position. For example, you go short sugar at 1201 and place your buy stop above the market at 1253 to limit your loss. You can always cancel and move your buy stop lower, in case the market moves in your favor.

Stops also can be used to initiate positions. They're used by momentum traders who want to enter a market moving in a certain direction. For example, if a trader believes that if gold is able to trade above the psychologically significant $2,000 mark, it will move higher. He places a buy stop at $2,001. If the market remains under 2000, the trader never enters the market and potentially avoids a "do nothing" or, worse, a losing trade. If the market reaches the 2001 level, he will be in at the next prevailing price. The hope is that the market keeps moving, to 2002 and on up. Once in, the trader can place a sell stop at, say, 1990, to limit losses should this turn out to be a false signal. Of course, the risk is that the market could run up to 2001 and back down again. In this case, it would have been better to limit the price at a lower level instead of using the stop to initiate the trade .

However, when used correctly, these can be useful orders to enter a new position. While a buy stop would be used to initiate a new position above the market on momentum (if not in the market), a sell stop would be used under the market. There additionally is a variation of a stop order called a *stop limit*. With a stop limit order, if the stop price is touched, a trade must be executed at the limit price (or better) or held until the stated price is reached again. The risk with the stop limit is the same as with a straight limit. In other words, if the market fails to return to the stop limit level, the order is not executed, so I normally do not recommend its use. It can, in a fast-moving market, defeat the purpose of the stop (to stop your loss).

Market if touched

Also called MITs, market-if-touched orders are the mirror image of stops. A MIT is placed above the market to initiate a short position and below the market to initiate a long position.

For example, say that you are long platinum at 1405, and you want to take profits at 1420. You could place a limit order to sell at 1420, but you cannot be assured that you will be filled if the price touches 1420. The market would have to trade above 1420 to have a reasonable assurance that you are out. An MIT at 1420 becomes a market order if 1420 is touched, which will ensure that you are out at the next prevailing price. MITs tend to be filled better on average than stops because you are moving with the prevailing trend. In a market that moves 1409.50, 1410, 1410.50, 1411, an MIT at 1410 would be filled at either 1410 or 1410.50. If the next tick after 1410 were 1409.50, you certainly could filled at 1409.50 (because the MIT became a market order), but it is more likely that a buy stop at 1410 would be filled at 1410.50 in this example. An MIT could also be used to initiate a new short position above the market. An MIT to buy is placed under the market to exit a short position or enter a new long. If the market is trading at 100, you might place an MIT to buy at 99, but you would place a stop to sell at 99. See the difference?

Exotic orders

So, these are the major types of orders you will use. There are other exotic orders I've not found useful in practice, with the exception of the OCO (which stands for *one cancels the other*). It is used on both sides of the market either to take profits or cut losses; one cancels the other. For example, you buy silver at 37.00, you want to take profits at 37.90 or cut the loss if the market trades down to 36.75. You could place one OCO order to sell at 37.90 or 36.75 stop; one cancels the other. In this way, you are assured that if one side is hit, the other side will be canceled. This is significant in volatile markets and markets that trade 24 hours a day since you'll be sleeping at some point. If you placed two separate orders, and the market first runs up to 37.90, takes out your position at a profit, then trades down to 36.75, you could be sold into a new short position you didn't want.

Another true story

This concludes our discussion of the basics. If this is your first exposure to commodity trading, you now know just enough to be dangerous. If you're a novice, hopefully this has shed some light on the game. If you've traded awhile, this is probably nothing new, but now you can get on to the more exciting stuff.

Let's conclude this chapter with a true story that happened to a commodity broker friend of mine. Remember, it is a common practice (and a good one) to place your stop loss order at the same time you place your trade, and a good broker will remind you of this. There is a belief that the traders will attempt to "run the stops," however, I've found the proper and judicious use of stops is essential to successful trading. The best markets will never reach your stop. I know that in my personal trading, a stop has many times prevented a bad trade from turning into disaster.

My commodity broker friend Tim tells the story of Elmer, a farmer client of his from rural Minnesota. Tim suspected that Elmer was growing a bit feeble, but then again, Elmer had been trading for many years, and he had always been the eccentric type. Tim recounts the day that Elmer called him prior to the market open.

Elmer to Tim: "Tim, a miracle happened to me this morning."

Tim to Elmer: "What's that, Elmer?"

Elmer to Tim: "Tim, I was shaving this morning, and as I looked in the mirror, the Holy Spirit came to me and said, 'Elmer, today you should buy 50 March wheat market at the open.'"

The way Tim tells it, he didn't hesitate, cross-examine, or stop before passing Go; he immediately queried, "Elmer, did he tell you where to place your stop?"

5

The Options Course

"The market can remain irrational longer than you can remain solvent."
—Lord Keynes

The proponents tout options as "the best of both worlds; unlimited profit potential with totally limited risk." Sounds terrific! Why would anyone trade anything else?

With options trading, as with every other financial instrument, there are advantages...but there is no free lunch. Actually, there are probably more ways to lose money when trading options than with any other financial instrument. This is because you give something up for the limited-risk feature, but in certain scenarios it's worth it to give this something up. I know folks who trade only options and wouldn't think of touching futures. Many of these people do quite well. I know others who have told me options don't work for them; they despise the added costs and point out that most options expire worthless. Like anything else in the speculative world, options requires good judgment, a sound game plan, and at times a bit of luck.

This chapter is an "Options 101" course for beginners (and those who want to brush up). In the first section, you'll learn the basics: what options are, how they work, the jargon, and the various ways to play. In the concluding section, we'll delve into some of the more advanced strategies.

An options primer

What is an option? An *option* gives a buyer the right, but not the obligation, to buy or sell a stated quantity of a commodity (or some other "asset") at a specified price on or before a specific date in the future.

Options are often compared to insurance. When you buy homeowner's insurance, for example, you pay a premium for certain rights. These rights are yours, but the policy can limit the payoff. To some extent, this analogy works for a hedger, but there are major differences when speculating. For example, an option buyer theoretically has unlimited profit potential. Insurance policies have a stated limit. Insurance is not transferable between parties and is usually specific to a person or property. Options are standardized and can be sold in the marketplace. Actually, Exchange-traded options are quite simple. There are two types—the call and the put. The features are fairly straightforward, and they can be utilized effectively under certain situations by both speculators and hedgers.

The cost of an option is called the premium. The premium is a one-time cost and represents the maximum exposure that the buyer has. No matter how far the price of the underlying asset rises or falls, the option buyer knows what his maximum risk will be. However, the profit potential is not fixed. As with futures, potential option profits are limited only by how far the market moves in the stated time period, minus the initial cost. Options are available for just about every futures market, from orange juice (an old adage says never sell call options during freeze season) to natural gas, gold, copper, heating oil, currencies…you name it. The most liquid and active futures markets, as you might have guessed, generally have the most liquid option markets.

Like futures, options trade in designated contract months. (You need to know your expiration dates because in many cases the options expire in the month preceding the futures month they correspond to.) March grain options, for example, expire the third Friday of February. For most of the cash-settled futures contracts, like the S&P 500 and Feeder Cattle, the options and futures expire the same day. You might have heard the term *triple witching hour*; it refers to the simultaneous expiration of stock index futures, stocks options, and stock futures options on the third Friday of March, June, September, and December. All this activity supposedly causes wild and crazy fluctuations, but in my experience, this has generally been a non-event. In many of the active markets, options are traded every month of the year. For example, the January, February, and March currency options all correspond to (and are exercisable into) the March contract. Consult the Exchange websites or your broker for the specifics on option months and expiration dates by market.

An option for what?

Options can be converted into the underlying futures contract at the discretion of the buyer; this is called the *right to exercise*. This is why the size of every option is exactly the same as the contract it represents. By exercising an option, the buyer receives either a long or short position at the option's strike price.

> An owner of a call option who chooses to exercise receives a long futures position. An owner of a put option who chooses to exercise receives a short futures position.

Advantages and disadvantages of options

For option *buyers*, the primary advantage is definitely the limited-risk feature. Unlike with futures, with options, the most you can ever lose as a buyer (not as a seller) is what you pay for the option. You could lose less by selling out prior to expiration, and you could even make a significant profit trading options, but you have a specifically defined and maximum risk. Additional margin calls are not a possibility, and you can avoid sleepless nights because you know the worst-case scenario the day you initiate an option purchase. The same is not true with futures.

For option buyers, the primary disadvantage is the premium. The premium must be paid up front, and this cost must be recovered in part or in whole through a favorable movement in price…or else you lose. When buying options, you can be correct in your market assessment, but if the market doesn't move far enough in your favor, you still lose.

Consider this: If you buy a wheat option good for the current market price for a premium cost of $1,000, and the market goes nowhere (it stays at the same price for the life of the option), you're out $1,000 plus fees. The market moved nowhere, and whoever sold that option to you keeps your $1,000.

To profit, the option *seller* only needs a stagnant market, a move in his direction, or an adverse move that does not cover the premium in full. If you buy a futures contract and hold it for the same time period in a market that goes nowhere, you're out nothing except the commission costs. In this case, the "limited-risk" option is definitely more costly than the "higher-risk" futures contract. Of course, in this simple example, we don't know what transpired in the interim period. The market could have sold off wildly, resulting in a margin call or a stop loss being hit in the futures and subsequently recovered. The futures trader could have been knocked out, perhaps more than once, while the option trader (not subject to margin calls) could sit it out. You see, there are no easy answers here, and we've only scratched the surface.

Types of options

Calls and puts are the two basic option types.

Call options are bought by bullish traders. A call option gives the buyer the right, but not an obligation, to purchase the underlying asset at an agreed-upon price (known as the *strike price*) within a specified time.

Put options are the mirror image of calls. A put option gives the buyer the right, but no obligation, to sell the underlying asset at an agreed-upon price (the strike price) within a specified time. Bearish traders who anticipate a weaker market would be the buyers of these options. What is the underlying asset? It is, for Exchange-traded options, the corresponding futures contract. Call buyers have the right to exercise into a long futures position, and put buyers have the right to exercise into a short futures option (at the corresponding strike price).

Strike prices

The option rules are set by the Exchange where the options are traded, and by convention, the Exchange determines the strike prices at which options trade. These prices are listed at set intervals.

For example, wheat options trade at every 10¢ per bushel: $7.50, $7.60, $7.70, and so on. (I am referring to Exchange-traded options in this book because these are the options available to the general public. Some brokers and institutions also offer over-the-counter [OTC] options, which are dealt off the Exchange. OTC options are completely flexible; the exact details, such as date and quantity, are freely negotiable between the buyer and seller. OTC options are common in the currency markets, for example but are generally available only to big players in lots of $1 million minimum.)

Exchange-traded options are standardized. The Exchange sets the strike prices, size, specifications, expiration date, and style (American or European). Most importantly, the Exchange eliminates the counterparty risk. If an Exchange member goes belly up, the clearinghouse guarantees performance. If the bank on the other end of your OTC option has one rogue trader too many, there is no guarantee you will be able to collect even if you are profitable. Although the risk of nonperformance by a large money center bank or multinational brokerage firm is slim, it is nevertheless a risk. Options written by Lehman Brothers in 2008 never were paid off by that option writer.

Another major advantage of Exchange-traded options is quotations, or transparency. This advantage may seem insignificant because you are able to get a quote from the counterparty for your OTC option. However, with the OTCs, the quote comes directly from the other party—and whose interest do you think is foremost in their mind? Quotes on Exchange-traded options are disseminated publicly by a third party—the Exchange—based on actual trades in an auction-like environment.

Styles of options

Two styles of options are available: American and European. The basic difference is in the rules of exercise. A buyer can exercise an American-style option at any time before it expires. A buyer can exercise a European-style option only on the expiration date. All other factors being equal, a European option is generally slightly cheaper than an American option because it can be exercised only on the one date and, therefore, involves less uncertainty for the seller. The vast majority of Exchange-traded options are American style, and the vast majority of OTC options are European style.

How are option prices quoted?

Option prices are quoted in terms of futures ticks. For example, a €122 call option might be quoted at 99 bid/102 offered. These are ticks, and because a tick for the euro contract on the Chicago Mercantile Exchange (CME) represents $12.50. If the 122 Euro option is priced at 101, it is worth $1,262.50. A 790 wheat call at 22¢ goes for $1,100. (It is a 5000-bushel contract, so each penny is worth $50.)

Buy 'em and sell 'em

Option buyers, for both puts and calls, pay a premium. Who gets it? The option seller receives the premium. In many cases, option sellers (also called option writers) are professional traders because the public generally prefers buying options. However, anyone can be an option seller. Why would you want to be an option seller? It places the odds in your favor. You receive the premium; it is credited to your account and becomes a cushion against an adverse market move. When would a trader not in the option market consider selling options?

- *Call options are primarily sold by bearish traders:* Call options are also sold by traders who expect a market to go nowhere over the specified time period. Call options are also sold, at times, by bullish traders who wish to receive protection, or cover, a long position or gain additional income from a long position.

- *Put options are primarily sold by bullish traders:* If the market moves up and remains above the strike price within the specified period, the put seller keeps the premium with no penalty. Put options may also be sold by traders who feel the market is going nowhere. At times, bearish traders who are looking for protection to cover a short position or to gain incremental income for a short position sell puts.

Advantages and disadvantages of selling options

The primary advantage of selling options is that the seller receives the premium income paid by the buyer immediately. All she needs to make money is either a quiet or stable market, or a market move away from the buyer, or a market move in favor of the buyer that is less than the premium received. In other words, there is a wider range of price movement in which the option seller profits. The odds are in the seller's favor, and this is why professionals like to sell them.

The disadvantage of selling options is the unlimited risk. Selling options is the mirror image of buying options: Because the market can move an unspecified amount away from the strike price, the risk cannot be predetermined. You can think of it like a Las Vegas casino, with the option seller as the house. You know the house has the advantage, but this doesn't mean any individual on any particular evening couldn't make a major hit against the house.

How options work

Let's look at an example of how options work. Say that you're bullish gold and want to play this market using options. You're a bull, so you can employ two basic strategies: You can either buy a call option or sell a put option. However, other decisions need to be made. It's like a kid who goes in to buy his first pack of cigarettes. The clerk asks him which brand he wants. The kid asks for Marlboro. Standard or Menthol? 100s or shorts? Box or soft pack? With his head spinning, the kid runs out of the store, rationalizing that cigarettes aren't good for you anyway.

Similarly, options come in a variety of flavors. The simplest way to participate is to buy a call (if you think the price will rise) or buy a put (if you're bearish). Suppose it's December, and the price of gold is $1,399 per ounce. You can buy an April 1400 call for, say, $26 per ounce. The option is exercisable into a standard futures contract, and this option has a size of 100 ounces, so $26 is equal to a cost of $2,600 per option. This option gives you the right, but not the obligation, to receive an April futures contract at a price of $1,400 at any time at your discretion, prior to the expiration date (which in this case is mid-March). You can pay less for an April 1420 call or more for an April 1380 call. You can pay more for a June 1400 call or less for a February 1400 call. You can pay much less for an April 1600 call or a lot more for a February 1340 call. The permutations are just about endless. Of course, you can sell any of these as well. Clients who have a market opinion often ask me, "Which is the best option for me to buy?" How do you determine this? It depends not only on your outlook but also your outlook for your outlook. There are a few other issues you will need to understand before you make your first option trade.

Time

The first issue you need to understand before you make your first option trade is time. You have to decide how much time you wish to pay for. A basic rule of thumb is—and this should be no surprise—that the more time you want the option to have before it expires, the higher the premium. You can go far out in time and receive a lot more time for your position to work, but this is generally a bad idea. Remember, there is no free lunch. Long-dated options are more expensive, and you tie up more money for a longer period of time. Instead, you could use that money for alternative transactions. Plus, the further out you go, the less liquid the option becomes. When trading a long-dated option, you are generally dealing with a market professional who will quote a wide bid-to-offer spread. If you want to liquidate the option in the options market (as opposed to exercising the option), you'll have to deal with this spread once again. In other words, the slippage is high, and these are additional hidden costs.

The cheapest options are the nearest options time-wise. The problem with a short-dated option—and this is obvious as well—is that you have a much shorter time for the market to move your way. Unlike with futures, with options the market not only has to move your way, but it needs to do so more quickly. This works at times, but the market doesn't always know your option's expiration date. There are no simple formulas that can tell you what is a fair price to pay for time at any particular point. A six-month option might or might not cost twice as much as a three-month option. You are dealing with the spreads of the underlying commodity, which can change. Many times the near month moves faster than the back months, and this is reflected in the option's cost.

Time decay

All else being equal, the time value of an option decreases slightly each day (provided that there is still a reasonable amount of time left before expiration). The rate of this decrease becomes more rapid as the option gets closer to expiration. This is termed the *normal time decay*, and it works to the detriment of the buyer and the benefit of the seller. As an option gets close to expiration time, the value becomes less and less. What matters is the relationship between the strike and the underlying commodity. This is because at expiration, the option can only be worth something or, alternatively, nothing—and that's it. Remember, you might buy a call because you think a particular commodity will increase in price, but you could show a loss even if you are correct. This happens when the extent of the rise is insufficient to compensate for the time it takes to occur.

In, at, and out of the money

If you look at an option price table, you will see two major categories: puts and calls. Then you will see listings for different months into the future. Under each month, you will see a variety of different strike prices. These are the prices at which the options can be exercised, an important feature of options that makes them more complicated than futures.

Let's look at gold as an example. Say that you are bullish gold and decide to purchase the April 1400 call when April gold is trading at $1,399. April gold futures subsequently rise to $1,425 per ounce. At this point, the option has *intrinsic value* because the price of the underlying asset (in this case, April gold futures) is above the strike price. At $1,425 per ounce, the 1400 call has $25 of intrinsic value. This is now an *in-the-money* call option—in the money by $25. Because a gold option is for 100 ounces, and every $1 is worth $100 per option, the value of this option is at least $2,500 ($25 times $100 per ounce). Another way to look at this is that the right to buy at $1,400, when the current price is $1,425 must be worth at least $25 because it is already profitable by this amount. It could be worth more if there is still time value.

Time value is that portion of the premium price outside of the intrinsic value. An option's price is dependent on time, but there are other factors as well that determine an option's value.

By definition, a call option is "in the money" when the market price of the futures is above the strike price of the option. A cocoa 2400 call is in the money when the futures are trading at 2458. A call option is out of the money when the futures price is below the strike. The same call is out of the money when the futures are at 2361. Because puts are always the mirror image of the calls, a put option is in the money when the market price of the futures is below the strike price of the option. A 2400 cocoa put is in the money at a 2361 futures price but out of the money at 2458. *Out-of-the-money* options have time value only.

How are option prices determined?

Like futures, options are traded in an auction-like environment. Futures traders are looking at whatever technical or fundamental factors they use to determine the value of the particular commodity they are trading, whereas the option traders are also looking at the futures. It goes without saying that the underlying asset determines an option's premium price. Dissecting this a bit further, you see that any particular option's premium has two basic parts: time value and intrinsic value. Options that are out of the money have only time value. That is, these options have no value other than potential value.

For example, in the earlier scenario, the April 1400 gold call was trading for $26 per ounce in December and would have cost the buyer $2,600. The price of April gold at that time was $1,399, so the option could not have been exercised at a profit. Nobody in his right mind would exercise an option to receive April futures at $1,400 when he could go immediately into the marketplace and buy it $1 per ounce cheaper.

So why, then, would anyone (in his right mind) pay $2,600 for this right? The reason is that this option has potential. To buy futures, the risk is potentially greater than $2,600. Yes, you could buy April futures at $1,399 and place a $26 stop. Although this would essentially provide the same initial risk without requiring you to fork over the $2,600, some major differences exist. For one thing, when you buy an option for $2,600, you know your maximum risk is guaranteed. If you purchase futures, with a $2,600 stop loss, the stop could be filled better at times, but it could be filled worse than your stop loss point. Another possibility is that the market could trade in a range. The market could fall $26 or more, stop you out of your futures, and then eventually trade back up to profitable levels. This underscores another main advantage of option purchases; staying power. The other side of the coin is the cost. If your analysis is right, and you are willing to take the risk of the futures, you are guaranteed to make more than you would by buying options. If the price of gold rises to $1,425, and you bought your contract at $1,399, you have the ability to cash in with a $2,600 profit per contract ($26 times $100 per ounce) minus fees. You have the right to sell your option and/or exercise it, but your profit has to be less than the $2,600. Remember, in our example, you paid $2,600 for time—or $2,600 for the potential to make a score. Some time has passed, and some time value will have disappeared. You won't get back that full $2,600, only a portion of it.

Let's review these concepts and clear up any confusion that remains. Calls that have a strike price above the market (for example, a 1400 gold call with the market at $1,399) and puts that have a strike price below the market (for example, a 1390 put with the market at $1,399) have premiums composed of time value only. In-the-money options (for example, a 1400 call with the market price at $1,425 or a 1440 put with the market at $1,425) have both time and intrinsic value. The more an option is in the money, the more valuable it becomes, so by definition, it becomes more expensive.

Another way of looking at this is with a simple formula:

Time Value = Premium – Intrinsic Value.

Time value increases for options with greater time to expiration. It makes sense, of course, because the more time an option has until expiration, the more potential the option buyer has for something to happen, and that increases the value of the option. The seller is taking additional risk (there's more time for something to go awry from his standpoint), and he demands additional compensation for this additional risk.

So, in-the-money options have intrinsic value and time value. Out-of-the-money options have time value only. You'll hear the term *at the money* as well; this term refers to an option for which the strike price is equivalent to the underlying futures price. In practice, at-the-moneys are options for which strike prices are close to the price of the futures. In the example with April gold at $1,399, the 1400s are "at the money." The 1410s are definitely out of the money, and the 1390s are in the money. The 1340s are deep in the money. What would you call the 2,500s? You could call them deep out of the money, or I would call these a long shot.

Long shots are generally cheap. You can buy quite a few out-of-the-money options for relatively little money, so if something extraordinary occurs, you stand to make a killing. A good analogy would be the Megabucks slot machines where I live in Nevada. The state's casinos link up for the Megabucks jackpot, where $3 can win $30 million or more. People do win these, but how many such people do you know? The jack does pop out of the box once every blue moon, however.

I once had a client who owned way-out-of-the-money wheat calls (worth less than a penny each, if I remember correctly) and only three days to go. It looked hopeless, and I felt he should have salvaged a few pennies so he could at least cover commissions. Then something called Chernobyl happened. We had never traded a nuclear accident before, and the rumors started to fly. The first rumor was that the entire Soviet wheat crop was wiped out. Wheat went limit up the next day and the day after. The options came back from the dead, and my client eventually cashed out each option on expiration day for 39¢ per bushel. In other words, options were selling for less than $50 each just days before and blossomed to $1,950 on expiration day. It was a good thing he had to sell that day (and that he didn't decide to exercise) because after the extent of the radiation damage was deemed not as severe as first feared, wheat prices came all the way back down a few days later.

You do hear rags-to-riches stories at times, as cheap options come to life. I personally owned some euro puts that were essentially worthless, and then the day of the Soviet coup, they blossomed to 50 points, or $625. When Yeltsin stood on the tank, and the coup failed the next day, they became virtually worthless again. Sometimes you need to be nimble. The point is, deep out-of-the-money options can hit at times, but they are long shots and generally a loser's game. I prefer both buying and selling at-the-moneys in most normal situations. With deep in-the-money options, you tie up capital that otherwise could be used for diversification. Deep out-of-the-moneys generally expire worthless. Given the choice, I also prefer to pay more for time.

Volatility

Okay, we have discussed how an option's value is determined—time and the relationship of the strike price to the underlying futures price. And there is another component: *volatility*. Very simply, as the volatility of a market increases, so do option premiums. This is an important determinant in pricing options. Sleepy markets supposedly have lower potential price movements, and option buyers bid less. However, some of my best option purchases have been "cheap" buys. When everyone is buying, the smart money is selling. The reason premiums increase with higher volatility is very simple: Option sellers demand higher premiums to offset the higher risks their options entail in a more volatile environment.

Many of the option pricing models place a great deal of emphasis on historic volatility. In determining "fair value," you are asked to input this number. For example, if the market is moving at a rate that equals 20% of the price annualized, this is your historic volatility. I have found this to be an academic exercise of limited value. It is only a prediction, and the past is not necessarily a good predictor of the future. My experience has shown the opposite: Quiet markets lead to more volatile markets and vice versa. When volatility is high, option prices are expensive, and although it takes guts, this is generally the time to sell. On the other hand, an old-timer once gave me some sage advice: "Never sell a quiet market." Let me sum this up another way. In general, the premiums reflect recent market conditions. In explosive markets, the premiums are larger than quiet markets. The risk equals the reward; however, in some situations, the majority does not see the change coming. Premiums could be tiny just before a major move comes; options are cheapest when they are the best buys. Conversely, at the pinnacle of expectation, decent opportunities to sell arise because premiums are at their highest.

One last point about volatility: On a percentage basis, volatility affects at- and out-of-the-money options to a greater extent than in-the-money options. Here's the reason: In-the-moneys have both intrinsic and extrinsic (that is, anything other than intrinsic—mostly time) value. Intrinsic value is not affected directly by changes in volatility. Therefore, a change of 10% in volatility might change an in-the-money option's value by 2%, whereas it would change an at-the-money's value by 10%. Out-of-the-moneys are affected most by changes in volatility because they can become profitable only when the market moves to them. A change of 10% in volatility could result in an option's price moving by up to 50% or more. This percentage move is also easier to accomplish for out-of-the-moneys because they are cheaper.

One final factor that determines option premiums is the cost of money, or interest rates. I won't dwell on interest rates here or discuss the various models for fair option pricing, because I have found these variables to be more theoretical than practical. In most cases, the professionals on the floor are able to exploit minor degrees in option mispricing, but this is not what we are playing for here. We are in this for bigger moves that can be exploited (or, for a hedger, options as a tool for price protection).

How changes in the price of the underlying commodity change an option's premium

All other things being equal, the basic rule of thumb for how changes in price of the underlying commodity change an option's premium are as follows:

- At-the-money options move at a 50% rate of change. For example, if the S&P moves 200 points, an at-the-money option will increase or decrease by about 100 points.
- In-the-money options move at a 50%–100% rate of change, depending on how deep in the money they are.
- Out-of-the-money options move at 0–50% rate of change, depending on how deep out of the money they are.

Again, these are rules of thumb. I have seen days in quiet markets when both puts and calls lose premium, regardless of the move of the market. Then again, in times of wild fluctuations or greater-than-normal expectations, both puts and calls can gain premium in the same day. However, in normal markets, these rules work fairly well. An at-the-money option moves at about half the speed of the futures. If a call (and an up day) the next lower strike price might move up 55% of the futures move , the next higher strike up say 45% of the futures move and so on. If a put, an at-the-money will also move at half the speed of the futures, the next lower strike up say 45% (if a down day) and the next higher strike up something like 55%.

If you trade options, you possibly will also hear the term *delta*, which is what I'm referring to above. Delta values range from 0 (for very deep out-of-the-money options) to 1 (or 100% for options so deeply in the money that they move just like the underlying futures). At-the-money options have a delta value of 50% (or .5). Calls have a positive delta, whereas puts have a negative delta. If, for example, a 400 copper call trading for 1250 points (or 12 1/2 ¢) has a delta of .6, a 1¢ (or 100-point) move in the copper price results in a move of 60 points in the value of the call to 1310.

You might also hear the term *delta hedging*. Professionals who specialize in selling options to the public strive to manipulate their position to always be neutral delta hedged. In this way, they look to maximize the benefits of time decay.

Gamma is an interesting concept in theory—it is the extent to which the delta itself is changing in relation to the underlying price move, or the change in volatility—but I've found it of no use in practice. The average trader needn't monitor gamma. For those who wish to achieve delta neutrality constantly, it is something to keep an eye on, but a more detailed explanation is beyond the scope of this discussion.

Exercising profitable options

When you exercise an option, you receive the underlying asset. In the case of a put option, you receive a short futures contract. (The seller or option writer receives the other side of the transaction, which is the long position.)

For example, let's say it is March. You feel that soybean prices are overvalued and purchase May $17.00 put options when the May futures are $17.02 for 30¢ per bushel. Then the futures fall to $16.85. The puts reflect the increased intrinsic value, in this case. They trade for at least 15¢, the difference between the strike price and the intrinsic value, or the amount the option is in the money. The put buyer could exercise her option, receive a short futures at $17.00, and, if desired, could cover the short futures at $16.85 in the futures market to realize the 15¢. She makes an automatic profit of 15¢ per bushel, or $750 per contract, which is the difference between the purchase price of the option and the futures profit. Of course, this example does not include time value or commissions, one of the basic reasons options are often not exercised. Instead of paying the commission to receive the futures and an additional commission when you offset the futures, it is much simpler and easier to sell the option back in the options market.

The great majority of option transactions take place entirely in the options market. When you are in the futures (which is what happens when you exercise), you assume the additional risks of futures. You can still lose more than your initial investment if you're not careful, and you must post margins required for futures. In fact, option buyers never have to get involved in futures at all. Option premiums reflect the change in value of the underlying futures. In addition, there is another good reason not to exercise options in normal markets. In most cases, you are giving up some additional money, which represents any time value remaining.

Let's look again at the above soybean put option example. The put value always includes any cash value, or intrinsic value, which is determined by the underlying futures. When the market is trading at $16.85, the $17 put is 15¢ in the money and has 15¢ in intrinsic value. Depending on how much time is left until expiration, this put also has some time value associated with it. It may be trading for 30¢ or more if a lot of time is left or perhaps 19¢ if just a few days are left. This is an in-the-money put in this example. The $16.80 also has a quoted value. With months left, it could be 30¢ or more, or with days left, it could be only a few pennies. This is an out-of-the-money option with no intrinsic value. Its total price consists of time value, or the potential to become profitable based on time, market outlook, and volatility.

In conclusion, the most profitable, least costly, and easiest way to liquidate an option is to sell the option back into the options market instead of exercising it.

Should you ever exercise an option?

There is really only one instance in which I would consider exercising a long put or call: on the last day, with no time value left. Options are priced according to their cash value. This also happens, at times, to deep in-the-money options prior to expiration. You might think you could always sell an option for at least its cash or intrinsic value, but this is not always the case. At the very end, you are most likely dealing with a professional trader. The public is not interested in selling in-the-money options on the last day. The professionals require a sweetener to take the other side of your transaction if you are looking to sell an option like this, and you may need to give up a small piece of the premium you earned to liquidate in the options market at an illiquid time.

Looking at the soybean put example once more, let's say the market is at $16.60, and you try to sell your 1700 put for 40¢ with very little time remaining. You might not get the order filled. You might need to price it at 39¢, which would guarantee the local a modest 1¢ ($50 per contract) profit. He just offsets the transaction in the futures market, and this guarantees him a profit. Another option is to buy the futures at $16.60, exercise the 1700 put, and be assigned a short futures at $17.00, which offsets with your long from $16.60 and results in a 40¢ futures profit. Your net profit in this example is the 40¢ minus your original option cost minus commissions. You need to consider whether this makes more sense than letting the local take the sweetener. Or, if you still feel the market is going to move in the direction of your option, consider exercising a profitable option on the last day. You don't need to even consider this prior to the last day, but on the day of expiration, you do. Remember that when you exercise, you are subject to the margining requirements of futures. In many cases, however, for a deep in-the-money option, you have this covered by the value of the option—at least temporarily. A greater concern is that you are now in futures, something option buyers have been trying to avoid. The risk is no longer limited, and an unfavorable move in the underlying futures can now wipe out your profit, so you should consider using a stop loss to prevent losing what you made.

If selling options puts the odds in my favor, why not do it?

Professional traders sell many more options than the public. Traders like getting the head start that selling (also called *option writing*) entails. Anyone can take the other side of an option purchase; however, the field is wide open. It is something to consider, but first think about this: The primary advantage of buying options is the option writer's disadvantage

When you sell an option, you agree to provide the option buyer with either a long position (when writing a call) or a short position (when writing a put). You receive the premium, but because the market could move an unlimited amount away from the strike price, the associated risk is also unlimited. The greater the premium received, the lower the risk to the option writer. The lower the volatility (not always an easy thing to predict), the lower the risk to the option writer. As a general rule, the less time that exists until expiration, the lower the risk to the option writer. The option writer is also subject to the risk of exercise. This is a right specifically granted to the option buyer, over which the seller has no control. When the buyer exercises a call option, he is credited with a long futures position at the strike price; the seller receives the short side of the transaction (at the strike price). When a put is exercised, the buyer is credited with the short and the seller with the long. A buyer exercises an option only when it is profitable to do so. Because profitability is the main reason a buyer is in options, there is no other reason to exercise the option. The buyer would just walk away from an unprofitable option, either by letting it expire worthless or by selling it back to the option market if there is time value left. By definition, when an option is exercised against the seller, it is unprofitable to the seller.

The only time it would not be unprofitable is if the seller sold the option in the aftermarket when it was already unprofitable to a previous seller.

The risk of exercise and the unlimited potential risk are the risks all option sellers must, by contract, accept. So, why take these risks? The reason is the option seller has a head start; she receives the premium. This insulates her risk to some extent, and she makes money in more situations than the buyer. The buyer needs a move in his favor. If he holds the option until expiration to realize a profit, the buyer needs not only a favorable move but also a move that exceeds the premium he paid. The seller can make money if there is a move favorable to her position (up when selling puts or down when selling calls). She also makes money in a quiet or stationary market, which is something an option buyer cannot do. Finally, she can profit even if the market moves against her, as long as it moves to a lesser degree than the premium received.

You will no doubt hear warnings against "naked" option writing. But just how risky is it to sell options? Well, it can be risky—certainly more so than buying—but it is actually less so than futures. It's risky because you receive a premium, and in the case of writing out-of-the-money options, you have the additional cushion of the gap between the market and the strike price. Furthermore, an option writer can use defensive strategies to protect himself. The writer can always buy back his short position, just as a short futures trader can buy back hers. He can use a stop loss in the option market, just as in futures. Some options are not all that liquid, and you need to take this into account, but many of them trade actively and are as liquid as the underlying futures markets. Finally, the option writer can buy (in the case of selling a call) or sell (for a put) a futures against his option if he gets into trouble. In many cases, professionals use this strategy to become more neutral.

For example, assume that you're bullish corn, and you are looking for an up move but not necessarily a major move. You can buy futures, buy calls, or sell puts. It is late September, and December corn is trading at $7 per bushel. You can buy the futures at $7, have unlimited upside, and (theoretically) have unlimited risk. You can buy the December 700 calls for 20¢ per bushel or sell the December 700 puts for 20¢. You project that the market will make a move to the $7.20 level, so you decide to sell the puts. If the market closes anywhere above $7 at expiration, you keep the entire premium, which in this case is 20¢, or $1,000 per option (minus the inevitable commission). If the market does close at $7.10, you keep the premium (because the 700 put expires worthless and is abandoned by the buyer). This is a profit, the same as for a futures buyer who buys at $7 and sells at $7.10. However, the put seller realizes the same profit—at a corn price of $7 at expiration, whereas the futures buyer only breaks even.

You can even be wrong and not lose. At expiration, if the market drops to $6.80, while the futures buyer is sitting with a 20¢ loss, the option seller can still get out of his obligation in the options market at approximately 20¢, or about break even…the seller was wrong about the market going up, yet no loss in this case. The beauty of selling options is that you can also be wrong and still profit. In this example, if the market falls to $6.95 by expiration, the option can be covered at 5¢, for a 15¢ profit. You can be wrong and still make a profit, which is an impossibility with futures or any other investment I can think of. The odds are in the option seller's favor because the majority of options do expire worthless and are never exercised. However, the payoffs are not as potentially high.

Here's the rub: The most an option seller can ever receive is the premium, and never a penny more. The risks are greater than with buying, and for some traders, the risks are just too high for the potential gain. This is the trade-off. Sellers have the odds in their favor, but buyers have the greater potential. This is not to say that sellers are stuck with the position. Just as in futures, the risks can be managed. As with a short seller in futures, a short option seller can get out by covering her position in the option market. Stop-loss orders are accepted in options. Should you write options? Nothing is wrong with it for those who understand the risks and how to manage them. Some traders, however, just cannot find it in themselves to cut the losses (one of the most important lessons) and should buy only options—nothing else. You know who you are.

Options as a hedging tool

Hedging is the offsetting of risks from other positions. Although as a speculator I personally prefer futures to options, I believe hedgers in may cases should consider options over futures. Options truly can offer the best of both worlds.

For example, a cattle feeder should know what his break-even cost is. He knows what he paid for the calf, and he knows his feed costs. (He hedged his corn, of course.) He knows his vet costs and labor, he has an allowance for death loss, and he can to the penny calculate his cost to finance the entire operation. Therefore, he would know that his break-even is 70¢ per pound for the finished product (a market-ready animal 120 days hence).

What the cattle feeder doesn't know is what his ultimate selling price will be on that date. After all, he is dealing with the unknown to some extent here. The futures 120 days out could be trading at 73¢, and by selling the futures today, he can guarantee himself a 3¢ profit. This isn't all bad, except that cattle feeding is a risky business. In periods of windfall profits, 30¢ per pound or more can be had. In other periods, 120 days of work and risk result in a net loss. If a 3¢ profit could always be locked in, a lot of the risk and uncertainty would be taken out of the equation, but in the real world, it's not always possible to lock in a profit.

The bottom line? You need the windfall profits at times to offset the marginal profits and losing periods that also occur. Futures hedges lock out the windfall profits. If you sell futures at 73¢, and the price at finish is 80¢, you have a futures loss of 7¢, which offsets the windfall cash gain of 10¢. The net result gets you back to your 3¢ profit. Today, most cattle feeders just accept the risk of the marketplace. They feed cattle and hope for a decent price in four or five months to reward them for their efforts. Sometimes it happens, but there are also many former cattle feeders out there. On the other hand, the big, profitable corporate cattle feeders use options. This should tell you something.

Here's how it might work. The feeder in this case could buy a 120-day live cattle put at, say, a 73 strike price for 2¢ per pound. In effect, he is "locking in" a 71¢ selling price (73 minus 2). If the price falls to, for example, 66 at expiration when his cattle are ready, he will take a 4¢ bath in the cash market. His break-even is 70, so a sale at 66 is a 4¢ loss. However, to offset this loss, his option will be worth 7¢, for a net profit of 5¢ before commissions (recall that he paid 2¢). Add the 5 back to the 66, and the feeder, in effect, gets back to his 71¢ in the worst-case scenario. So the feeder is giving up 2¢ of potential profit for the ability to avoid catastrophic loss. The real beauty of options, unlike futures and unlike forward contracting in the cash market, is that the upside is totally unlimited. If prices rise to 80, the feeder reaps a 10¢ profit in the cash market. This is reduced by the cost of the option, in this case 2¢, down to 8¢, but the upside is unlimited. The bottom line is that the feeder has a tool in which he can guarantee himself a price floor, a worst-case scenario, while not constructing a ceiling (which is what he is doing with futures hedges).

Precious few opportunities exist for the feeder to reap windfall profits, and he needs them to offset the mediocre or worse-than-mediocre years. Options are a powerful tool that, when used properly, achieve this goal.

This concept works just as well in financial futures. Say that a U.S. company receives an order from Germany for equipment not yet built, with the U.S. company receiving euros on delivery in six months. The euro is trading today at 125 to the dollar. The profit margin is good, but it could be wiped out by exchange-rate fluctuations. Also, a windfall gain could be possible if the currency moves up in relation to the dollar within the time period. The company is not in the business of currency speculation; its business is building equipment. The common practice is to hedge in the currency forward by using the interbank market (the electronic market between banks for foreign exchange trading). This might be prudent, and it certainly makes more sense to a manufacturing business than floating in the wind. Options can be just as prudent, and they offer something else, a sweetener—the possibility of improving on a position while limiting the risk for a predetermined cost.

The company can purchase an option, giving it the right to sell euros at, say, 125 to the dollar in six months for 300 basis points—a 125 put. A standard contract traded at the CME is for €125,000. The minimum tick is for $12.50 per contract, so a quote of 300 points would cost the company $3,750. If the order is for €1 million worth of equipment (today's exchange rate), the company might buy about eight of these puts—as profit insurance, so to speak. If the euro rises, the company loses the premiums, but it can reap an additional currency profit that is theoretically unlimited. If the euro falls, the company sells the put for a profit, and this offsets the cheaper currency. Ultimately, the company is willing to pay the $30,000, which reduces its bottom-line profit to ensure a profit.

Finally, let's look at this from the other side. If a company places an order for merchandise or equipment and is required to pay for it on receipt sometime in the future, this firm also has a currency exposure. A rise in the value of the euro, or yen, or any other currency means higher costs. A fall reduces the cost of the purchase and adds to line profits. Unless the firm's purchasing people are gamblers, who can end up being heroes or bums (and bums don't keep their jobs), they will hedge this risk. The traditional method is to forward contract in the interbank market or buy futures. Both methods lock in a price or cost of the currency. However, buying calls might be a better way to go—establishing a ceiling price on costs while allowing for windfall profits if the currency falls by more than the option price in the time period.

Stock index options

How many times have you been right about the direction of the stock market, but your stocks went nowhere? Well, you guessed it, there's a simple way to gamble on the stock market without having to be a stock picker. A trader who is bullish can buy S&P 500 (or any of the other) stock index call options. A bear would, of course, buy the puts. Or, when the premiums are high, a sale might be warranted. Much of the volume in the S&P is institutional, where a portfolio manager uses the futures or options for protection, but any individual can use S&P at-the-money puts for price protection. They allow the buyer to sell the S&P 500 Index (the 500 biggest stocks, representing more than 80% of the U.S. market) at today's market price. If prices rise by expiration, the purchase price and commissions are lost, but no additional funds are required. This is a hedge, however, and if you lose on the put, hopefully your stock portfolio rose. If the market falls by the same amount as the premium, you'll get your purchase price back. In other words, you're protecting your portfolio from a fall of greater than the premium paid. If the market falls by a greater percentage, you lose on your portfolio but gain on the put option. Why wouldn't a bear just sell his stocks? For long-term investors wary of a market dip, this is cheaper and easier. Selling a large portfolio of stocks would involve numerous and costly commissions. The commission on each S&P option generally is cheaper. Plus, you need not forgo dividend income on your stocks or worry about long-term capital gains taxes, and, if your stocks outperform the market in general, you have a relationship gain. If the market declines, the investor/hedger can sell his put at a profit and hold onto the stocks. If the market rises, the stocks will be worth more, and the put has to be considered insurance that just never needed to be used.

Advanced option strategies

Thick books have been written about options. Many of them get too precise for practical real-world trading, covering such academic topics as complex butterfly spreads and other strategies that might look good on paper but in practice I've seldom found useful. Here, I'll cover some basic strategies I feel worthy of your consideration.

Buying options to protect futures

Buying options to protect futures involves buying a put with long futures or buying a call with short futures. This strategy is also known as *creating synthetic options* because a put combined with a long futures is similar to a call, and the call in conjunction with the short futures is similar to a put. You can make a case that if you buy an at-the-money call option while simultaneously holding a short futures position (synthetic put), or you buy a put option while simultaneously holding a long futures position (synthetic call) that the overall position will act just like a put or a call (so why bother?). Because this can be a better strategy since it gives you added flexibility.

For example, say that you are fundamentally bullish the hog market, but you are concerned that the upcoming Hogs and Pigs Report could move the market substantially (hopefully in your direction, but there are no guarantees). In fact, the Hogs and Pigs Report, released quarterly by the USDA, has a reputation for moving the market's locked limit, at times consecutive multiple limit days in a row. Lock-limit moves (or abnormal moves in markets without limits) is a risk every futures trader has to accept. If the Hogs and Pigs Report is a bearish surprise, you could lose many times your initial margin because you might not be able to liquidate the first day or even the second. This can become a real nightmare when you're caught on the wrong side of a three-day lock-limit report, and it does happen.

Of course, the Hogs and Pigs Report could confirm your fundamental bias. If you are not in a position, and the market starts moving limit in your intended direction, you might be unable to enter at a reasonable price. You could buy a call, of course, but here's a more flexible approach.

Say that you buy the hogs at 72 and simultaneously purchase a 72 put for a premium of 180 points, or $720. If the report is bullish, you can abandon your put for whatever the market will offer and reap your profit on the futures. If the report is bearish, you are protected, and regardless of how many limit moves the market makes, you know your worst-case scenario—in this case, a $720 maximum risk plus fees. If worse comes to worst, you can exercise the put, and you will be assigned a short futures position that automatically offsets your long futures. You always have the right to sell your 72 purchase for 72—in other words, a wash in the futures. You are out, at most, the cost of the put.

This is the point where flexibility comes in. These reports are unpredictable, and I've seen markets open limit in the direction of the report and close totally opposite by day's end. The markets trade off the reports initially; however, the reports are not always right, and the smart money uses the news as an opportunity. It is almost always a significant sign when a market closes opposite the direction a report indicates it should. Let's say, in this case, that the consensus was looking for 3% more hogs, and the report indicates there are 7% more—in other words, quite bearish.

You're glad you had the foresight to buy the put because the newswires are talking two, perhaps three, limit days down. The market opens limit down at 69. The put increases in value from 180 to 450 at the open. The market should theoretically remain limit down, and if two days down, the put should theoretically trade up to 550 or higher. You place a sell stop on the put at 320. Remember, if the market rises, the put loses value. The only way for the stop to be hit is for a rally to occur sometime during the day. If the market remains weak, your plan is to leave the put in place, but if the market starts to rally, you're stopped out of your put at a profit of 140 points, and you still own the long futures.

In effect, you are long the futures in an environment where the market is trading; the abnormal situation is more normal and, therefore, more manageable. You can now place a stop loss under your futures. If the market keeps rallying, you have a good position. The Hogs and Pigs Reports have been proven to be inaccurate 40% of the time, but nobody knows for sure until six months down the road, when the pigs actually materialize—or not. In this scenario, you have protection if the report proves unmanageable. In effect, if it is a favorable report to your position, this protection becomes a "mistake" you are happy to make because the futures would rise more than the put would deteriorate. Bottom line: You have a lot more flexibility than just buying a call or being naked long futures.

Using options in conjunction with futures can give you staying power while allowing you the choice of lifting one side or another at any time. If your technical or fundamental bias changes, you can always lift one side and keep the other. If you reach your profit objective on the futures, you can liquidate your futures position and hold the option. At times, "dead" options return from the dead and earn you a double profit.

Another variation on this theme involves buying options to protect profits for a position that has already moved your way. You see, I'm a big fan of riding a trend for all it's worth. In a big move, a market always seems to go further than logic alone might warrant. However, at the end of a move, a market can get overheated, and when you know the top is in, it could be too late. When you feel the end is near, but there is no fundamental or technical reason to liquidate, why not just buy an option to protect profits? It could be money well spent, and if you are too early, this is the kind of mistake you like to make because you will make more on the futures than you spend on the option.

Writing options as a hedging strategy

Previously, you learned how a company with foreign currency risk could purchase options to hedge this risk. A more sophisticated strategy involves the selling of options to generate additional income.

For example, what if a company needs to buy Japanese yen and is happy with today's rate of exchange? To generate additional income, the manager could sell at-the-money put options. Let's say the yen is trading at 100, and the 100 puts for 60 days are priced at 200 points. By selling the puts, the company's account is credited with the premium—in this case, $2,500 per option. In effect, the company is saying it is willing to buy yen from the option buyer at 100. If the value of the yen rises, the puts remain unexercised at expiration, and the company keeps the entire premium. This is a hedge, in that the money can be used to offset the higher yen.

If the yen rises by less than 200 points, the company is money ahead. If it rises by more, the company can buy calls or futures, or forward contract at an appropriate spot (if it is unwilling to accept additional risk in the marketplace). If the yen falls, the company simply honors its commitment to purchase yen at the higher price. (It will be assigned long futures at 100, a price it was willing to live with.) But the company still keeps the 200 points that effectively lowers the purchase price to 98.

This strategy works best if the outlook is for a stable, slightly rising, or slightly falling market. By receiving the premium, the traditional costs of hedging are not only reduced, but at times they can be totally paid for plus a bonus.

Covered option writing

As we've discussed, the advantage and attraction of buying options is that your risk is limited and predetermined, and the profit potential is unlimited. However, the majority of options expire worthless, and the premiums eventually disappear. Therefore, buying options is generally a losing proposition. This is not to say that you cannot make good money in a major bull or major bear market, but be advised that professionals primarily sell options (generally to the public). They might hedge these sales with a ratio of long or short futures, but the public generally likes to purchase premium. The advantage of selling options is that you can capitalize on the time decay of options. Because the premiums that people pay for options eventually rise to option heaven, the option seller gains these premiums. While writing options is generally a winning strategy, the big disadvantage is that the risk is unlimited, while the profit potential is limited to the premiums received. When option premiums are high, the general rule of thumb is that it is better to sell options than to buy them.

The advantage of futures is the unlimited profit potential, but the risk is theoretically unlimited also. You should, therefore, use risk-management techniques (stops). Stops are not foolproof, but they generally work efficiently. The main problems with stops is that they can be filled away from your intended risk level at times and in a volatile market you can be stopped out only to have the market eventually go back your way. On the other hand, if you do not have stops, you cannot predetermine what your risk is.

Covered option writing can allow you to take advantage of the decaying option premiums just like the professional sellers, but it is less risky in a volatile market. It basically involves selling call options and buying futures or selling puts and shorting futures. For example, in a recent bull soybean market, I bought the November beans at $18.00 and sold the 1800 calls for 60¢. This gave me 60¢ in downside protection. At expiration, if the market was anywhere above $17.40, I would still profit on this trade. If the market was anywhere above $18/bushel at expiration, I would keep the 60¢, or $3,000 gross per covered contract position—not a bad profit.

The disadvantage of this strategy is that the most I could make on each transaction was 60¢, or $3,000 gross per covered contract. So, if the beans ran up to $22, the covered positions would allow only a limited profit. Here is how I overcame this disadvantage: My plan was to pyramid the position approximately every 50¢ up. So, if the market moved to, say, $18.50, I would look to buy more futures at $18.50 and sell the 1850 calls for approximately 60¢. At this point, my lower buys are safer. I could theoretically ride these 1800 covered writes back down to $17.40, so the market would have to fall $1.10/bushel before I was in major trouble. If I happened to have the 1750s on at this point, they would look even safer, and so on.

Now, if the market appreciates rapidly and we add every 50¢ up, taking in an average of 50¢ each time, we make $1.00 (or $5,000/contract) for every $1 move up if the market remains strong. With a call option, if you pay 60¢ and the market moves up $1, you will make only 40¢ at expiration. So, this pyramiding technique is actually a more profitable strategy than just buying calls in a major bull move. And during corrections to the major up trend, you are better able to ride out the fluctuations than you would be with uncovered futures. In a sideways market, you would make money with this strategy also, whereas you would lose when just buying calls. Of course, with this strategy, there is no predetermined risk if the market goes down more than the short premium, whereas with option purchases, the risk is limited. With the covered position, the risk is less than futures, but you'll need to monitor the position and use a risk point on the futures/option combinations if the market again looks weak.

Option spreads

Futures can be spread in various ways, and options can be spread in even more. Only with options can you spread two different contracts of the same month. Option spreads can be constructed in a variety of ways to fine-tune market outlooks. Although personally I rarely spread options, some of these strategies are very popular and fit in nicely with some trading styles.

Vertical call spreads

With a vertical call spread, you have two options of the same month but with different strike prices that are spread against each other. The vertical call spread is bullish, and the vertical put spread is bearish. For example, you're bullish wheat, it's March, and May wheat is trading at $4.20. You buy the May 420 call, pay 22¢, simultaneously sell the May 450 call, and take in 7¢. Your cost (excluding commissions) is the difference between the two premiums—in this case, 15¢, or $750. The difference (always a debit) is your maximum risk. If the market at expiration closes below 420, you lose the 22¢ and keep the 7¢, a maximum risk of 15. Your maximum profit is the difference between the strike prices minus the debit. In this case, 450 – 420 = 30 and 30 – 15 = 15. At expiration, above 450, you lose penny for penny on the 450 what you make on the 420. So, your maximum profit is at or above 450. Returning 30 for your 22 investment is the lower-priced call, but you keep the 7¢, for a total of 15¢.

Why spread vertically? In one respect, bull spreading calls offer the best of both worlds. The risk, as in buying options, is strictly limited. You lower your overall cost by benefiting from the time decay of selling premium. You are selling premium on the greater out-of-the-money option, which is more likely to expire worthless than the lower-priced option. The main disadvantage is that the profit is limited, and this eliminates one of the main advantages of buying options. There is still a premium cost, one of the main disadvantages of buying options, and you incur double commissions.

Vertical put spreads

The vertical put spread is the mirror image of the call spread. For example, say that you are mildly bearish in the stock market. It is July, and the mini September S&P is trading at 1750. You buy the August 1740 put (which keys off the September contract and expires the third Friday in August) for 1,800 points and sell the 1710 for 450 points. Your maximum risk is 1800 points minus 450 (1,350 points = $675). You lower your maximum risk over just buying the 1740 put for $900. Your maximum profit takes place under 1710 and is the difference between the strike prices (in this case, 30 points, or $1,500 minus the debit of $675, which is $825, excluding commissions). By writing a lower-priced put against a higher-priced put, you take on less risk for a lowered potential profit. For call spreads, by writing a higher-priced call against a lower-priced call, you do the same thing. There are quite a few variations, but in practice, if you use a call that is priced too high or a put priced too low, you will not receive enough premiums to lower the cost sufficiently.

Calendar spreads

Also known as time spreads, *calendar spreads* take advantage of the tendency of nearby options to decay faster than distant options. This strategy involves the sale of an option in one month and the simultaneous purchase of an option (usually, but not necessarily, the same strike price) in a later month. For example, you might sell a September 2500 cocoa call and buy a December 2500 cocoa call for a net debit. If the market remains fairly stable, you eventually gain the premium in the nearby to cheapen the ultimate cost of the distant, or there will be a net gain on the entire position after some time passes. (You can, of course, liquidate both sides or just one side at any time.) One of the potential pitfalls in this strategy is that the spread values of the underlying commodity can change, perhaps favorably, but contrary to expectations as well. Many times, the nearby month, which affects the short side of the spread, moves more dramatically because of higher open interest and greater speculative play. The risk cannot always be predetermined to an exact level like the vertical spreads; however, there is merit in this strategy if it is monitored and used correctly.

Straddles and strangles

Straddles and strangles are option spreads that involve both puts and calls. A *straddle* involves buying or selling puts and calls at the same strike price. During the life of a straddle, it is a certainty that one or both of the options will be in the money at any point in time. A *strangle* involves different strike prices, so it is less likely that both or even one of the strangle legs will be in the money at any point in time. However, it is certainly quite possible. There are two sides to each of these market plays, so let's examine the four possibilities.

Buying a straddle

Say that it is late September, and the December T-bonds are trading at 10503. You buy the December 105 call and the 105 put. The call is trading for 2 full bond points and 1/32. The put is trading for 1 full point and 31/32. Your cost is the sum of both premiums—or in this case, 4 full points, or $4,000 (plus commissions). To be profitable at expiration, bonds must move more than 4 points, above 109 or below 101.

The advantage of this strategy is that you know, to the penny, your maximum risk on the trade. The disadvantage is that you must overcome double premiums to be profitable. Why do this? The only situation in which this makes any sense is when you anticipate a volatile market but do not have any idea which direction the market will move. Suppose there's a big unemployment report coming out that will determine Fed policy. You know this report will move the market, but you have no clue as to how it will come out or how it will be received. After the report, you can decide whether you want to cut the losses on the bad option and let the good one roll, or whether the move is dramatic enough for the good one to cover both premiums. In practice, I've found this strategy works only if you are willing to manage it. To overcome the time decay of two options, you need to be very right over time. At times, after a move of significance, it could make sense to take a profit on the good side and hope the other one returns from the dead, or to cut the loss on the unprofitable side and look to maximize the good side. There are no hard-and-fast rules here. It takes management and smarts. Back to the example, the report is released, and unemployment is up dramatically. Because this indicates a weakening economy, the thought is that the Fed could lower rates, which means bullish bond prices.

Next, you observe how the market reacts to the report. Remember that it is not the news but how the market reacts to the news that is important. In this case, bond prices move up, rallying more than 2 1/2 points, to close at 10718. The call gains about 1 1/4 points, and the put loses 1 point. Because of the delta pricing of options, the first leg of the move is the least profitable for this strategy. As your profitable option moves deeper into the money, it acts more and more like a futures contract, and this strategy becomes increasingly profitable. The out-of-the-money loses comparatively less because it has less to lose. Of course, at any time, you have the choice of selling out one leg of the straddle or both. If at some point your indicators tell you the move is over, you might wish to take profits on the call and hold on to the put, hoping the move reverses to the downside. You could, if you are looking for a major bull market to unfold, cut your loss on the put and hold on to the call. In this case, you would realize a loss of about one point, and you would most likely be out about $1,000 or so on the realized side of the equation. If at expiration the market falls back under 105, you would lose your entire call premium, and this "limited-risk" trade would cost you more than $3,500 per straddle. For this reason, it is important to protect profits on the good side of the spread. You could place a stop on the call at break even (for the call side), and this action would limit your risk on the entire position to approximately the put loss while leaving your upside open. After you are out of the put, you would need a move (at expiration) to more than 108 to show a net profit. Every point move above this level results in a $1,000 profit per point per straddle. The important thing to remember is to use sound judgment and good money management when employing a strategy like this. At expiration, one side of the straddle expires worthless, so you'll need to make this up.

Selling a straddle

In the previous example, there was someone on the other side of either or both options. Most likely, the buyer of the straddle bought from two different sellers, but you could be a seller of the straddle, too. This is a strategy that places the odds in your favor but raises the risk level. In the previous example, the seller of the December T-bond 105 straddle receives both premiums, or in this case, about

4 points. If the market doesn't move, and at the expiration date it closes exactly at 105, the seller gets to keep both premiums. The odds of this outcome are small, but as long as the market remains within a range, the seller makes something. In this example, he has 4 points to work with. If the market stays within the relatively wide range of 101 to 109, some profit is possible. The market must move outside the range for the straddle writer to lose. The problem with this strategy, in many cases, comes in the timing of the move. If the market moves fast (in either direction) and volatility increases, the seller could get in trouble. Just as with any other limited-profit/unlimited-risk strategy (in this example, the profit is limited to an absolute maximum of $4,000), it needs to be managed. If the unemployment report results in a ho-hum reaction, you might want to stay with the entire position. If there is a dramatic move, it certainly could make sense to cut the loss on the unprofitable side but then look to lock in a profit by using some form of risk-control measure (a stop comes to mind) on the profitable side.

Buying a strangle

A strangle is similar to a straddle but with an important difference. A strangle player uses different strikes, usually at either side of the market price. As a buyer, your risk is limited. Your leverage increases because a major move results in a greater profit on funds at risk. Let's go back to the T-bond example. In the straddle, you purchased the 105 call and the 105 put, with the market trading about 105. The strangle buyer might buy, as one of numerous examples, the 108 call for 1 point and the 102 put for just under 1 point. Therefore, your cost is perhaps $2,000 instead of $4,000, and your risk is cut in half. Your outlook is most likely the same as the straddle buyer's; that is, you are looking for a substantial move in a volatile market but don't have a clue as to direction. The disadvantage is that the market must move substantially for you to show a profit. In the straddle example, at expiration, the profit zone is outside 109 or 101. For this strangle, the range has widened to 110 on the upside (108 plus the 2 points in premium paid) and 100 on the downside. However, if bonds soar to 118 at expiration, this strategy results in a gross profit of $8,000. The 102 put expires worthless. The 108 call would be worth $10,000. The cost is $2,000, resulting in a gross profit of $8,000, or 400%. In the straddle example, the gross profit would be $9,000 at 118. The 105 call would be worth $13,000 minus the $4,000 cost, which equals $9,000. Although the gross profit is higher, the leverage is lower. On a $4,000 risk, the net profit is 225%. For the same risk, you could have purchased two strangles, resulting in a gross profit of $16,000. Don't forget, I am hypothetically assuming a major move here. Such moves do happen, but don't count on them.

Selling a strangle

Selling a strangle, which would involve taking the opposite side of the previous example, is profitable the majority of the time because most out-of-the-money calls expire worthless—or at least they do not totally overcome the premiums paid. In this case, you are writing two out-of-the-money options, but this does not necessarily put the odds doubly in your favor. If a major bull or bear move takes place, the strangle seller could find himself in big trouble. I cannot stress enough how important it is to manage these option spread strategies, especially when you are a strangle writer. The risks are less, but they are still there, and they are very real. Strangle writing has a lower potential profit than many other plays.

In conclusion, a strangle buyer pays less than a straddle buyer, but her profit potential is lower. The strangle seller has better odds of a profit, but his risks are higher. The strangle and straddle sellers can do quite well in quiet, trading-range type markets. The buyer does well during major bull or bear moves and particularly well in runaway moves. Your market outlook is not as important using these strategies as the degree of the move is. Premiums vary by market conditions, so you need to vary your strategy based on these conditions and your outlook. The one rule that always holds true is that the rewards are higher with the risks!

Ratios

Ratios involve buying or selling a greater number of calls or puts on one side of the transaction than the other. They are basically a combination of strategies already discussed and are useful in certain situations.

Ratio writes

Simply stated, a ratio write involves selling a greater number of options than the underlying futures position, with the most common number being 2.

For example, say that it's September 15 and you buy December cotton at 8055, and you simultaneously sell two December 86 calls for a premium of 130 each. You are taking in 260 points in premium. (For cotton, 1 point is worth $5.) Therefore, this strategy gives you $1,300 in downside protection. The downside risk still exists here, but it is less than in an outright futures position. The market at expiration must move below 7795 for this strategy to produce a loss (not including commissions). With the futures, any move under 8055 results in a loss. Profits are also higher on a normal bull move compared to an outright futures position. If the market on option expiration date closes at 8305, a single futures position shows a gross profit of 250 points, or $1,250. The ratio write shows a much more impressive profit of $2,550 because the 86 calls expire worthless, and these premiums are kept in full. It should be noted that this profit is also greater than naked call writing. In this example, the naked call seller receives the $1,300, not the $2,550.

The rub? This ratio write has a two-sided risk, which is not seen in either covered or naked writes. If the market falls substantially, the risk on the futures is not limited. If the market rallies substantially, the upside risk is unlimited as well, because there is an extra naked call to contend with. A ratio call writer has a neutral to slightly bullish outlook. A ratio put writer (short December cotton and also selling two December puts) has a neutral to slightly bearish outlook. I've stressed this before, and I'll do so again: This is a strategy that can be quite profitable but must be managed. A ratio writer should know her break-even point, both above and below the market, and she should manage the position when it appears threatened. The best positions are those that have a wide enough profit range to allow for defensive action should it become necessary.

Ratio spreads

A 2:1 ratio call spread involves buying one lower-priced call and selling two higher-priced calls. For example, with May beans trading at $16.89, you might buy a May 1700 call for 34¢ and sell two 1750 calls for 14¢ each. Under $17, there is no real risk other than net cost of 6¢. In fact, if you can establish the spread at a credit initially, there is no downside risk. The maximum profit occurs at the upper strike price at expiration. If the market expires exactly at $17.50, you keep the 28¢ plus show a net profit of 16¢ (50 minus 34) on the 1700. The 44¢, in this case, is the maximum profit.

The profit potential is reduced above the upper strike price because the loss is theoretically unlimited for the naked portion of the spread. The greatest risk for ratio call spreads always lies above the market. Ratio put spreads have their greatest risk below the market. Ratio spreads and ratio writes are similar in that they both involve uncovered writes, and both have predetermined profit ranges. The difference is the downside risk (for ratio call spreads) or upside risk (for puts) is small and in some cases nonexistent. Again, you would use this strategy in a neutral or mildly bullish or bearish environment. Virtually unlimited permutations of ratios and strike prices can be used; just remember to use good judgment and monitor the market in question.

Reverse ratio spreads

As the name implies, a *reverse ratio spread* is a strategy opposite the more commonly utilized ones; therefore, you don't hear much about it. It involves selling a call or put at one strike price and then buying a greater number of calls at a higher strike price or buying a greater number of puts at a lower strike price. This is also commonly called a *backspread*. Look for backspreads that you can establish for a credit if possible, and in a market where you anticipate a relatively substantial move for the best profits.

For example, say that it is February, and May sugar is trading at 1112. You sell an 1100 call for 65 points and you buy two 1200 calls for 23 points each. The spread is established at a credit of 19 points (plus 65 minus [23 times 2]). If May sugar expires under 1100, then all the calls will expire worthless, and the credit of 19 points will be the profit. While you don't put on a bull backspread anticipating a down move, still if you are totally wrong and the market falls you can still earn a slight profit. This strategy has limited risk. The maximum loss comes at expiration at the purchased calls. In this case, at 1200, the 1100 call sold will show a loss of 35 points (100 points of intrinsic value minus the 65 received), and the 1200 calls will expire worthless. Therefore, the total risk on this one is 35 plus 46, or 81 points. The risk is never more than this.

The real profit potential comes when the market moves above 1200, with no limits on the maximum profit potential. If the market expires at 1300, the short call will show a loss of 135 points. However, each of the 1,200 calls will show a profit of 76 (for a profit of 17; 76 times 2 minus 135), a relatively small profit, but at this level, the profit potential is now unlimited should the market continue to move in the anticipated direction. One short and one long call offset each other, but the added call gains with the futures market. At 1400 in this example, this strategy results in a 117 point profit, at 1500, it results in a 217 profit, and so on. The profit range (without fees) is anywhere below 1119 and anywhere above 1283, but not in the middle. Very simply, this is a bullish strategy, one that is hedged to an extent by the short sale. The profit is unlimited on a major upside move, and yet there is a wider range of potentially profitable outcomes because the trader can also profit to an extent when totally wrong. As with all these other plays, this one can be performed with puts when bearish. It should be used when the outlook is for a relatively large move in a volatile market. It generally makes more sense with more time, and it ties up less money than just buying options. The drawback comes with a relatively normal move in the direction anticipated. If the move is not large enough, a loss will result.

Eight winning option trading rules

So, it may appear your options when trading options are seemingly infinite. How do you sort through all the strategies to find what works best? These eight rules just might help you.

1. Avoid deep in-the-money options

The two key advantages of buying options are leverage and limited risk. If an option is deep in the money, it cuts down on your leverage and adds to your risk. Even though the risk is still limited, you're paying more and therefore have more to lose. You cut down on your leverage because you need a bigger move in the underlying asset to generate a significant profit. The whole idea of leverage is to take a small amount of money and own an option to exercise into an asset worth many times as much. When buying deep in-the-money options, you tie up a lot more money that can be used for other opportunities. I don't like selling deep in-the-money options either. You tie up a considerable amount of capital this way (since you need to margin the position). The biggest advantage to an option seller is time decay, and deep in-the-money options have less time value; therefore, you have less to gain the easy way and more risk with the intrinsic value component. Bottom line: I stay away from deep in-the-money options when buying or selling. Of course, when buying options, your objective is to turn an out-of-the-money, at-the-money, or slightly in-the-money option into a deep in-the-money option. Your objective when selling options is to avoid turning your sale into a deep in-the-money. This is an effective way for your wallet to go deep out of money!

2. Avoid deep out-of-the-money options

The illusion is that deep out-of-the-money purchases give you a lot of leverage. In reality, they give you a lot of hope, encourage overcommitments, and generally offer little profit opportunity. Yes, they do hit at times—and so does the Powerball lottery—but this is a game of probabilities, and the odds are certainly against you when buying deep out-of-the-moneys. You have to be realistic. If the premium appears cheap, there's usually a reason. Of course, you could buy an August 1200 soybean call in July when the beans are at 600 and hope for a crop failure. You could probably buy a lot of them because they'd be cheap, maybe just $100 each. But, it would be unlikely for beans to rise $6 per bushel in just three weeks. It makes somewhat more sense to purchase a deep out-of-the-money option if you have sufficient time—but, then again, you lose some leverage because you are paying for that time. The odds are greatly in your favor when you sell deep out-of-the-money options, but the expected reward is minuscule in relation to the risk. You could be profitable 99 out of 100 times when selling deep out-of-the-money put options on the stock market, but that crash will inevitably come on some unexpected event when you least expect it. Unless you wish to be "the house," the entity capitalized sufficiently to cover its lottery or slot machine jackpot, stay away from deep out-of-the-moneys.

3. Trade slightly out-of-the-money, at-the-money, or slightly in-the-money options

The reasons here are the opposite of the reasons for avoiding the deep options. Slightly out-of-the-money, at-the-money, and slightly in-the-money options have a reasonable chance of proving profitable when buying; you gain from the maximum possible time decay when selling; and they are generally the most liquid of the bunch, resulting in a tighter bid/ask spread, which in turn saves on transaction costs. The one variation on this theme has to do with selling options; in this case, it is certainly fine, and even advantageous, to sell out-of-the-money options—with this one caveat: The premium received must warrant the risk. What price might this be? There are no hard–and-fast rules; you just need to use good judgment. It is also advisable to use good judgment when cutting losses. This involves taking a reasonable or small loss when covering short options that are not working. It is important, as well, to cut losses in long options that aren't making you money. Human nature makes it all too easy to become complacent when buying options. I've seen too many people play them out all the way to expiration when all the indications say the play isn't working. This is just another form of hope, and hope is not a recipe for success. The fact that most options expire worthless should be a strong clue to the buyer to sell out prior to the end in cases of nonperformance. This is easy to do—just click to "sell!"

4. There is a time for all seasons

What I mean by "there is a time for all seasons" is that you need to have a feel for market conditions prior to implementing any option strategy. I've known traders who have initial success with one or another strategy and think they've found the holy grail. I met a doctor who was lucky enough to turn $5,000 into six figures during the bull corn market of 1996. His first trade was a long shot that worked—the purchase of deep out-of-the-money calls for March that turned deeply in the money by expiration. He took his profits and rolled them into at-the-money Mays that also went deeply into the money, then once again into Julys, and that worked, too. He caught the best kind of market for this strategy and then proceeded to give all his profits back in a dull period of flat markets. I've also seen people win 9 of out 10 times when selling out-of-the-money calls or puts, only to fall flat on their faces later.

In the early 1980s, a firm called Volume Investors became one of the largest option players in the gold pit by continually selling premium. It worked beautifully for years, but it took just one unexpected, volatile spike to wipe them out—to the tune of $6 million. The lesson: Know your market. Option writing can be extremely profitable in dull, flat markets. If the tone changes, cover fast before that catastrophic loss. If option premiums feel too low to give you an adequate cushion of income, they probably are. The common wisdom is to "sell flat markets," but I suggest this is just the time to start thinking about buying. Avoid selling in periods of rising volatility. Option purchases will start to become more expensive, but then the rising volatility will work in the buyer's favor. Only when volatility reaches wild proportions should you think about selling—just make sure you're adequately margined to take the heat.

5. Covered call writing is a decent strategy for a bullish environment, and covered put writing is generally good for the bear

This is one of the few strategies where you use futures and options together and have the ability to profit on both legs. The strategy works well in a modestly bullish or bearish environment as well. It is not risk free, but it is less risky than the outright purchase or sale of futures. Furthermore, by using my limited pyramid strategy discussed previously, you have the flexibility to capitalize on a major move when using covered positions.

6. In "normal" markets, write straddles and strangles

Selling puts and calls works in most market environments. It is a good strategy, as long as it is managed properly. "Normal" is a term I am unable to define specifically; it's more of a feeling you will develop after trading for a while. In most cases, the premiums received when writing straddles and strangles give an adequate cushion to weather most storms. However, when the typhoon hits and your margin balance is diminishing, run for the exit door.

7. Find opportunities to backspread

Backspreading is a seldom-used strategy, but it has potential to make you rich. Recall that this involves selling a call or put at one strike price and buying a greater number of calls at a higher strike price or buying a greater number of puts at a lower strike price. Look to establish backspreads for a credit to benefit from time decay, and only consider markets with the potential to move big. This strategy always has a predetermined and limited risk and is one of the few that can still prove mildly profitable (keep your equity together) when you're dead wrong. The profit is unlimited on a major upside move. It is not the holy grail, and there certainly is risk here as well, but I know of one S&P option trader who traded backspreads only. He held his equity together quite well over many years and was always positioned for a major move in either direction. During the stock market crash of 1987, his bear backspreads worked so well he was able to retire!

8. Use options to hedge a profitable futures position

If you are a trend-following trader, like me, and you're lucky enough to catch a major move that is showing massive unrealized profits, the great dilemma is when to cash in. You know you inevitably will have to give up a large portion of your paper gains if you wait for confirmation of a trend change. But top and bottom picking are very hard things to do. There is only one top, and there is only one bottom in major moves of importance, which could develop over hundreds of trading sessions. Many times, the most important leg of a major move takes place in the last 48 hours. Why not use put options to lock in bull-move profits and calls for the bear-move profits? Commercial hedgers use options all the time. Trading is a business, and options can be a prime tool to hedge your profit while still allowing for additional profits. For example, say that you own soybeans in a dry period. You're in at $7, and the market is now $9. There is no rain in the forecast, it's mid-July, and with another two weeks of this, the old rallying call of "beans in the teens" will again become a reality. Options aren't cheap, but this is a situation in which I would buy premium anyway. The $9 August puts are running 40¢. Buy them. This is a no-lose situation. It's cheap insurance at 40¢: You assure yourself a $1.60 profit per contract—$8,000 per contract—and that's not bad. This is insurance you hope you never need to use. Let the good times roll if the forecasts prove correct! They're not always correct, as I've found out.

During the drought of 1988, no weather service that I know of called the end. It was a long holiday weekend, and when we went home on Friday, it was more than 100 degrees with "zero chance of meaningful precipitation for at least two weeks." Soybeans were approaching $11, with "beans in the teens" a virtual certainty. It remained hot and dry Saturday and Sunday, with not a cloud in the sky. Then, seemingly out of nowhere on Monday afternoon, with the markets closed, the skies opened. It poured rain over a wide area, and we were greeted with a multiple-limit-down situation beginning with our return Tuesday at the open. If I had only used puts to lock in the significant paper profits, and it had turned out to be a mistake, it would have been the kind of mistake I would have been happy to make. Plus, buying options to lock in profits on futures is the best way I know of to avoid premature "profit-taking-itis." This affects us all at one time or another.

Bottom line: Options can be wonderful tools. They're not a panacea, but at one level, options *can* offer you the best of both worlds. Be alert for ways to use them to your benefit!

6

The Intermediate Trading Course (Or Just Enough Knowledge to Be Dangerous!)

"Please don't think that I am showing off when I say that I know the secret of how not to lose but win. I really do know the secret; it is terribly silly and simple and consists of keeping one's head the whole time, whatever the state of the game, and not getting excited. That is all, and it makes losing simply impossible...but that is not the point: The point is whether, having grasped the secret, a man knows how to make use of it and is fit to do so. A man can be as wise as Solomon and have an iron character and still be carried away."
—Fyodor Dostoyevsky, *The Gambler*

A broker took on a customer with whom he was told to be extremely careful with. The money was thought to be from organized crime. The customer opened the account with $50,000 and initiated a long platinum position. The market went down, and the customer bought more. The market went down even more, and it was margin call time. The broker was becoming a bit nervous with the position, but when he called the customer, the reply was, "Sure, we'll send you more money. No problem." When the margin call went that easy, the broker felt much more relaxed. The market kept going lower, the customer kept adding to the position, the margin calls continued, and the crime boss continued to send in the money. The broker was talking with his customer one day and confided that he was not sure platinum was going to rebound any time soon. The response was simple, "Let's get this straight. You can have all the money you want; just remember, we don't take losers!"

Fundamental analysis

There are basically two macro-methods you can use to analyze and therefore trade the markets: fundamental analysis and technical analysis. Both the fundamentalist and the technician are trying to solve the same problem: to predict future price movement. However, they approach this problem in different ways.

Fundamental analysis basically is the study of supply and demand. The fundamentalist says that the cause and effect of price movement is explained by supply and demand.

Here's an example of how fundamental analysis might work: Fundamental statistics are available in market reports. You might read new copper mine production this year will be 300,000 tons, manufacturing demand is projected to be 400,000 tons, and "above-ground" supplies available to the market are 50,000 tons. A fundamentalist would conclude that these statistics project a coming supply deficit of 50,000 tons. Therefore, logically copper prices must rise to ration or diminish this impossible level of demand. Fundamental analysis appeals to our logic. After all, if Brazil is suffering through a drought during the flowering phase of the soybean plant, one can rationally explain why bean prices are rising. A good fundamentalist is able to forecast a major price move well in advance of the technician. Some fundamentalists have what amounts to "inside information" (which is perfectly legal in the futures markets). If Cargill has a scout in Africa who identifies a cocoa-killing fungus that is devastating that crop, odds are Cargill will act on this information long before you or I hear about it.

Fundamentalists are able to trade the courage of their convictions and are not shaken out as easily during false market movements. They are better able emotionally to maximize positions because fundamentals can take a long time to change. In late 1995, with corn trading in the mid-$2-per-bushel range, I noticed China (formerly the third-largest corn exporter, and the largest exporter in Asia) had turned into a corn importer. This was the first time in history China had imported corn from the United States. China's livestock production had grown to a rate that could not keep pace with its reduced crop production of that year. In my mind, this was a significant fundamental, which was a major reason corn prices were able to hit new all-time record highs within a six-month period. No doubt, fundamentals can be powerful and allow a trader to stay with a position longer than he otherwise might stay. However, they also can prompt a trader to stay with a position longer than he should stay.

Technical analysis

On the other hand, a technician is concerned with market action only. The basic issue is not that fundamentals are what ultimately moves price; the technician concedes this point. The technician believes that it is virtually impossible for most of us to know all the fundamentals that affect price at any given time. By the time the news reaches most of us, it has been disseminated so widely that it has been discounted in price. Because a trader makes or loses money via price movements, the technician believes this is what should be studied. In other words, the technician believes price is the ultimate fundamental.

In early 1997, corn had retreated back to the 1995 lows—in the mid-$2.50 per-bushel range. The price was low because the fundamentals were decidedly bearish. Supply was dramatically up, with an excess of a 1-billion bushel carryover supply projected, which was large for that time. The livestock numbers were sharply reduced. Exports were falling, and China had once again turned into a corn exporter. However, the market traced out a technical "bottom formation," and certain commodity funds bought. Other funds, seeing the price action moving up, bought more. One day in February, they bought 100 million bushels. Many of the commodity and hedge funds trade technically. It seemed they all saw the same price action at the same time, and they acted on it. The 100-million-bushel purchase pushed prices higher, despite the bearish fundamentals. The higher prices attracted more technical buying, and this new buying hit price stops above the market. Undercapitalized shorts could not meet margin calls and had to cover their positions, and this meant more buying. The commercial firms were selling into the market, but the funds bought more as additional price objectives were hit. In a four-day period, the funds added another 150 million bushels to their initial purchases. Prices soared by 50¢ per bushel, more than 20%. Farmers started to notice that prices were rising and began to hold back on their cash corn sales as they became bullish and waited for higher prices. In this case, a technical move actually resulted in the fundamentals changing (that is, a restriction of supply due to less farmer selling). Eventually, the market fell of its own weight, but there is no denying you could have made a nice profit in a case like this by ignoring the fundamentals and just listening to the sounds of the market.

In many ways, technical analysis can be said to include fundamentals. However, the reverse is not true; a pure fundamentalist does not look at charts. The best fundamentalist tends to make the most money, but she also tends to lose the most when she misses something. In the 1970s, there was a phenomenal pork belly trader who had amassed a fortune amounting to several hundred million dollars. When short-term interest rates started their rise from 4% to 10%, this guy began to short T-bill futures under the fundamental belief that rates at this level were unsustainable. By the time they reached 18%, he was broke. He was ultimately right in his analysis as rates eventually plummeted, but not before he lost all his money.

Which is best: fundamental or technical analysis?

Correct fundamental analysis can make you money, and so can a good technical plan. In either case, a good forecaster can go broke if he is not a good trader. A good trader can make money regardless of whether he can identify the correct fundamentals or technical tone of the market. My belief is that a trader should be aware of the underlying fundamentals, but a primarily technical approach combined with a sensible money management plan, produces the best results over time. In my experience, the best trades come when solid fundamentals (as we see them) agree with the technical action of the marketplace. My "advanced trading course" in Chapter 8, "The Advanced Trading Course," covers how to use technical indicators in your trading. However, you should know what it is you're trading (although I know a soybean trader who had not even seen what a soybean looked like until after he had spent his third successful year in the pit).

The 4 futures groupings

While there are hundreds of Exchange-listed futures contracts globally, and most of them have liquid options markets, the major futures markets basically can be arranged in four groupings:

- Financial futures
- Energies
- Agriculturals
- Metals

Financial futures include three major subsets: the interest rate futures, the stock indices, and the currencies. The agricultural markets include the grains, the meats, and the softs. The "softs" are markets such as cocoa, cotton, sugar, coffee, and orange juice. The metals are classified as either industrial (copper, aluminum, tin, lead, zinc) or precious (gold). Some are both precious and industrial (silver, platinum). For any of the markets you have an interest in trading, I suggest you consult the website of the Exchange where that particular market is traded for detailed fundamental data. The following is a quick and dirty overview.

Financial futures

Financial futures can be broken down into three basics: interest rates, stock indices, and currencies. Many of the fundamentals that affect one group affect the others. Obviously, interest rates affect stock prices and currency valuations. Governments allow interest rate futures to exist so that hedgers can neutralize or shift some of their price risks. A mortgage banker can transfer his price risk to a speculator, just as a corporate comptroller can lock in her cost of borrowing funds. The best way to think of any hedge is as a temporary substitute for a transaction that will occur at a later time in another market. When talking about interest rates, some hedgers are interested in protecting against higher rates in the future, and some lower. Speculators are trying to profit from the inherent risks in changes in the cost of money. Of course, in a global economy, rates can be moving in one direction in Japan and another in the United Kingdom. The fundamentals that move interest rates and, therefore, interest rate futures, are varied and dynamic. Human emotion is just as important a fundamental as credit flows.

Futures have been traded on commodity exchanges for more than 100 years. The first interest rate futures contract was introduced in 1975. Yields reflect interest rates in various money market investments. It goes without saying that the yield on a short-term instrument is, in most cases, dramatically different from longer-term "paper." You will sooner or later hear the term *yield curve*, which measures the relationship of the yields of various securities against their maturities. The eurodollar is based on a short-term, 90-day debt issue. Technically, a eurodollar is defined as any U.S. dollar on deposit outside the United States (generally dollar deposits at London branches of major world banks) that, therefore, falls outside the reserve requirements of the Federal Reserve. Actual eurodollar time deposits are securities available in a short-term maturity time frame for either taking or placing deposits. In reality, this market has become the benchmark for short-term interest rate price discovery for shorter-term U.S. rates. The eurodollar prices are quoted in terms of an index. The index is based on the difference between the actual eurodollar yield. There is no dollar sign here, just the number 100. For example, a yield of 3.00% is quoted as 9700. If yields rise to 3.50%, the index falls to 9650 (the difference between 100 and 96.50). The contract size is $1 million, but because this is a 90-day instrument, 1 basis point is worth $25 per contract (.01 of 1%). So, if yields rise by 1%, the price falls by 100 basis points, or $2,500 per contract (100 points times $25 per point).

The 10-year, 5-year, and 2-year T-note futures and options consistently rank in the top in terms of volume. Treasury bonds futures are designed to reflect prices of longer-term interest rates (such as mortgage rates). These contracts are based on a security with a face value (par amount) of $100,000. Bond and note prices are a mirror image of interest rates. When interest rates rise, bond and note prices fall (and vice versa). There are interest rate futures on European paper, Japanese paper, Canadian paper, and on and on. The fundamentals that determine interest rates are central bank manipulation, with the central banks supposedly basing their decisions on the levels of unemployment, inflation, and economic activity. There are all kinds of statistics the fundamentalist can analyze, everything from housing starts to balance-of-trade figures, car sales, and retail sales. The problem a fundamentalist has is that there is just too much information out there, and the economy is too complex to make consistently accurate price predictions of interest rates or stock movements.

There are dozens of stock index trades, the primary U.S. index in terms of futures volume being the S&P 500 Index, followed by the NASDAQ and Russell. Traded on the Chicago Mercantile Exchange (CME), the S&P 500 represents the 500 biggest U.S. stocks, accounting for about 80% of total U.S. shares traded. It is a weighted index composed roughly of 400 industrial companies, 40 utilities, 20 transportation companies, and 40 financial companies. It is "weighted" because a bigger company carries proportionately greater weight in the index. The E-Mini S&P is the most actively traded contract in terms of dollar volume and is one of the day trader's favorites because it is liquid and can be volatile. Day-trading margins are generally much smaller, but a trader is always obligated for the difference between entry and exit. In other words, if you lose, you must pay the piper by the end of the day.

The major stock market fundamentals are the same as for interest rates, but throw in political considerations and investor attitudes.

Let's face it: Any one thing (war, a leader's death, an interest-rate hike, a major company's earnings) could affect the stock market on any particular day. The stock markets of the world generally move together; however, any one market can certainly move opposite the pack, based on internal considerations. One thing seems clear: Attitudes and economic trends tend to last for a while; therefore, the major trends of the stock market tend to last for a while. It's those minor trends that can kill you or make you rich.

The very first financial futures contracts were based on foreign currencies. It should be noted that the spot (or forward market) is much bigger than the futures market. The forward market, also known as the interbank market, is dominated by currency dealers at major global banks. While the spot market's volume towers over the listed Exchange volume, this vehicle is not available to the average investor. The average unit is $1 million. Currencies also can be traded at retail FOREX-type outlets. The active futures contracts at this time are the euro, yen, Swiss franc, British pound, and Australian and Canadian dollars. The U.S. dollar is traded as an index, and of increasing importance are currencies such as the Brazilian, Indian, Russian, and Chinese currencies. Throw in the New Zealand dollar, the South African rand, and other Asian currencies, and there is a currency market for just about every currency trader.

The price of a currency is determined in the same way as the price of any other commodity. Currency users have risks. If a currency depreciates in value and a manufacturer is to receive this currency in payment for a product that he will deliver six months hence, he loses money. If not hedged, his entire profit margin could be wiped out. If the people in the United States demand more Japanese-made goods, the demand for the yen goes up in relation to the dollar, and Americans will have to pay higher prices to induce holders of yen to sell. If interest rates go up in Germany in relation to the United Kingdom, the euro will look relatively more attractive as an investment than the British pound.

Fundamentalists look at trade balances, a country's wealth, budget deficit or surplus, interest rates, inflation, and political factors such as tax rates.

In addition, central bank intervention to support (or not support) a currency is definitely a market-moving factor. At times, a country can move alone to support its currency, and sometimes an orchestrated group effort is under way to attempt to support some currency. The central banks are huge, but they're not always larger than the speculative community. If the ultimate fundamentals are opposed to artificial support, a currency can still move contrary to the wishes of the central banks. This was demonstrated when George Soros was able to break the back of the British pound and successfully challenge the Bank of England in the late 1980s; he profited to the tune of $2 billion.

Obviously, some of these factors are subjective, whereas others are hard to predict in advance. Ultimately, capital flows are the major fundamental that determines what a currency is worth, and these are determined by the consensus of the world's traders.

Energies

There are two major energy exchanges. The ICE trades an active Brent Crude Oil, and the CME trades an active WTI (West Texas Intermediate) Crude Oil contract.

When I first entered the business, a part of my training program at Merrill Lynch was a tour of the Exchange floor. The New York Exchanges were housed in the same building, and after touring the wild and woolly COMEX (where the metals were traded—now a wholly owned division of the CME), we passed a pit with four or five traders, not one of whom was shouting out bids or offers. (In fact, a few of them were reading the paper.) We were told this was the NYMEX, the "poor man's Exchange," also called the "Potato Exchange," where platinum was the major contract. You could have bought a seat for $2,000, but then the $100 per month dues made this appear to be a losing deal. A few years later, they had the foresight and good fortune to register their No. 2 Heating Oil contract with the Commodity Futures Trading Commission and start trading it in 1978. The NYMEX became one of the world's major Exchanges, and when the Exchange went public, a seat was worth in excess of $3 million. (If only we had known in those "poor man" days and had picked up a few of those cheap seats!)

Crude oil is the world's largest cash commodity in terms of dollars and volume. (The annual value exceeds $500 billion.) Over 20% of the world's entire trade is in oil. (Only currencies are bigger.) The WTI is a light, sweet crude, preferred by refiners due to its low sulfur content. Most of the world's supply is sour (high-sulfur) crude, but because the sulfur content varies widely, the contract based on WTI is one of the two pace setters for world oil prices in general. Brent Crude is also liquid and active, based on the European North Sea variety but a benchmark for much of the oil traded in Europe and Asia. Both are 1,000-barrel contracts. If you think you have a pretty good idea who the top oil players, the top producers, and the top users are, you just might have to rethink some of your assumptions. The key countries in oil as of this writing are as follows:

- Producers—Saudi Arabia, Russia, United States, Canada, Venezuela, Iraq, Iran, China, Nigeria, Kuwait, United Arab Emirates, and Mexico
- Consumers—United States, China, Japan, Germany, India, Brazil, France, Russia, South Korea, United Kingdom, and Spain

Of course, these rankings are dynamic (constantly changing). When my last book went to press, for example, Japan was the number-two global consumer, but it has been replaced by China. The United States as we go to press is far from energy independence, but that is the goal (and as older gas guzzlers are retired, more efficient cars are helping toward that goal). That said, there are a lot of common misconceptions. Did you know the United States is the 3rd-largest crude-oil producer in the world? When asked, most people don't place the United States in the top 10. The U.S. problem is not that production is all that small. It had declined for over 20 years, from 1985 to 2005, but since then has been growing again. In 2012, for the first time in history, oil production in North Dakota surpassed that in Alaska. Texas by far remains the highest-producing state. The United States produces more oil than any other country globally except Saudi Arabia and Russia. The problem is that the United States gulps the stuff, every day burning through much more than it produces domestically. The United States still consumes four times more oil per capita than the second-largest global consumer. In 2010, however, for the first time in history, total oil imports as a percentage of total domestic consumption was higher in China than in the United States. Were you surprised Kuwait and Nigeria are not among the top seven producers? Iraq is the second-largest country in the world in terms of proven reserves (112 billion barrels).

The newest star in terms of production—very close to Saudi Arabia because of investment in improved technology—is Russia (along with some former Soviet states). Russia is not an OPEC member, so OPEC is far less important today than it was 30 years ago. As OPEC has lost market share, it's lost its price control as well to free-market forces.

China's production (were you surprised to see China in the top seven?) has also been increasing; however, its consumption is increasing at a far faster rate. In 1993, China turned into a net oil importer. Japan has the biggest problem because it has no domestic production at all and is totally dependent on imports. China has the same problem as Japan and the United States, because it is dependent on imports to fill the gap, but its rate of consumption versus its production is accelerating at the fastest rate in the world. The ramifications of the increasing industrialization and economic growth of China, India, and Brazil will have the most profound of all dynamics on oil prices in the coming years. Realize that China has five times as many people as the United States, yet today, it uses just one-fourth of what America uses. What happens as this gap closes? It's clear that while oil prices will continue to fluctuate, in the next few years, demand will increase at a faster rate than new supply. Unless alternative energy sources take hold, the cheap prices of years past are going to remain a memory.

For many years, the NYMEX heating oil contract was the second-most-liquid energy contract, although in recent years, it has been overshadowed by natural gas. It is also known as the number-two fuel oil and accounts for about 25% of the yield of a barrel of crude. This contract also is used by hedgers of diesel fuel and jet fuel, both of which are chemically similar to heating oil. The contract size is 42,000 gallons, and a 1¢ move equals a profit or loss of $420.

Futures prices for unleaded gasoline might appear to be too cheap when compared to the pump price, but they are based on the wholesale price for delivery at New York Harbor. The price you pay at the pump has all those costs added to get it to the station, including local and national taxes. Unleaded gasoline is by far the most important product, accounting for almost half of the yield from a barrel of crude. The contract size is also 42,000 gallons, with a 1¢ move (100 points) equal to a profit or loss of $420 per contract.

Thirty years ago, seven major oil companies owned 50% of the world's oil reserves and produced two-thirds of its crude and products. Today, these same seven own less than 10% and produce less than one-third of the products. OPEC is still a factor but no longer the major price setter. The major price setter is now the marketplace. The following factors are important and must be considered in any fundamental analysis of the energy markets: weather, inventory reports, OPEC, and other "political" actions.

For many years, U.S. natural gas prices were subject to government price controls; it has only been recently that the chains have been broken. The contract, which started trading in 1990, is now the second-most-actively traded energy contract. Of all the natural gas that is produced, industry (including utilities) uses about two-thirds, and homeowners use one-fourth. An 80-year supply of natural gas is available under American ground, and it is virtually "free" to tap, except for the transportation and storage costs, with middleman profits in between. The contract size is 10,000 MMBtu (million British thermal units), with price quoted in dollars and cents per MMBtu. The price of natural gas was about $1 in 1992 and above $10 during the winter of 2000 (when it was freezing cold in both North America and Europe) exchanges. Then, the price dropped under $2 a year later and once again rallied over $10 during the winter of 2003.

Agriculturals

Futures were invented in the sixteenth century for the Japanese rice trade. The agricultural markets continued to dominate futures trading throughout the first 75 years of the twentieth century. Today, agriculture, while still important, accounts for perhaps one-quarter of global futures trade.

Humans and animals require fat, protein, and carbohydrates for survival. Although meat is generally thought of as the predominant protein source, much of the world's human population and a majority of the world's livestock populations obtain their protein from soybeans. Corn is the predominant carbohydrate source used for animal feed.

Oilseeds

Soybeans were mentioned in ancient Chinese records prior to 2000 B.C. The United States, now accounting for under 50% of the world's output, was the world's largest soybean producer until 2004. Prior to the 1980s, the United States accounted for 80% of the world's output, but Carter's grain embargo prompted the Japanese, who were looking for a more reliable supplier, to fund the Brazilian soybean industry. In 2000 the United States planted about 65 million acres of beans. In 2012, that number was up to 80 million. The acreage keeps growing, but so does the world's population (which is growing at over 80 million—the size of a Mexico—each and every year). Today, more than 50% of the world's soybean crop is grown in South and Central America, primarily in Brazil and Argentina. China accounts for most of the rest of the world's production, but it remains a major importer most years. Called the miracle crop, soybeans are used in thousands of applications, primarily crushed for meal (used as an animal protein feed) and oil (for human consumption and as a cooking oil). Financially, it is generally the most volatile of all the grains, although, technically, it is not a grain but a legume (also known as an oilseed). The contract size is 5,000 bushels, with prices quoted in dollars and cents per bushel. A 1¢ move is worth $50 per contract.

The richest protein source of all the oilseeds is soybean meal; a feedstuff suited for cattle, hogs, and poultry. One bushel of soybeans weighs about 60 pounds and yields about 48 pounds of meal. Sixty percent of U.S. production is used domestically, and the balance is exported. A contract's size is 100 short tons (2,000 pounds per ton), with prices quoted in dollars and cents per ton. A $1 move equals plus or minus $100 per contract.

The contract for the other major "product" of the soybean, soybean oil, is sized at 60,000 pounds. One bushel of beans produces about 11 pounds of oil. This is an edible vegetable oil and competes in the world market with other edible oils, such as palm, peanut, canola, corn, olive, and sunflower, and even fats such as lard. Prices are quoted in cents per pound, with a 100-point or 1¢ move equal to a profit or loss of $600 per contract. The major oilseed grown in Canada is canola. Canola, the oil of choice among the health conscious, generally will have price moves in the same direction as soybeans, although at a different speed.

Palm oil is the world's second-most-heavily produced vegetable oil, and it is traded in Malaysia. Production is dominated by Malaysia and Indonesia. Palm oil competes directly with soybean oil and canola oil, but it generally trades at a discount because of health concerns about saturated fat in tropical oils. Palm oil is attractive to countries with expanding, low-income populations.

Grains

Traditionally, the highest volume of the grain contracts is corn, the major U.S.-grown crop. The contract specifications call for feed corn, not the variety used for human consumption. In recent years, in excess of 85 million acres of corn have been planted annually in the United States, producing crops that can exceed 13 billion bushels in a good year and accounting for one-half of the world's production. The United States consumes 70% of its crop domestically (75% of this is used to feed animals, and 25% is used to produce ethanol), with the balance exported.

The oat market is generally a slower-moving, more thinly traded market. Oats is the only major crop that the United States imports, primarily from the Scandinavian countries, Argentina, and Canada. Milling quality (used in oatmeal and other forms of human consumption) and feed oats are the two major varieties of oats. The contract, which is for 5,000 bushels, tends to act more like a feed contract, based on the delivery specifications that favor delivery of lower-quality oats. A 1¢ move per bushel equals plus or minus $50 per contract.

Wheat is the "staff of life'" and is grown in more than 80 countries. The United States, Russia, the Ukraine, Canada, China, Argentina, and India are the major producing countries. The Chicago contract is the highest volume contract in the world. The deliverable grade is Soft Red Wheat, used for cakes, pastries, and cereals. This crop is grown in the area around southern Illinois and Missouri. The Kansas City and Minneapolis varieties are deliverable on the Chicago contract; however, because they generally trade at a premium price and have freight considerations, this does not happen often. However, if Chicago prices ever trade at a greater than 20¢ premium to Minneapolis (the cost of freight from Minneapolis to Chicago), it has not been unheard of for a major grain company to load a unit train of wheat (100 rail cars) and send that train south. The contract size, as it is for all the CBT contracts, is 5,000 bushels, so a 1¢ price move equals plus or minus $50 per contract. The Kansas City Board of Trade is where Hard Red Winter Wheat is traded. This bread wheat is the most important class of wheat grown in the United States, accounting for half of the production, but the volume there is lower than in Chicago. This wheat is grown primarily in Kansas, Oklahoma, and Texas. It is planted, like the CBT wheat, in the fall and harvested in early summer. It lies dormant over the winter, and that's where the name comes from. The contract size is 5,000 bushels, and a 1¢ move also equals $50.

The primary contract of the small Minneapolis Grain Exchange is Northern Hard Spring Wheat. This wheat is a high-protein, milling-quality-type wheat grown primarily in Minnesota, North and South Dakota, Montana, and Canada. It is used in specialty bakery products such as croissants, French rolls, and bagels. It is planted in late spring (hence the name) and harvested in late summer. Because it is a higher-protein wheat, it generally trades at a premium, from 20¢ to up to dollars per bushel above the Chicago Exchange. I have seen it trade at prices below Chicago (1996 was a very poor winter wheat crop and a bumper spring wheat crop) and as much as $12 over in 2008 when Minneapolis traded as high as $25/bushel on a devastated spring wheat crop. The Spring Wheat contract, like the others, is for 5,000 bushels.

White Wheat, the fourth major wheat variety, represents 10% of the U.S. crop and is grown in the Pacific Northwest. It is used in crackers and pita bread.

For the grains and the soybean complex, fundamental analysts set up tables and debate where the ending stocks ultimately will be at the end of the crop year. If it looks like stocks are too low, higher prices are needed to "ration demand." If stocks appear too high, lower prices are the result, as farmer selling overwhelms demand. The supply-and-demand table for soybeans, for example, includes the following:

- *Beginning stocks:* This is what the government says will carry over from the previous year.

- *Production:* This is the crop estimate for the current year. During the growing season, the USDA releases the weekly Crop Progress Report, which shows the condition of the crop.

- *Imports:* Because the United States is an exporter, this is generally a small number for the U.S. table.

- *Total supply:* This is the beginning stocks plus production plus imports.

- *Crush:* This is the domestic demand by the "crushers," who buy raw soybeans and crush them into the products, meal, and oil.

- *Exports, seed, and residual:* These are the other sources of demand. Each year, 3% to 4% of the crop is held back for the next year's seed use. Export data is released twice weekly by the USDA. There is a Monday report, called Export Inspections (after the close), and there is a similar Thursday report, called Export Sales. Exports also can be affected by the strength or weakness of the dollar and other major currencies. If the dollar falls dramatically, it makes these commodities cheaper to foreign buyers and helps to stimulate export demand (and vice versa).

- *Total demand:* This is the sum of the crush, exports, seed, and a "residual" number for other use.

- *Ending carryover stocks:* Total supply minus total demand equals the carryover, or ending, stocks. This is the important number everyone talks about. A supply-and-demand table can be set up for a single country or the world.

These tables theoretically could be constructed before the crop is in the ground. If production falls by just 100 million bushels (a couple bushels per planted acre), the ending stocks could drop to an "unsustainable" number. ("Pipeline supply" is considered to be ending stocks somewhere in the neighborhood of just over 100 million bushels for soybeans.) This would be perhaps a few week's supply. On the other hand, if yields in a year increased by just a few bushels per acre because of favorable growing conditions, the ending stocks would rise to perhaps 300 million bushels (which is a comfortable level). Basically, a fundamental analyst constantly adjusts these numbers based on weekly export and crush numbers, as well as his determination of how the crop is maturing. Benchmarks for where prices have gone before are based on various carryover levels, but every year seems to be completely different.

The following are some other important fundamentals:

- *"Deliverable stocks" of grain:* The Exchange distributes information on the following in a weekly report: the quantity and change of bushels of corn, wheat, soybeans, and oats in the elevators licensed to deliver on the futures contracts. The report is useful in determining whether there is the potential for a "squeeze," where the shorts are not able to find the grain to deliver. If all the corn is primarily on the farm and very little is available for futures delivery, this is short-term bullish (even though the longer-term fundamentals could be bearish). If there is a large supply deliverable and the commercial players have no export business, the best place for them to sell might be a futures delivery (to speculators who really don't want the grain), and this is bearish. These numbers are most useful for analyzing the nearest futures month.

- *Government policy:* Government farm programs can expand or restrict acreage in general or for a specific crop. Price support programs can pull supply off the market, and "export enhancement" programs can stimulate exports.

- *Weather:* This is the biggest factor when analyzing future supply. Nothing affects soybean, corn, and wheat prices to a greater degree than weather. A "weather market" occurs when drought or flooding moves the market. These can be the most emotional of all markets. In the spring in the United States—and, in fact, in most of the Northern Hemisphere—the market watches the planting progress (for soybeans, corn, and spring wheat). In the summer, the market monitors the crop development, and in the autumn, it keeps track of the harvest progress. In the North American winter, the market watches the planting progress and crop development of the South American crops (during their summer). In the spring, it watches their harvest progress. A wet harvest can cause delays and hurt yields. In the winter, the market watches the weather affecting the dormant Winter Wheat. The wheat needs snow cover, or else it is susceptible to "winterkill," if the temperatures drop too low without the insulating effect of snow. Weather is so important that services for hire provide weather advice and predictions.
- *Seasonality:* All other factors remaining equal (a bold statement), the grains and oilseeds do exhibit certain seasonal tendencies. Soybeans and corn tend to put in a high in the May-to-July period, at the height of the "weather scare" period, and bottom out at harvest time in the October to December time frame. Cotton exhibits the same seasonal tendency. Winter Wheat tends to bottom out in the June-to-July period (harvest time) and peaks in January to March, when supplies are depleted to an extent but before the new crop is available. I am not a "seasonal" trader—with two exceptions. These are what I term "super seasonals."

The Voice from the Tomb (super seasonal #1)

"I'm not afraid of dying; I just don't want to be there when it happens." —Woody Allen

When you have traded as long as I have, you acquire a lot of knowledge. Unfortunately, not all of it is useful; however, I believe this might help you. I have discovered two seasonal tendencies that could help you capture profits: one in the soybean market and the other in the wheat market. The "Voice from the Tomb" is a wheat seasonal.

Between 1983 and 1995, my trading business was located on the floor of the Grain Exchange, where I met a very successful old-time trader. Other traders would ask this man's opinion, which was highly regarded because he was known as a successful trader. His response often was, "Listen to the 'Voice from the Tomb.'" Over the years, I befriended him and finally got up the nerve to ask him what he meant by this statement. He told me that the Voice from the Tomb (VFTT) was one of the secrets of his success, and the legend goes something like this:

Years ago, a millionaire grain trader lost his wife and dedicated his life to his three children. But as in many second generations of self-made people, the children were lazy and thought they would inherit all his money. As he aged, he began to look at his children as wasteful, and he believed they took him for granted. When he died, he left nothing to the children and instead gave all the money to charity. All he left them in his will were dates of when to buy and sell. The will stated that if they strictly followed his advice, they would have the fortune they had always expected to inherit.

Then, my friend shared the VFTT dates for the wheat market:

- Sell March wheat on January 10.
- Buy May wheat on February 22.
- Sell July wheat on May 10.
- Buy December wheat on July 1.
- Sell December wheat on September 10.
- Buy March wheat on November 28.

He told me these dates worked for him 80% of the time (a remarkable percentage for a trading program), but he never shared exactly how he used them in his own trading. So, I went back and studied the wheat charts.

I researched 35 years' worth of records and found that the VFTT was historically profitable approximately in 75% of the trades, based on the criteria I developed. I used the Voice from the Tomb dates simply: Originally, I would buy or sell at the close of each date and risk 15¢ per bushel, or $750 per contract, to make 15¢, or $750 per contract. If a date fell on a Saturday, I would take the trade on the Friday close; if the date fell on a Sunday, I would use the Monday close. I started trading it with real money in 1999, and it worked nicely for eight years, up until 2007. The actual results were as follows (number of profits in six trade signals annually):

- 1999—Five out of six
- 2000—Four out of six
- 2001—Six out of six (see Figure 6.1)
- 2002—Four out of six
- 2003—Four out of six
- 2004—Three out of six

- 2005—Five out of six (see Figure 6.2)
- 2006—Four out of six

So, during this eight-year period, I experienced 30 profits and only 12 losses. And in 2001, it was perfect: six trades and six profits. The overall result was more than 70% profitable—a nice little program.

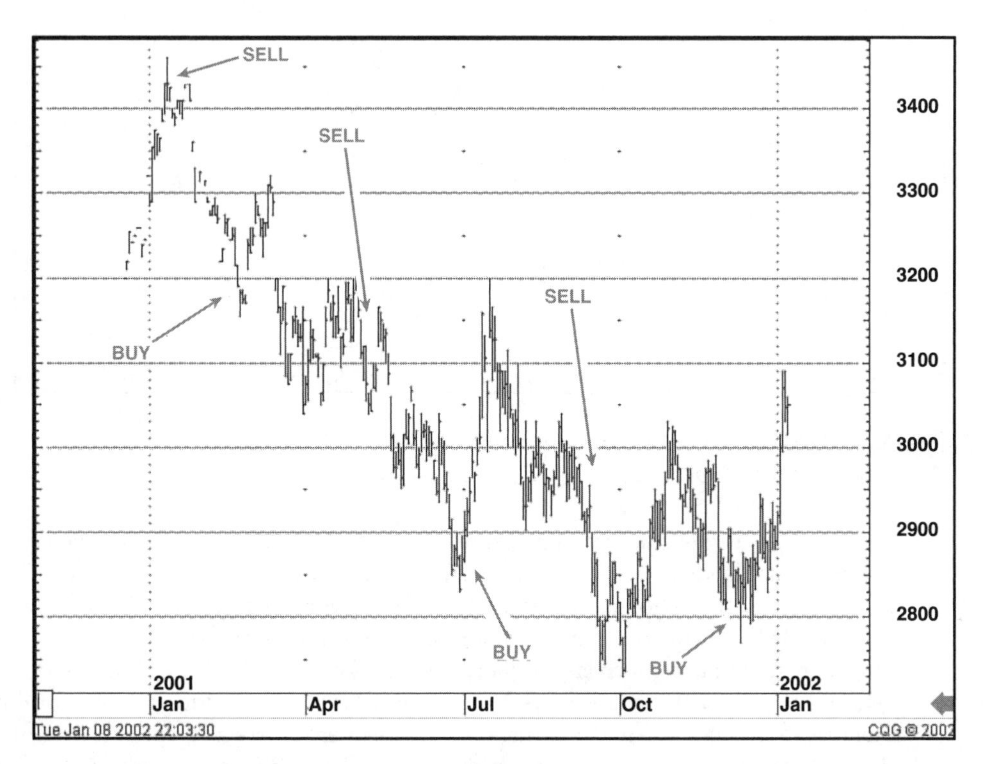

Figure 6.1 2001 wheat market (Voice from the Tomb)
Source: CQG, Inc. © 2008. All rights reserved worldwide.

In 2005, it resulted in five profits and only one loss, as shown in Figure 6.2.

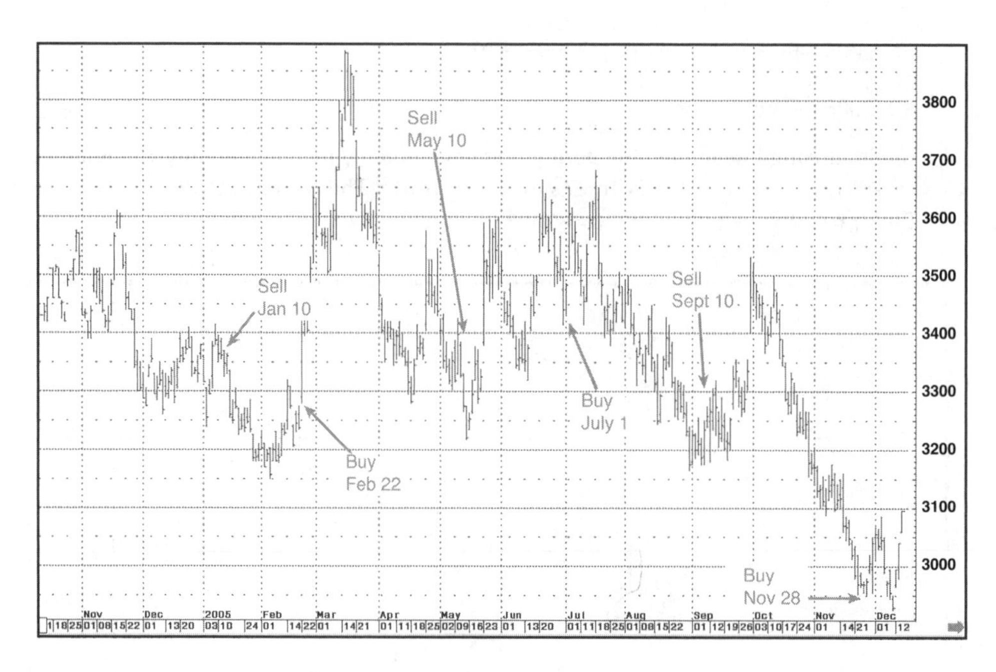

Figure 6.2 2005 wheat market (Voice from the Tomb)

For the time I began trading with real money until 2007, I had one break-even year, seven profitable years, and no losing years. In 2007, the system self-destructed: The results were only two for six. What made that year worse was that the first trade was a short sale that came out the day before a major crop report. The crop report was bullish, resulting in a sharp gap higher at the market open the day of the report and creating a 27¢ loss on our 15¢ stop. Now, I needed two wins just to make up for that one loss, but, unfortunately, the next two trades were losers as well. This was also the first and only time since I had been trading the VFTT that it had three losing trades in a row. I told my clients that something had changed, something was not right. After eight years of a winning program, I retreated to the sidelines. As it turned out, two of the three remaining trades that year worked, but overall, this was the year the VFTT didn't work.

Then in summer 2008, a client of mine who had been on the program for years and was still monitoring it asked if I had been watching the VFTT. He said that after we quit, it was working nicely again. During the last three trades of 2007 and the first four trades of 2008, it was five for seven and right back on track. So, I took another look at the program that had been so good for so long, and this is what I discovered.

Remember the bad trade in January that took place right before a major crop report? If the signal had taken place one day later, at the close the day of the crop report, it would have worked. The May signal didn't work, and I gave up before the July signal, but that one worked like a champ. The September signal would not have worked, but if it had taken place one day later, it would have worked. And the November signal worked just fine. This told me that the basic seasonal tendencies still seemed to work, but something was off a day or two for certain signals. That something was the major *crop report* in both January and September, which skewed the program. And guess what? For decades, the crop report had come out on the 10th of the month. But due to date changes, the January report had come out a day later than the usual date, as had the September report. I believe the VFTT works because it's based on normal seasonal tendencies for the wheat market. For example, the July buy signal takes place about the time the winter wheat harvest is approximately half over. Because many farmers sell their wheat crop right out of the fields at harvest time, the tendency is for prices to fall into the harvest period because there are greater-than-normal supplies available to the marketplace at that time of year. The futures market anticipates the end of harvest and generally bottoms, and then it starts to climb as the harvest period turns the corner and unwinds.

When a crop report comes out, traders react to it. A bullish report might be released during a normally weak seasonal period and might spike the market higher. However, in a normal year, the market tends to move along the normal seasonal path of least resistance after the news is out. Based on its stellar past, it was time to revisit the VFTT program, but with one major modification: looking at the trading calendar to determine when the monthly crop report will be released. If a signal is due to take place the day before the report, we wait a day and buy or sell at the close the day *of* the report. My theory is this: If the seasonal is bearish and the report is bullish, we will short the artificial spike and then let the bearish seasonal take over. If the report is bearish and we end up selling lower, the normal seasonal trend will bail us out anyway. This improvement would have turned a 2-and-4 year into a 4-and-2 year in 2007 and maintained the winning streak. Using my new rules, the subsequent results were as follows:

- 2008—Four out of six
- 2009—Four out of six
- 2010—Five out of six (see Fig. 6.3)
- 2011—Three out of six
- 2012—Four out of six

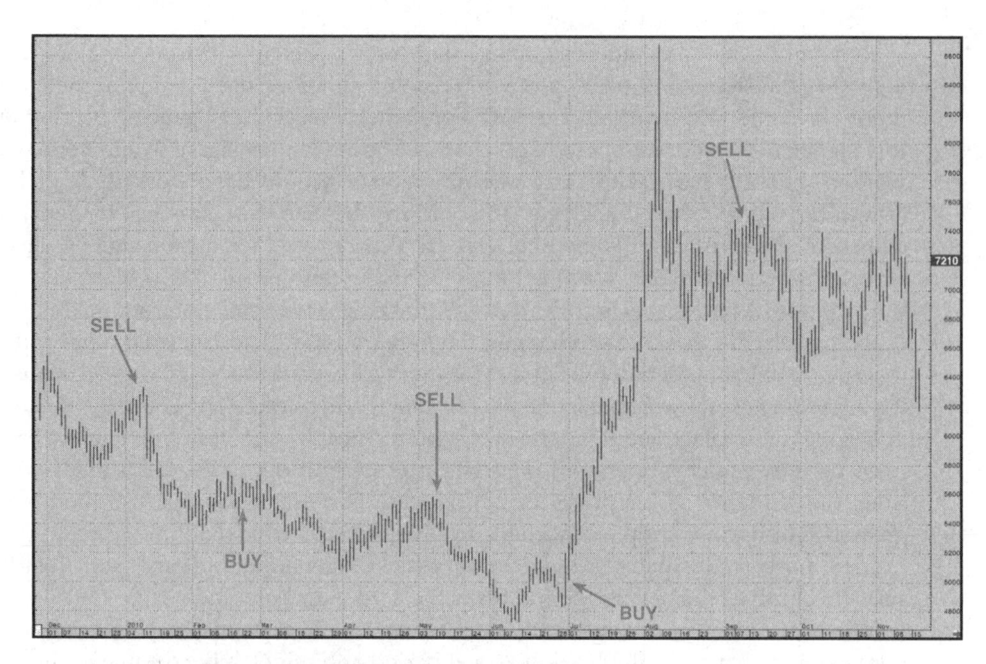

Figure 6.3 2010 wheat market (Voice from the Tomb)
Source: CQG, Inc. © 2012. All rights reserved worldwide.

One last observation: Think of my 15¢ rule as an optimization rule. The trend often moves much farther, and you can make considerably more than the 15¢/bushel. Sometimes, you need to take 15 to 20, and other times, you can make a lot more. For example, consider the 2008 February 22 signal: The buy came at $10, and with zero risk on that signal, the market rallied above $12, or 200¢ ($10,000 per contract traded), *in just three trading sessions* before the first significant correction occurred. So, you might want to wait and watch a bit when the profit target is met, and use a trailing stop. One method is to raise your stop to ensure a modest profit when the 15 number is reached, and try to maximize the trade.

Bottom line: I believe the VFTT will put the odds in your favor. Just watch out for those crop reports.

Some traders believe that seasonals exist in many markets, such as gold, but in my experience, I've observed them successfully only in the grain markets. By the way, Voice from the Tomb dates occur for corn as well. But, my experience is that they're not as accurate as those for wheat, which is why I didn't include them here. However, I have discovered my own extremely reliable seasonal for the soybean market.

Soy secret (super seasonal #2)

"Three may keep a secret, if two of them are dead."
—Benjamin Franklin

I want to share with you another super seasonal I call *the soy secret*. The soy secret is simply this: *Soybeans exhibit an extremely strong tendency to form a seasonal price bottom during October.*

The large number of farmers who tend to sell their crop right out of the fields to generate cash at harvest time results in selling pressure and creates this bottoming tendency. Sometimes, particularly in high-priced years, this market behavior is more pronounced than in others. *After the harvest selling pressure subsides, the soybean market tends to exhibit a post-harvest rally, offering a profitable trading opportunity.*

When I quantified the probabilities for a soybean price rise post-harvest, I discovered something quite exciting: My database covers 43 years, beginning with the 1968–1969 crop year. In the spreadsheet shown in Figure 6.4, I sorted this data by the *percentage gain* (last column on the right) the July soybean futures contract made from its October low price to the July contract high price for each year. The "Risk" column refers to the maximum price break (in cents per bushel) for that crop year *under* the October low price (post-October), and the "Gain" column measures (in cents per bushel) the highest price achieved after the October low was registered for the contract.

YEAR	OCT LOW	DATE of OCT LOW	POST OCT LOW	DATE of LOW	CONTRACT HIGH	DATE of HIGH	RISK	GAIN	% GAIN
1981-82	722	27-Oct	602	7-Jul	755	12-Oct	120	0	0.0%
1990-91	649	1-Oct	519	10-Jul	NA	9-Oct	130	0	0.0%
1968-69	259	4-Oct	NA	NA	272	7-May	0	13	5.0%
1985-86	541	7-Oct	497	24-Nov	576	26-Dec	44	35	6.4%
1983-84	828	27-Oct	720	14-Feb	899	25-May	108	72	8.6%
1988-89	780	26-Oct	751	18-Nov	847	5-Jan	29	67	8.6%
2000-01	490	30-Oct	422	25-Apr	534	19-Dec	68	44	9.0%
1984-85	627	1-Oct	551	2-Jun	685	1-Nov	134	58	9.3%
1991-92	578	11-Oct	563	6-Jan	637	1-Jun	16	59	10.2%
2006-07	585	10-Oct	565	28-Nov	650	4-Jan	20	65	11.1%
1998-99	555	1-Oct	402	9-Jul	618	30-Nov	153	63	11.4%
2005-06	585	10-Oct	565	28-Nov	650	4-Jan	20	75	12.8%
1974-75	803	28-Oct	490	3-Jun	NA	11-Nov	313	106	13.2%
1979-80	713	29-Oct	595	2-Apr	816	17-Jul	118	103	14.4%
1971-72	319	5-Oct	313	13-Jan	366	18-Apr	6	47	14.7%
1994-95	564	7-Oct	559	1-Feb	649	17-Jul	5	85	15.1%
1989-90	579	16-Oct	578	29-Jan	672	1-May	1	93	16.1%
1970-71	300	1-Oct	290	26-Apr	351	19-Jul	10	50	16.7%
1993-94	628	8-Oct	NA	NA	733	23-May	0	105	16.7%
1997-98	643	1-Oct	607	9-Jun	753	11-Nov	36	110	17.1%
2008-09	867	16-Oct	796	5-Dec	1291	11-Jun	71	149	17.2%
1999-00	497	29-Oct	465	13-Dec	583	3-May	32	86	17.3%
1982-83	570	26-Oct	NA	NA	673	11-Apr	0	103	18.1%
1969-70	250	1-Oct	NA	NA	299	29-Jun	0	49	19.6%
1980-81	856	3-Oct	673	29-Jun	1024	28-Nov	183	168	19.6%
1986-87	497	7-Oct	477	27-Feb	604	15-Jun	20	107	21.5%
2009-10	891	6-Oct	NA	NA	1092	1-Dec	0	201	22.6%
2002-03	531	9-Oct	NA	NA	658	20-May	0	127	23.9%
1978-79	675	2-Oct	673	16-Nov	859	22-Jun	2	184	27.3%
1995-96	663	3-Oct	NA	NA	856	12-Jul	0	193	29.1%
2004-05	535	18-Oct	506	4-Feb	696	16-Mar	29	161	30.1%
2001-02	442	22-Oct	425	2-Jan	600	10-Jul	17	134	30.3%
1973-74	529	30-Oct	520	5-Nov	696	26-Feb	9	167	31.6%
1996-97	681	31-Oct	668	12-Nov	902	7-May	13	221	32.5%
1992-93	555	8-Oct	NA	NA	755	19-Jul	0	200	36.0%
2010-11	1069	4-Oct	NA	NA	1474	9-Feb	0	405	37.9%
1977-78	539	21-Oct	NA	NA	758	30-May	0	219	40.6%
2011-12	1190	4-Oct	1026	12-Dec	1679	9-Jul	164	489	41.1%
1975-76	515	28-Oct	466	15-Dec	757	7-Jul	49	242	47.0%
2007-08	965	9-Oct	NA	NA	1596	3-Mar	0	631	65.4%
2003-04	639	6-Oct	NA	NA	1064	5-Apr	0	425	66.5%
1976-77	619	18-Oct	617	15-Nov	1064	22-Apr	2	445	71.9%
1987-88	546	20-Oct	540	3-Nov	1100	23-Jun	6	554	101.4%
1972-73	344	13-Oct	NA	NA	1290	5-Jun	0	946	275.0%

Figure 6.4 July soybeans (ranked by percentage gain, low to high)

For example, the July 2008 soybean contract followed this pattern (see Figure 6.5). The contract low was made on October 7, at $9.65 per bushel, and a dramatic uptrend ensued, with an interim high the following March at just below $16 per bushel. (The actual contract high was reached during the delivery period in July, at $16.60 per bushel.) Bottom line: It would have been hard not to make at least some money that year using the soy secret.

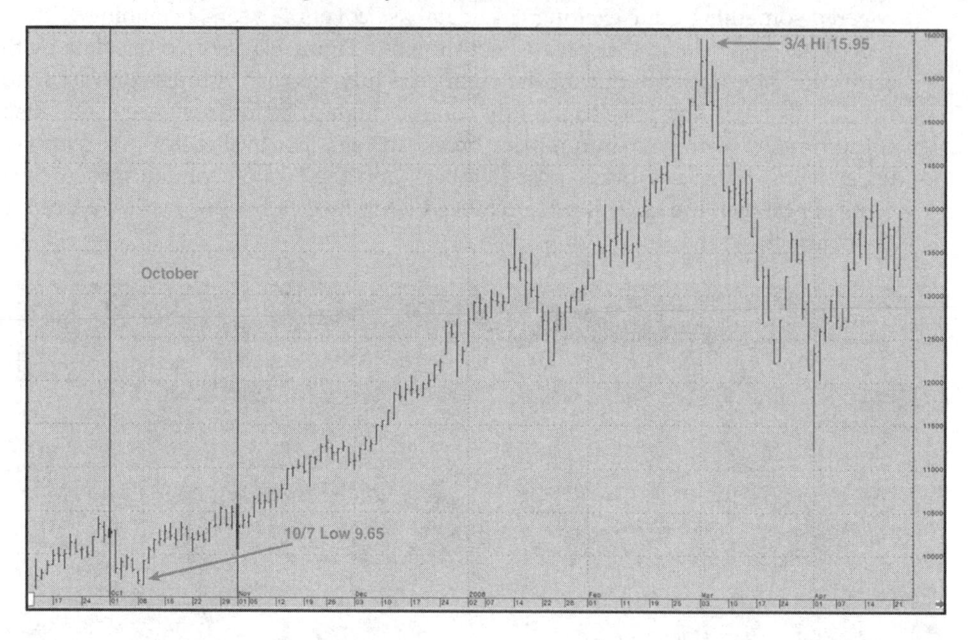

Figure 6.5 July 2008 soybeans

Now, let's analyze the spreadsheet data to develop a trading plan.

Looking at the last column first, we see only two years with zero gain, which means there were only two years when the month of October was a high-priced period for the July contract. For 41 of the 43 crop years, at least *some* price gain occurred above the October low. In other words, over 95% of the time, this market exhibited a rally off the October low before the July contract went off the board. This has to be more than random chance, wouldn't you think?

However, trading is never as easy as just buying in October and selling at a profit sometime later; we need to be realistic, based on some risk-to-reward criteria. In the real trading world, I've identified nine years (1974–1975, 1981–1982, 1983–1984, 1990–1991, 2004–2005, 2005–2006, 2006–2007, 2008–2009, and 2011–2012) when I made the assumption that a trader who knew about the soy secret still might not have profited since a measurable price drop occurred at some point from the October low before any big gains. Take, for example, 2011–2012 (see Figure 6.6); even though the market eventually gained a huge 41% from the October 2011 low, I placed this year in the losing category because the market made a lower low in

December. This December low was followed by a big rally, so it is certainly possible that a trader actually would have profited this year on the soy secret. However, to be conservative, I placed years like this one in the losing category.

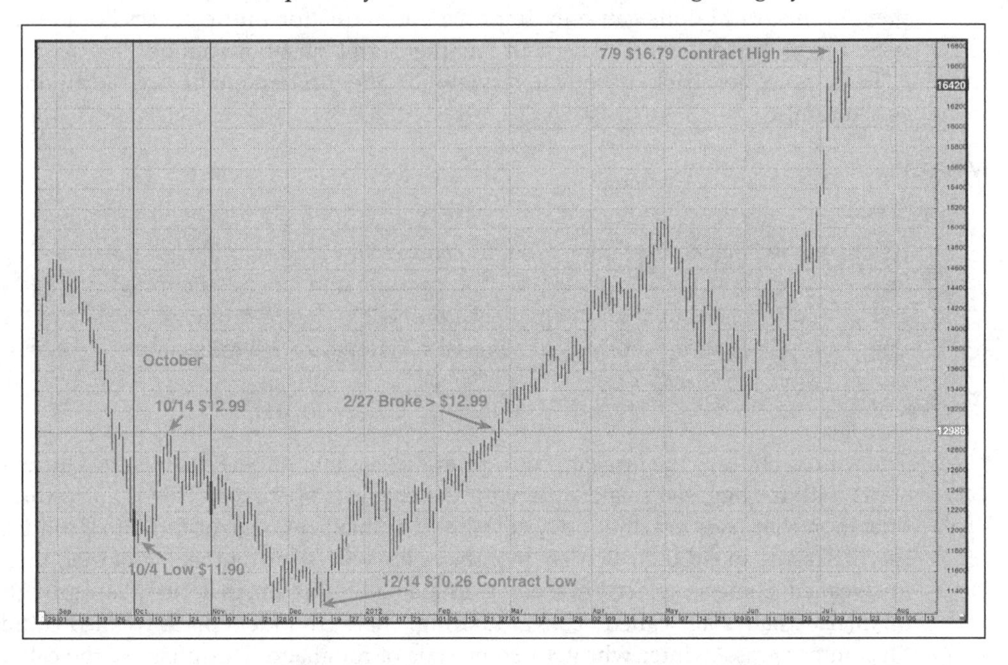

Figure 6.6 July 2012 soybeans—market made a lower low than the October low prior to a huge rally

Yet, even if we place years like this one in the red category, overall there was an excellent chance to make a nice profit with minimal risk by buying in October—over 80% of the time (35 of the 43 years).

Now, here's a clue on how to turn a "red" year into a "black" year: In the great majority of the years that did register a lower low after the October low (the 9 years I placed in the losing column, to be specific), in 7 of those 9, the market eventually rallied above the October low price. The eventual gains were anywhere from 9% to over 40%. The key to profiting in these years is to note if and when the market was eventually able to trade above the October *high* price. For example, in the 2012 market, the October high price was $12.99. Once the market was able to break above and close above that level (late February), the market continued to rally. In other words, this "breakout" level generally signaled a low-risk entry point during the "red" years.

Of course, every year is different, and you have no guarantee or sure path to profit. You might want to study the fundamentals of a particular year (acreage, yield, carryover supplies, and projected demand), but knowledge is power, and understanding historical odds can only improve your odds for future success. And one last thought: How about we keep our "market secret" just between us?

Let's now get back to our overview of the fundamentals for additional agriculturals.

Meats

Here's another real-life true story. A buddy of mine was at Costco the other day, and he saw some guy in the parking lot, loading package upon package of meat into a pickup. My buddy thought he was being cute when he says to the guy, "You should buy a cow!" The guy looked back at him and said the following three words: "This is pork."

The United States is the largest producer and consumer of beef. Just as the chicken starts with the egg, the steak starts with the cow/calf operation. This is a breeding operation that uses grazing land, cows, and a small number of bulls to produce calves. Calves spend their first six months of life with their mothers, and then they are weaned. Some are placed in feedlots immediately, but the majority pass through an intermediate stage called "backgrounding." Backgrounders place weaned cattle on summer grass, winter wheat, or some type of roughage. This phase of the calf's life might last from 6 to 10 months, or until the animal reaches a desirable feedlot weight of 600 to 800 pounds. After the animals are ready to be placed in the feedlot, they are termed *feeder cattle*. Usually, feeding continues until the animals weigh from 1,000 to 1,300 pounds, at which time they are slaughter-ready animals. The CME Live Cattle contract consists of 40,000 pounds of slaughter-ready animals. The customer for these animals is the meat packer who buys the livestock and sells the meat and other products, such as hides.

Prices are quoted two ways, either cents per pound or dollars per hundredweight (hundred pounds), which really are the same thing. Almost all feedlot cattle are steers (castrated males) and heifers (females who have not calved). Because some heifers are retained on ranches to replace cows that get too old, there are always more steers than heifers. Feedlots can be as small as 100 head or as large as 100,000. Some feedlots are farmer owned, and some are commercial operations. The commercial operations (cattle hotels) account for less than 5% of all lots but 80% of all cattle marketings. A feedlot operator might buy feeder cattle for his own account, or, for a fee, he might "custom feed" for farmers or other cattle owners. These feedlot-ready animals make up the CME Feeder contract, which has a size of 50,000 pounds. The specifications call for approximately a 750-pound steer; therefore, the contract represents about 60 animals. Prices are quoted in either cents per pound or dollars per hundred weight. Unlike the cattle contract, the feeder contract is cash-settled, just like many of the financial futures. It is based on an index, which the contract will equal on the last day. The index is compiled by the USDA, based on a weighted average of feeder cattle cash market sales.

Like cattle, the pork industry can be divided into segments, but there are important differences. The preslaughter phase of hog production is usually combined into what's called the "farrow-to-finish operation." In the hog industry, the backgrounding phase does not exist. In other words, the hog generally stays on the same farm from birth to finish. (Eighty percent of all hogs are produced this way, and 20% come from a breeding-only operation to the farm.) Hogs are taken to market when they weigh 220 to 240 pounds, and this takes about six months. Most beef is sold as fresh meat; however, a large portion of pork is processed further and becomes storable as ham—smoked, canned, or frozen.

Pork bellies are the raw material for bacon and can be fresh or frozen and stored for up to a year. The hog contract represents 40,000 pounds of carcass and is cash-settled based on an index of prices collected by the USDA. For over 50 years, we also traded pork bellies, highlighted in the movie *Trading Places*. The belly contract was *notorious* for numerous limit moves and volatile, erratic behavior. It was a speculative favorite when I started in the business in the 1980s, but alas, due to declining volume, the contract was de-listed in 2012.

Here's a trivia question for you: How many bellies does a hog have? The answer is two.

Major meat fundamentals

Accumulation or liquidation? During the accumulation phase of the cattle cycle, ranchers are building their herds by holding back cows. This method can temporarily create a short supply of market-ready animals, but it is bearish longer term. During liquidation (for example, in times of drought, which kills off the grazing pastures, or high feed prices), cows are sent to market. This is bearish from a supply and price standpoint in the short run but bullish longer term. This tactic works the same way for hogs as cattle. During the expansion phase, an increased number of gilts and sows (female breeders) are withheld from slaughter to become part of the breeding herd. During contraction, females are culled from the breeding herd, and the female portion of the total slaughter rises.

A fundamentalist would analyze the following data:

- *Seasonality:* Although it does not happen every year, feeder cattle sales tend to peak in the fall, with the end of the grazing season. At the same time, calf/cow operators tend to sell off unproductive cows, which increases the total beef supply and depresses prices. Hog prices tend to be the highest in the summer months because the December-through-February time frame is traditionally a low-birth period. Also, the demand for pork tends to peak during the summer months.

- *Corn and feed prices:* The rule of thumb is that high feed prices result in liquidation and low feed prices result in accumulation. The other variable here is the market price of the finished product. If sale prices of cattle or hogs are high, then more money can be spent on feed. In 1996, when corn prices soared to a then all-time record high of more than $5 per bushel, many cattle feeders found it more profitable to sell their stored corn and take their cattle to market (including breeding animals). Others could not afford the high feed costs, and this added to the liquidation. Prices of cattle spiked downward under the weight of the burdensome supply, but this turned out to be bullish for the longer term. This is pure economics. When it is profitable to raise or feed animals, this is what producers do; when it isn't, they don't.

- *Feeder costs:* In cattle feeding, the feeder's cost accounts for, in many cases, more than half of the total cost of production. Higher feeder costs lead to lower placements into feedlots.

- *Weather:* Tough winter weather can result in death loss and weight loss, which can reduce supply permanently or temporarily. At times, when the temperatures in the major feeding regions get extremely cold, cattle eat more and gain less. Animals that were to be ready for market at a certain date are "pushed back," creating a temporary shortage, and there is a glut later when they reach market weight. This fundamental is more important for cattle than hogs because the majority of hogs are now fed indoors.

- *Consumer tastes:* This can be approached in a macro sense and a micro sense. The per-capita consumption of beef or pork and how it changes over time affects price; this is a macro fundamental, and it has to do with dietary considerations and media news. On a more focused approach, hot summer days increase barbecue demand, and holidays increase the demand for hams.

- *Exports and income levels:* When a country achieves a higher level of income, the demand for red meat increases. Exports to Asia have become a much more important factor in recent years, and unexpected new export business can, at times, result in price spikes. China is a major soybean (and at times corn) importer due in large part to its large and expanding hog industry.

- *The substitution effect:* Beef, pork, chicken, turkey, and fish are substitutable commodities to a major extent. For example, if the price of chicken plummets, sales increase, which takes away demand from the other meats.

- *Cattle on Feed Report:* This is an important and much anticipated monthly report released by the USDA. Three major parts compose the report: cattle on feed (the total numbers in the feedlots), placements (of cattle into feedlots the previous month), and marketings (out of the feedlots the previous month). Because a placement of a 700- to 900-pound animal into a lot will become a market-ready animal in 120 to 160 days, this report can give a good indication of future market-ready supplies. Marketings out of feedlots can vary based on economic considerations because cattle feeders can move cattle ahead a bit or feed them a bit longer at times.

- *Cattle Inventory Report:* This is a count of the total numbers of mature animals as well as the country's "calf crop." It is an important report but is released only twice a year, in January and July.
- *Hogs and Pigs Report:* This is the most important report for the hog futures. The market often moves "limit," sometimes for days, after this report is released when it shows numbers higher or lower than expectations. It shows the total numbers (the pig crop), the breeding herd (numbers kept back for breeding), the farrowings and farrowing intentions (the numbers actually bred and anticipated breeding levels), and the market hogs (those intended for market). Weight classes also give clues about total future supply. It should be noted that although the Hogs and Pigs Report moves the market, it is often wrong. However, this fact cannot be verified for up to six months in the future when the animals either show or don't.
- *Daily Slaughter Levels:* This report gives an indication of how many animals are processed by the packers on a daily basis.

Sal, my feeder cattle broker in the pit days, once told me a story of a successful hog trader, who had a brother-in-law who was struggling in the pit. The successful one wanted to help his sister, who was promised a new house by her husband (the brother-in-law), but he could never seem to come through. The day after a very bullish Hogs and Pigs Report, the struggling trader saw 100 long hog contracts in his account. Thinking it was some sort of error (and not inquiring why they were in his account), he proceeded to trade out of them right after the open.

After a $7 run-up in hog prices, the successful one walked up to his brother-in-law and told him to go and buy that new house for his wife (the successful one's sister). The brother-in-law responded, "With what?" The successful one said, "What do you mean with what? Take the profits on those 100 longs I put in your account two weeks ago!"

Softs

The commodity subclass termed the *softs* has also been referred to as the *breakfast commodities* because it includes coffee, cocoa, sugar, and orange juice. Cotton, while not consumable, is also in this class because it's soft. And although lumber is hard (although it can be classified as a softwood or a hardwood) and has nothing to do with breakfast, we'll place it in this category because there is no other where it fits.

Sugar is grown in more than 100 countries around the world. Most sugar is consumed in the country in which it was grown and produced under government pricing arrangements. The sugar that is not subject to government restrictions is freely traded among nations, corporations, and traders. This free market is typically 15% to 25% of world production. A 5% change in production can mean a 25% change in free market supply.

The two main types of sugar grown in the world are cane and beet. Both produce the same type of refined product. Sugar cane, a bamboo-like grass, accounts for about two-thirds of world production. Cuba, India, Thailand, and Brazil are the leading cane producers, whereas Russia and the EEC are the major beet producers. The largest sugar exporting nations are Cuba, the EEC, Australia, Thailand, and Brazil. The major importing nations are Russia, the EEC, the United States, China, and Japan. A contract is for 112,000 pounds, with prices quoted in cents per pound. A 1¢ move equals a profit or loss of $1,120 per contract.

Coffee is traded in London, but the most active contract is in the United States, which is also the major consuming nation. Coffee is classified into two types: Arabica and Robusta. The Arabica areas produce 60% of the world's output, with Brazil and Columbia accounting for one-third of the world's exportable supplies. The Central American countries of Costa Rica, Mexico, Guatemala, Honduras, and El Salvador are also important producers, as are Uganda, Indonesia, and Vietnam. The US contract calls for delivery of Arabica coffee. Robusta, with flavors generally not as mild as the Arabica, is produced in the hot areas of Africa and Asia. The London contract is a Robusta contract. It takes approximately four years for a coffee bush to produce a useful crop. The fruit is green at first, and as it ripens, it changes to yellow and then red. It should be picked only when red, and the work is extremely labor intensive. Coffee beans do not ripen simultaneously, even when on the same branch, so the crop needs to be handpicked in most cases. In New York, the contract size is 37,500 pounds, or roughly 100 bags. A 1¢ move equals a profit or loss of $375 per contract. Note that most of the Central American varieties are deliverable on the contract at par, but if you deliver Colombian coffee, you receive a 2¢ bonus because it is considered a premium product.

The cocoa tree is a tropical plant that grows only in hot, rainy climates. As a result, the major producing countries are (in order) Brazil, The Ivory Coast, Ghana, Malaysia, and Nigeria. The fruit of the cocoa tree appears as a pod on the tree's trunk, which when ripe is cut down and opened, and then the beans are removed. Cocoa butter is extracted from the beans for use in cosmetics and pharmaceuticals, but its primary use is for the manufacture of chocolate. Cocoa is consumed primarily in countries of relatively high income. It was first brought to Europe as a luxury drink in the seventeenth century. The leading importing nations are (in order) the United States, Germany, France, the Netherlands, and the United Kingdom. These five countries account for about two-thirds of the world's consumption. Cocoa trades in London, but the U.S. contract traded on the InterContinental Exchange, commonly known as the ICE; the leading Exchange for cocoa. The size of the contract is 10 metric tons of cocoa beans, with prices quoted in dollars per ton.

Cotton is grown around the world and has been used for 7,000 years. Since the Civil War, cotton has been the major cash crop of the American South. When I wrote the first edition of this book, the United States was the largest world producer, but as of this writing, the United States is third, behind China and India. Other major producers include Pakistan, Brazil, Australia, Uzbekistan, and Turkey. The cotton fiber is used to produce fabric, and the seed is used for cooking oil. The major consumers (some are users for manufacturing) of cotton are, in order, China, India, Pakistan, Turkey, Brazil, and the United States. The contract calls for 50,000 pounds of U.S.-grown white cotton. A 1¢ move is equal to plus or minus $500 per contract.

Oranges are second only to apples among fruit in production. The United States used to be self-sufficient in production; however, a series of killer freezes in Florida sparked the growth of the Brazilian orange industry. Now up to 50% of U.S. consumption is imported from Brazil. The New York contract is based on a U.S. grade of frozen concentrated orange juice. In years of crop problems (primarily a freeze), prices can trade well in excess of $2 per pound. In years of high production, they trade below $1. This is a relatively thin contract, with a size of 15,000 pounds.

Woods are classified as hard or soft. Softwoods account for 85% of total lumber consumption. Most harvesting of lumber is done by the mill on land leased for timber rights by private parties or the government. The bark is removed, and logs move to the head saw. The contract calls for construction-grade random-length two-by-fours manufactured in the Pacific Northwest or Canada. The contract size is 80,000 board feet, with prices quoted in dollars and cents per board foot. A $1 move equals plus or minus $80 per contract. Like orange juice, this is a relatively low-volume, thin contract.

The following are major fundamentals for the softs:

- *Stocks-to-usage ratios:* The level of sugar supplies in relation to demand, the stocks-to-consumption ratio, is the major statistic traders talk about when measuring the degree of "tightness" in the marketplace. For sugar, a ratio of 20% to 30% is considered low and is consistent with higher prices. When prices spiked above 25¢ per pound in 1980, this ratio was in the mid-20s. When the ratio rose above 40% in the mid-1980s, prices fell as low as 3¢. Because the free-floating supply of sugar is comparatively low, it does not take a big move in the stocks-to-consumption ratio to result in a major price move. Candy sales are important, as is the price of corn. (High-fructose corn syrup is a competitor of sugar.)

- *For cocoa, the "grind" is the term used to measure consumption:* Higher grinds indicate rising demand and vice versa. From time to time, the International Cocoa Organization (ICO) forges an agreement intended to support prices. The ICO is a group of producing nations that purchases cocoa for its own account and stores it to push prices upward. When a shortage develops, the ICO releases stocks onto the market. Coffee consumption is believed to be more inelastic, with a major price increase needed to curtail demand. However, the sharp rise in coffee prices in 1996 to 1997 was met by a commensurate reduction in consumption. Americans consume close to double what the Germans drink (they are number two), followed by the Chinese, the French, the Japanese, and then those from the other major EEC countries. Consumption trends need to be followed closely. In the late 1940s, the United States accounted for two-thirds of world imports, but because of the growing popularity of coffee globally, this number is down to one-third.

- *Crop yields:* Weather, disease, insects, and political and economic conditions in the producing countries all affect production rates. For example, the great freeze in 1994 caused coffee prices to surge from less than $1 per pound to close to $3. For coffee, the International Coffee Organization provides useful statistics, such as number of bags produced by country.

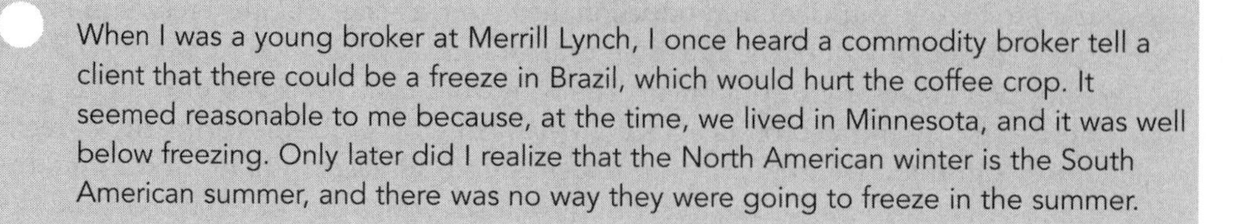
When I was a young broker at Merrill Lynch, I once heard a commodity broker tell a client that there could be a freeze in Brazil, which would hurt the coffee crop. It seemed reasonable to me because, at the time, we lived in Minnesota, and it was well below freezing. Only later did I realize that the North American winter is the South American summer, and there was no way they were going to freeze in the summer.

Metals

There are two major subsets to the metals category: precious and industrial. Although gold certainly is used in the jewelry industry and electronics and other industries, it is considered precious due to its traditional role as a medium of exchange (in other words, money). Silver is considered both precious and industrial. Metals such as copper (sometimes called the poor man's gold) are considered to be in the industrial class.

Precious metals

Unique and therefore precious, gold is its own asset class. Prices are quoted alongside securities in the major financial media, and many believe gold to be a global reserve currency as well as a commodity. Gold is a hedge against asset erosion in times of inflation and political unrest. It was always popular as a store of value in India, and it is becoming increasing popular as an investment vehicle in China, as wealth there grows. In 1816, Great Britain, the world's major superpower, backed its currency exclusively with gold, which in turn forced other nations to follow its lead. Today Great Britain is not even one of the top 10 gold holders. The metal formally entered the world's monetary system in 1944, when the Bretton Woods agreement fixed all the world's paper currencies in relation to the dollar, which was tied to gold. Then, on August 15, 1971, President Nixon canceled the dollar's convertibility to gold, which likely led to the hyperinflation of a decade later. Gold now trades freely, in accordance with supply and demand.

I consider gold an asset class unto itself, with money flowing into the metal as a store of value, particularly when inflationary expectations heat up or in times of money printing. This is a list of the rankings of gold holders as we go to press, starting in first place: The United States (with over 8,000 tons), followed by Germany, Italy, France, China, Switzerland, Russia, Japan, the Netherlands, and India (about 600 tons). If the International Monetary Fund (IMF) were a country, it would rank third, as the IMF holds approximately 3,000 tons. If the euro zone were one country, it would rank first, and some estimates place "private" holdings in Indian households way up in the rankings (perhaps at first place), but there is no hard data on this.

Today, some of the world's central banks are divesting themselves of a portion of their gold reserves, while others (notably Russia, Korea, and China) are adding. For over 40 years, beginning in 1965, the world's central banks were selling gold in aggregate. As we go to print, however, the world's central banks are increasing their gold holding (in aggregate). South Africa is the world's largest gold producer, accounting for more than 25% of the world's production and 50% of the in-ground reserves. The next five major producers (in order) are Russia, the United States, Canada, Australia, and Brazil. When the first edition of this book was printed over a decade ago, the all-time futures price high was $1,026 (reached in January 1980 on the October 1980 contract when the spot price hit $875). As this edition goes to press, the all-time high futures price was $1,921 in September 2011. I have no doubt there will be a new all-time high price in the future as currencies depreciate. When the gold futures contract was listed in 1976, it came "on the board" less than $100. The most popular futures contract is a 100 troy-ounce contract, and there are also minis in 50-, 33-, and 10-ounce sizes. Prices are quoted in dollars and cents per ounce, with a $1 move equaling a profit or loss of $100 on the "big" contract.

In the summer of 2011, my wife booked a three-day Class IV river raft trip for us. This was during a major bull market for gold, and the day we left, I was long gold for myself and numerous clients. I had a problem in that we were told there was no Internet or cell phone reception where we were going. The market was extremely volatile at that time. Gold was trading at about $1,885 right before we left, and because I would be unable to monitor the market, I sold out our entire position. Just before we departed from the hotel to meet the guide, I received one last price quote; gold had just traded above $1,900 for the first time in history. Damn, I thought; it's on its way above $2,000. But there was nothing I could do, so we left for the trip; it was relaxing, and I tried not to think about the markets. The first thing I did, however, when we again reached civilization was power up the iPhone for a gold quote. It flashed $1,755 (actually on its way down to the $1,500s in the next few weeks). The clients thought I was pretty smart, selling out just one day before the top. Sometimes being lucky is as good as being smart.

Although an industrial metal (used in the automotive industry and in chemicals, petroleum refining, and electronics), platinum is considered a precious metal because only 80 tons of new production reach the world annually. Ninety percent of the world's production takes place in South Africa and Russia. South Africa still accounts for 85% of the world's in-ground reserves, with its two largest production companies setting the producer price. However, the futures sets the free market price with a 50-ounce contract, which is worth $50 per $1 ounce move. Platinum (and palladium, platinum's poor cousin) are also actively traded on TOCOM (Tokyo Commodity Exchange). Until 2012 platinum always traded at a premium to gold, and the platinum/gold spread is a popular speculation.

Silver is truly a hybrid industrial/precious metal. In the 1980s and 1990s, many of the world's dedicated silver mines could not operate profitably below $8 per ounce, so much of the production was the result of a by-product of copper, lead, and zinc mining. However, in recent years, new dedicated silver mines have been brought into production. Mexico and the United States are the world's largest producers, followed by Peru and Canada. Fourth and fifth in production are Australia and Russia. In recent years, silver consumption has outpaced new production, with the balance being met by above-ground supplies. This probably cannot occur forever without either demand falling, production rising, or prices rising. The major silver futures contract is sized at 5,000 troy ounces. Prices are quoted in dollars and cents per troy ounce, with a 1¢ move equaling a profit or loss of $50 per contract. When the Hunt brothers felt the world would run out of silver and attempted to corner the market from 1979 to 1980, they were able to run prices as high as $50 per ounce, a price silver did not hit again until 31 years later. Silver was 35¢ per ounce during the Great Depression in the 1930s.

Here are the major metals fundamentals:

- *Central banks and inflation:* Watch what the central banks are doing. At times, the central banks are aggressive sellers, and at times, they are absent from the market. When they are printing money, gold by default rises (more currency units in circulation require a higher gold price per ounce). Keep an eye on the global political climate and how gold reacts to it. In times of instability, gold is considered a store of value. War or a loss of confidence in traditional investments can cause a shift of funds into gold. Watch China, India, and other growing economies. As income growth increases there, so has gold demand. Most importantly, keep an eye on inflation and inflationary expectations. In the long run, the prices of gold and all other precious metals are sensitive to inflation. Regarding silver, watch the price of gold, but also watch the prices of copper, zinc, and lead. Because much of the new production of silver comes as a by-product of these three metals, if the price of the three is depressed and production curtailed, silver output will suffer as well. The reverse is also true. Watch Indian imports. Silver is a precious metal of choice in India, and a strong economy there increases demand.

- *Platinum:* Regarding platinum, watch Japan. In Japan, platinum is the precious metal of choice, with more of it used for jewelry than gold. A strong economy in Japan is good for platinum prices. This is an industrial metal and a precious metal, and the demand for platinum is somewhat dependent on the health of the automotive, electrical, dental, medical, chemical, and petroleum.

Now, let's briefly discuss industrial metals:

- *Copper:* The red metal, copper, is traded both in New York and in London at the London Metals Exchange. The LME contract is for 25 metric tons, or 55,000 pounds; prices are quoted in dollars and cents per ton, with a $1 move equal to a profit or loss of $25. The CME contract is for 25,000 pounds or 12 1/2 "short tons." The price is quoted in dollars and cents per pound, with a 1¢ move equaling a profit or loss of $250 per contract. Copper is the third most widely used metal, after aluminum. It is mined all over the world but primarily in the United States, Chile, Mexico, Australia, Indonesia, Zaire, and Zambia.

- *Aluminum:* The British call aluminum (and spell it) aluminium ("al-you-min-e-um." They include an extra *i* and an extra syllable in the word. We Americans call it aluminum ("al-ou-min-um"). Aluminum is the world's second most widely used metal, after iron. The LME lists an active, liquid contract. The contract size is 25 metric tons, or 55,000 pounds. Prices are quoted in dollars and cents per ton. In the United States, prices routinely are quoted in cents per pound. To convert from dollars per metric ton to cents per pound, you divide the price by 2,204 (the number of pounds in a metric ton). The LME also trades a scrap aluminum contract; the aluminum alloy is a 20 metric ton contract.
- *Zinc, nickel, and lead:* Zinc is used as an alloy with copper to make brass. It also is used with iron or steel in a process called galvanizing, which is the largest use. The former USSR countries, Canada, the United States, and Australia are the major producers. The LME lists a 25 metric ton (55,000 pound) contract, which is quoted in cents per pound. Most of the nickel production is used in stainless steel. It also is used as a coating for such varied applications as helicopter rotors and turbine blades. Nickel is also used in coins and rechargeable batteries. The major producers are Canada, Russia, and Australia. The contract also is traded on the LME, in 6-ton lots, with prices quoted in dollars and cents per ton. The major uses of lead include car batteries, ammunition, fuel tanks, and as a solder for pipes. The United States is the largest producer, followed by Canada, Mexico, Kazakhstan, and Australia. Because it is extremely toxic, there has been a concerted effort to "get the lead out" of many products in recent years. The United States, Japan, Germany, and the United Kingdom (the common link here is a major automotive industry) are big consumers. Lead also is listed on the LME in 25 metric ton contracts quoted in dollars and cents per ton.
- *Tin:* Tin is manufactured into a coating for steel containers used to preserve foods and beverages and other forms of electroplating. China is the largest producer, followed by Brazil, Indonesia, Malaysia, Bolivia, and Thailand. However, more tin is smelted in Malaysia for export than any other country. It can be volatile at times. Traded on the LME in 6-ton contracts, prices are quoted in dollars and cents per metric ton.
- *Palladium:* Palladium is a member of the platinum group, used in the automotive, electrical, and medical industries. Russia is the world's largest producer, with South Africa a close second. The two countries account for about 93% of the world's supply. Palladium futures are thinly traded in 100-ounce contracts. Every $1 per ounce of price movement results in a $100 profit or loss per each contract purchased.

The following are major industrial metal fundamentals:

- *Economic activity:* Watch the economies of the major industrialized nations that comprise the prime demand fundamentals of this group. Each of the metals, of course, has its own fundamentals (zinc and lead are generally mined together, for example), but industrialized demand is the key. If there is a threat of an economic slowdown, this will be reflected in lower prices.

- *LME stocks:* Every day, the LME releases its widely watched stocks report, which is a good measure of supply. It lists the stocks in the Exchange-approved warehouses for aluminum, copper, zinc, tin, and lead.

- *Mining strikes, production problems, and war:* Demand traditionally soars for the industrial metals in times of increased defense spending. Copper has been called the "war metal."

- *Inflation:* The industrial metals have, at times, been called "the poor man's gold," and they heat up in an inflationary environment.

When I was a novice commodity broker at Merrill Lynch, my biggest client was a retired former top executive of a major software company. When the company went public, his stock was worth more than $15 million. In retirement, his hobby was trading commodities. He traded a bit differently from most of us, in that he had the funds available to back his convictions until they eventually worked—and they usually did. For example, he once started to short wheat at $3 per bushel. The market went against him, and he added to the position, at $3.50. He added to his short position at $4 and more at $4.50. When the crop finally came in, he covered the entire position at $3—a nice profit. This is not a recommended way to trade, mind you, but it worked for him. He was a strict fundamentalist and never looked at charts.

In 1979, when silver first crossed $8, he started to short the market with a modest position of five contracts. He was a former metallurgical engineer, and he had a theory that above $8, the technology was available to extract silver from the slag heaps alongside the mines, and the market would be flooded with supply. Remember, at this point, we did not know that the Hunts and their Arab partners were accumulating silver bullion and silver futures in their attempt to corner the market. At $8.50, my client shorted another five and another five at $9. By the time the price crossed $10, he was short 25 contracts, with an unrealized loss of more than $125,000. He was determined to keep shorting; "whatever it takes," he told me, until he finally beat this one; this was his style. By the time the market reached $12 (an all-time high), he was short approximately 50 contracts, with an average price of $10 and an unrealized loss of $500,000. I was getting very nervous and concerned, but he was adamant. All we knew at that time was that there was a broker from the now-defunct Conti Commodity firm who would come into the pit, almost daily, purchase a huge position, and leave the pit for the day. Many times, his buying would put the market up the limit. (There was a 50¢-per-ounce limit at the time.) When he left the pit, the market would drift a bit and usually close higher on the day, but not up the limit.

I started to have silver nightmares, afraid my big client would go down with the ship, but I didn't really know what to tell him. At the time, there wasn't a good fundamental explanation that could convince him he was wrong.

I then remembered that there was a Merrill Lynch executive who was also on the board of directors of the COMEX (metals exchange). The next morning I called him, explained I had this big client short silver with a big loss, and he just wouldn't get out. I still remember the call: The Merrill Lynch executive's response went something like this: "Look, there's big money behind this market. If you're short, GET OUT. That's all I can tell you—don't call me again!" Then, he hung up.

About 10 minutes prior to the open, with my heart pounding, I called my client and told him about this conversation. I must have sounded daft as I heatedly told him, "The guy says, 'If you're short, GET OUT,'" because he calmly told me to "Reverse the position at the open." I said, "You mean, not just buy your 50 to cover, but buy 50 more?" He said, "Yes. If we're wrong to be short, then we should be long."

Now I was really nervous. What if I convinced my client to cover and then he bought at the top? He could lose well over $1 million, and I could lose my best client. Still, it was too late to do anything but put the order in to buy 100 contracts at the open.

Guess what happened? The market opened limit up, at an all-time high price somewhere around $12.50. Then, it started to drift down. So, he covered his 50 at a loss in excess of a cool half-million, and because of my phone call, he now owned 50 contracts at what was an all-time, record-high price—and the market was drifting down!

To make a long story short, the market drifted another 10¢ or so lower, but then reversed up to close that day up the limit price (so at least he was not showing a loss on the new position at the close that day). As it turned out, the next $2 to $3 higher came fairly easily, and when he recouped his total loss, plus a modest profit, he got out of the 50, in the $15 to $16 range. Of course, if he held on to the 50 up to the highs, around $50, he could have made more than $9 million. Then again, he could still have been there on the descent back to $5. In any case, disaster was averted.

He never traded silver again, but continued to trade actively (even from his hospital bed) until the day he passed away about three years later.

Continuing your commodity trading education

Concluding our introduction to the fundamentals, is there anything else you need to know? Well, there's an old saying, "To make a small fortune in commodities, start with a big one." And I may be giving you the impression that the odds are stacked against you with all the computer algorithms and professional hedge fund managers, but I don't feel that way. It's true that most people lose when trading commodities, but it's not because the odds are stacked against them. Every buyer of every losing trade could have been a seller and made money on that same trade, and every seller of every losing trade could have been a buyer and made money on that trade. A profitable minority is doing just that. Not on every trade, mind you, but on balance. So what's the key? Is it how you analyze the market?

We will discuss various indicators and methodologies shortly, but the real determinant of success or failure is the trader's state of mind, his or her psychology. All winning traders understand this. Trading emotionally, or on gut feelings, will fail. You need to understand mass psychology because this is the reason markets move in trends. You also need to understand when the trends are turning and why the majority is wrong at turning points. The key to this whole equation is smart money management.

If emotions can kill you in the markets, then the opposite must be true: Being unemotional enhances your prospects. Years ago, a friend of mine whom I respect as a successful trader cashed in on what I knew was a major score in the wheat market. I saw him in the members dining room, and I said to him something like, "You must be feeling damn good having cashed in at the top." He was a calm sort of fellow, and he said, "George, when the markets treat me well, I don't dance in the streets, and when they don't, I don't beat myself up. Always remember these words: Slow and steady wins the race." Years later, I know what he meant by this. What a trader needs to do is not to think about the money but instead to concentrate on trading correctly. If you trade properly, the money will come. If you trade incorrectly, you're doomed.

A loser hopes too much. She has an inability to get out of a losing trade early enough because she keeps hoping the market will turn back her way. Sometimes it does, but too often, the margin clerk is the one forcing her out. Invariably, after she's forced out, the market comes back the way she thought it would, but by then, it's too late.

The volume of trade generally swells at major bottoms and major tops. Why do so many people sell at the bottom or buy at the top? It's because they're acting emotionally instead of intellectually. One simple way to avoid this is to not get attached to a position. Trading should not be an ego thing. There is always another market tomorrow.

I've witnessed literally thousands of trades from hundreds of brokerage clients over the years. I've seen what those who make money do, and I've seen what the losers do. Invariably, the losers make the same mistakes. They may make money initially, and they might even have more winners than losers, but there always seem to be those large losses that wipe out whatever good came before.

Many years ago, the CME had an ad campaign in which it tried to teach the public how to trade—an impossible undertaking. One of the full-page magazine ads pronounced, "Do not risk thy whole wad." How profound. And yet, this is the one major mistake the majority of novice traders make. They bet too much on one trade or on one market, which brings us to the first tenet of good money management: You must know in advance how much you are risking on a trade, and unless it is a small percentage of your total risk capital, don't take it.

I could go into theoretical probability here, but common sense works better. Some of the most important advice I can give you in this book is to plan for slow and steady gains and look to minimize the draw-downs. The way to do this is to cut the losses quickly on the bad trades. So, how much should this be? It should probably not be more than at most 10% of your total trading capital per trade, and ideally no more than 2% to 5% per trade. Think of it this way: If you risk 5% on each trade when you start trading, you will need to be wrong 20 times in a row to be totally wiped out. You would need to be using a very poor trading system to do this.

Consider this: If you win on just half of your trades, but your net profit is 10% of trading capital on each winning trade, with your net loss of 5% on each losing trade, you're up 50% on your first 20 trades. Not bad for being right only half of the time. On the other hand, if you risk 25% of your capital on each trade, it takes only four losing trades in a row before you're done. And that's a certainty; the time will come when you have four losing trades in a row. The key here is to avoid major draw-downs. Plus, I have a couple of other tips.

For one, diversify. Don't put all your eggs in one basket, and don't place all your chips on a single roll of the dice. This lessens the opportunity for any one trade to be your last. Stick with the trades that are working and cull the ones that aren't. If you don't have the discipline to get out of the bad trades when you need to, make it your own personal rule to immediately and physically place a stop loss order in the market the moment you enter any trade. Believe me, your stops will not be hit on the very best trades. And once you have a reasonable paper profit on a trade, move your stop so that it never turns into a loss.

Contrary opinion theory

At times, it pays to be contrary. And because you should avoid doing what the losers do, which generally is what the majority is doing, this is a good time to introduce contrary opinion theory. The concept is simple: If all the bulls have already bought, there are no bulls left to buy, and the market falls because of its own weight. If a piece of bullish news fails to move the market up, this is your clue. When all the bulls decide to run for the exit door, there will be no cushion of new buyers to soften the decline, and the decline will be particularly severe. The reverse is true if "all the bears" have already sold.

Contrary opinion is not a hard-and-fast trading system. The way to use it is to watch closely for signs of a turn in the marketplace when the majority of what you read is very bullish or very bearish. I am always on alert when everyone knows the story or when the story is on the front page of the of *The Wall Street Journal* or the *Financial Times*, or pictures of burned-up corn are on the evening news. In the summer of 1993, when the floods hit the Midwest and thousands of acres of crops were under water, it seemed everyone was bullish soybeans (including myself). The consensus was over 90% bullish. *Newsweek*, when it still was a major print magazine, ran a cover story on the floods. The cover had a picture of a farmer up to his neck in water. Looking back, we now know that issue came out on the very day the contract high *for the next decade* was reached in the grains.

Spreads

Using *spreads* (at times called *straddles* or *switches*) is a more sophisticated way of trading, and it fits well into the game plan of many traders. I know some traders who trade only spreads because they feel spreads are the best way to limit some of the risks inherent in futures and options. Actually, this is the main purpose of spreading: to reduce risk.

When you enter a spread, the objective is not necessarily to make money on a rise or fall in the market in question but rather to make money from a change in the relationship between different prices.

When you put on a spread, you buy one contract while simultaneously selling another. You are long and short in either two related commodities or two different months of the same commodity at the same time. The relative change between the two determines your profit or loss.

The two major categories of spreads are *intramarket* and *intermarket* spreads.

Intramarket spreads

Intramarket spreads consist of buying one month in a particular commodity and simultaneously selling a different month in the same commodity. Examples include buying July corn and selling December corn, buying March crude oil and selling April crude oil, and buying May cotton and selling December cotton. Since you are trading two different months in the same commodity—one long and the other short—their prices tend to move in the same direction. So how can you possibly make money in a spread? Well, although spreads tend to move in the same direction, they don't have to. And even when the two months move in the same direction, they generally tend to move at different speeds. Many times, when you gain on one side of a spread, you lose on the other. What you're looking for is a bigger gain on the winning side than loss on the losing side.

Let's look at an example. Assume that you put on a spread between March copper and July copper in December of the previous year. You are buying the March and selling the July. When you buy the near month and sell the distant, it is called a *bull spread*. A *bear spread* (short March and long July) is the mirror image. In a bull spread, you are predicting that the near month either will rise faster than the distant or fall slower. Either outcome is profitable. Spreads can be more reliable and more predictable than outright positions, which is precisely the reason many traders like them. Spreads are not sure things, but they can put the odds in your favor.

For example, most years, the March copper tends to gain on the July because of seasonal considerations. March is historically a high-demand time of the year for copper because of inventory rebuilding prior to the peak building season. Suppose that when you "place" the spread in December that March is trading at 302 and July is trading at 301. You have put on this bull spread—long the March and short the July—with the March trading at a 100-points (1¢ per pound) premium to the July. (If the March were trading at 300 and the July at 302, you would say you were long the March and short the July, with the March 200 points discount to the July.) A few months pass, and in February, copper has risen in price, with both months appreciating—but at different speeds. The March is trading at 315 and the July at 310. The spread has now widened from 100 points premium the March to 500 points premium the March, and you sense it is time to take your profits. To exit, you would do the reverse transaction—that is, sell the March and buy the July. This offsets both sides of the spread and effectively wipes your slate clean. Let's look at the result. The March has risen from 302 to 315, so you have a 13¢, or 1300-point profit, on this side of the spread. The July (the short side) has risen from 301 to 310, so you have a 9¢, or 900-point loss, on this side of the spread. The difference between what you gained and what you lost (1300 minus 900) is your profit, which in this case is 400 points. Note that you don't need to calculate both sides to determine your profit; this works out neatly to be the spread differences: 500 minus 100 is 400. Because 1 point in copper is worth $2.50 per contract, this is a gross profit of $1,000 per spread.

You might be asking yourself why you'd want to trade the spread when you could make more money by simply buying the March outright. In this case, March rallied from 302 to 315, a 1300-point move, or $3,250 profit versus $1,000 profit. It all has to do with the risks versus the reward. Spreads generally move slower. Yes, you can certainly lose in a spread as well, but at times you can gain even when the market doesn't move the way you plan. What if the economy weakens and March copper falls 1300 points? If you were long, you would lose $3,250 per contract. The spread could certainly fall 400 points, but it is also possible that traders would turn bearish the whole market, and both months could go down the same amount, thereby resulting in no loss. When spread trading, you are more interested in the difference between the months than the outright flat price movements.

The ability to profit in both up or down situations is one of the advantages of spread trading. Also, the margin requirements for spreads are generally much smaller than outright positions because the Exchange recognizes that, in most cases, spreads are less risky. If you are long May corn and short September corn, and the president declares a grain embargo, odds are that both months will be down sharply. In other words, you are somewhat insulated from dramatic news with the resulting price shocks when spread trading. In addition, spreads tend to move slower, giving you more time to react, and many traders believe spreads are more predictable.

Intermarket spreads

Intermarket spreads consist of buying one commodity and simultaneously selling a related commodity. Two examples are buying silver and selling gold and buying Minneapolis wheat and selling Chicago wheat. In these examples, the two markets are related, and they generally move in the same direction because the same market forces affect both. However, they move at different speeds.

For example, you may decide to buy July corn and sell July wheat. Both are grains, both can be used for animal feed, and both are export commodities. They will tend to move in the same direction. However, if the fundamentals are opposed, the two could move in opposite directions. Let's assume that it is March and that you believe the supplies of corn are tight but that wheat supplies will grow larger as the market moves closer to the harvest in the early summer. July corn is at $3.10 and

July wheat is at $4.50, so you buy the corn and sell the wheat, with corn at a 140 discount to the wheat. (Be sure to read the order with the long, or the buy side, first.) Intermarket spreads cannot be classified as bull or bear, like intramarket spreads. Suppose that a few months go by, and both corn and wheat fall in price—corn to $2.80 and wheat, because of harvest selling pressure, to $3.60. You decide it is time to unwind the spread. You buy the July wheat and sell the July corn, which offsets both sides of the spread and wipes your slate clean. The long side (the corn side) shows a loss of 30¢, and the short side shows a profit of 90¢. Your gross profit is the difference, 60¢, and because in grains a penny move is worth $50 per contract traded, this is a profit of $3,000. Note that you put the spread on at a 140 discount and took it off at an 80 discount; the difference between 140 and 80 is 60. In this case, you wanted the spread to narrow; you wanted the lower-priced corn to gain on the higher-priced wheat, and it did. If the corn fell by 40¢ and the wheat by 20¢, you would have lost 20¢ on the spread. If there were weather problems with the new wheat crop, and the spread widened to 190 (wheat went up 40¢ and corn fell 10¢), you would have lost 50¢, or $2,500 per spread.

Certain spreads are actively and commonly traded. The Exchanges generally gives traders a break on the margin rates for trading the common spreads. For example, although margin might be set at $1,700 to margin a wheat contract, because Kansas City and Minneapolis recognize intermarket spreads between their two respective wheat markets, a long Minneapolis wheat and short Kansas wheat spread might require only $1,500 total (or $750 a "side," not $3,400).

In the grains, the new crop/old crop spreads are popular among traders who try to determine how the relationship will change between one crop that has already been harvested and another that is either in the ground or yet to be planted. Here are some common examples:

- Long May or July corn/short December corn
- Long May or July soybeans/short November soybeans
- Long May or July soybean meal or oil/short December soybean meal or oil
- Long May or July oats/short December oats
- Long March or May wheat/short July or December wheat

Popular intermarket grain spreads include these:

- Long or short wheat versus corn
- Long or short corn versus oats
- Long or short soybeans versus corn or wheat

Soybean processors use the soybean crush to lock in profit margins, when available. This involves the purchase of soybeans (the raw material) and the simultaneous sale of the products: soybean meal and soybean oil. The reverse crush involves the purchase of the products and the sale of beans.

The new crop/old crop July cotton versus December is popular and can be volatile.

In the meats, the hogs versus cattle, cattle versus feeder cattle are the most popular. Some traders like to trade the cattle crush, which involves a purchase of corn and feeder cattle (the two raw ingredients) versus the sale of live cattle (the finished product).

By far the most popular energy spread is the purchase or sale of heating oil versus the unleaded gasoline because traders try to take advantage of the seasonal tendencies of these two products to move toward or away from each other. The Crack Spread is the simultaneous purchase and sale of the crude oil contract versus the products, gasoline and heating oil.

In the metals, the gold/silver ratio spread is calculated by dividing the price of gold by the price of silver. It represents the number of ounces of silver required to equal the price of 1 ounce of gold. In 1980, when gold was $850 and silver $50, the ratio was 17; however, in 1996, with gold at $350 and silver at $5, the ratio was 70. I'm not sure there is an average or a correct number here, but recently the ratio has traded between 30 and 70, with the average for the past century at 32.5. The purchase or sale of platinum versus the purchase or sale of gold is another popular metal spread, with a margin break for buying one and selling the other.

A popular interest rate spread is the NOB (Treasury notes versus Treasury bonds), or the spread between the U.S. Treasuries and the Bund (German Government Bonds), or the Eurodollar versus the Note spread (the relationship between short-term and longer-term rates).

Limited-risk spreads include carrying charge spreads. Carrying charges are the costs to hold a commodity from one month to the next and include storage costs and interest. For example, if it costs 3¢ per month to hold wheat, and the July/September wheat spread is trading at 8¢ premium to the September, by definition the risk on this one, is low. Unless interest rates rise dramatically, the likelihood that September would rise much more above July is minimal. However, if a bull market develops in wheat due to limited nearby supplies, there is no limit as to how far July could rise above September. These are spreads to watch for. Limited-risk carrying charge spreads can be found only in storable commodities. On the other hand, there is no limit to how spreads can vary in either direction for perishable commodities such as live cattle.

And yes, you can "leg off" a spread (meaning you can liquidate one side and leave the other intact), but it is generally not a good idea. You normally enter the spread because it is a lower-risk transaction. Novice traders, when a spread isn't working, have been known to take off the profitable leg, leaving the unprofitable on, in hopes that it will come back and profits can be realized on both sides. For some unexplained reason, this usually doesn't work. (It would be better, in most cases, to take off the unprofitable side because this is the side that isn't working.) No matter which side you take off, however, if you exit one side of a spread, you immediately incur the risk of an outright transaction. You can think of this like splitting sixes in blackjack, because you don't like a 12 against a dealer's ace. Although it might work at times, in the majority of situations, you're just asking for trouble. (Incidentally, when you leg off a spread, you immediately lose your margin advantage, and your account is charged full margin for the remaining outright position.)

Note that spreads can trade with the front month higher than the back and vice versa. You can use this fact as a valuable forecasting tool: Generally, markets like this are bullish. I'll end this particular discussion of spreads with a caveat: Because the margins are generally much lower on spreads, there is a natural tendency to overtrade or put on too many. Just because spreads are limited risk does not mean there isn't risk; on occasion, spreads can actually entail greater risk than outright positions. A number of years ago, a friend of mine had the long July/short December cotton spread. One afternoon, after the market's close, a change in a government policy was announced. Although I've forgotten the specifics, I remember that the next day the market opened limit down in the July and limit up in the December—the result being that my friend was hit to the max on both sides!

Finally, here's another true story from the pit days of the Chicago Mercantile Exchange. One morning before a major USDA Cattle Report, a large trader in the cattle pit bought 100 contracts at steady money on the day to initiate a new long position. Several smaller traders in the pit also bought, figuring this guy knew something and that they could "coattail" him. Then, the first wave of selling hit the pit. The market moved 50 points lower on the day. Instead of panicking, the large local bought more. So did the coattailers. Then, the second wave of selling hit the pit. At 100 points lower, the big guy bought more. So did the "coattailers"—but at this point, their coattails were feeling a bit tight. Then, the third wave of selling hit the pit. The market went limit down, at that time 1.5¢ per pound under the previous day's close. If there had been more sellers than buyers, the market could have ended the day "lock limit" down, with traders conceivably being locked into a position until the next day. Still, the big guy bought even more. This time, however, the coattailers ran for exits; they just couldn't take it anymore. Just as they sold out, they heard the big guy say, "Now we've got 'em right where we want 'em." Only one coattailer had the guts to hang on. As it turned out, that third wave of selling was the last wave of selling, and the market ended up closing higher on the day!

Perhaps this is where the following old-time trader's expression comes from: "I bought the first break; I bought the second break; I was the third break."

7

Algorithms Eliminating People

"Relax," said the night man,
"We are programmed to receive.
You can check out any time you like,
But you can never leave!"
—The Eagles, "Hotel California," 1976

An electric tension fills the air as Louis Winthorpe III and Billy Ray Valentine muscle their way through the crowd of traders lining the New York Board of Trade's orange juice trading pit. The traders are sweating from heat generated by more than 100 tightly packed bodies, nervous with the anticipation of what's to come. The clerks, manning the phones surrounding the pit, are on high alert.

The crop report will be released in five minutes. When those numbers are released, the market will move big time, creating (and destroying) fortunes in the process. Winthorpe and Valentine are now standing shoulder to shoulder with other traders and eyeing their arch nemesis, Clarence Beeks. Beeks believes he already knows the actual crop report numbers, since he illegally obtained an advance copy of the report in his quest to corner the orange juice market on behalf of the infamous Duke Brothers. However, our heroes learned of Beeks's plan, they managed to steal the real crop report back from Beeks...and secretly delivered him a fake version.

The "real" crop report will show a record-large orange harvest, resulting in huge supplies that will ultimately move the traders to yell, "SELL!"

Beeks believes the numbers in his false report and is looking for the orange crop production to be sharply lower. He is planning to "BUY!" in his quest to corner the orange juice market for the Dukes. Commodities can be volatile on any day, but particularly so on crop report day.

The opening bell rings, and the decibel level explodes. (In the 1980s, all the trades in OJ were made in the pit by the "open-outcry" process, in which the traders yell out their bids and offers.) Beeks starts hitting all offers, screaming, "Buy, buy, buy!" Most of the traders in the pit are sheep looking to hop on for the ride. Seeing Beeks bidding the market up, they believe he knows something and join in his buying frenzy. The rumors have started to fly: "The Duke Brothers (with Beeks as their agent) are looking to corner the market!"

FCOJ prices are now on a tear, rising as high as $1.45 per pound. Until now, Winthorpe and Valentine have been lying in the weeds. With perfect timing, they begin to scream, "Sell, sell, sell!"—right at the top of the market. The true crop report numbers are then revealed. The market begins to crash, and at the optimal low point of 29¢ per pound, our boys reverse course and start screaming "Buy, buy, buy!" They are now covering their short sales. The majority of these sales were made well above $1 per pound, and they are covering from 25¢ to 46¢ and netting millions. The Dukes, who bought near the top, are left holding the bag.

The classic 1983 comedy *Trading Places* is one of my all-time favorites. Winthorpe is beautifully portrayed by Dan Aykroyd as a rich commodity broker turned homeless, with Valentine played by the comic genius Eddie Murphy as a homeless man transformed into a rich commodity broker. Many people believe that the story was inspired by the silver market's incredible rise and ultimate fall in 1980, when the Hunt brothers of Texas tried unsuccessfully to corner that market. Silver prices crashed in March of that year, when the brothers were unable to meet their last $100 million margin call.

What really made *Trading Places* exciting was the trading pit itself, filmed in the actual pit at the New York Board of Trade (NYBOT), where real traders played themselves in the movie. The climactic scene (in most viewers' minds) is the chaotic buying frenzy that took place in the pit (although some male viewers might argue that the climactic scene was when Jamie Lee Curtis took off her sweater). In any case, the movie would not have been as visually exciting or nearly as suspenseful without the trading pit. It's hard to imagine any excitement if our heroes were just clicking a mouse in front of a computer screen.

Trading Places is now more than 30 years old. The NYBOT, where cotton, coffee, cocoa, sugar, and orange juice were traded, was established in 1870. On a rainy Friday, October 19, 2012, the floor traders in cotton, coffee, cocoa, sugar, and orange juice donned their trading jackets and yelled out their bids and offers for the last time. You see, this was the final day of "open-outcry" trading. Open-outcry trading, the backbone of the Exchange for more than 100 years, was permanently silenced. It was progress, but the pit closing put 1,000 traders and support staff out of work. One veteran pit trader told a *New York Post* reporter, "Most of these people really don't know how to do anything else, and now we will all have to find our place in the world." However, other than these folks, the closing had little to no effect on the dealings in these key global commodities. Or did it?

Open outcry is dead

When I wrote the Introduction to my book *The New Commodity Trading Guide: Breakthrough Strategies for Capturing Market Profits* in 2008, I discussed the upside of replacing the pit trader with computers. There was no need for traders to leave their homes in the morning. No need to maintain a downtown facility with the associated high rents and utility costs. No need to hire runners, phone clerks, and trading clerks. And above all, no need for the pit trader. I used to pay a good pit trader an extra $2 to $5 per contract (above normal clearing fees) to execute my trades, and I was glad to do so. If the guy was louder or bigger or quicker than my competitor's floor broker, I would often get the better price. So, the cost savings of computerized trading is obvious, but it also brings the benefit of a level playing field. Ernest Hemingway once said, "The best way to find out if you can trust somebody is to trust them." In the old days, you really had to trust your pit broker.

Years ago, I was using a floor broker in the New York silver pit to execute my trades there. All was going well until one day, when I placed an order to buy 50 silver contracts at a price that should have been easily filled. After a few minutes had elapsed, the market surged higher, netting me a tidy profit...at least that's what I thought. I had been waiting for the pit broker's phone clerk to call me back with the fill. He hadn't called yet, so I called the floor. The broker got on the phone and denied I had ever placed the order. I asked to listen to the tape recording of the transaction, but it had been mysteriously erased. To this day, I have little doubt that he filled the order and pocketed my profit for himself. My only recourse was to never use this guy again, and subsequently I did find a pit broker I could trust. This kind of problem doesn't occur with electronic trading because the computer can't lie.

And there are other benefits. You can place orders faster—as fast as a mouse click. During a fast-moving market in the olden days, it was entirely possible to miss a price by the time the runner delivered the order to the pit broker. Even with using a market order (required to be filled at the next available price) during a wild pit session, we might not have known for hours what price we were filled at. In erratic market conditions, a good fill was often the luck of the draw. Today these doubts are gone; fills return to the trader instantaneously. The computer can also manage multiple orders and price fills more efficiently than a human. Clearing firms like computerized trading as well because credit and risk management are automated. The computer can cut off an out-of-control trader before the trader's account moves into an unsecured debit position.

Reduced cost and speed, enhanced information management, the expansion of markets globally with 24-hour trading...isn't technology terrific? Other than the loss of a few jobs and the romanticism of the bygone era of the pits, are there any downsides?

Over time, at least to me, the downsides have become more evident.

The legendary trader Livermore once said something to the effect that technology might change, but the markets never will because markets are made by human beings, and human nature doesn't change. Traders today still make the same mistakes traders made 50 or 100 years ago. Markets will continue to trend up and trend down.

"The trend is your friend" is a basic theme of some of my other books. This truism has not changed and remains a primary theme for successful trading in this book. I can cite literally thousands of examples of markets that have trended long and far and, in the process, made some people rich and wiped out many others. You might have heard about the poor soul who lost his farm. I can almost guarantee that guy was bull-headed and fought the prevailing trend of the market until he finally ran out of money.

In the 1920s, for example, the New Haven railroad was the premier blue-chip stock of the day and sold as high as $279 per share. In those days, you could trade stocks on 5% margin, as we trade futures today. When New Haven sold 50 points off the top, it must have looked cheap at the time. How many traders would have had the guts to sell it short when it crossed below 179, 100 points from the top? Better yet, who would have had the guts, or the vision, to sell this investment-grade security short at 79, or 200 points from the top? It must have looked extremely cheap at 79 because, remember, this was the Apple of its day. Yet the trend was down, and after the crash of 1929, it traded as low as 12.

In the year 2000, a friend of mine bought a "new technology" stock at the offering price of $66. He added to his position at $150 a share, again at $200, and then again at $300. I suggested he use stops to lock in his profit, but he "knew" this company was only going up (his daughter worked there), and he told me it would ultimately trade at $1,000. It did keep going up beyond what I imagined it ever could, and he added to his position at $450 and $500. It actually traded as high as $600. Today, it has been delisted, going off the board at $0. He lost much more than his original investment because he was trading on margin.

Remember Enron? This was a "blue-chip" energy company and the largest contributor to the 2000 Bush presidential campaign. At that time, the stock was trading at $90 a share. Today, it no longer exists. If you still own the stock, you can use your certificate as wallpaper. *The trend is your friend; do not fight it.* Electronic trading will not eliminate trends or eliminate future Enrons or silver crashes. The keys to successful trading are still, and always will be, successfully identifying the trends and practicing good money management, combined with the essential qualities of patience and discipline.

While I have long subscribed to Livermore's belief that markets do not change because human nature does not change, eliminating people from the middle of the equation *has* made some difference in price movements.

Rogue algos

Knight Capital is a firm that specializes in executing trades. On a Wednesday morning in August 2012, the firm was testing a new electronic trading algorithm, and somehow in a 45-minute period, the firm managed to lose $440 million. This was not caused by a rogue trader, or even human interaction. It was blamed on a "bad algorithm" in the computer software. If not for a cash infusion by certain customers, the firm would have become insolvent. This disaster was all done by the computer, at 40 trades per stock per second over hundreds of stocks. Buying too high, selling too low, and attracting other computers to take the other side, moving the markets and causing chaos. Trades occurred at "abnormal" prices, both above and below the prevailing market; on Knight's appeal, the Exchange let the great majority of the trades stand. Somebody made the $440 million, but many other innocent traders were caught in this web as well. If you had a stop working to cut a loss, it might have been hit. If you had a limit order to buy or sell "away" from the market, it could have been filled that morning. Bottom line: The computers can create weird market actions, and at times they even do this by design in normal trading. Some firms program their algorithms to create wild swings, to set off stops and move markets to points they've engineered to profit. It's all market action and may have nothing to do with news or fundamentals of supply and demand. It seems that every day, I see market actions that never would have occurred when the trades were done in the pits.

As traders, we have all had to adjust to these new market realities in stocks and commodity futures, and you will need to adjust your methods as well.

Exploding volatility

One consequence of eliminating people is *volatility.* Speed and volume have combined to make the markets more volatile than they have generally been in the past. Volatility can lead to trader anxiety; however, an anxious trader will not be a successful trader. Succeeding in trading today requires the ability to cope with exploding volatility.

Are you old enough to remember the good old days when gasoline was less than $1 a gallon? Consider Figure 7.1.

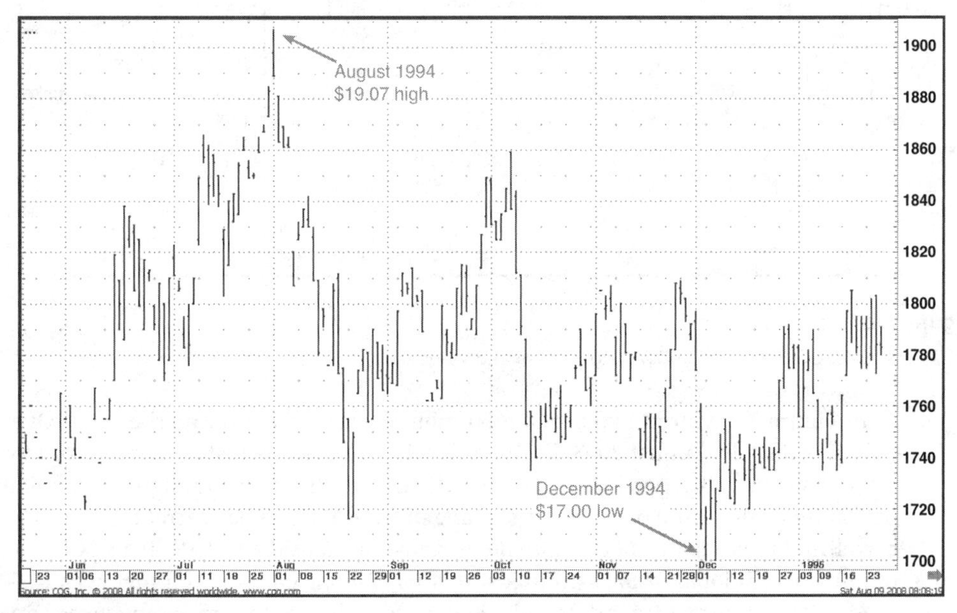

Figure 7.1 1990s oil

Source: CQG, Inc. © 2008. All rights reserved worldwide.

This is a daily chart of the oil market for the 1994–1995 trading period. Each vertical line represents one full day of trading. You are looking at nearly one full year of oil futures trading. The chart appears to illustrate a volatile market with big ups and downs throughout this period. However, it all depends on how the chart is scaled.

The price range during this 10-month period was an extreme high of $19.07 per barrel in August and an extreme low of $17 in December. This is a $2.07-per-barrel range from high to low within this entire period. The size of one oil futures contract is 1,000 barrels; therefore, every $1-per-barrel move equals $1,000 profit or loss per contract traded. During this 12-month period, we saw approximately a $2,000-per-contract range in price movement between the two extremes—not an atypical year for that period.

Today, the oil contract size is exactly the same; however, volatility has exploded. Consider the recent example shown in Figure 7.2.

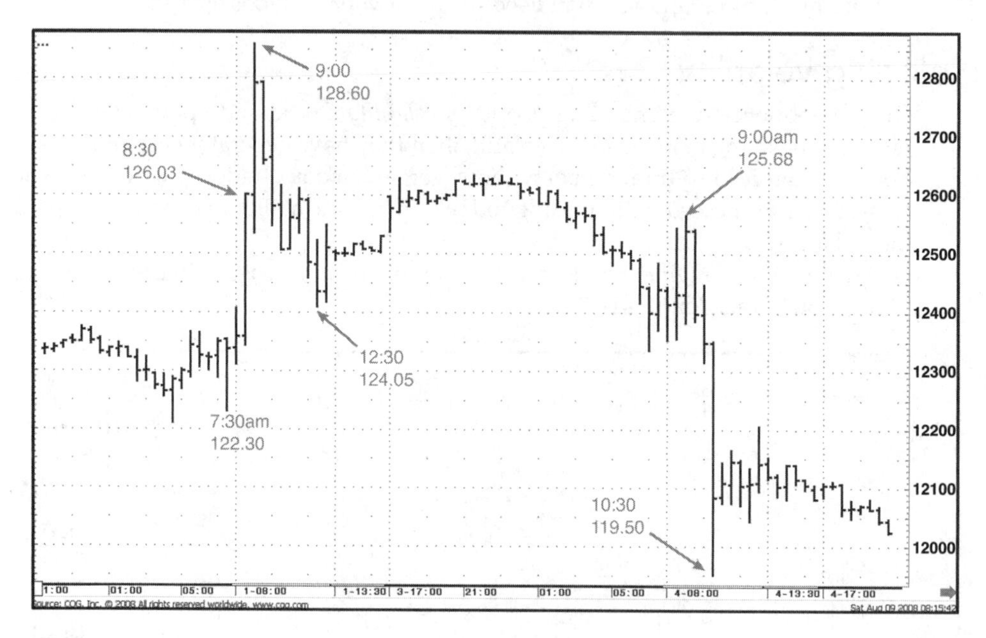

Figure 7.2 Today's oil

Source: CQG, Inc. © 2008. All rights reserved worldwide.

In Figure 7.2, you're looking at a 30-minute chart of the oil market that covers only two days in August 2008. Each vertical line represents just 30 minutes of trading (versus one day per line in Figure 7.1). During the first highlighted one-hour period (two 30-minute bars), the price ranged from $122.30 per barrel to $126.03 per barrel, and *in just one additional 30-minute period* (from 8:30 A.M. to 9:30 A.M. CST), oil ran up an additional $2.57. Within just this 1 1/2-hour period, the range was $6.30, or $6,300 per contract traded. In only 90 minutes this day, the price range was triple the range of the entire 1994–1995 trading year. The next day, a similar dollar move *in exactly the opposite direction* occurred. This is not atypical for the current market environment. In fact, oil now moves the same amount in an average day that it moved in an average year before 1990.

Why this dramatic rise in volatility? Screen trading is the major culprit; however, reasons other than electronic trading are to blame, too. Commodity demand has multiplied in recent years due to the dramatic industrial revolution in a number of countries, notably China and India. This demand increase (with a dose of inflation) has resulted in higher prices. Higher prices lead to larger ranges for the same percentage moves. For $19 oil, a 10% move equals $1.90, but for $90 oil, a 10% move equals $9. So, this is part of it, but it doesn't fully explain the velocity and ferocity of today's market movements (let alone the volatility).

Speeds accelerating

Are you old enough to remember the days when you heard a song on the radio and wanted to buy the album? The process involved physically going to the record store, finding what you were looking for, and returning home to play it. This process took time. Now you can find and download music in seconds. The main reason for the increased speed of market movements is the Internet, a direct result of the dramatic shift during the past few years away from nearly 100% pit trading to pretty much 100% electronic trading.

Until recently, this is the way I would place an order in the commodity markets: I would pick up the phone and dial a trading floor. Hopefully, the clerk would pick up the phone call in a timely manner, but in a fast-moving market, sometimes it would ring for what felt like forever, and this could be maddening. When the clerk did pick up the call, I would read my order, and the clerk would write it on an order ticket and then time-stamp the ticket. Good procedure required the clerk to read back my order to me for confirmation and consistency before she sent it off. The clerk would then pass my order to a runner (hopefully the runner was near the phone clerk and not out having a cigarette), who then physically walked it to my broker in the trading pit (or, at times, the broker's clerk, adjacent to him in the pit). The pit broker would cue the order, and when the market approached my price, the pit broker would yell out the buy or sell into the trading pit, looking for an offsetting trade via the open-outcry process. After the order was filled, the process would reverse from runner to clerk, with more time stamps, and eventually it would be phoned back to me. This all took time. From today's point of view, it is amazing that we operated this way—and in most cases efficiently.

Now with electronic trading, orders are disseminated and received instantly. Orders of all sizes from around the globe are now entered instantly, eliminating this entire human-based process.

This volatility enables many opportunities, but it also geometrically increases the risks compared to the old days. So, how does a human trader cope with this rise in volatility? The answer is you must have a plan.

Today, a trader needs to compress his time parameters and use computing power over shorter time spans. A plan will not eliminate the volatility and speed of today's markets, but it will help you compete.

Melding the old with the new

One objective of this book is to meld the necessary adjustments for the current market environment while maintaining those timeless methodologies that have worked in the past and will continue to work in the future because of human nature. Fear and greed ultimately move markets. And no matter what machines we utilize, these human traits will never go away. Speed can be our friend or our enemy.

There is hardware available today that can make trades in extremely tiny fractions of a second. The truth is that you and I are not going to compete with that, nor do we need to. Maybe we do not want to. Remember that Knight Capital was rich enough to afford that degree of computing power.

What we need to do is focus on methodologies that can work for us. We need to develop trading methodologies that utilize human traits for success. One of the objectives of this book is to help guide you through these waters.

As the legendary trader W.D. Gann once said, "Most people are in too big a hurry to get rich, and as a result they go broke." This hasn't changed.

In 1841, Charles Mackay penned *Memoirs of Extraordinary Popular Delusions and the Madness of Crowds*, in which he wrote: "Men, it has been said, think in herds; it will be seen that they go mad in herds, while they only recover their senses slowly, and one by one." This hasn't changed.

The pit trader may have "gone the way of the dodo," becoming an extinct species. (They were good to eat and easy to catch.) However, human nature hasn't changed.

It is interesting to note the change in how the mainstream views commodities. During most of my trading career, which spans more than 30 years, futures trading was viewed as a casino. Now, many financial planners treat commodities as an asset class, and they allocate a portion of their portfolios to commodities, alongside traditional stocks and bonds. While the commodity markets may act differently now than they used to, many time-tested methods do still work.

A few years after the 1929 stock market crash, the great trader and philanthropist Bernard Baruch wrote a foreword to a reprint of Charles Mackay's classic. As the title indicates, Mackay's book chronicles various investment manias from the 1500s through the 1800s. From the tulip craze to the Mississippi and South Sea bubbles, the basic underlying premise is that manias (economic and otherwise) are a condition of the human species. They will come and go over time but never disappear. The reprinted edition of *Popular Delusions* that I own was published in October 1932, right in the thick of the Great Depression. In this quote from the foreword, Baruch refers to that most recent mania he termed the "1929 market madness in America:" "I have often thought that if, in the lamentable era of the 'New Economics,' culminating in 1929, even in the presence of dizzily spiraling prices, we had all continuously repeated, 'two and two still make four,' much of the evil might have been averted." Those very words could be used today; just substitute the dates and the market you want to insert.

Panics, manias, and bubbles

The 1929 panic and eventual recovery from the Great Depression that followed were not firsts for America. Crashes and market panics had previously occurred in 1837, 1857, 1861, 1873, 1893, and 1901. The 1857 panic was preceded by the California Gold Rush. The 1873 panic was preceded by a speculatively induced bubble in railroad stocks, just as the panic of 2008 was preceded by a speculative boom in housing prices that created the subprime mortgage debacle. Still, more has been written about the 1929 crash than any other crash in history because more people in the newly minted middle and upper classes were affected, and also because few people saw it coming. People held a widespread belief at that time in the "new economics;" a period of permanent prosperity had arrived. Certainly, the 1920s was an unprecedented period of prosperity, with new wealth created from the automobile industry and the accompanying boom in road building and travel. A plethora of new technologies and new household electronic appliances, such as the radio, were born. To top it all off, the 1920s saw the creation and widespread use of installment credit products. Perhaps this was one of the main unsung underlying causes of the crash. Looking at modern history, we can point to the dot-com mania of the late 1990s. Maybe gold will be the next bubble; and while we can't know whether it will be the next bubble, we can count on the fact that bubbles will continue to grow and pop. Obscure manias pop up nearly every year but fail to reach the mainstream media because they affect only a few who are directly involved.

One shared trait of all manias is that the majority of players never see the crash coming. If you read the financial press from 1929 to 1931, all during the period the market was falling, respected analysts continually considered it a correction that would soon be over. When stocks finally did hit bottom in 1933, more than 80% of all value had been lost. Will this be how the current commodity boom ends? The answer to this question is, yes, it certainly will end badly because all economic bubbles eventually burst. The only question is "When?" It will take place after any bull market move in a particular commodity market morphs into a mania. This will be the time when the general public is totally immersed in the story of the day. It's never "different this time:" It always ends the same way—badly for the general public.

So, when analyzing any market move for a top, ask yourself whether the market you're looking at is currently spiraling. Does it look similar to a flagpole reaching up to the sky (which the laws of physics tell us cannot last indefinitely), or has it recently been cleansed and purged via a healthy correction? In the middle of a move, some of the air (the buying) that was pumped in flows out before new air is pumped in. One of my goals for this book is to teach you how to recognize the early signs of a new bull run and also how to recognize the end of the run. It doesn't matter if the move was created by computers or human beings. The result will be the same.

One type of top is the blow-off top, a formation that occurs at the end of a sustained bull market run. How can you tell if a market is in a blow-off top? Close to the end of the move, during the top formation, the market surges higher, with only shallow corrections. Compared to the norm, volumes are huge. Technical indicators, such as the Relative Strength Index [RSI], run up to extremely high (overbought) readings, but although these readings appear to be in unsustainable territory, the market continues moving higher than anyone believed possible. Then you'll hear outlandish price predictions in the mainstream media, along with talk of shortages in this or that. The talk will be that the world is going to run out of X commodity. In many cases, the last 48 hours of a major move can be the most feverish and therefore the most lucrative for the bulls. This final surge that forms the actual blow-off is the most painful for the bears. Their capitulation (short covering) creates the final high prices. Nobody I know of is able to pick the exact top in a situation such as this. However, in markets that show these signs, if you have been fortunate enough to be on for some of the ride, it's time to be vigilant because the end is near. The top price will come when nobody is looking and generally when the news is as bullish as it can get.

Most people will see the first break from the top price as a normal correction, just a temporary break within a bull that is nowhere close to being over yet. The market might have a secondary rally after the first break, but then it will be unable to register new highs. Without most of the players realizing it's happening, the air will be let out of the bubble. Then one day, whoosh! Bullish news might continue during much of the move back down. The bull turns into a bear, the decline accelerates, and ultimately there's *blood in the streets*. This is the time when the news will turn very bearish, there will be a multiyear surplus of this or that, and it will appear that the bear has settled in for the long pull. In reality, as only the smart money will see during blood in the streets, the bear is losing the game and will soon be replaced by a young bull.

Explosive commodity demand

At this writing, the macro forces of global commodity demand appear to remain in force. The balloon is inflating, not deflating. Sure, there have been, and will continue to be, plenty of healthy corrections along the way, but at this time, consider these merely temporary tops.

We know explosive demand growth exists in the developing world, and there is no easy way to turn this train around. More than 1 billion consumers are moving up to a higher level of consumption, demanding the comforts the West has enjoyed since the Industrial Revolution that began in the early 1900s. For many decades, 1 billion of Earth's human inhabitants have consumed two-thirds of Earth's developed resources. The other 6 billion have gotten by on the remaining one-third. Now, led by China and India, the developing world is eating better and living better, and this requires massive commodity consumption. These people are transitioning from being mainly producers to a combination of producers and consumers. From a macro sense, this places upward pressure on commodity prices. Sure, there will be crashes and busts along the road, but this is an overall macro trend that likely will continue throughout our lifetimes.

More people drive more cars and consume more protein and more electric power. This year, more than 5 million new cars will be produced every month—more than 60 million for the year. Heating, lighting, air conditioning, and appliances require power plants. New buildings, roads, ships, ports, trains, trucks, and buses...the list goes on. Energy needs, food requirements, textiles, copper to build new electrical grids, corn and soybean meal to feed growing populations of pigs, chicken, and cattle. Soybeans, cotton, rice, sugar, and corn for food and fuel, with more fertilizer needed to grow these crops.

This year, there will be more than 100 million new births before the month of October. Net of deaths, the global population is growing at more than 80 million people annually. This is the equivalent of adding one Mexico to the world every year. The areas of the world with the greatest population percentage increases are moving toward the consumption patterns of the developed world. And while all this is taking place, the developed world continues to consume. And it's not just India and China that are players in this industrial revolution. Other rapidly emerging Asian nations, Eastern Europeans, and South Americans (with Brazil at the forefront) are creating massive new consumer middle classes.

North and South American farmers have experienced great growing weather for the majority of the past 100 years. This benefit, combined with improvements in agriculture, has resulted in abundant crops most years. You have to go back 800 years to find a period of such favorable weather for such a long time, and it is not going to continue like this. As the U.S. drought of 2012 has demonstrated, with one crop failure anywhere around the world, prices of corn or soybeans can easily triple. With another Mexico being added to the world's population each year, the demand side of the equation will not solve this problem. When the world again experiences a year of bad weather (whether too much rain or too little, temperatures too hot or too cold), food prices are set to surge again.

Despite the computers taking over the volume, all these factors underscore the reason many investors need to diversify and become commodity traders—at least with a portion of their portfolio. But the question still remains: "How can we best compete with the computers?"

George Soros once wrote, "The most important fundamental is credit flows," or, more simply, *money. Money flows* move markets, and this is the most important determinant of price action. My premise is that you need to correctly analyze only this one fundamental—which direction the money is flowing—to be successful. How do we do this? My answer to this question lies with technical analysis, which the balance of this book focuses on.

But, no matter how you decide to trade, remember that commodities are necessary for life and comfort, and as a result will be traded as long as the human race exists. Every economy has experienced long periods of negative growth when commodity prices have been depressed. Then the bull cycles occur. Mini cycles, such as the commodity decade of the 1970s, have lasted about 10 years. However, long-term charts beginning in the 1700s tell us that major bull cycles in commodities generally last decades.

America, and by contagion much of the rest of the globe, will certainly continue to have their share of future financial crises. In 2008, when the major investment banks Bear Stearns and Lehman Brothers, both in business for over 100 years, disappeared, and the U.S. government bailed out Fannie Mae, AIG, and General Motors, countless paper assets plummeted in value. Yet commodity prices remained relatively strong because they are necessary to sustain and enhance life. I anticipate that commodities will continue to be a hot asset class for years to come because the world has entered a period of tightening commodity supplies with increasing demand. The planet's resources are limited, and commodities can play a role in your asset-allocation decisions. However, there will be downtrends as well, so just realize that bear cycles can be as profitable as their counterpart, and they can move much faster.

Bottom line: Follow the money flows.

8

The Advanced Trading Course

"How do we know when irrational exuberance has unduly escalated asset values?"
—Alan Greenspan, 1996

Fundamentals versus technicals

If you work for a global commodity trading firm like Cargill or Glencore and have access to accurate, timely (and expensive) fundamental intelligence, the odds are it's better information than the rest of us are getting. It's Nestlé's business, for example, to know the condition of the cocoa crop in Ghana or Brazil. Although you might read some brokerage house report that discusses the "witch's tail disease" and its potential to devastate the crop, Nestlé has their man right there in Ghana, with another in Brazil walking the fields. Nestlé and Hershey both have better intelligence for just how good or bad the crops are than you'll ever have (and they have no reason or obligation to share this information).

Suppose the cocoa crop is deteriorating. A confidential communiqué is sent to Switzerland, and the folks in charge of cocoa purchasing for Nestlé get busy. One aspect of their job is to hedge by buying cocoa futures in London and New York. Protecting against future price risk is what hedging is all about. The Nestlé traders will, as quietly as they can, accumulate new crop cocoa futures long before you know what they're up to…but there's a catch. Nobody is able to accumulate a large position, either on the long or short side, without leaving "footprints in the sand." Large, significant, "informed" volume is reported according to Exchange rules and inevitably will move price. This is what technical analysis is all about—analyzing current price action to project future price action. So, if you and I are unable to compete on the fundamentals, perhaps a technical approach is warranted?

Does technical analysis really work?

My more than 30 years of experience proves that technical analysis works. Solid technical analysis is, in my opinion, a tool that can give an individual trader a decent chance against the professionals. You might not have the research capabilities of the commercials or the execution advantages of the millisecond computer quants. However with technical analysis on your side, you have the luxury of not having your trading size affect price. You have a different perspective, and you don't have to be subject to false trend movements—"noise" that takes place on the screen when the computers are "spoofing" or "beating the beehive." And you're not stuck trading just one market (which might or might not be moving). You can sit back, relax, and analyze your charts in the comfort of your home or office.

Pure technicians believe that the most important factor necessary to the markets is price action. They do not look at crop size, export data, money supply, or employment numbers. They don't care if it's raining in Brazil or if the head of the European Central Bank just made a speech saying he's in favor of raising interest rates. Technicians basically care about price action.

This is not to say that technicians don't believe that fundamentals move the market. They concede this fact. A technician might know that soybean prices are rising because drought is devastating the Brazilian crop. He also will tell you that price will signal when the diminished supply has finally been rationed by diminished demand, and this could happen long before the drought has broken.

The technician believes that all the pertinent fundamental information, perhaps thousands of bits of data impossible for any mortal to assimilate, is reflected in price action. In essence, the price action reflects the consensus of the market players far better than the mainstream fundamental information available to the public trader.

Some pure fundamentalists dismiss technicians as merely "chartists," insinuating that technical analysis is voodoo. They point out that "every sunken ship carried a chart." I should point out, however, that charts are an integral part of most sciences, from engineering to medicine.

There are four reasons that technical analysis makes sense:

1. "Footprints in the sand": The smart money (who are generally the big players) cannot hide. They might be better informed, but their buying or selling has to show up in price, volume, and open interest.
2. The market discounts all fundamentals in price.
3. History does repeat, and if you don't learn from it, you are bound to fail.
4. Markets do move in trends, and these trends are more likely to continue than not. It is the goal of technicians to determine the trend.

While I feel a mix of fundamental and technical analysis makes the most sense, a primarily technical approach is more important for you and me. I know of many successful traders and funds, people who consistently take money out of the markets, who are purely technical.

The trend is your friend

This rhyme might sound like an oversimplification, but don't underestimate it. When talking about successful trading, these five words are some of the most profound around. A successful trader once told me, "If you can correctly determine the trend of a market, you *will* make money." Although this might sound like a simple concept, it's not easy to accomplish in the real world. The reason you'll make money when you correctly identify the trend is that the odds favor your position as you should show a profit in short order. Even if your timing is initially off, if you have correctly identified the major trend, many times the trend will bail you out. On the other hand, when you attempt to pick tops or bottoms, you must be extremely nimble in booking any available profits because they'll be fleeting when the trend reasserts itself. My experience has been that contra-trend profits tend to quickly evaporate.

Just as it's much easier to swim with the current than against it, and it's easier to walk with the wind than against it, it's generally easier to trade with the trend than against it. The trick is how to determine the prevailing trend and determine it early enough to reap the benefit.

It's a paradox that the trend is always pointing up at the very top and down at the very bottom, and people who are somehow able to pick tops and bottoms certainly make the most money. I profess that I'm unable to do this (I personally know of no one who can do it consistently), but the good news is that you don't need to capture a full move to make money; a portion of a move will do just fine.

In the long run, fundamentals determine price. However, as Lord Keynes said, "In the long run, we're all dead." My primary goal in trading is to determine the true trends of the markets I trade. My premise is that if you are able to accurately determine a trend, you will (over time) make money, and you can determine the trend using technicals.

Basic chart analysis

A price chart is your road map, your primary trading tool. Charts come in different flavors, from point and figure to Japanese candlestick and the most popular, the bar chart.

Most of you are no doubt familiar with bar charts. Although they're fairly easy to construct, they are not always that easy to analyze for maximum profitability. A bar chart can be in any time frame a trader prefers. A day trader might use a five-minute time frame, whereas the long-term "position trader" might look at a weekly time frame.

All the charts are constructed basically the same way. For example, on a daily bar chart, each day is plotted as a vertical line (or bar), with the range of the day's trading represented by the length of the bar. In other words, the top point of the bar is the day's high, and the low point is the day's low. On a standard bar chart, the horizontal axis measures time, and the vertical axis measures price. A small horizontal "tick mark" (or "flag") is plotted on each daily bar "waving" to the right to indicate the closing price. Some bar charts also reflect the open via a small horizontal flag (or tic mark) plotted on each daily bar waving to the left.

In this chapter, I present the most significant chart patterns. In Chapter 9, "The Moving Averages Primer," I discuss a specific technical approach I use in the markets. The following pages should give you a good basis for additional study, but I do not mean to imply that the price patterns discussed are the gospel—far from it. Every one of these price patterns will provide you with false signals at times. In a way, however, this can be beneficial, because even false signals are useful signals, if you know what to look for and how to react.

The trendline

The trendline is perhaps the most popular of all chart tools. Remember that if you can determine the trend of the market, you'll make money. This is what the trendline is designed to do: determine the trend of the market and keep you with the trend until it changes.

Trendlines basically are one of two types: the up trendline and the down trendline. In an uptrend, the market tends to make higher lows and higher highs. A down trend is characterized by lower highs and lower lows. You can prove to yourself that markets move in trends by simply looking at charts and doing an "eyeball." Note how the moves of significance are characterized by a series of higher highs/higher lows or lower highs/lower lows.

Certainly, hindsight is 20/20. It is not always easy to know just what a trend is in the thick of the battle or, if you can accurately determine the current trend, just how long it will last. This is where the trendlines come in.

A trendline is drawn on the chart you are analyzing along the tops or bottoms of the price bars in the direction of the significant trend. In a bull, or rising market, the trendline is drawn by connecting a straight line that connects higher lows. At least two points are necessary, but I recommend a minimum of three to add validity. (See Figure 8.1.) In a bear, or falling market, the line connects two (but preferably three or more) highs.

The rule of thumb is that the more points you have connected, the more "valid" the trendline. But here's the rub: The more "valid" the trendline, by definition, the more price data you have to use, and, therefore, the older the trend and the closer it is to its inevitable conclusion. A broken trendline (that is, price action moving below an up trendline or above a down trendline) is a danger signal that the trend has reversed (see Figure 8.2). This is how technicians use trendlines. When an up trendline is broken, longs should be liquidated and new shorts established. Shorts should do the opposite when a down trendline is broken. Many traders place stops just under an up trendline or just above a down trendline to exit positions. If a trend is of significant duration, a trailing stop can be used, where the risk is reduced gradually daily as the stop loss is moved in the direction of the prevailing trend. In this way, the first risk is the greatest risk. The objective is first to achieve a break even, and then if everything goes according to plan, a modest profit is locked in. Over time, additional profits are locked in until the trendline is finally broken. The best and most reliable trendlines are older and, therefore, by definition, longer.

The problem with using trendlines is that, in practice, markets are not always all that orderly. A straight line assumes some sort of symmetrical series of higher lows and highs, or the reverse. In the real world, markets can act this way for a time, but because of human nature or computer programs, there will be sharp and meaningless reversals in trend, which in the long run generate false trendline reversal signals. False trendline reversal signals are more likely to occur when a trendline is too steep. Steeper trendlines are generally those of shorter length; therefore, they are shorter in duration and, by definition, most likely to be violated. (See Figures 8.3 and 8.4.)

When a trendline is broken, it certainly can be used as a danger signal. But what do you do if the market in short order resumes back in the direction of the major preceding trend? You can construct a new trendline by using the new significant low or high. *Technical Analysis of Stock Trends* by Edwards and Magee, first published in 1948, is often referred to as the "bible of technical analysis." The basic premise of this book is that prices of stocks and commodities move in repeating and identifiable patterns, the result of the ebb and flow of supply and demand. Although some of the concepts presented in the book at that time were new, many had been around since the turn of the century. Although markets might have changed dramatically since the 1940s, human nature has not; therefore, many of the patterns presented by these two groundbreakers remain valid today.

Note: I sourced all the charts in this chapter using real market data on a CQG, Inc., platform. All rights reserved worldwide.

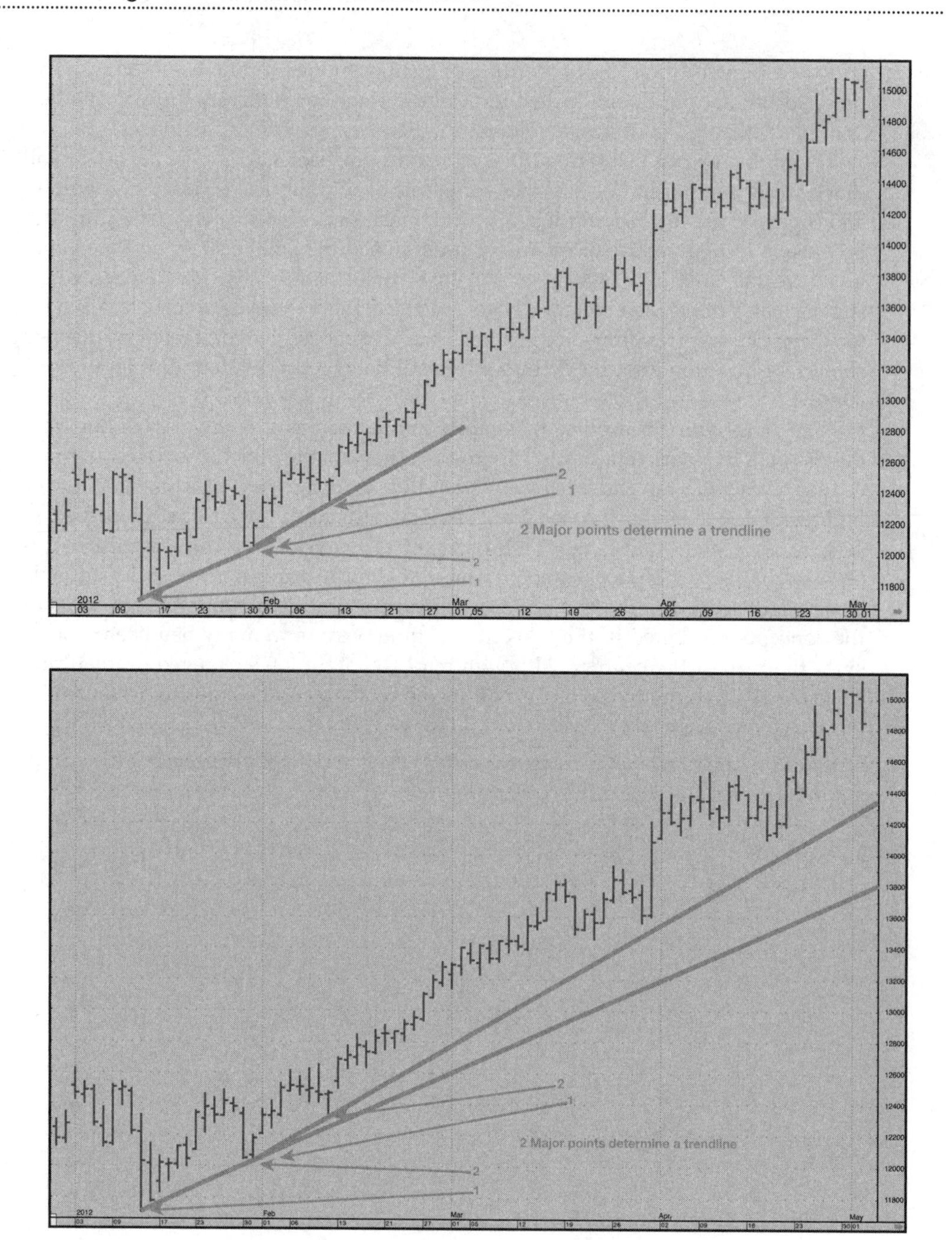

Figure 8.1 Classic trendlines

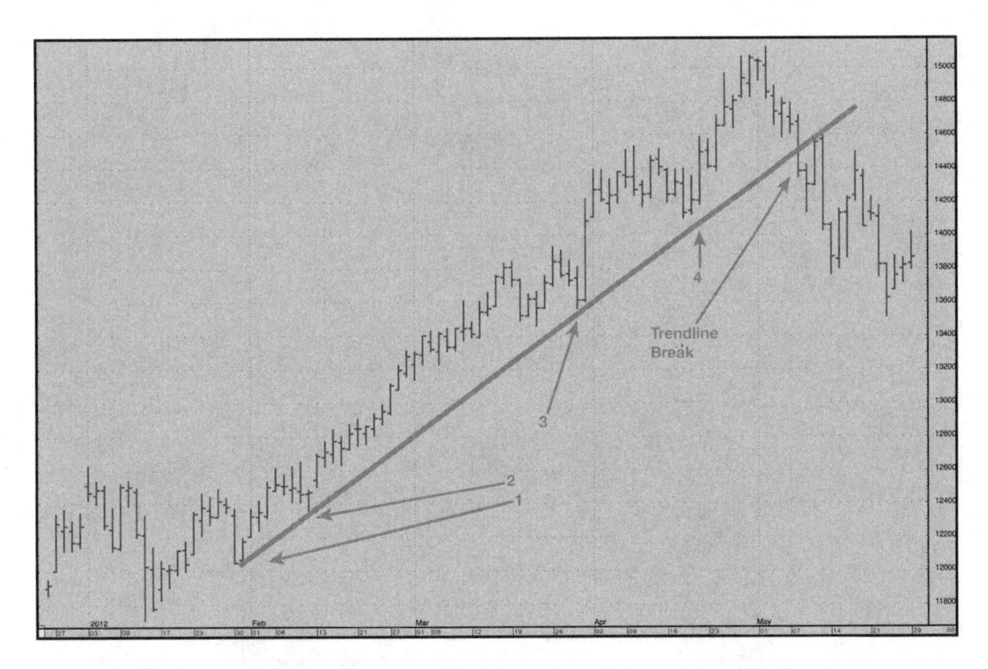

Figure 8.2 Classic up trendline and trendline break

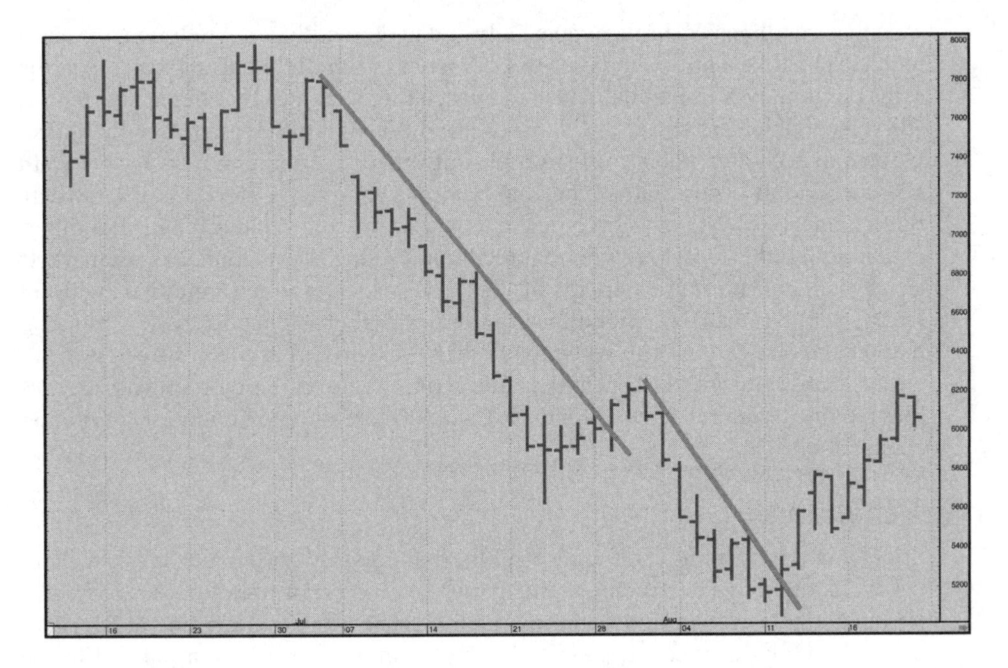

Figure 8.3 Classic down trendline

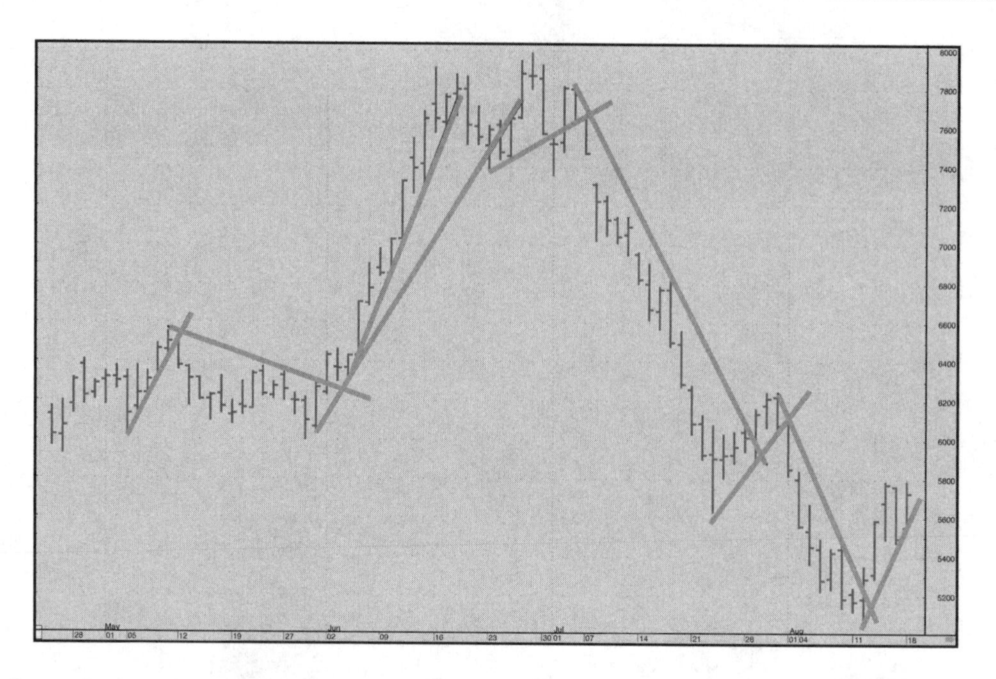

Figure 8.4 Redrawn trendlines after a trendline "break"

When trendlines are broken repeatedly and new trendlines are redrawn, the chart tends to look like a fan (as in Figure 8.4). A series of trendlines, all starting out at the same point, moves in parallel. This fan effect either indicates that the major trend is still intact (albeit less steep) or the major trend is actually changing. Good interpretation and analytical tools come into play at this point; some traders have a sixth sense when this occurs. Others need to rely on a completely mechanical approach. Bottom line: It is best not to become too reliant on any one technical tool. Trendlines are helpful, but I do not see you making money using them alone. Not all markets trend well, and no market trends all the time, which is when trendlines will not work at all. Nevertheless, trendlines can indicate the basic tendency of a trending market and also can tell you when the trend has exhausted itself. However, by combining trendlines with other chart patterns plus some of the more powerful tools like moving averages (covered shortly), you'll increase your odds for a winning combination.

Trend channels

Prices in a classic trend commonly tend to trade roughly within a channel. A channel is identified by constructing a line parallel to the major trendline. If a market is trending higher and an up trendline has been constructed, the top line of the channel is drawn by connecting progressive highs. In a down trend, a parallel to the down trendline is drawn, connecting progressive lows and a channel is born (see Figure 8.5). As long as the market remains within the channel for the most part, the market is behaving normally during a trending-type period. Nimble traders look to buy on the trendline and sell toward the upper channel line (assuming that they're in an up trend). Active traders might also look to reverse at the channel lines, but this generally is not recommended, because they would be fighting the trend.

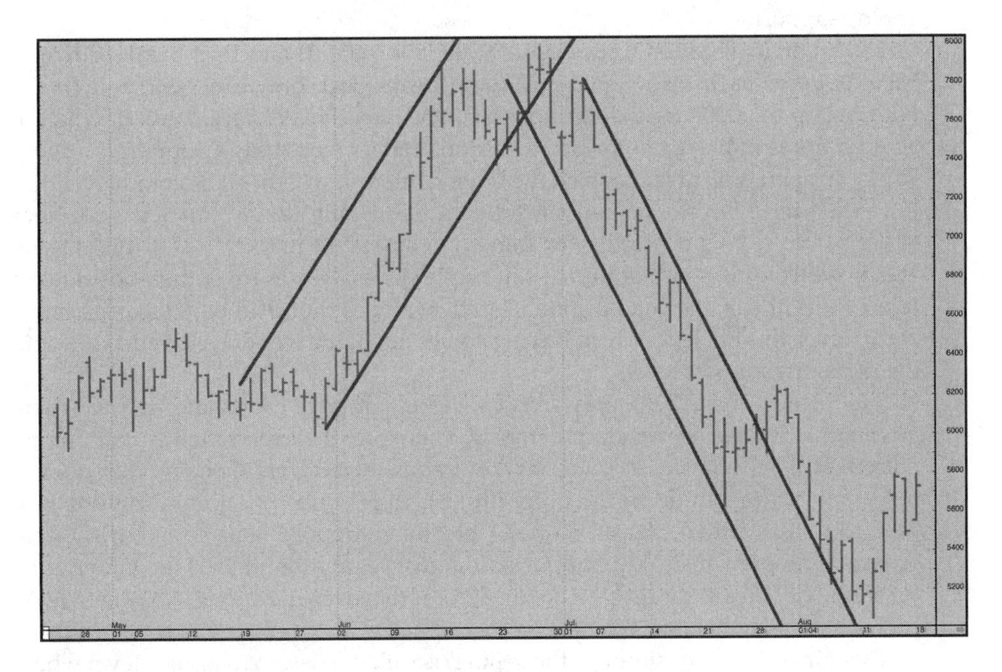

Figure 8.5 Trend channel

Markets will eventually trade outside the bounds of the channel. This can be a significant clue to subsequent market action. The general rule of thumb is that when a market trades above the upper channel line (in an up trend) or below the lower channel line (in a down trend), odds are that the market is entering an accelerated phase in the direction of the major trend. In other words, a significant change in the normal supply and demand balance has taken place. With bona fide breakouts of channels, the market tends to move faster, with price action becoming more dramatic. Stops can be tightened, positions can be pyramided, and your "antenna should be up" for any signs of a subsequent trend reversal. The accelerated phase of any market can be the most profitable and most exciting time to play, but it also can be the shortest. Don't fight it; go with it but remain alert. If acting right, after it has broken out, the market should not fall back into the channel because this would be the place to exit and reevaluate.

Support and resistance

Support and resistance levels are price points that can clearly indicate at what price levels the demand or the supply for a particular commodity rests. Think of them as floors and ceilings. Simply put, support is a significant area in which buying interest develops, has developed, or is expected to develop based on past history. Support becomes evident on a price chart, as the market "bounces off support" or "holds support."

For example, if cotton trades up to 9900 (99¢/pound) and then breaks down to 9500, bounces back up to 9700 and then breaks back down to 9490, and finally bounces up to 10000 (one dollar/pound), and then breaks back to 9510, where it again starts to move in an upward direction, traders would say, "Support is around 9500." Support is an area in which the buying interest, whether it be commercial cotton users, fund buyers, or bargain hunters (it actually doesn't matter who) have either placed resting buy orders or step up to buy at the market. It also might be an area in which a big short, or perhaps multiple shorts, look to cover their positions to take profits or exit a losing position. Don't get all caught up on why the price holds at this level; this is a level where buying comes out of the woodwork, and as a result, it is termed a support level.

Support levels can be plainly seen by looking at price charts and appear where buying interest has shown up previously. Therefore, the expectation is that buying interest will be there again if the market trades there again. If the market doesn't hold on a return run (as in the preceding example, with cotton breaking down to 9400 the fourth time), this is termed "breaking support" and is a bearish sign. Traders who previously had supported the market at around 9500 are either gone (or all the significant shorts have covered), or if they were new longs, they are weaker this time than the new sellers.

The mirror image of support, the ceiling, is called *resistance*. This is a level where the market has a hard time moving higher or where a market has trouble getting above a certain point. If cotton rallies to 10000, then tails off to 9700 and back up to 9995, and it does this more than once, this is the level (at least temporarily) of resistance. In other words, resistance is an area in which the selling interest is greater than the demand.

Support and resistance levels can be drawn graphically by using a horizontal line on a bar, chart connecting the floor points, in the case of support, and ceiling points, in the case of resistance. These are important levels that indicate the areas you would expect a market to hold or to fail. As with trendline points, traders are cognizant of where support and resistance levels are. As a result, they can become a self-fulfilling prophecy, at least in the short run. If a market continues to fail at a certain resistance level, the sellers become bolder every time that price is reached, and the buyers assume that this is the place to exit.

For many years, corn prices were unable to trade above $4. This was considered a ceiling price in years of big demand and in years of drought. In 1996, when China for the first time turned from a corn exporter into a major importer, corn prices broke the $4 "glass ceiling" (and didn't look back until they hit $5.50).

Extended periods of support and resistance both holding simultaneously can lead to one of the most powerful (one of my two favorite) of all chart patterns, the "breakout from consolidation." You can see this in Figure 8.6, and we'll spend a bit more time on this one.

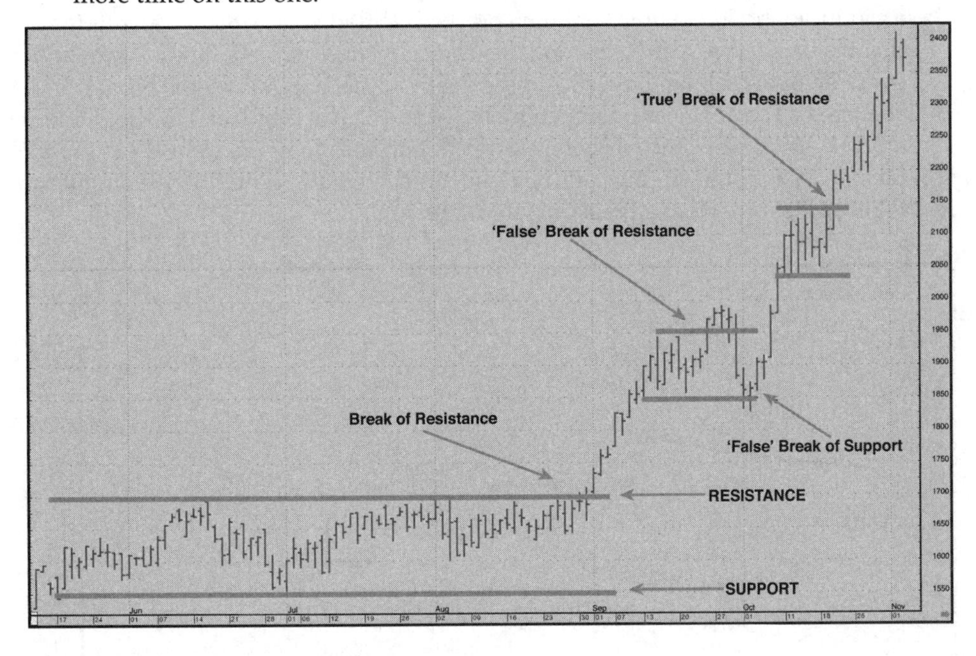

Figure 8.6 Support and resistance examples

Breakouts from consolidation

Think of a market bouncing off "support" as being similar to a ball bouncing off the floor. If the floor is a deck four stories off the ground, the ball will bounce as long it remains on the deck. But, if it subsequently falls off the deck, it drops lower. Alternatively, "resistance" is similar to a ceiling, but if a glass ceiling is smashed, the birds are free to fly higher.

Support and resistance levels are very important to traders. When a market is in a relatively flat range (holding at support and failing at resistance), it's called *consolidation*. Consolidation is an inability by either the bulls or the bears to win the battle. When the market holds at some level, rallies, and then again retreats to that same level, it then appears cheap. Bulls that missed the first rally feel as if they have a second chance at "cheap" levels and step up to the plate. The shorts, especially those who are scalping and selling at higher levels, see the market start to bounce, and they're induced to cover their shorts before their paper profits disappear. This additional buying (short covering) adds fuel to the bull move. The reverse occurs when the market rallies to the level of previous failure—the resistance point. Some of the longs who previously purchased at support might feel that the market is looking expensive and cash in. Bears, who missed selling the last rally, will consider this a "second chance" and start selling. The market starts its retreat, and other longs (who do not want to see their paper profits disappear) sell out, adding fuel to the bear fire. We know that if a market fails at a resistance level on numerous occasions and over a significant period of time, and then proceeds to trade above that level, this is a sign that the bears have lost the battle. The buying interest was finally strong enough to overwhelm the selling interest, and the defensive ceiling built by the bears has been shattered. (The opposite is happening if a support level is broken.) In simpler terms, a break above resistance or below support indicates that a major shift is probably taking place in the supply and demand fundamentals of the market in question. Figure 8.7 shows what a breakout looks like.

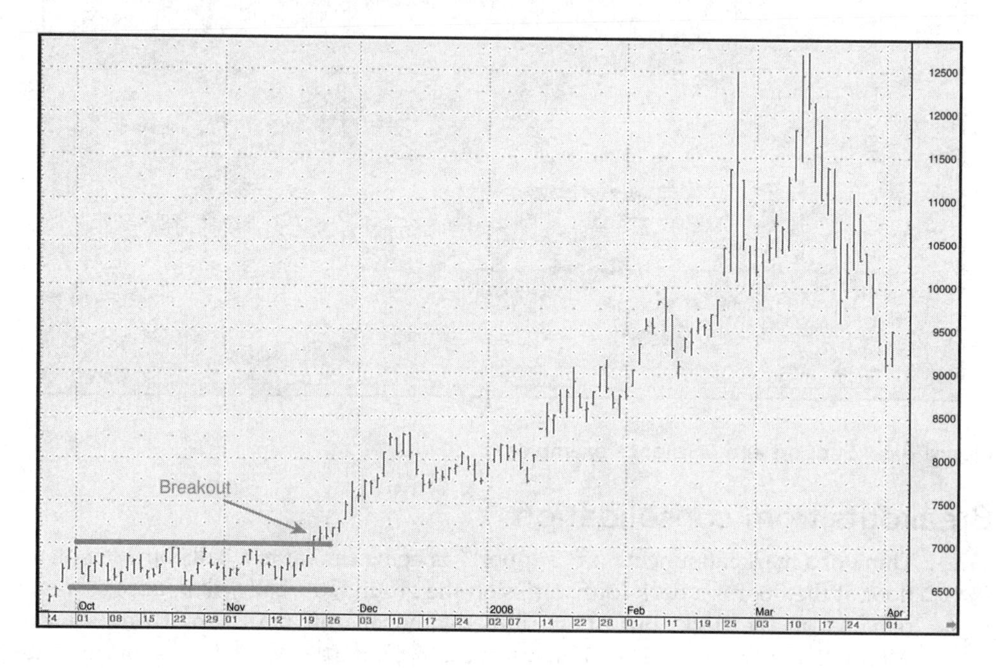

Figure 8.7 Breakout from consolidation

Take a look at Figure 8.8, which shows the 1988 oats chart. This monster oats rally drove prices to all-time highs that were not exceeded for the following 20 years. Look at the length and beauty of the consolidation that preceded this bull move.

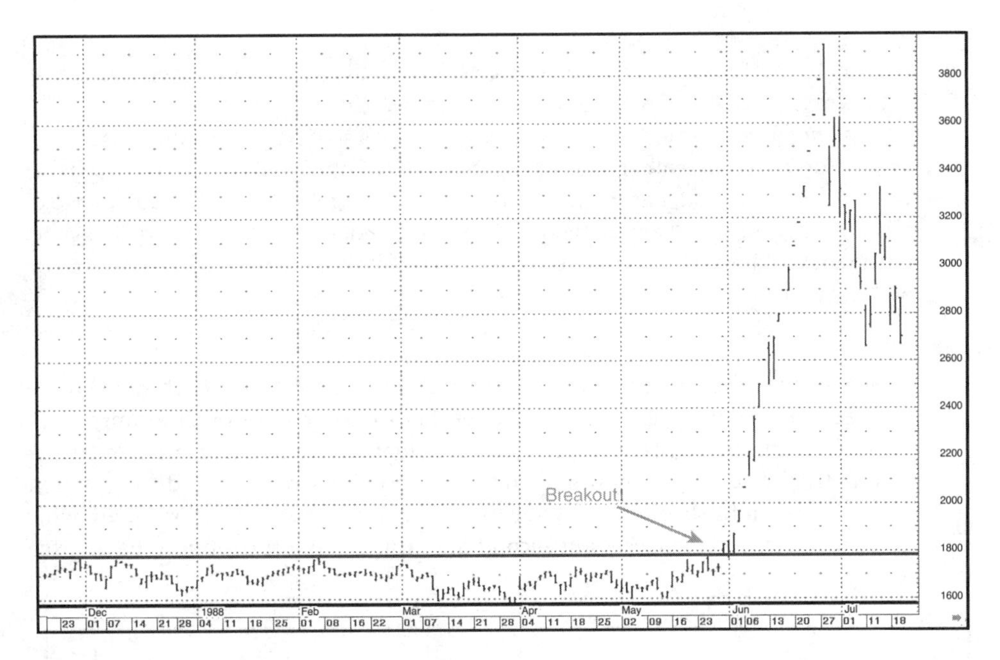

Figure 8.8 July 1988 oats breakout

I have a soft spot in my heart for this 1988 oats move. This is a true story:

I had a wealthy client who was stubborn and gutsy, and who would not get out of his March 1988 oats contract because he believed oats were too cheap. He owned 2 million bushels (the limit an individual could buy at that time), and I told him that if he didn't get out, he would get delivery. I liked the oat market but suggested that he roll his March contracts into July. No, he told me he would take the delivery, even though when delivery takes place a trader is required to put up the full value of the contract and is no longer on margin. So he took delivery of the 2 million bushels at approximately $1.60 per bushel in March. He wired the $3,200,000 into his account. From that day on, my job was to look for a buyer to sell the oats in the cash market, but neither of the big players (General Mills nor Quaker Oats) seemed interested.

The market continued to trade in the consolidation range for a few months, and then it got hot and dry. (That's what caused the breakout from the long consolidation you see in Figure 8.8.)

The drought of 1988 is history now, but let me tell you the result to the market. The oat crop in the Dakotas was devastated, and the futures price traded up to approximately $4 per bushel. On June 28, the all-time record-high day for oats, I got a call from one of the large processors. He asked if the delivery oats were still for sale. I told him yes, and he promptly offered $4 per bushel for the entire 2 million. I called my client, who told me to reject the $4 bid but offer the whole lot at $4.40, "take it or leave it." When I called the processor back, he immediately said "Sold!" My client sold

2 million bushels of cash oats 40¢ per bushel higher than the futures price and at the all-time record price to that date. The client cleared a cool $5 million.

Months later, when I asked the grain man why he was so quick to buy the oats at a record-high price (remember, these are oats he didn't want at $1.60) of $4.40 (which was obviously too high, based on the futures price), he told me this: "I had the choice of closing down the mill and putting 200 people out of work because I didn't have any oats to make oatmeal or paying 'too much' and bumping the price of a box of cereal by 10¢. What would you have done?"

Bottom line: These patterns are powerful, but they are also fairly uncommon. And they can occur in varying time frames. Let's look at a few other examples. The wheat example in Figure 8.9 illustrates a potentially false breakout (which later proved true) and how breakouts from consolidations can occur during a trend move, not just at the beginning. I have found that a potentially false breakout, which later proves true via a successful second attempt, usually turns out to be an excellent signal.

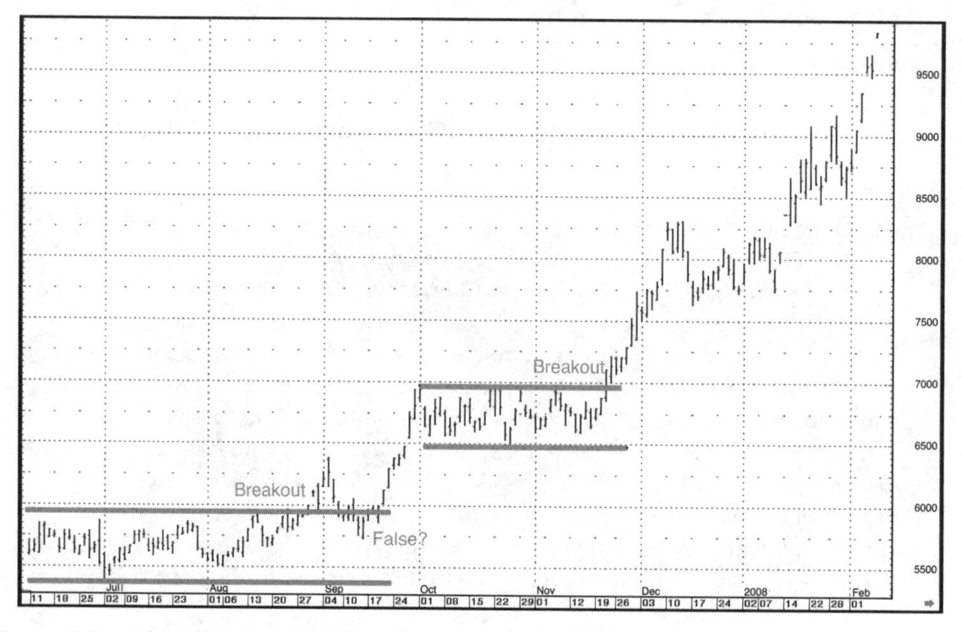

Figure 8.9 Wheat false and true breakouts

Certainly, these patterns can signify breakouts to the bear side as well as the bull side, as the cattle example in Figure 8.10 illustrates.

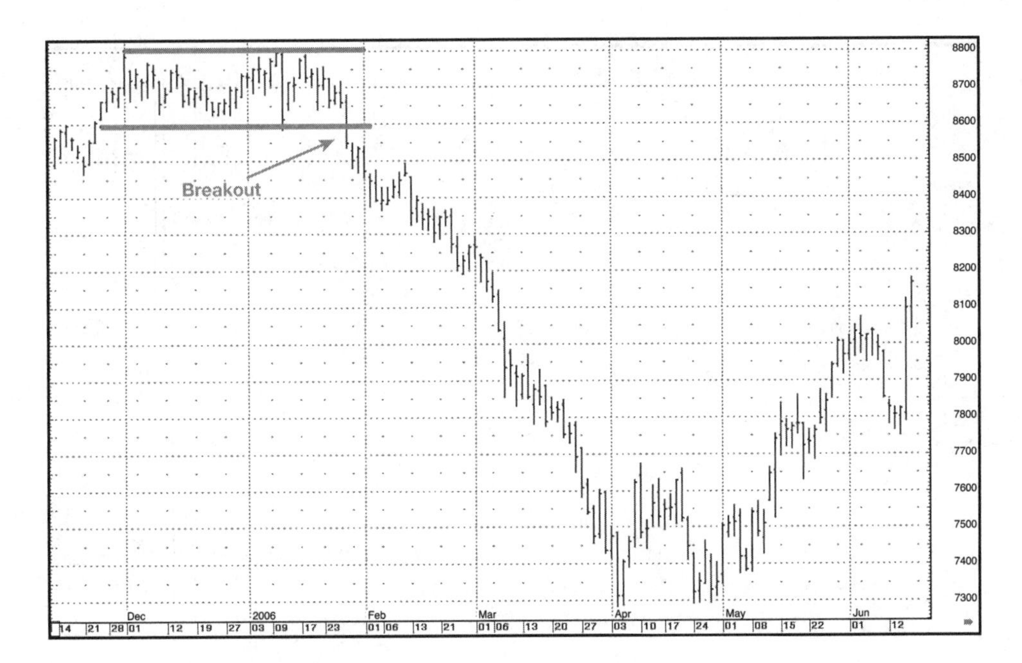

Figure 8.10 Cattle downside breakout

The previous charts are all daily charts (so one bar equals one day's trading). In today's electronic age, breakouts can occur in any time period, and traders need to be ready. Take a look at Figure 8.11, which shows a breakout on a five-minute chart (where one bar on this chart equals five minutes of trading).

Figure 8.11 illustrates a sleepy Cinco de Mayo, with London closed due to a holiday, the New York copper market was in a tight consolidation between \$3.83 and \$3.86. The breakout above consolidation occurred at 7:10 A.M. above the \$3.86 level. Within 20 minutes (four 5-minute bars on the chart), the market traded as high as \$4.27, representing a move of 41¢, or \$10,250 per contract. The margin for one contract at the time was \$7,763, so this was well over a 100% return in less than a half-hour. Don't even try to calculate what the annualized return would look like; it would be a ridiculous number. Ten minutes later, the market was back below \$4. The news? There was none. Stops were hit all the way up, and the market eventually ended back where it started by the next day. A move of this magnitude would not have occurred in this short of a time period during the pit days because professional pit traders would have stepped in to blunt the rally at an earlier stage. Still, the time-honored breakout from consolidation signaled the way to go on this one.

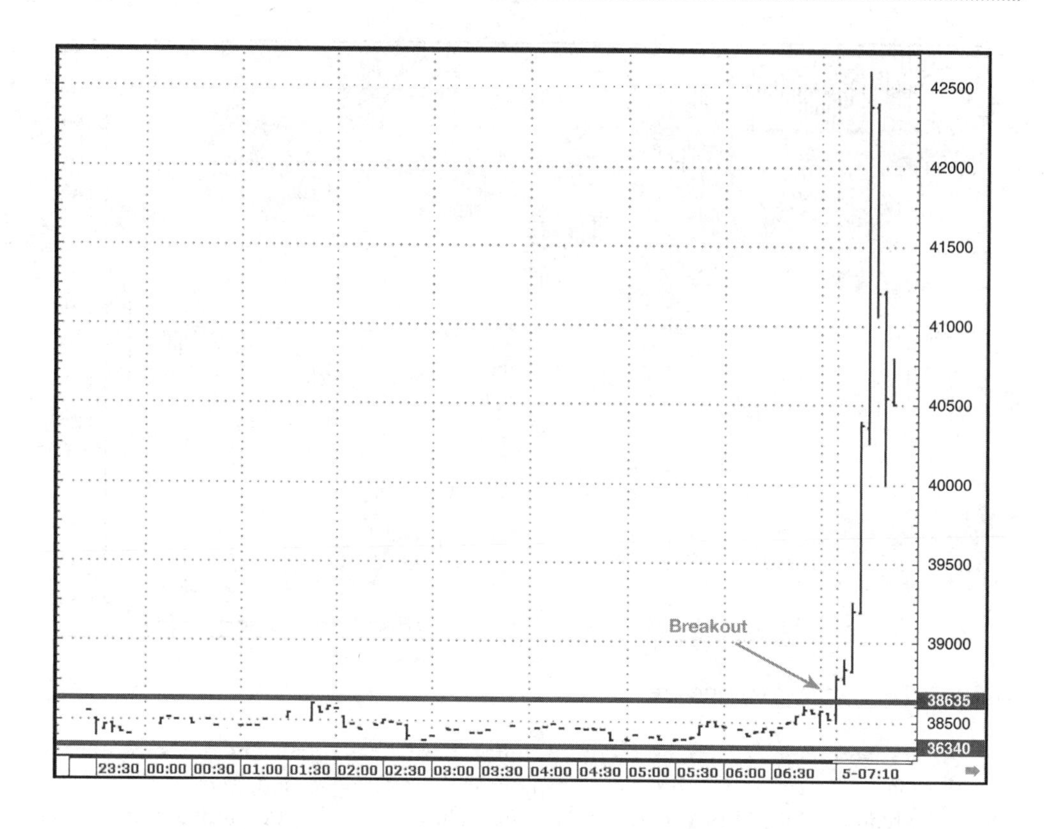

Figure 8.11 Copper (five-minute chart)

Although this stuff is good, and I believe it works, you didn't think this would be all that easy, now, did you? When I first discovered technical analysis, I studied the profitable examples in the books and thought this trading gig would be a piece of cake. Unfortunately, as with all of life, it doesn't work all the time. I must tell you that false breakouts from consolidation have occurred and will continue to occur. Many traders are well aware of how powerful a tool these patterns can be. As a result, they look for these breakouts. Many technicians will place stops just under support to limit losses or establish new short positions. "Beating the beehive" is one strategy designed by the computer nerds to trigger these stops. It's not sinister; the computer algorithms make an educated guess on where the stops reside. For example, if a market has held numerous times at 95 and it approaches that level again, what's to stop a professional computerized trader from offering the market down to 94.90? The objective is to uncover the sell stops. A sell stop is a resting order to sell at some predetermined level. If the stops are actually "resting" at 94.90 (numerous orders representing hundreds of traders from various unrelated firms), the selling commences.

Sometimes, this action can feed on itself. The sell stops in place at 94.90 immediately begin to work. The resting orders to buy at 94.90 are filled, so the market is offered lower (94.80, 94.70, 94.60), but everyone seems to be selling, and it's all on stops. The scalpers love this, especially in a quiet or thin market. They will come back in and bid at 94.50 and 94.40, for example, and cover their shorts at a quick and tidy profit. Because no fundamental substance caused this price action, the market quickly bounces back above 95 again as the shorts are covered, and commercial traders and bargain hunters step in. For a speculator, getting caught in a false breakout is frustrating. Seeing your stop hit and knock you out of a good position, only to watch the market quickly reverse in the direction you though it was going in the first place will steam you. If you trade long enough, this will happen to you, so keep your cool. Place your stops carefully, where you don't think everyone else's stops are.

Six rules for trading breakouts from consolidation

Breakouts from consolidation are such powerful indicators of potential trend changes that you should never become complacent when they occur just because false breakouts exist. Here are my six rules for trading breakouts from consolidation:

1. The longer it takes to form a consolidation, the more significant the breakout and the bigger the expected move to follow. A breakout on a daily chart is more powerful than a breakout on a 30-minute chart, and a breakout on a weekly chart is even more powerful. A breakout from consolidation on a yearly chart is the most powerful, signifying some major fundamental change in the supply-and-demand balance of that market.

2. After a breakout occurs, the market can retrace back to the breakout level, but it really shouldn't trade back into the consolidation zone. If it does, the odds of a false breakout increase.

3. The breakout should remain above the breakout level for a significant amount of time. After it moves above the resistance or below the support, you shouldn't be in much trouble if you went with the breakout. If profits are not forthcoming in a reasonable amount of time, be wary. A quick failure is a symptom of a false breakout.

4. Watch the volume on the breakout since a true breakout is generally associated with a sharp rise in volume. Sometimes this high-volume level might precede the breakout by a day or two; however, false breakouts are usually associated with modest volume.

5. When trading a breakout using stops, never place your stops just below support or just above resistance. All the amateurs do this, and they become bait for running the stops. It's generally better to take a bit more risk (what I term a "buffer") and place your stop at a slightly greater distance.

6. A basic rule of thumb, which truly does work (use some judgment here), is that when a market breaks out from consolidation, it will move roughly the distance up or down equal to the horizontal distance of the consolidation phase. I term this phenomenon "the count." The longer the consolidation,

the bigger the count. To determine the count, measure the horizontal distance of the consolidation and then measure upward from the resistance breakout or downward from the support breakout to get an idea of the price objective for the coming move. (See Figure 8.12.)

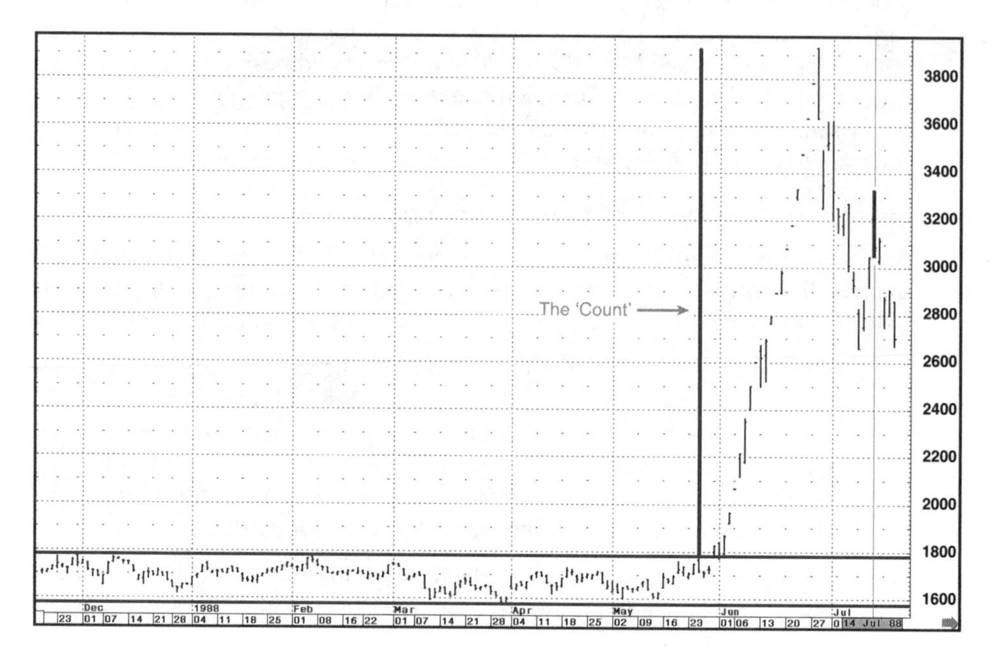

Figure 8.12 The count

Additional classic chart patterns

Chart patterns basically fall into two groups:

- Those signaling a reversal in trend
- Those signaling a continuation in the prevailing trend

Reversal patterns include the head and shoulders, double tops and bottoms, rounding tops and bottoms, and reversal days. Continuation patterns include flags and pennants. Certain patterns are hybrids that can signal either or both; gaps and triangles for example. The following sections explain the classic patterns, which I have found remain valid today.

Double tops and bottoms

Double tops and bottoms are reversal patterns, many times associated with major tops and bottoms. Double tops occur when prices rally from an area close to a previous high, but then the market fails, with an inability to continue decisively into new high territory. I'm trying to be careful in my choice of words because many novice traders believe a double top is valid only if a market fails under the previous top. I've found, in practice, that many times double tops are formed when a market just nicks or even at times moves slightly above the previous high and then fails. Think of double tops as the letter M, with the right mast at times a bit lower or a bit higher than the left.

Double bottoms are the mirror image of the tops. Think of them as the letter W. The market makes a major bottom, rallies, fails, and holds slightly above or slightly below the previous bottom, and then it reverses. (See Figure 8.13.)

The one problem with double tops and bottoms is that they don't always occur at the top or the bottom. You have to be careful because, many times, you'll see these in the middle of moves (which obviously doesn't help in identifying a top or a bottom). As I've stated before, there is no holy grail. All you can hope to do is place the odds in your favor, using good money management to cut the losses on the trades that don't go according to plan. To avoid false signals, it is important to wait until the pattern is completed. This removes some of the profit potential but also improves your odds. Make sure you look for double bottoms and tops only after a major top or bottom is made and then wait for the market to test the low/high and then rally/break significantly, which increases its validity. How much is "significant"? Unfortunately, I can't give you a number, but after you have been doing this awhile, and after studying hundreds of charts, you'll get a feel for this in various market situations.

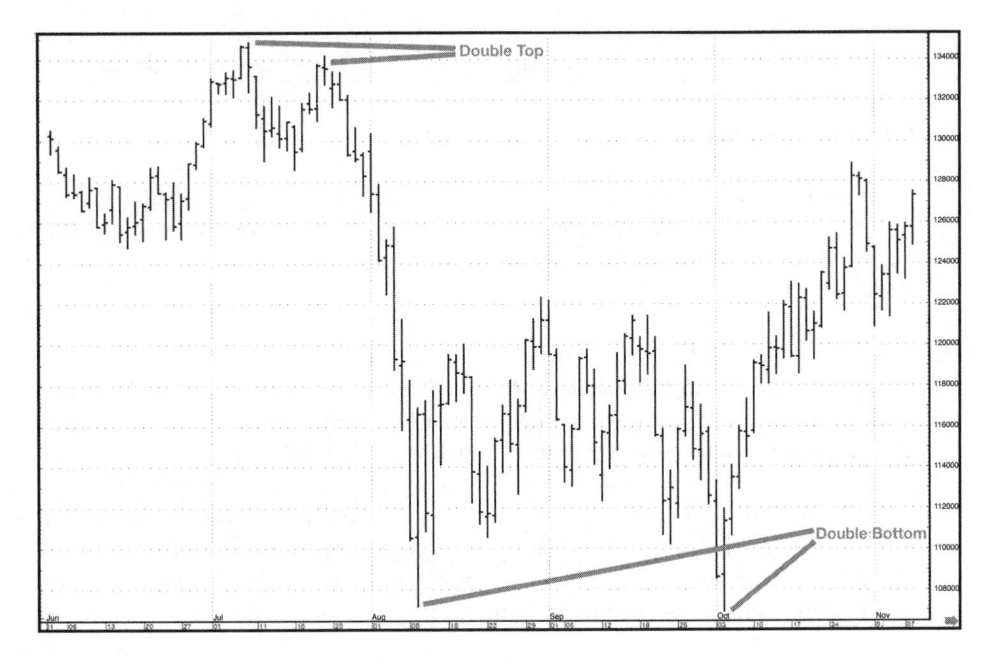

Figure 8.13 Double top and double bottom

Rounding tops and bottoms

Rounding bottoms are sometimes referred to as saucer bottoms. Although you'll rarely come across these, they are reliable reversal-type patterns. Figure 8.14 shows a rounding bottom.

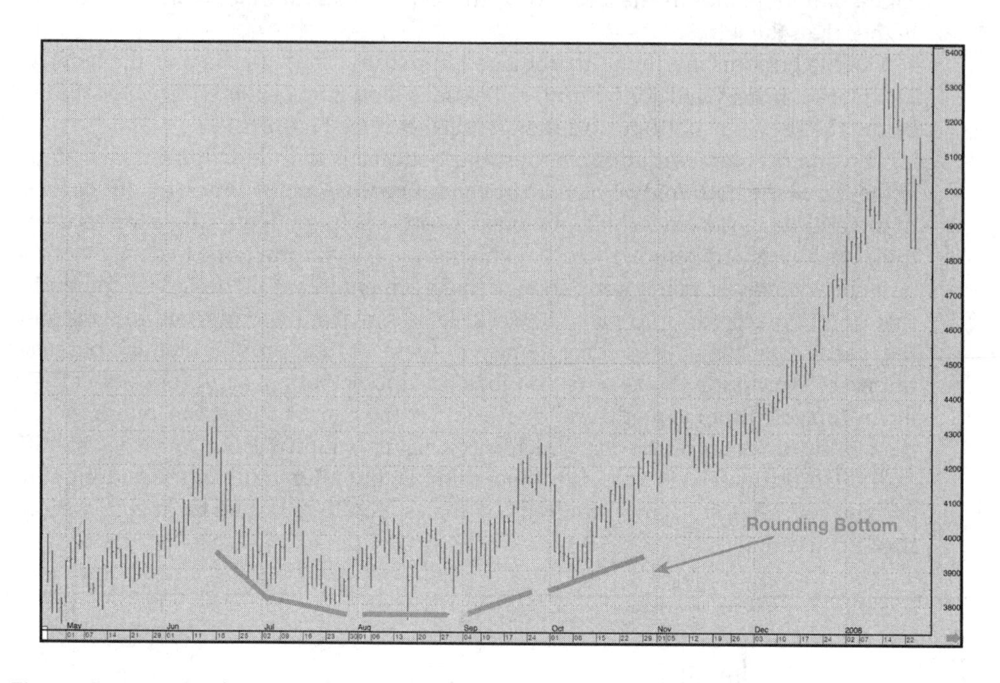

Figure 8.14 Rounding bottom

These usually take quite a bit of time to form properly, and again, it's important to wait for the pattern to be completed. False rounding tops or bottoms, when they occur (evidenced by a higher high or lower low), often precede the final top or bottom.

Flags, rectangles, and pennants

Flags, rectangles, and pennants are three relatively common *continuation* patterns. They generally occur in the first third, middle, or second third of major moves and can be good formations to pyramid from using fairly tight stops.

Rectangles, at times called "boxes," are formations where the market pauses and proceeds to trade in a tight range. A rectangle is like a consolidation but much smaller in length. Unlike a consolidation, a rectangle occurs after a move is under way—not at a top or bottom. It is generally a price movement that is contained between two horizontal lines, as shown in Figure 8.15.

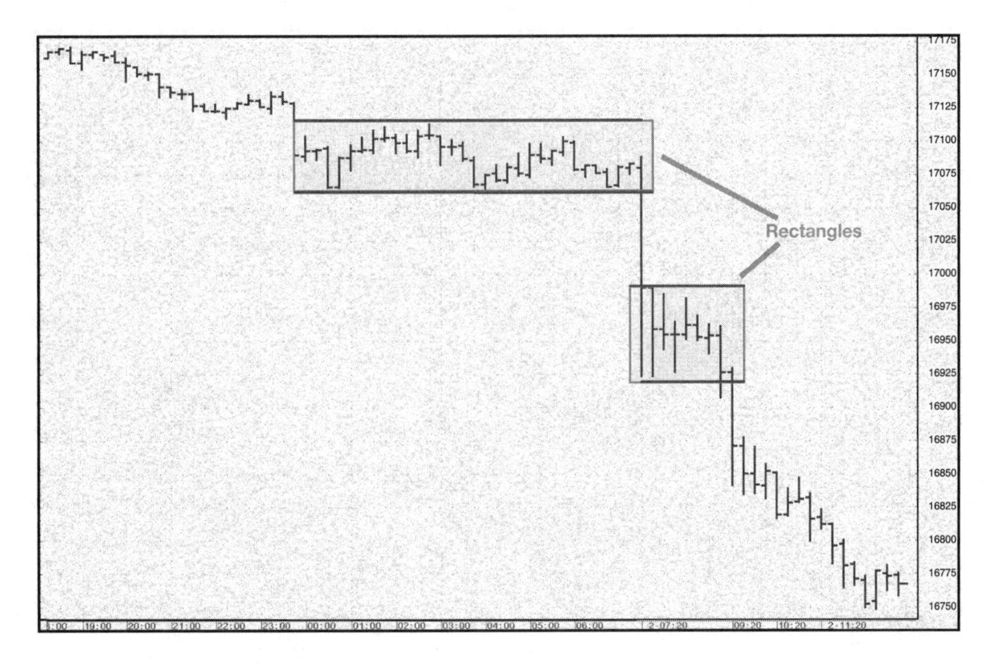

Figure 8.15 Rectangles

The upper line of the rectangle is the resistance line, and the lower line is the support line. The plan is not to anticipate but rather to go with the flow. In an up trend, buy on the break of resistance, and in a down trend, go short on the break of support. Rectangles basically represent pauses in the major trend; the market remains fundamentally bullish or bearish, but it has to first undergo a "healthy" round of repositioning or profit taking before resumption of the move. Volume generally dries up during this box-like formation and increases on the breakout. Just like in the neckline of the head and shoulders (explained shortly), many times the market returns to the breakout level after it takes place. Rectangles provide an excellent time to pyramid a winning position. I look to add to profitable positions after the breakout, moving my stop on the total position to above or below the opposite boundary of the box.

One drawback of rectangles is that they are continuation patterns, which at times can revert into reversal patterns. Once again, be warned: Keep an open mind and be nimble.

A flag is basically a rectangle whose boundaries slant upward or downward. The boundaries are parallel, like a rectangle (see Figure 8.16). The "flag" is, again, a pause due to profit taking by the weak hands, a rest stop before the train once again rolls out of the station.

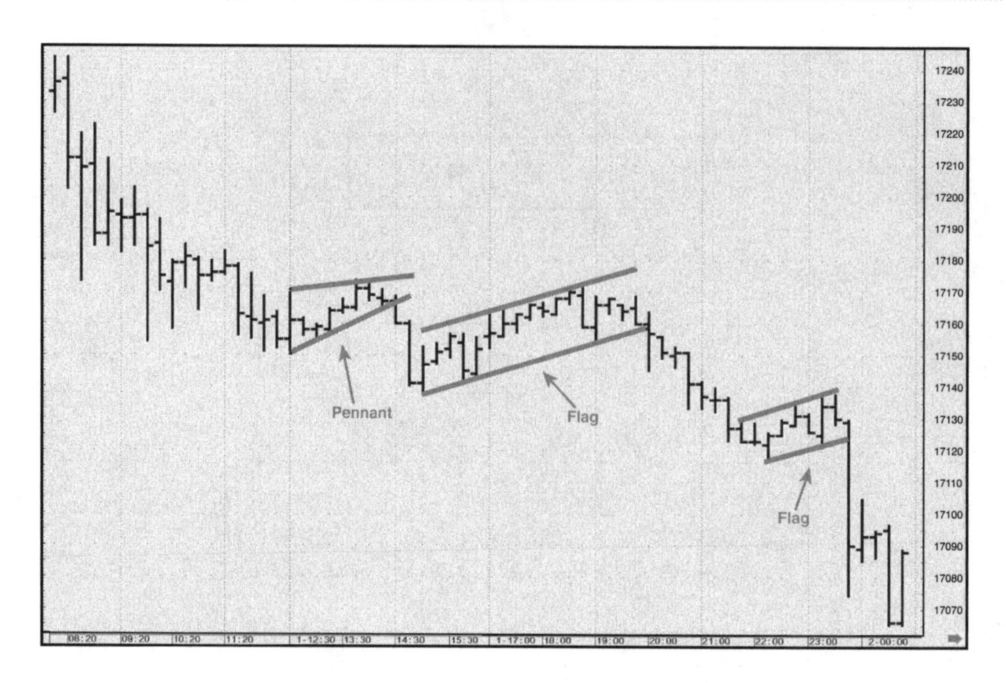

Figure 8.16 Flag and pennant

The general rule is that the slant of a flag will run opposite the direction of the major price trend, but this isn't always the case. Actually, contrary to popular belief, I've found that many powerful moves out of flag congestions come from those slanting in the direction of the major trend.

Pennants work just like flags and rectangles. The basic difference is that the boundaries are not parallel. This difference is illustrated in Figure 8.16.

All these continuation patterns work best when they are tight, fast, neat, and formed on relatively light volume. Be wary of flags, pennants, or triangles that don't meet your expectations quickly. Take a look at Figure 8.17, which shows the drought corn market of 2012, a market where technical analysis helped me immensely in capturing a fair share of this move.

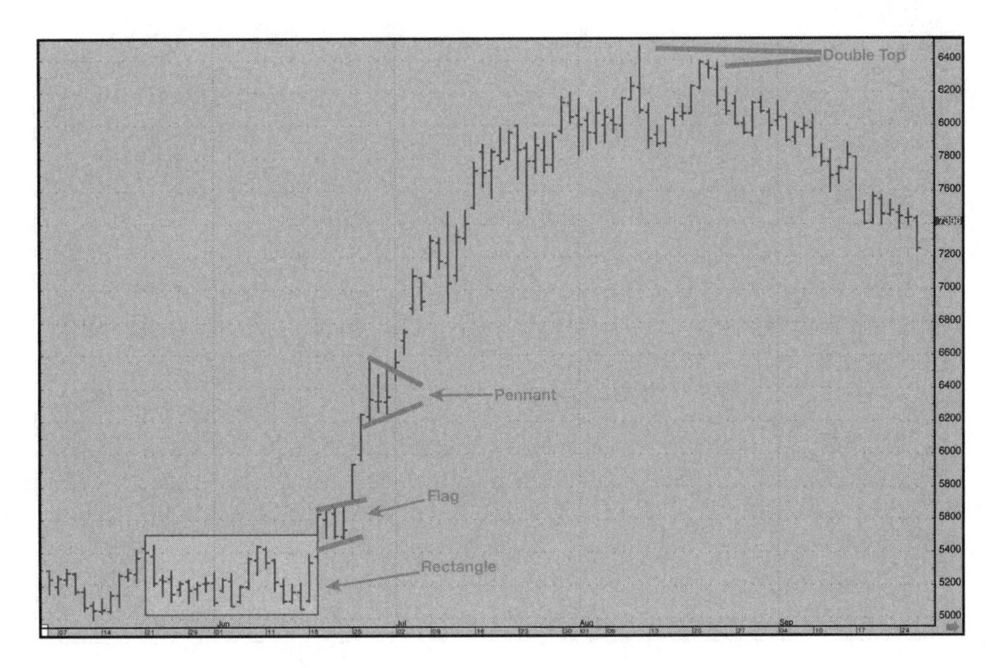

Figure 8.17 Corn move

Triangles

Triangles are congestion patterns that can signal either continuation or reversal. They come in three distinct varieties: symmetrical triangles, ascending triangles, and descending triangles.

A symmetrical triangle has an upper line that slopes downward (it looks like a down trendline) and a lower line that slopes upward (it looks like an up trendline). These lines converge at a point. With all congestion patterns, there is a war going on between the bulls and the bears. Within a triangle, the sides are matched fairly evenly, with neither side winning. (See Figure 8.18.) However, at some point, as time goes forward, one side will win. The market will break out of the triangle, and this is the time to act because the breakout signifies the direction of the next major move.

The general rule is that the most valid signals will come when the market breaks out prior to reaching the end, termed the *apex*. The best breakouts generally occur approximately two-thirds of the way along of the length of the triangle. Also, as with most of the other patterns, volume should increase on the breakout. You know you're caught in a false move, a "trap," when the market trades back into the triangle after the breakout, and all bets are off when it moves over to the other side.

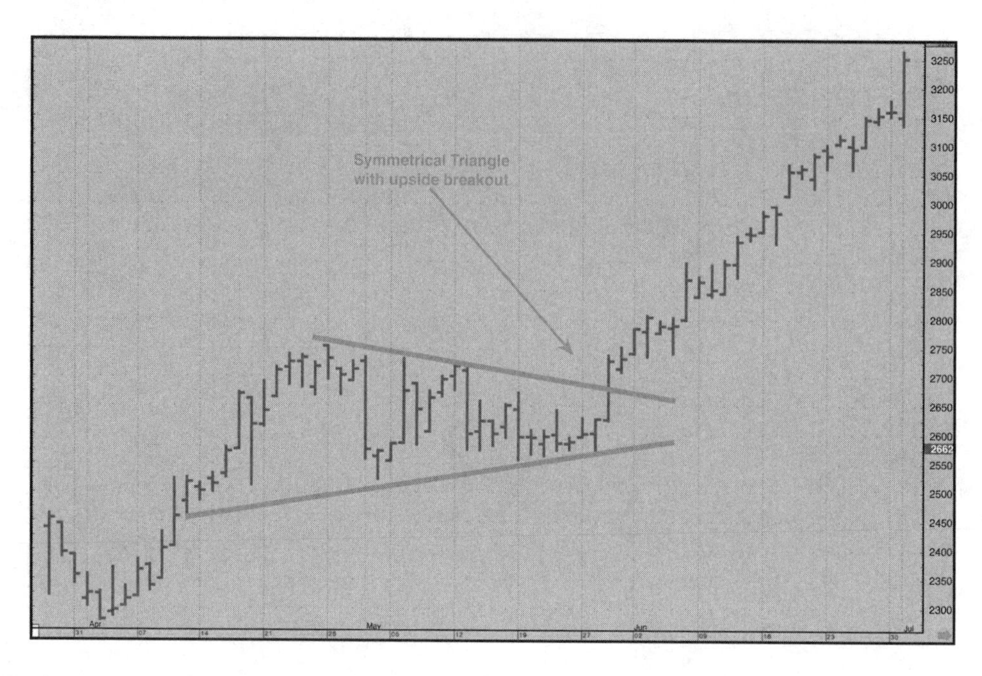

Figure 8.18 Symmetrical triangle

Ascending triangles and descending triangles are like their symmetrical brethren, except they work toward a breakout in the direction of their respective names. The ascending variety has a flat upper boundary with a rising lower boundary that can be defined by an up trendline. The bulls are able to support the market at successively higher lows, while the bears are making a stand at the upper resistance level, with the result more likely to be a breakout to the upside. This is generally a continuation pattern, most likely to be seen during a major up trend. The descending variety is the mirror image, with a lower horizontal support line and successively lower highs that can be connected by a down trendline. Examples shown in Figure 8.19.

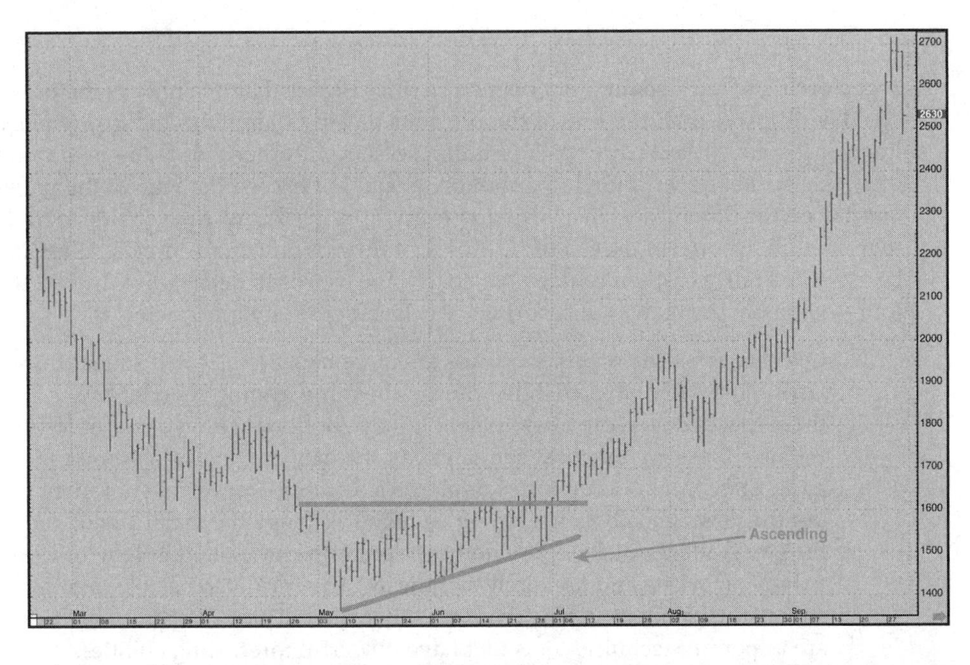

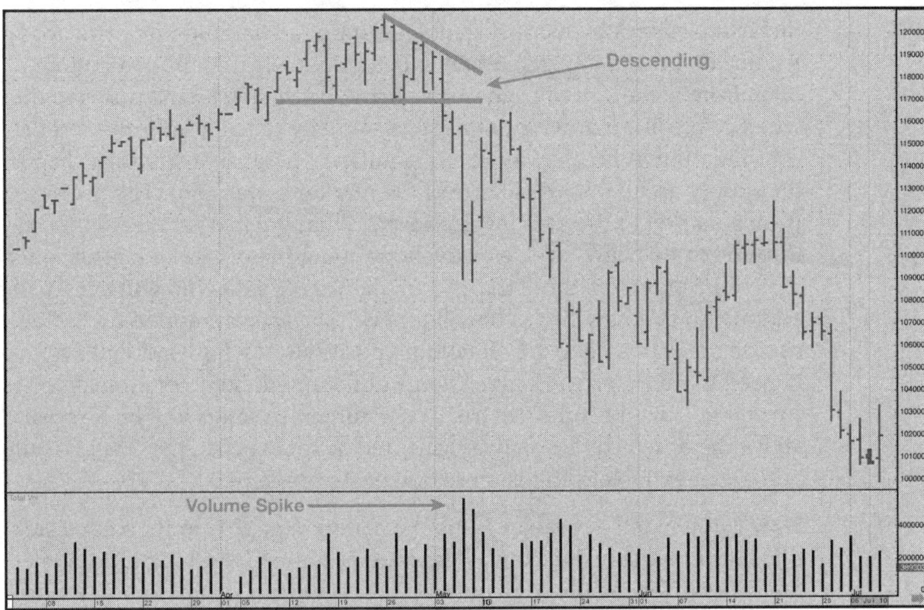

Figure 8.19 Ascending (part a) and descending (part b) triangles

Volume characteristics match the other patterns; many times, volume will jump on the breakout. The bigger the triangle, the bigger the move to follow is likely to be.

Gaps

A gap occurs when a commodity opens at a price higher than the high of the previous day or lower than the low of the previous day. By definition, the gap remains intact if it's not "filled" during the trading session. In other words, on a "gap up day," the market never traded low enough to equal or exceed the high of the previous day on the downside. On a "gap down day," the market was never able to trade high enough to equal or exceed the low of the previous day on the upside. Gaps can be identified fairly easily on a daily bar chart. The trick is to determine which of the four—common, breakaway, measuring, or exhaustion—you are looking at.

1. *Common gaps:* The majority of gaps are more likely to be filled sooner than later. Most daily gaps are filled during the same trading session, and of those that aren't, more often than not, they are filled within a day or two. Because these are the most common variety, they are known as common gaps. They might occur, for example, as a result of a government report, but the news usually is not strong enough to change the major trend, and the gap is filled quickly. Common gaps are seen quite often in thin, or low-volume, markets and are rarely significant. The trick is to be able to differentiate the common variety from the other three. The other three varieties are important technical tools that have powerful forecasting abilities.

2. *Breakaway gaps:* A breakaway gap develops at a beginning of a new move. An upside breakaway gap occurs when prices jump up from a bottom, often from some sort of congestion area. A downside breakaway gap occurs when prices jump down from a top, also many times from some sort of consolidation. A breakaway gap is significant because it signals a change in the supply and demand balance of the market in question. The pressure to push a market to the next level is so great that the market literally has to leapfrog to this new level, effectively trapping many market participants on the wrong side. It is those trapped on the wrong side who will eventually add fuel to this new fire as they liquidate. The shorts trapped under the upside breakaway gap are all holding positions at a loss and will eventually need to find a place to cover. Some of them will hope for a break to cover, but it won't come. Alternatively, numerous longs will be trapped above the downside breakaway gap, and at some point, they will be selling out. The inevitable result is more downside pressure.

   How can you tell a breakaway from a common gap? Common gaps are filled fairly quickly. Breakaway gaps are not filled for a long time, sometimes never for the life of a contract. They signify the start of a new and major trend move. Many times they form out of a consolidation or during blow-off highs or lows. The breakaway day is accompanied by greater-than-normal volume, usually at least 50% greater than the average volume of the preceding two weeks. These are significant and powerful tools that you should be alert for constantly. Particularly, watch for them when a market appears to be "cheap" or "expensive." The market could be basing for a major bottom or climaxing for a major top.

3. *Measuring gaps:* A measuring gap is found at approximately the midpoint of a powerful trend move. Such a gap forms one day, often on news, but unlike with a common gap, the market continues on its way without filling the gap. Once again, volume is usually large. Measuring gaps serve to trap many players who are on the wrong side even more deeply in the muck, and these traders provide some of the fuel for the next leg up or down. The interesting thing about these gaps is that they tend to occur when a move is just about half over. If the breakaway came at 100 and the measuring is at 140, you can project that this move will run to about 180. The measurement rule is certainly not written in stone. At times, there will be more than one measuring-type gap in powerful moves, perhaps one at 33% of the move and another when the move is about 60% to 67%. However, the 50% rule is usually pretty close, so it can help you determine approximately where you are in the move. Exhaustion gaps can do this, too. (See Figure 8.20.)

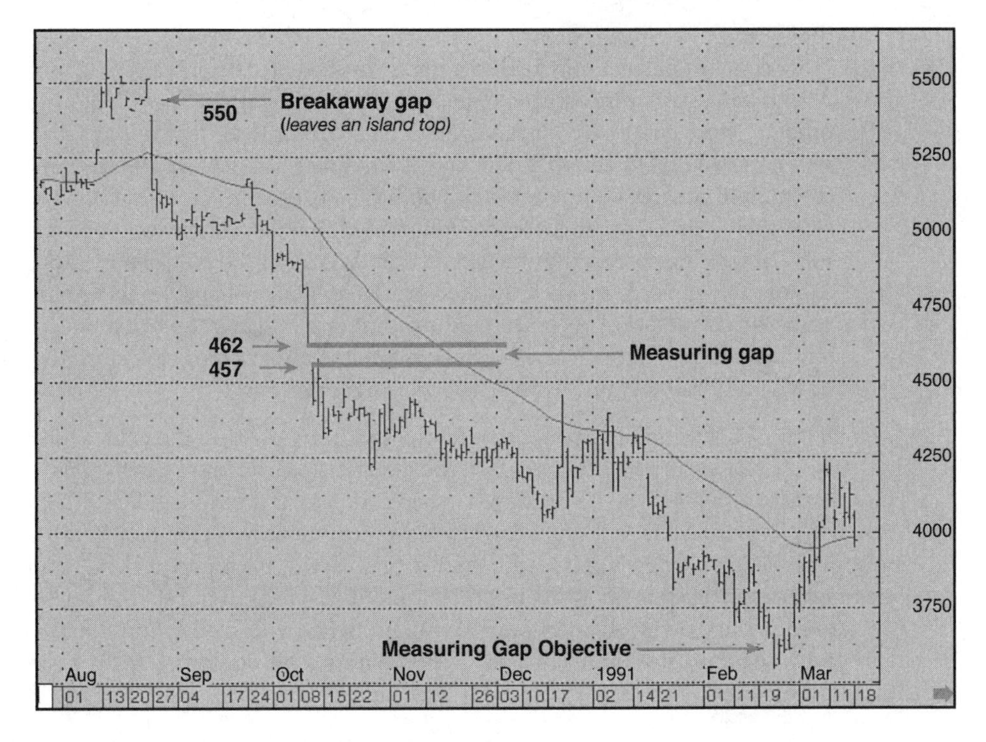

Figure 8.20 Breakaway and measuring gaps

4. *Exhaustion gaps:* An exhaustion gap forms near the end of a move. In a major up trend, the market gaps up to new highs, generally on bullish news. In a major down trend, the market gaps down to new lows, perhaps on new bearish news, sometimes based on final panic liquidation. In both cases, many times these gaps follow wide-ranging or limit-type moves. In markets that still have limits, the exhaustion day might even trade at the limit at some point in the direction of the major trend. Unlike with the other gaps, however, this is the beginning of the end. The market has run out of steam, even though most of the participants do not realize it on that day. One way to explain this is that on the day of an upside exhaustion gap, the last of the weak shorts have thrown in the towel and are covering their positions. The last of the "uniformed" longs are entering the party believing this market still has a long way to go. However, the news is always the most bullish at the top, and the market is satiated. High prices are starting to ration demand, and supply is beginning to come out of the woodwork. With a downside exhaustion gap, the last of the under-margined longs have given up. Many times, panicky conditions prevail as the red ink flows. This, too, is the beginning of the end because low prices have begun to stimulate demand.

   How can you determine whether a gap is of the exhaustion variety? Unlike with breakaway or measuring gaps, an exhaustion gap will be filled fairly quickly. More commonly, the market will churn for three to five days, but it will generally be filled fairly quickly—sometimes the next day. Many times, the high of the exhaustion top day will not be exceeded, or with a downside, there will be no lower lows. Volume will be high, but it was probably high in the days preceding the exhaustion day, too. Like breakaway gaps, exhaustion gaps are powerful indicators. Keep your exhaustion gap antenna up when a market becomes wild-eyed after a long run up or panic stricken after a long run down. Remember, it is always darkest before the dawn and brightest just before the sun starts to recede.

Finally, no discussion of gaps is complete without mentioning the island formation. Islands can be formed in part by either exhaustion or breakaway gaps. An island bottom is formed by a gap down, price action at a basing level, and then a breakaway gap up. An island top is formed by a continuation or exhaustion gap up, some price action at new highs, and then a breakaway type gap down (or vice versa). Islands are easy to spot because they look like islands in the sky (or the sea). They are rare, but powerful, and you'll know one when you see it! Figure 8.21 is a daily cocoa chart illustrating examples of each variety, all occurring within a two month time period.

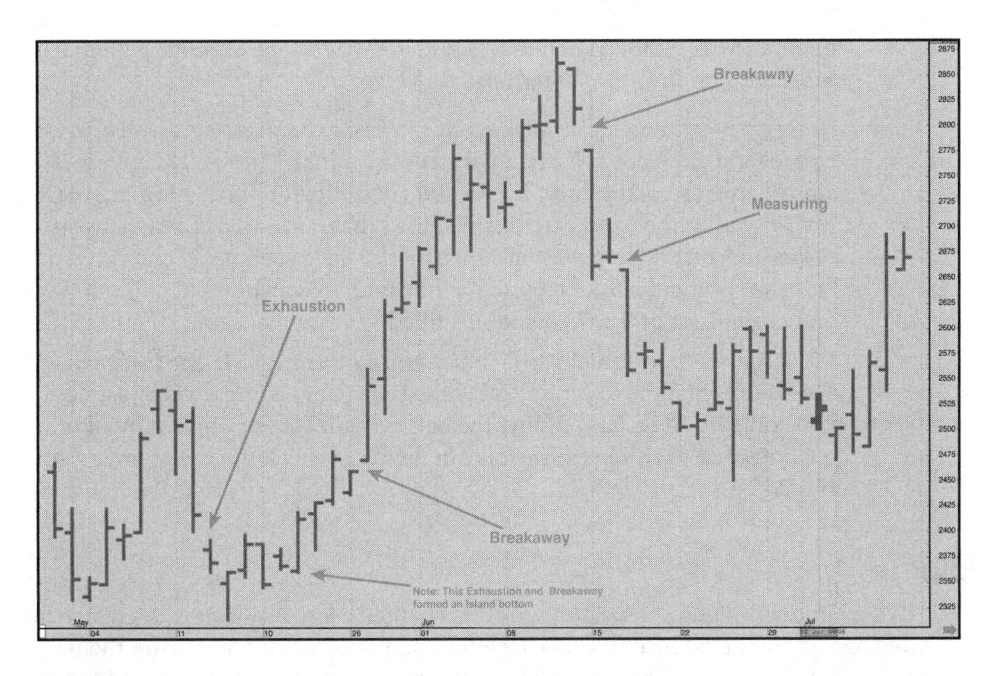

Figure 8.21 Gaps

Five rules for trading gaps

The following are five useful rules for successful gap trading:

1. *The majority of gaps are common and will be filled.* Do not look for significant gaps at nonsignificant times. If a market gaps on minor news, low volume, or what doesn't appear to be a major top or bottom, assume that it will be filled. Scalpers can fade these common gaps and look to take profits when they're filled. If a gap is not filled fairly quickly (within two to seven trading days), begin to treat it as a significant gap (either a breakaway, measuring, or exhaustion gap—depending on where the market is in its cycle).

2. *When a market is forming a long base, place a buy stop above the base to catch a breakaway-type move.* Many times, breakaway gaps occur when they're least expected; at times, they occur on no news. I've observed on breakaway-up days that the lows are generally registered right at the open. If you are stopped into a new long position in this way, place your sell stop at the low end (the fill) of the gap. If it is any good, it should not be filled, and you should be in close to the lows for maximum potential profitability.

3. *Measuring gaps offer an excellent opportunity to pyramid a position.* If you spot a measuring gap and are already in on a base position, it is time to double up and move your stop loss on the entire position to the fill of the measuring gap. Your average price is better than the market, and your risk on the

new "add" is minor. When they work, you have a lot of profit potential remaining on the new, larger position.

4. *Never anticipate exhaustion gaps—wait for them to be filled to take a new position.* Exhaustion gaps occur in the final stages of a major move. This phase is almost always volatile, and it is extremely difficult to pick a top or bottom. It is only after the exhaustion gap is filled that you can define what your risk is and that it truly was an exhaustion. I have seen occasions when the bullish sentiment is so frothy that it forms an exhaustion but still can work higher for days or weeks before it's filled.
5. *When you see a significant gap (a breakaway, measuring, or exhaustion gap), act!* This is not the time to hesitate; it is the time to act aggressively. Just do it! If you wait, you'll be left holding the bag. Significant gaps generally offer good reward to risk because you can define fairly closely what your risk should be.

Volume

I've mentioned volume repeatedly in this chapter because when it is greater than average, it adds evidence to other technical signals. The one recurring theme you might have noticed is that significant days generally are associated with greater-than-average volume. Gap days, breakouts from consolidation, and support or resistance penetrations are many times associated with greater-than-normal volume. To know what greater than normal is, you need to know what average volume is for the market you're trading. All markets are different, and you need to know what the average is. A rule of thumb is that a significant volume day is at least 50% higher than the 30-day average.

I've identified three major volume rules:

1. In a major up trend, volume will tend to be relatively higher on rallies and lower on declines or trading ranges (consolidations).
2. In a major down trend, volume will tend to be relatively higher on declines and lower on rallies or trading ranges (consolidations).
3. Volume will tend to expand dramatically at major tops and bottoms. Major bottoms can be characterized by climax-type selling. Blow-off tops will be associated with climatic volume, too.

Open interest

Open interest (OI) analysis is a powerful trading tool that futures traders use. (Stock traders do not have access to this tool.) *OI* is simply the number of contracts outstanding—the total number held by buyers *or* (*not* and) sold short by sellers on any given day. The OI number gives you the total number of longs and the total number of shorts because, unlike in stocks, in futures, the short interest is always equal to the long interest. Each long is willing to either accept delivery of a particular commodity or offset a contract(s) sometime before the expiration date. Each short is willing to either make delivery or offset a contract(s) before the expiration date. With this in mind, you can plainly see that OI is a measurement of the willingness of longs and shorts to maintain their *opposing* positions in the marketplace. It is a quantitative measurement of this difference of opinion.

OI numbers go up or down based on how many new traders are entering the market and how many old traders are leaving. OI goes up by one when one new buyer *and* one new seller enter the market. *This act creates one new contract.* OI goes down by one when a trader who is long closes out one contract with someone who is already short. Because this contract is now closed out, it disappears from the OI statistics. If a new buyer buys from an old buyer (who is selling out), total OI remains unchanged. If a new seller buys back, or *covers* from a new seller entering the market, OI also does not change. The old bear had to buy to cover, with the other side of this transaction being a sell by the new bear.

Let's look at an example. If heating oil has a total OI of 50,000 contracts, and the next day it rises to 50,100, this means 100 new contracts were created by 100 new buyers and 100 new sellers—or perhaps 10 new net buyers and sellers of 10 contracts each, or whatever it takes net to create the new 100. During that day, many people closed out and many entered, and the net result was the creation of new OI. The market has 50,100 contracts' worth of shorts and 50,100 contracts' worth of longs at the end of the day. Theoretically, one short who had 100 new contracts sold (probably the smart money) could have taken the opposing side of 100 others who each bought one (the majority, probably the dumb money), but the short and long interest are always the same on any particular day.

The exchanges release OI figures daily, but they are always for the *previous* day, so they are a day old. You can chart OI on a price chart, and the direction it is changing can tell you some interesting things.

OI statistics are a valuable tool that you can use to predict price trends and reversals. The size of the OI reflects the intensity of participants' willingness to hold positions. Whenever prices move, someone wins and someone loses—a zero-sum game. This is important to remember because when you think about the ramifications of changes in OI, *you must think about it in the context of which way the market is moving at the time.* An increase in OI shows a willingness on the part of the participants to enlarge their commitments. Let's say the market is moving lower and OI is increasing. You can assume that some of the hurt longs have left the party, but they are being replaced by new longs, and many existing longs are still there. If they were liquidating en masse, OI would drop. Likewise, if the short holders were primarily taking profits and leaving the party, OI would also drop. However, because the OI is increasing and the price is dropping, you can assume that the bulls are losing money, but many must be hanging in there or they are recruiting buddies at an increasing rate. What are the ramifications of an OI decline? It is a sign that the losers are in a liquidation phase (it doesn't matter which way the market is moving), the winners are cashing in, and new players are not entering in sufficient numbers to replace them.

Six rules for trading OI

The following sections describe six profit rules for analyzing OI.

1. If prices are in an up trend and OI is rising, this is a bullish sign

In this situation, the bulls are in charge. They are adding to positions and making the money, thus becoming more powerful. Shorts are also being stopped out, but new sellers are taking their place. As the market continues to rise, the longs get stronger, and the shorts get weaker. (See Figure 8.22.)

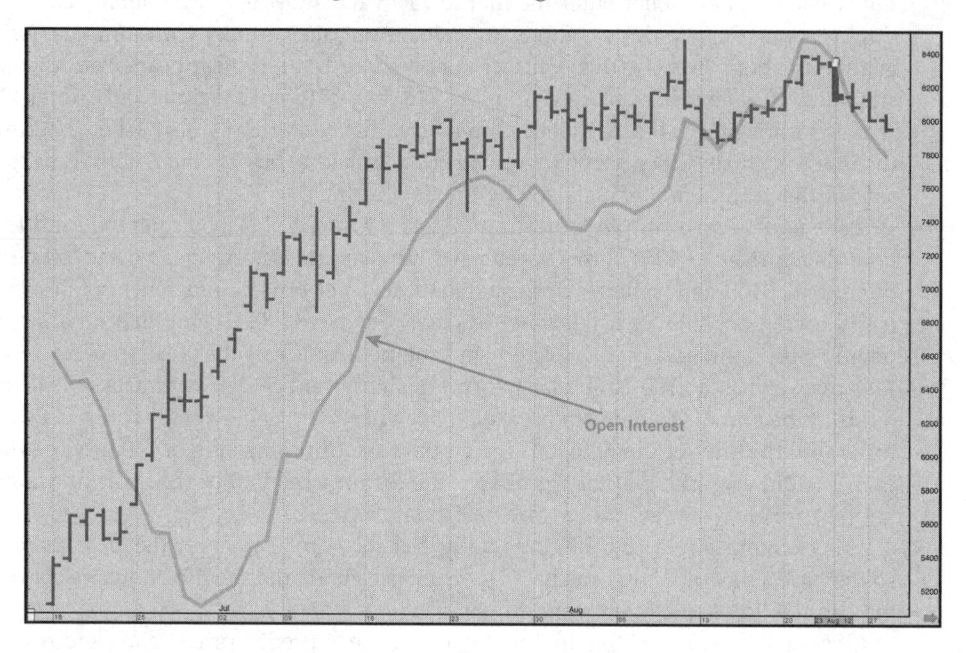

Figure 8.22 Bull market OI

2. If prices are in a down trend and OI is rising, this is a bearish sign

The bears are in charge in this case. They are adding to their positions, and they are the ones making money. Weaker longs are possibly being stopped out, however new buyers are taking their place. As the market continues to fall, the shorts get stronger, and the longs get weaker. Another way to look at the first two rules is that, as long as the OI is increasing in a major trend, it will have the financing it needs to draw upon and prosper.

3. If prices are in an up trend and OI is falling, this is a bearish sign

The old longs—the smart money (I call them "smart money" because they have been right to this point)—are taking profits and liquidating. They are replaced by some new buyers who will not be as strong on balance, but the declining OI is an indication that the weak shorts are also bailing. They will be replaced to some extent by new shorts who are stronger than the old shorts were.

4. If prices are in a down trend and OI is falling, this is a bullish sign—the mirror image of rule 3

The smart money, the shorts, are covering or liquidating. They will be replaced to a degree by new shorts who are not as strong as they were, but the declining OI indicates that the weakened longs are largely throwing in the towel. They will be replaced by fresh longs who were not as weakened by the lower prices. Another way to look at Rules 3 and 4 is that when the pool of losers is depleted, the party will be over.

5. If prices are in a congestion range and OI is rising, this is a bearish sign

This situation is a bearish sign because the public generally plays the long side. Rising OI in a trading range affair assumes that the commercials and professionals are taking the short side, and the uniformed public will most likely lose out in the end.

6. If prices are in a congestion range and OI is falling, this is a bullish sign

This situation is a bullish sign because the professionals, who are more likely to be short, are covering. The weak hands are throwing in the towel.

RSI

Oscillators are a group of technical indicators that are popular with traders as overbought or oversold indicators. The most commonly used oscillator is the relative strength index (RSI). RSI was developed originally by Welles Wilder in the late 1970s. When you hear the words *oversold* and *overbought*, here's what they're talking about: Markets do not go straight up or straight down forever without corrective moves. There comes a point where the market is ready to turn, either temporarily or for good. Overbought basically means the market is too high in the respect that it's running out of buyers; in effect, it's about to fall of its own weight. Oversold is the antonym: The market is too low, running out of sellers (at least for the current time period), and ready for a bounce. Oversold is not a scientific term and is bandied about somewhat arbitrarily. The RSI attempts to quantify the degree of oversold or overbought.

To determine the RSI, a trader selects the number of days; nine is the standard, or default, in most programs. To calculate the nine-day RSI, you need to average the change of the previous nine up days and divide this number by the average of the change of the previous nine down days. The RSI ranges from just above 0 to just under 100, but it is extremely rare to see a number close to either of these extremes. The RSI spends most of its time fluctuating between 25 and 75. At extremes, it moves under 25 or over 75. These are the standard oversold (less than 25) and overbought (greater than 75) areas.

How do you use the RSI? When this number gets too small or too large, it is time to put your antenna up. The market could be getting close to a reversal point. Some traders attempt to buy when the RSI wanders into oversold range and sell in the overbought range. My opinion is that if you attempt to do this, you better have deep pockets. At times (range bound markets), this can be an excellent way to pick tops and bottoms. However, in the major moves and at extremes (the most profitable time for the trend follower), the RSI can remain in the extreme ranges for long periods of time and for quite a few points. (And, hey, it's "only" points, right?) This is the major drawback of the RSI: It works in normal markets, but when the market is in the blow-off or panic stage, it can remain in overbought or oversold territory for an extended period and become quite costly.

Still, I do believe the RSI is a useful tool, but only when used in conjunction with other indicators. You need to know what type of market you are in (trading-range or trending, young or mature). If you can determine this, the RSI can help you identify the point in the life cycle of the market. The RSI tends to get high in the mature stages of a bull market and low in the mature stages of a bear, but there is no magic number that signals the bottom. In fact, I've found it is a good practice to watch for the RSI to turn up after it falls under 25 to signal a bottom and vice versa for the bull. Yet, even this tactic tends to lead to numerous false and money-losing signals because the RSI is a coincident indicator. It moves with price. A minor upswing has to turn the RSI up.

The best way in my opinion to use the RSI is to look for divergences. These occur when the RSI doesn't make a new low or a new high coincidentally with the market. For example, suppose that coffee rallies from 128 to 158; the RSI registers a high for the move of 83 at 158 (so it is in overbought territory). The market then falls back to 152, a normal correction, and the RSI falls back to 71. Subsequently, the coffee market continues its bullish ways and reaches a new high of 161. Up until this point, the RSI has moved with price. Each day, coffee registered a new closing high for the move, and so did the RSI. However, on this occasion, the RSI moved up to only 79, a lower high. The market made a new high; the RSI made a lower high. (See Figures 8.23 and 8.24.)

This is classic divergence, and I've found that the best signals come from RSI divergence. The very best signals come from triple divergence, in which the market makes a third higher high or third lower low, while the RSI makes a third lower high or a third higher low. I've also seen quadruple divergence and even more divergences. This can be another dilemma when using RSI. Double divergence can be seen many times just before a turning point, but in the most powerful moves (the ones you really want to be on), there is nothing to say the market cannot keep going in the direction of the major trend. This is something to look at daily, because it can give you some useful information, but I would use RSI as a confirming indicator only, not as a stand-alone trading method.

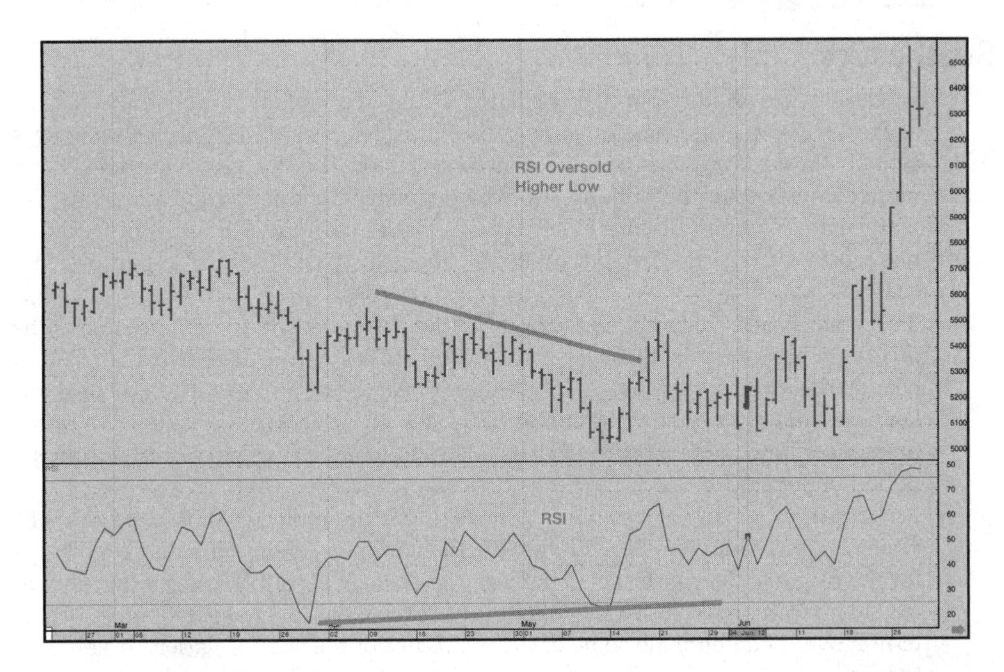

Figure 8.23 RSI divergence

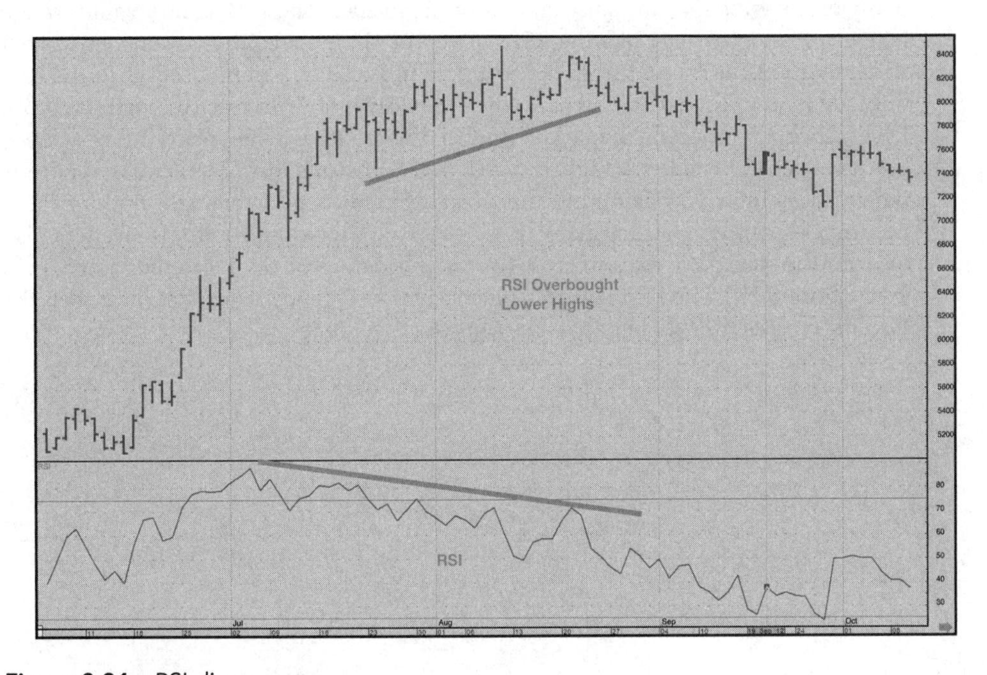

Figure 8.24 RSI divergence

Stochastics

Stochastics are another popular oscillator. While George Lane is generally credited as the developer of stochastics, some in the industry contend that Ralph Dystant was actually the creator of this widely followed indicator. The stochastics formula is a bit more complex than the RSI and is readily available for those who want to see the mathematics. I won't discuss it here (you can let the computer figure it out for you, like most other traders do), but I will talk about the basics of how to interpret stochastics data.

The stochastics formula measures how the close impacts the trend. Here is the theory: In bull markets, the close is more likely to occur near the day's high, and in bear markets, the close is more likely to occur near the day's lows. The way the market closes determines how the stochastic trends. In essence, stochastics are a measurement of how the most current close relates to where prices have been during the period under study.

Stochastics consist of two lines: the %K, which is more sensitive, and the %D, which is slower moving. As with the RSI, the trader can choose the number of days for the formula. Shorter terms (5 days is popular) are sensitive and act quickly but lead to many more whipsaws. Longer terms (14 day is widely used) identify longer-term moves and eliminate some of the whipsaws of the shorter variety. If you plan to work with stochastics, the computer will plot the "fast" and the "slow" versions. The slow version is likely a better way to go because it is smoothed to eliminate many of the whipsaw and false signals of the former. The stochastic's values range between 0 and 100, just like the RSI's. Overbought is generally considered to be a value in excess of 80, and oversold is less than 20. They can be used as in the RSI, but they tend to give better signals when they diverge from price (as with the RSI). Divergence can precede the market. Bullish divergence is when prices hit new lows, but the stochastic makes a higher low than its previous low. Bearish divergence is when prices hit a new high, but the stochastic makes a lower high. Both of these occurrences can give strong indications of market tops and bottoms. Traders also look for the stochastic lines to cross to exit an existing position or enter a new one. (See Figure 8.25.) The best signals come when divergence is present, and then the %K line crosses the %D line that confirms the divergence.

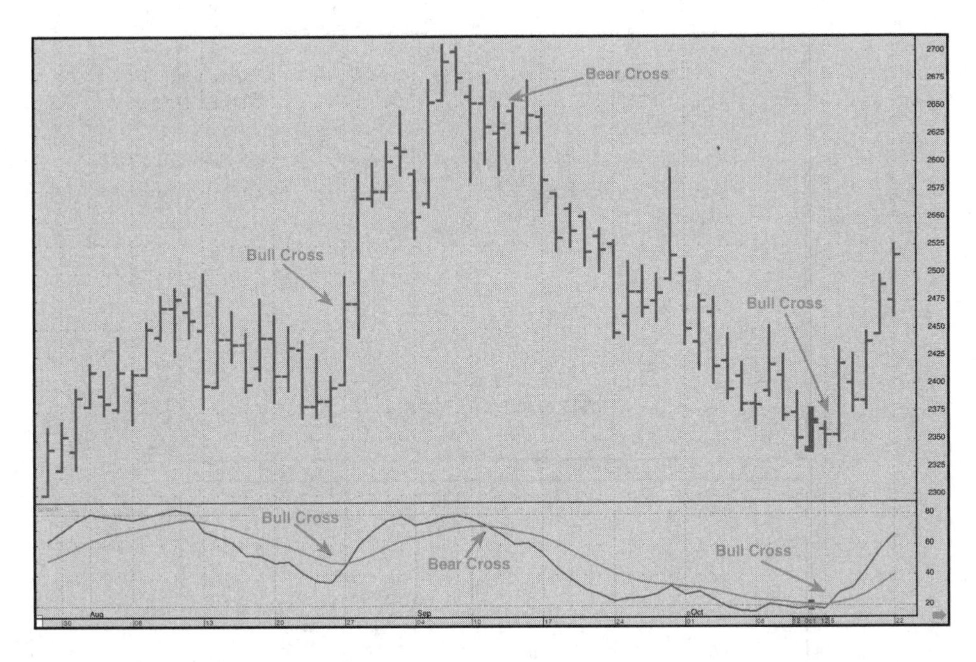

Figure 8.25 Stochastics

Elliot wave analysis

Ralph Elliot was an accountant who developed his theory on market cycles in 1939. Basically, Elliot believed that there is a "natural order" to the markets and that they travel in predictable cycles. He believed that the market rallies in five waves when in an up trend and falls in three-wave corrective moves. When in a down trend, the main trend is five waves down, with three-wave corrective up moves. This five-wave pattern is made up of three odd-numbered waves—1, 3, and 5—which are connected by two corrective waves—2 and 4. Each major odd-numbered wave can be subdivided into five waves, and corrective waves can be broken into three parts (the ABC correction). (See Figure 8.26.)

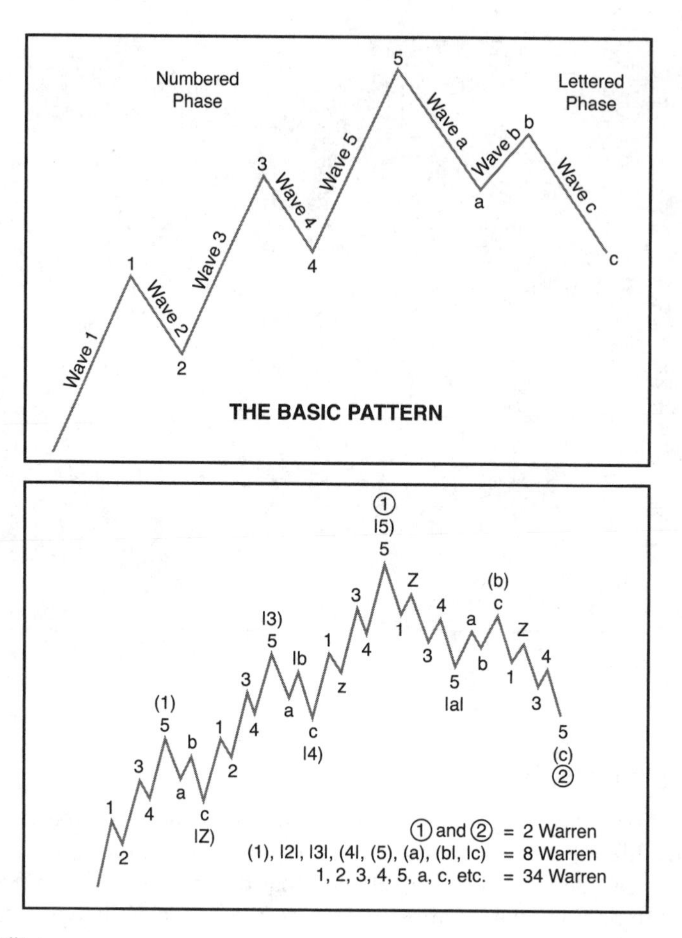

Figure 8.26 Elliot wave

At times, I have looked at longer-term charts of major trends and been able to see exactly what Elliot was talking about. Other times, it just hasn't happened. The main problem I personally have had with Elliot wave analysis is that I find it difficult to determine what wave the market is in during the heat of the battle. If you delve deeply into Elliot wave analysis, you'll find numerous rules that explain away every wiggle on the charts. There are subsets of subsets of waves, and when an Elliot wave theorist misses the count, he revises his analysis to say wave 3 was actually not wave 3, but a subwave 4 of major wave 2, and this is the reason for an ABC correction, which he didn't expect. I'm not trying to be critical here, because I do believe there is validity to Elliot's work, but I personally have had trouble using it. Every trader must use what works for him. Two traders can have entirely different approaches, and both can still make money.

Point and figure charts

The point and figure (P&F) is another type of price charting; the unique thing about P&F is that it ignores time. Time is irrelevant; only price matters. Xs and Os indicate price signals. A P&F chartist uses Xs to illustrate rising prices and Os for falling prices. As long as the price is rising, Xs are added. Os come into play when they are dropping. The decision to start a new column of Xs or Os is based on the market making a price change of a certain amount designated by the technician. This would be a box. The technician also must designate (in addition to the size of each box) what determines a reversal.

For example, a popular reversal size is three boxes. So, if you use a scale of 10 points for cattle, a reversal size would be 30 points. The values for the box and reversal are arbitrary, depending on how sensitive the trader wants the P&F chart to be.

The larger the box size and reversal values, the less sensitive the chart is and vice versa. A 1¢ box for wheat is obviously more sensitive than a 10¢ box. If the chart is too sensitive and the boxes too small, you increase the chances of being whipsawed by insignificant fluctuations. If the boxes are too large, you miss out on significant portions of some moves and take too much risk. Figure 8.27 illustrates a typical P&F chart.

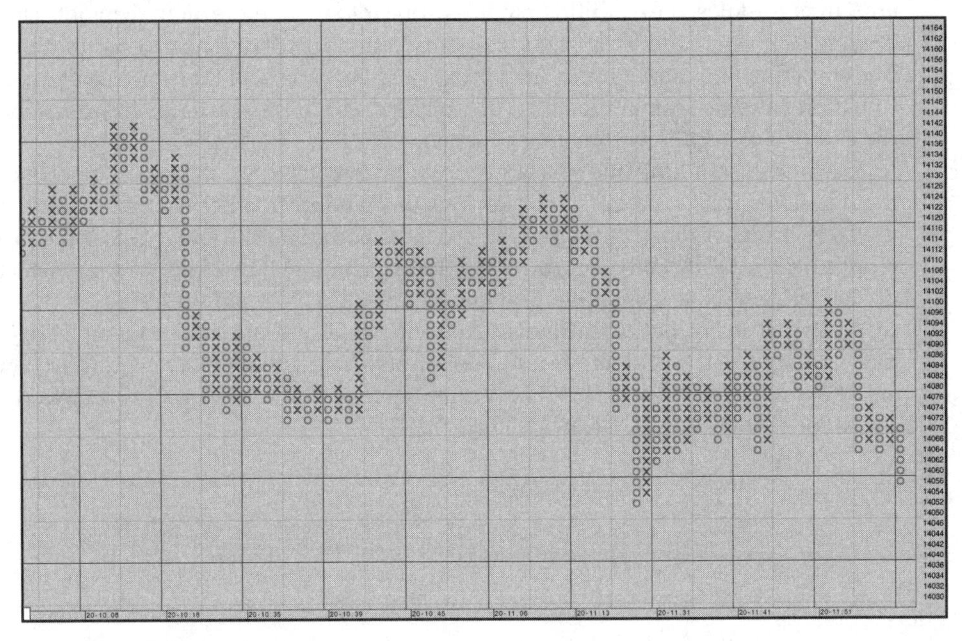

Figure 8.27 Typical P&F

Although I personally do not use P&F charts, I knew a number of successful floor traders who did. This is why I want to at least mention them in this book, so a serious student who wants to pursue the P&F can research further.

Japanese candlestick charts

Candlestick charts are the third major charting method available on most charting programs. The Japanese used candlestick charts before charting ever became popular in the West (rice futures were active in Japan as early as the 1700s), and they are the earliest form of technical analysis. Whereas bar charts use bars and point and figure charts use *X*s and *O*s, candlestick charts use rows of candles with wicks on either end. The body of each candle is the distance between the opening and closing prices. If the closing price is higher than the open, the body is left empty or white (or it could be one color, like blue). If the closing price is lower than the open, the body is filled in with black (or another color, like red). The upper wick represents the high, and the lower wick represents the low. The wicks are not as important as the body. In other words, candlestick chartists are not as interested in the day's high or low as they are in the relationship between the open and the close. I am not an expert on candlestick charts; entire books have been written on the various patterns for those who want to delve deeper.

While I've decided that candlewick charts do not fit my personal style, a number of interesting patterns appear to have some validity. They have colorful names, too. Candlestick chartists refer to "hanging men," "tweezers tops," and "dark cloud covers." In my studies, the engulfing patterns appear to work more often than not. They seem to be able to identify tops and bottoms better than standard reversal patterns. The engulfing line can be seen at major tops and bottoms, and there also can be continuation patterns seen in the midst of a major trend. In many cases, they do signal the end of a correction within a major trend.

The bullish engulfing line consists of a white (or colored in, at times empty) body that totally engulfs, or covers, the previous day's body. In other words, the high of the body is higher than the high of the previous body, and the low is below the previous low. The white body is formed by a low opening met by strong buying, which pushes price to close above the previous candle. This is a bullish indicator that is seen often at major bottoms. Bearish engulfing lines are the mirror image seen at tops—a long black (or colored in, at times empty) candle that totally engulfs, or covers, the previous day's candle. This is often seen at a blow-off top. It is a powerful signal for candlestick people. (See Figure 8.28.)

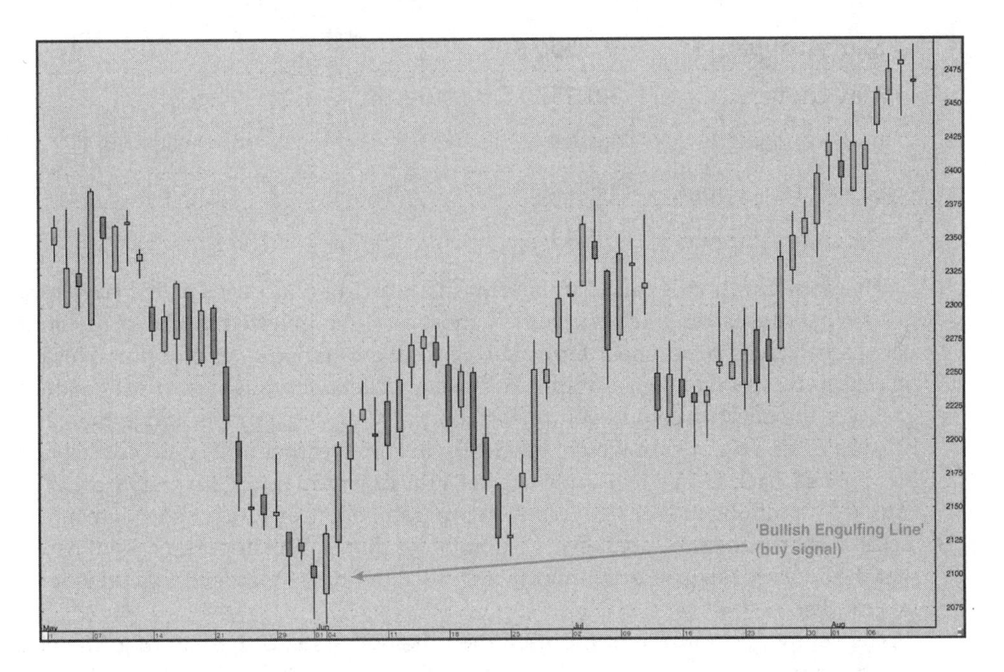

Figure 8.28 Typical candlestick pattern

Spreads—a valuable forecasting tool

I've found that by monitoring the spread action in many of the actively traded physical commodities, a trader can get valuable clues about how bullish or bearish a market is. Spreads also can be used to predict the market path of least resistance. Typically, commodity futures markets are in "carrying charge" or "normal" configurations. (In London, they would say the market is in *contango*.) This is when the distant months sell at a higher price (or premium) to the closer months.

Here's a typical example of what a "normal" copper market might look like:

March copper	299.05
May copper	300.15
July copper	301.95
September copper	303.25
December copper	305.10

Because it costs money to store copper from one month to the next (storage costs, insurance, and interest), this is reflected in the configuration of futures prices. However, at times, markets take on the opposite configuration, in which the near month is trading at a premium to the distants, as illustrated:

March copper	303.50
May copper	301.25
July copper	300.05
September copper	298.15
December copper	295.95

This configuration is called an *inverted* market. (In London, it's called *backwardation*.) What causes a market to invert? In most cases, an inverted market is the product of a perceived or real near-term shortage of the commodity in question. This can be caused by weather. For example, cold weather tends to push the nearby natural gas over the back or could even push the nearby cattle contracts above the backs because cattle do not gain weight efficiently in cold weather and could conceivably be "pushed back"—not ready for market in a timely manner. Inversion could be caused by a mining strike, a government program, big near-term export demand, or a classic short squeeze—actually, any number of things. The important point here is that the spreads can give you important clues about the strength or weakness within a market.

Here's my general rule of thumb: When the bull spreads are working (the near months are gaining on the back months), this is a bullish sign. When the bear spreads are working (the near months are losing to the back months), this is a bearish sign. As with every rule, there are exceptions. For example, November beans might be gaining on July beans in June, because the new crop, which will be harvested in the fall, is burning up due to drought; however, there are adequate near-term supplies. As a rule, however, this works. I'm usually skeptical if I'm short a market and the bull spreads are working—something is wrong.

Here's another powerful trading tip: Watch for spreads to cross "even money." I've noticed that when spreads "cross zero," more times than not, this indicates a significant indicator of a change in the supply-and-demand balance of the commodity being studied. My advice is to go with the flow. If the spread in question crosses zero to the upside, play the bull spreads (long nearby, short the deferred) or play the market from the long side. If the market crosses zero to the downside, play the bear spreads (short the nearby, long the deferreds), or play the market from the short side. For example, consider the spread between May 2003 sugar and March 2004 sugar, shown in Figure 8.29. Note that this action took place during mid-2002 into early 2003 (the 2004 contract is listed two years prior to its expiration).

This spread crossed the zero line in August 2002, which turned out to be just a few weeks before a major bull run began in the sugar market. The price at that time was 574. The market on that day really did not "show its hand"; what I mean by this is there were no real indications of the major move that was to follow. Still, the spread (by the mere act of inverting) turned out to be an excellent leading indicator of a major bull run.

This particular bull spread continued to work nicely, peaking on January 29 at 132 points May over the March. On that date, May sugar closed at 822, so the market had moved 248 points, equivalent to a profit of $2,777 per contract traded. The spread itself had rallied 132 points above the zero mark, for a spread profit of $1,478 per spread traded. Considering that the spread margins are generally much lower—in the case of sugar, only one-third the size of an outright contract—trading three spreads for every one contract would have yielded an additional 50% profit. Of course, on that date, there was no way to know that this was the highest this spread would run; however, when the spread started to turn south, our antenna should have been raised. My experience has been that more times than not, spreads lead price action—spreads can be a powerful indicator. Note that after the spread peaked on January 29, the sugar market continued to rise, and the contract high was registered February 20, at 884. On that date, despite the May contract making a new high, the spread was already fading, trading at 115, or equal to 17 points below its peak. On March 10, the day the spread broke below its 50-day exponential moving average, May sugar was trading at 801.

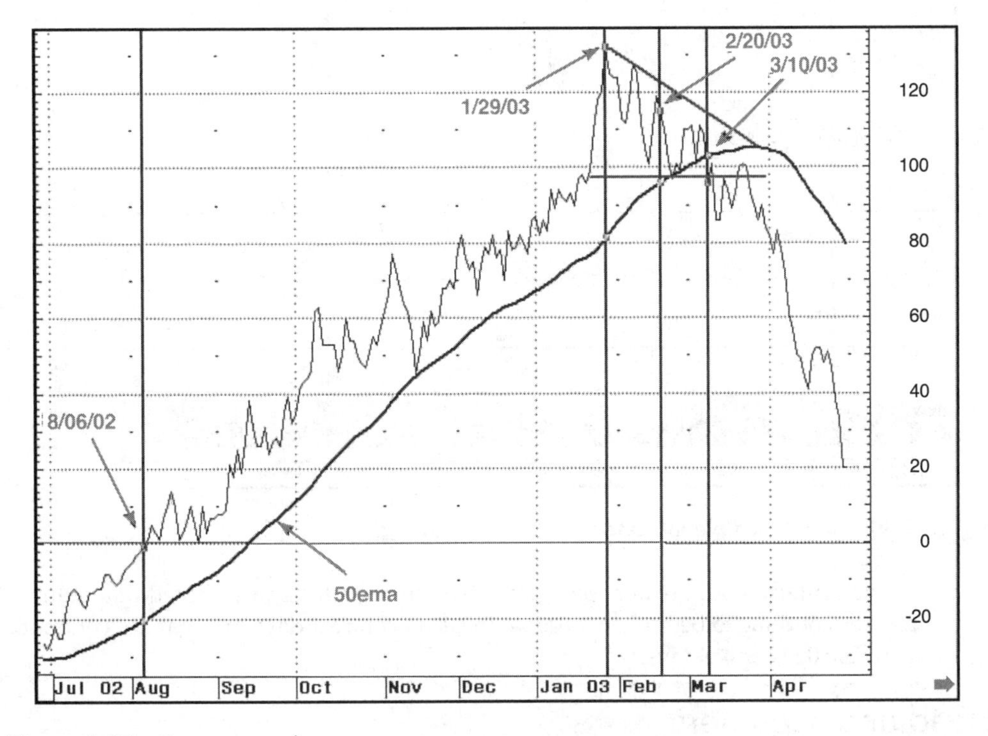

Figure 8.29 Sugar spread

Certainly, there were other clues that the bull had run its course. For example, open interest was rising nicely during the bull run, but it peaked on February 13, a full week before the price peaked. The price rising and open interest fading with the bull spreads declining were two powerful signals that together could have been used to predict the end of this bull run. The icing on the cake was a volume spike on February 19, one day before the top. On that day, volume hit close to 74,000 contracts, the only time that year it was above 70,000. High-volume days can come at turning points, and historically, sugar volume tends to expand just prior to and coincidentally with the beginning of a bull move. This day turned out to be the third-highest volume day in sugar's history to the date. The previous highest were January 5, 1999, and February 24, 1998. Both of these registered over 80,000, and both came at major tops, with the market trading above 9¢ per pound. (See Figure 8.30.)

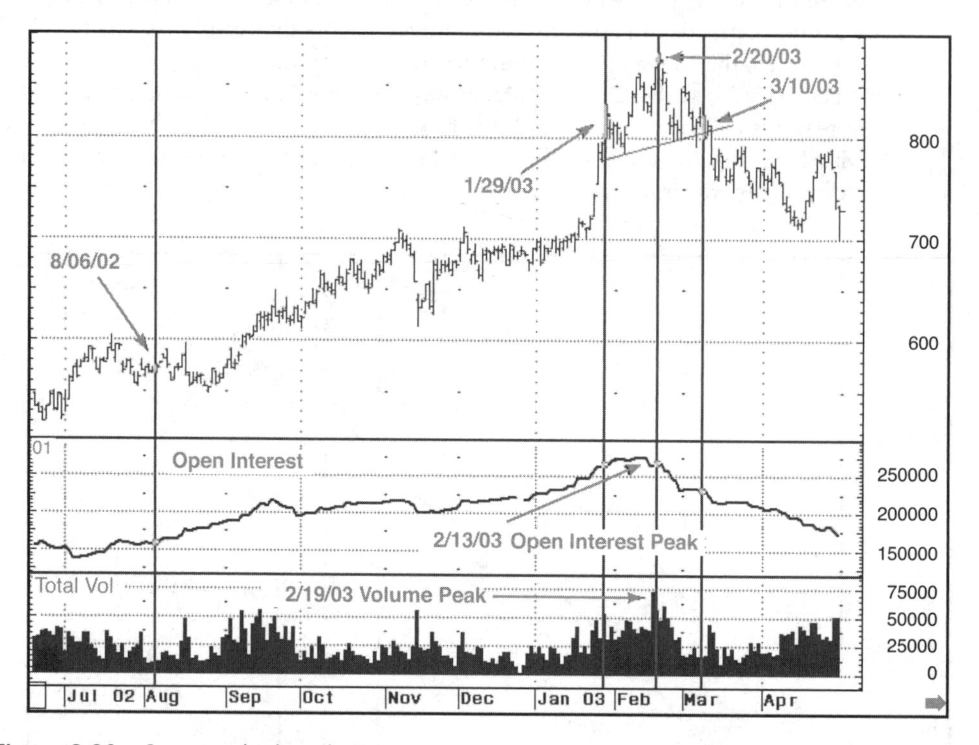

Figure 8.30 Sugar multiple indicators

Incidentally, with greater speculative participation today, I've noted that volume records continue to be broken. (Today, 100,000+ contract days in sugar are common, with 200,000+ spike days.)

Head and shoulders

Next to the breakout from consolidation, the classic chart pattern the head and shoulders (H&S) is my other favorite. Edwards and Magee made the H&S pattern famous in their 1948 book *Technical Analysis of Stock Trends*, and it still remains a valid and useful indicator today.

The H&S is a reversal pattern that signals a change in the prevailing major trend. We'll take up some ink reviewing this concept here because, in my experience, it remains one of the most reliable. (I also will add my own twists to identifying and analyzing this pattern.)

When you see an H&S pattern, it's time to either exit and take your profits, cut your losses, or establish a new position in the new direction. An interesting characteristic of the H&S is that it not only tells you a market is making a top or bottom, but it also tells you how far the ensuing move will travel. The H&S does not actually pick *the* top or *the* bottom, but it gives you the sign after the top or bottom is in place.

Because a picture is worth 1,000 words, let's start with a two charts that illustrate the H&S pattern (see Figures 8.31and 8.32).

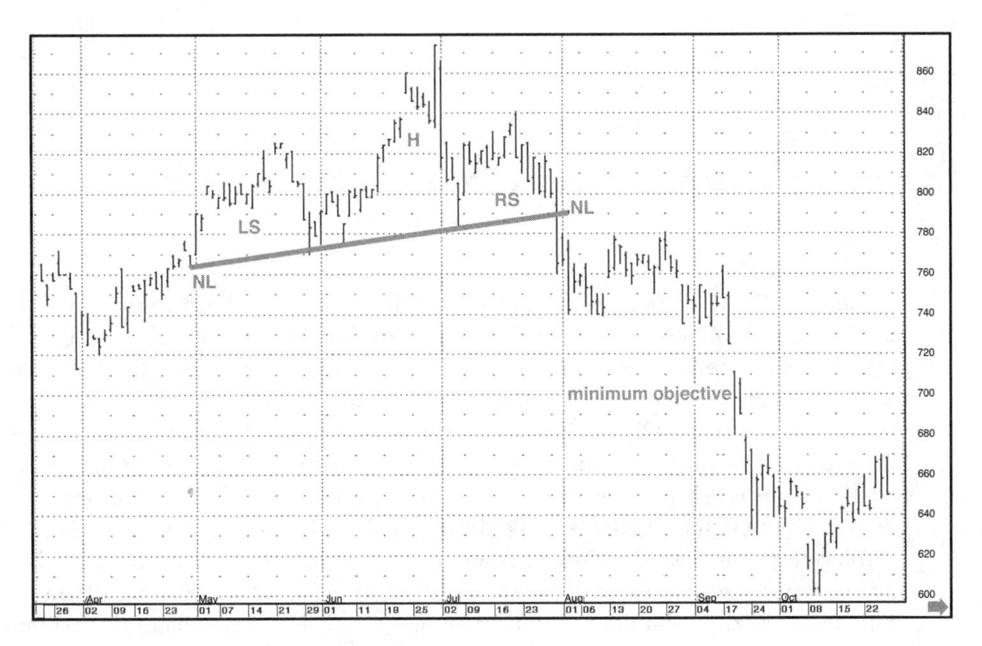

Figure 8.31 Sugar H&S top

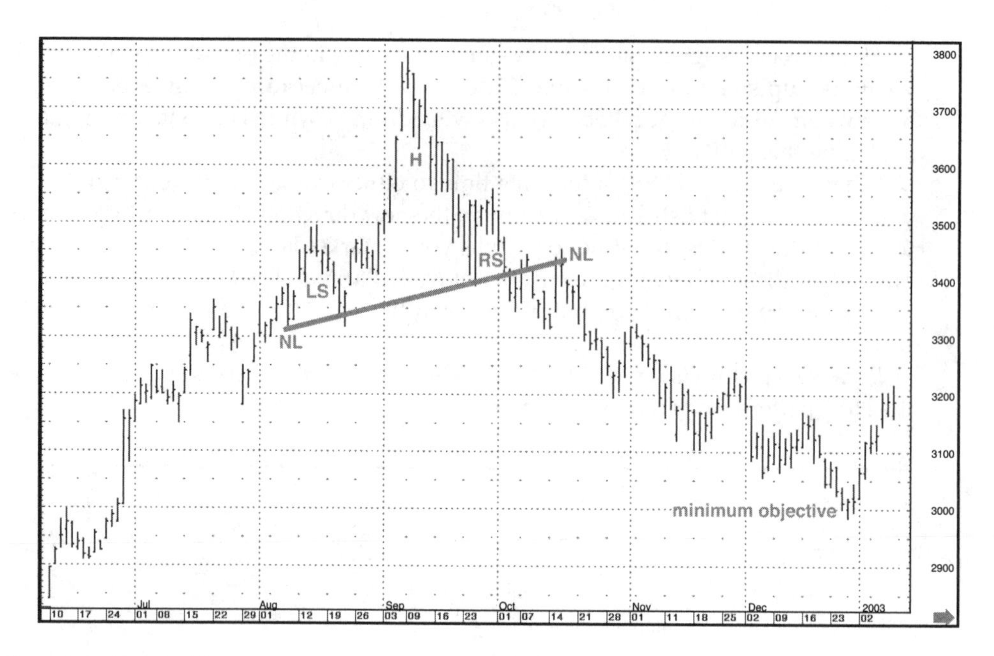

Figure 8.32 Gold H&S top

The head (H) is a price peak; another peak lower than the head to the left is the left shoulder (LS), and another peak lower than the head to the right is the right shoulder (RS). The line connecting the lows of the declines from the shoulders and the head is called the neckline (NL). In a classic H&S, the neckline is often horizontal (similar to a support line). However, it can also be upward sloping (as in Figures 8.31 and 8.32), similar to an up trendline, or downward sloping, similar to a down trendline. This is where your analytical skills come into play. Many of the best H&S patterns are mutants, which resemble the original but in a skewed way.

You can spot an H&S developing when the left shoulder and the head are in place and the market starts to rally from the neckline. If it fails at a lower high than the major high, the right shoulder is in formation. A classic H&S often has a right shoulder of the approximate same size and duration as the left. However, it can be lower or higher, longer or shorter, but its peak will ultimately end up lower than the head. The pattern is not complete until the right shoulder is completed *and* the decline from the right shoulder's peak breaks under the neckline. When that happens, a top is presumed. It is time to exit longs and go short. After the initial breakout below the neckline, the market often rallies back up to approximately the neckline, giving the trader an excellent low-risk shorting opportunity. H&S patterns can also sometimes provide false signals. Suspect a false signal if the market is able to rally back above the peak of RS (this is the place to initially set your risk point). This will not occur with the best H&S signals; most will not rally beyond NL. If the market trades above the peak of the right shoulder, you can safely assume that all bets are off and this one isn't "right."

There's a bonus that comes with the H&S: It also provides a *target* that is generally reliable and more precise than most technical techniques. If you measure from the top of the head to the neckline and bring this measurement down from the neckline, you have a target for a *minimum objective,* where prices will subsequently end up. The market can certainly move farther than this count for the objective, but it gives you a minimum objective that could prevent you from exiting prematurely.

H&S patterns occur in all time frames, and you can often find them in the short-term mini S&P chart. With a smaller pattern, you usually need to shoot for a smaller objective. Figure 8.33 illustrates a short-term complex H&S pattern on a 45-minute chart (where each bar represents 45 minutes of market activity) that I traded successfully from the short side.

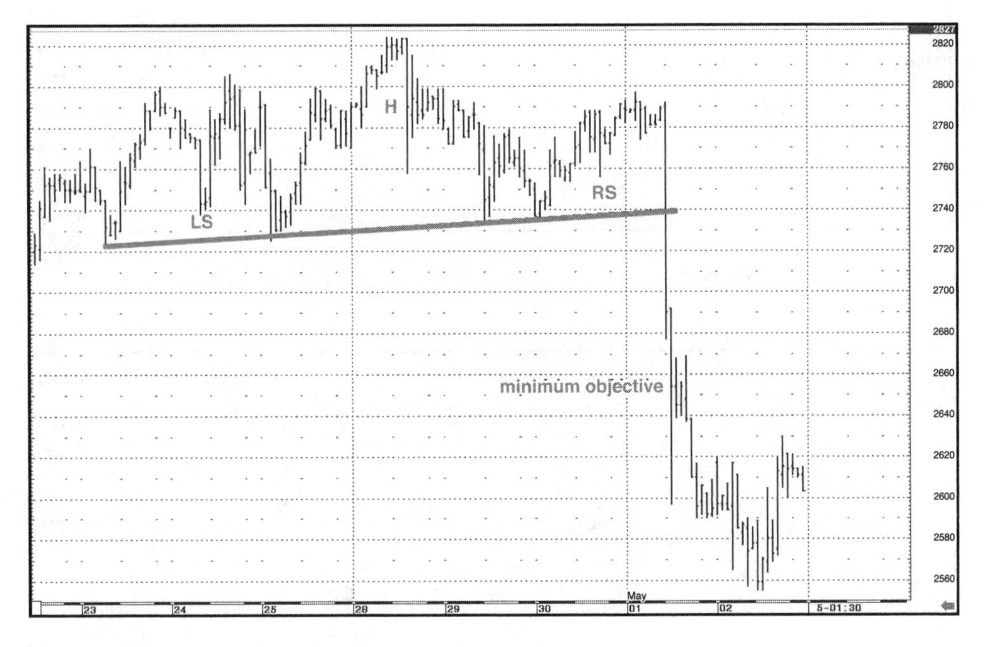

Figure 8.33 Cocoa H&S

Watch volume to confirm the pattern. Volume often will tend to spike at the head and usually is higher than average at the break of the NL.

An H&S occurs at major bottoms as well and looks like the mirror image of one that forms at the top. Some traders call these *inverted head and shoulders* or *reverse head and shoulders.* In this variety, the head is at the lowest point, with two higher shoulders, one on each side. Other than the fact that these are the mirror image of the tops, you trade them the same way. The gold H&S bottom shown in Figure 8.34 is of the simple, classic variety; the soybean is more complex. Note how the extended and complex bottoming pattern illustrated in Figure 8.35 signaled the start of a major move that greatly exceeded the minimum objective.

Figure 8.34 Gold H&S bottom

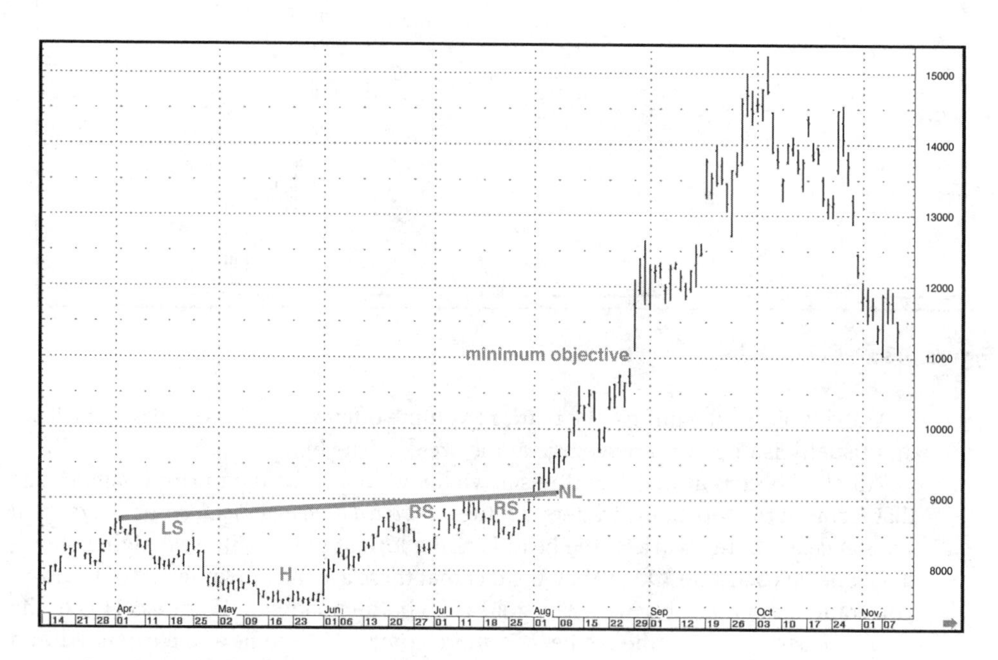

Figure 8.35 Soybean H&S bottom (inverted complex)

10 rules for trading H&S

Here are ten rules for successfully trading using H&S patterns:

1. Never anticipate. When I first discovered H&S patterns, I had a great trade, but then it seemed I started finding them everywhere. I would start to sell after a right shoulder and a head developed, only to lose money. I would see complete H&S patterns develop and take action *before* penetration of the neckline, only to have my head handed to me. As Yogi Berra said, "It ain't over till it's over." Wait until the pattern is completed before you trade it.
2. The bigger the H&S pattern and the longer it takes to develop, the bigger the subsequent resulting move.
3. The count is a *minimum* measurement. Odds actually favor the move carrying much further. However, a warning here: As with all other chart patterns, you are not dealing with a certainty here. If your count says the market will fall 400 points, and it falls 380 and starts to reverse, it would be a shame to let all your profits evaporate over a lousy 20 points.
4. After the market breaks the neckline, watch for the return move back to the neckline. This occurs in at least half of all valid cases and offers a place to enter with a close stop.
5. Watch the slope of the neckline. Downward-sloping necklines for H&S tops increase the odds for a more powerful bear move to follow. Upward-sloping necklines for inverted H&S bottoms increase the odds for a more powerful bull move to follow.
6. Be volume aware. The most reliable neckline breakouts are accompanied with higher-than-average volumes. I have sometimes seen the highest daily volume days of the year associated with H&S patterns.
7. Watch for the head to also form an "island" (see Figure 8.36). This combines two very powerful patterns and geometrically increases the validity of the signal.
8. When the pattern is complete, it should act correctly. These patterns are fairly reliable and do not often deviate from their true purpose, unless, of course, they are false. How can you tell if a pattern is false? One good indication is that your margin account will start to show a loss. Don't freeze when it's not acting properly; when in doubt, get out. Be suspicious if the pattern occurs on low volume. Remember that the market can retrace to the neckline (this is normal and a good place to position), but if the pattern is good, the retracement really shouldn't go much further.

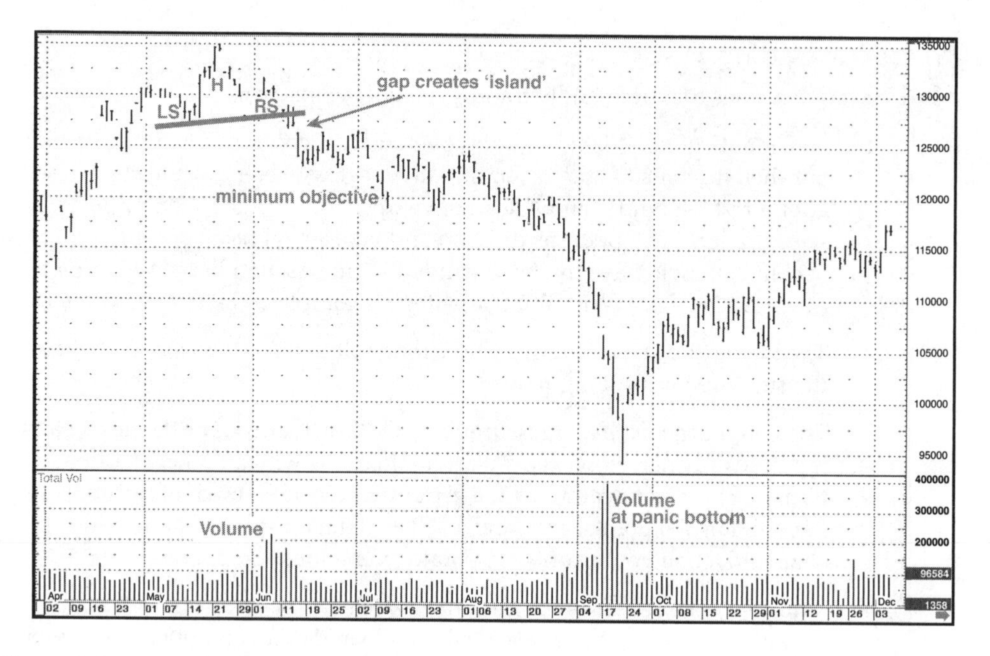

Figure 8.36 Island H&S top

9. If it's a false signal, look to reverse your course. I've found that a classic H&S failure often offers an excellent opportunity to get back in sync with the major trend. If the market again trades above the right shoulder's top (or below the right shoulder's bottom for a reverse H&S), odds favor, at a minimum, one last thrust to a new high or new low. I would buy the market at this point, with the objective of a new high, risking to under the neckline. For an inverted H&S failure, sell the market under the low of the right shoulder, with a minimum objective of a new low, risking to above the neckline.
10. After a false signal is confirmed, watch the market action closely as soon as a new high or low is registered. I've noticed that an H&S failure that turns out not to be the final high or low, ultimately leads to a new contract high or low in short order. The H&S was telling us we were close to the major top or bottom, but the bulls or bears were able to mount one last hurrah. If the market is unable to show much follow-through after this climatic top or bottom (following an H&S that didn't work), be ready to take action because a major top or bottom is now in place.

GK's significant news indicator

"First the doctor told me the good news: I was going to have a disease named after me."
—Steve Martin

As long as markets have existed, savvy traders have paid attention to the market's reaction to significant (potentially market-moving) news. This was true in the days of the ticker tape and is still true in today's electronic age.

Significant news should, by definition, result in a significant market reaction. But it doesn't always happen, and many times the reaction is opposite of what's commonly expected. In this section, I present my "significant news indicator" (SNI). The SNI will help you trade the market's reaction to news. It's as much a trading philosophy as an indicator, but because we're able to apply specific rules to news reactions, the SNI can be as useful as any mathematical indicator.

To introduce the concept, consider this statement: What matters is not the news but how the market reacts to the news. Certainly, the news sets the public perception, but you must be alert for divergences between the news and market action. It's *expectation versus reality.* Look for the divergence between what's happening and what people think is supposed to happen. When the big turn comes, the general public will always be looking the wrong way.

Six rules for trading news

The following are six news rules:

1. If bad news is announced and the market starts to sell off in large volume, it's a good bet that the market's going lower.
2. If the market fails to react to good news, it has probably already been discounted in the price.
3. Moves of importance invariably tend to begin before any news justifies the initial price move. When the move is under way, the emerging fundamentals will slowly come to light. *A big rally (decline) on no news is usually very bullish (bearish).*
4. It is generally not a good practice to buy after very bullish news or sell after an extremely bearish report because both good and bad news can already be discounted in the price.
5. Always consider whether the trend is down or up when the news is made known because a well-established trend will generally continue, regardless of the news. As an example, I remember getting caught in the emotion of a very bullish corn report in January 1994. Looking back, this news was the very top. An opposite (very bearish) report the following year turned out to be the springboard for one of the biggest corn bull markets in history and led me to develop the SNI.

6. When unexpected news occurs (news that the market has not had time to prepare for) and the market opens in a wide range or "gaps" lower or higher, sell out your longs or cover your shorts and wait. Watch the market for 30 minutes to an hour. If the market opened sharply lower with heavy selling and was not able to trade much lower than that, it's into support and you can buy it with a tight risk point. Watch the market closely at this point and note the tone of the rally. If it's small and the market is able to again fall under the levels made when the bad news came out (or rise above the levels made when the good news came out), it's safe to assume the market is going lower (higher).

I recall the big bull coffee move of 1994. One day, the market was trading in the mid-80¢ level. I was long when unexpected news hit the wires about the surprise government release of massive Brazilian stockpiles of coffee. These stocks were supposed to be held in reserve and off the market, but Brazil needed foreign exchange at the time and changed its policy. The market gapped lower at the open and proceeded to trade down 400 points, stopping me out in the process. It remained weak for a day or so, but as soon as the market was able to cross above the mid-80¢ level again (the price registered before the unexpected bad news hit), it basically went straight up. This was the time to reenter. It was up to about $1.40 before the first freeze hit. The full move wasn't over until coffee prices hit close to $2.75, and the monster bull run began when the market, on no news, crossed the level made before the release of the bad news.

In the summer of 1999, the British Central Bank announced that it was going to auction off half of its gold reserves, calling gold a "barbaric relic." The price was $250 per ounce, and although this news was bearish (flooding an already weak market with massive additional supply), this was a major bottom.

With this type of market action in mind, it was the bearish crop report of 1995 that led to me to develop the SNI (although I did not formally put a name to it at the time). We were moving from Minnesota to Lake Tahoe and driving along Interstate 80 on the day of the report—August 11, 1995. I had a large long position in December corn for clients and myself. At that time, the crop was looking good, and nobody knew the weather would turn unfavorable late that summer, creating a short crop. I must have had my reasons for being long, but my hopes were dashed when the crop report was released before the market open that day. I remember calling my assistant from the road when he told me "limit down." The crop report was so bearish in reporting an increased size of the upcoming crop that the early calls were for the market to open down the (then) 10¢-per-bushel limit. And not only limit down, but the early banter was that the market would open limit down and "lock," meaning we could be stuck in our position with only offers to sell limit down and no bids at that price. I was uncomfortable as I sweated out the hour and a half before the market's open, trying to decide how I'd work out of this mess from the road. I asked my assistant to call me right before the market opened and give me a blow-by-blow.

The market did open sharply lower—7¢ lower, to be exact, but not limit down, to our surprise. The market gave me, and anyone else who was long, a chance to get out and save our skins before a limit-down move. But, instead of trading lower from the 7¢ lower open, my assistant told me corn was beginning to trade up from the open. It felt as if a cloud was lifted, and my nervousness disappeared. I told him to place a stop on our entire position just below the opening price of 270. See Figure 8.37.

Figure 8.37 December 1995 corn

I continually checked in that day, but the stop was never hit. When the market was trading higher for the day, I instinctively knew I was safe. That 270 low registered that day because of the bearish news was a major low that was never challenged again the rest of that year. It actually turned out to be a significant low that held up for years, and it was the springboard for one of the biggest bull moves in history. By the next year, due to crop problems in the United States and globally (China turned from the largest corn exporter in Asia into an importer), corn prices had doubled.

The SNI is a fairly simple, but powerful, concept: *The SNI is the price at which a market is trading just before the release of a significant market news event.* The news is generally a preplanned event; however, it can also be unexpected.

Four rules for trading SNI

Here's how to successfully use the SNI in your trading:

1. If the news is considered bullish, the SNI is your major support number and, if acting properly, the market *should* remain above it. If the market is acting properly after a bullish event, you can enter a long position with a stop just below the SNI.
2. After a bullish news event, a move below the SNI generates an automatic sell signal, and you can immediately enter a short sale with a tight stop just above the SNI.
3. If the news is considered bearish, the SNI is your major resistance number, and the market *should* remain below it if acting properly. If the market is acting properly after a bearish event, you can enter a short position with a stop just above the SNI.
4. After a bearish news event, a move above the SNI generates an automatic buy signal, and you can immediately enter a long position with a tight stop just below the SNI.

In other words, when the SNI is crossed, it tells a trader when to enter and where to place a protective stop. However, it doesn't tell a trader when to exit a profitable position. (Other technical indicators or a trailing stop should be used for that.)

It's important to know what the market is expecting before the release of a news event so that you can accurately judge whether the market is acting properly. For example, if a crop report is to be released and the market is expecting an increase in soybean acreage of 2 million acres, an increase of 1 million is bullish news. You would need to know the average "guesstimate," or expectation, before the release to accurately evaluate the report and the market's reaction to it.

I've instinctively or knowingly used the SNI after every crop report for many years now. I simply evaluate the market's reaction versus expectation.

For example, the October 2006 crop report was considered bullish corn. The market was anticipating a record-large (bearish) corn crop estimate of more than 11 billion bushels on the USDA report; however, the crop size was reduced by 2% and was well under this figure. The market closed the day before the report at 284 (this was the SNI) and opened limit up at 304 the day the report was released. (See Figure 8.38.)

Figure 8.38 December 2006 corn

The market was not able to remain limit up that day and gave ample opportunity to enter a new long position, based on our first rule. The sell stop should have been placed at just under 284, the closing price before the report's release. For the remainder of that year, countless opportunities arose for traders to take a decent profit entering *after* the bullish news was well known to the marketplace. Note this action also created a measuring gap.

In contrast, that same report was considered very bearish for soybeans. The market was looking for an unchanged soybean crop estimate; however, the USDA report indicated that the crop size was more than 3 billion bushels for the first time ever. This was up 3% from the September report and was record large.

The January 2007 soybean futures closed the day before the report's release at 577; however, the market opened higher, at 588, after the "bearish" number. The SNI was therefore 577, and a higher open was an immediate and automatic buy signal according to our fourth rule, with an initial sell stop just below 577. The market continued to climb until the end of November. Even though the number was considered "bearish," the Chinese turned out to be major buyers of soybeans for the remainder of the year, pushing prices much higher (although a trader could not have known that at the time of the report). However, the market certainly knew this, leaving countless 'footprints in the sand'. (See Figure 8.39.) Also note, on the day of the "bearish" report, you'll also see a beautiful breakout from a consolidation. The news didn't matter as much as how the market reacted to this news.

Figure 8.39 January 2007 soybeans

The SNI works not only with crop reports but also with financial reports and other news events, both expected and surprise.

Every Wednesday, the oil inventory report is released at 10:30 A.M. EST. This number typically moves the oil market, sometimes sharply. This is an example of a typical reaction to a bullish supply number: On this report day the first week in June, just before the release of the number, the nearby oil futures were trading at 12230. The market was looking for a slight drawdown in weekly oil stocks, but the actual number was a 5-million-barrel drawdown—bullish. The market immediately traded higher and, within a minute, was trading above 12300. The market exhibited a bullish reaction to the news and was acting properly. (See Figure 8.40.)

After the market moved quickly higher, many traders would have shied away, believing the news was already out and discounted. However, this was an opportunity based on our first rule. The chart looked good, the market was acting correctly, and you could enter a long position with a stop just below the 12230 SNI (the price just prior to the release of the news). After all, if the market is any good it shouldn't be able to trade below the point just before the release of the bullish news. Subsequently, the market ran above 12400, corrected, made a higher low at approximately 12300 (at which time the stop could be raised to just below this higher low), and a trailing stop could have be used. During the following 48 hours, this particular move ran up to 13900—over $13/barrel, or $13,000 per contract, before the first significant correction took place.

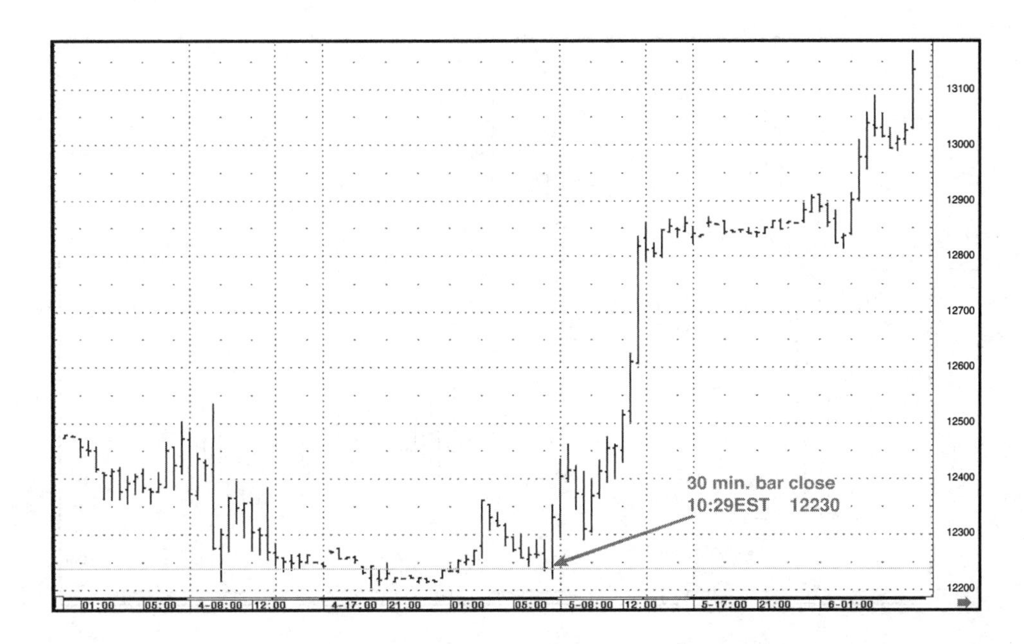

Figure 8.40 June 5 oil

Two weeks later, another "bullish" inventory report was released with a higher-than-anticipated drawdown. Just before the release, the market was trading at 13700. That was the SNI. The market immediately traded higher (in other words, acted properly), up to 13836. However, within an hour after the number was released, the market reversed and quickly moved below the 13700 SNI (see Figure 8.41). Unlike two weeks earlier, it had been able to trade below the point before the release of the bullish news. This is bearish action, according to our second rule. A trader could have gone short on a stop just below this 13700 number and, if filled, place a buy stop just above.

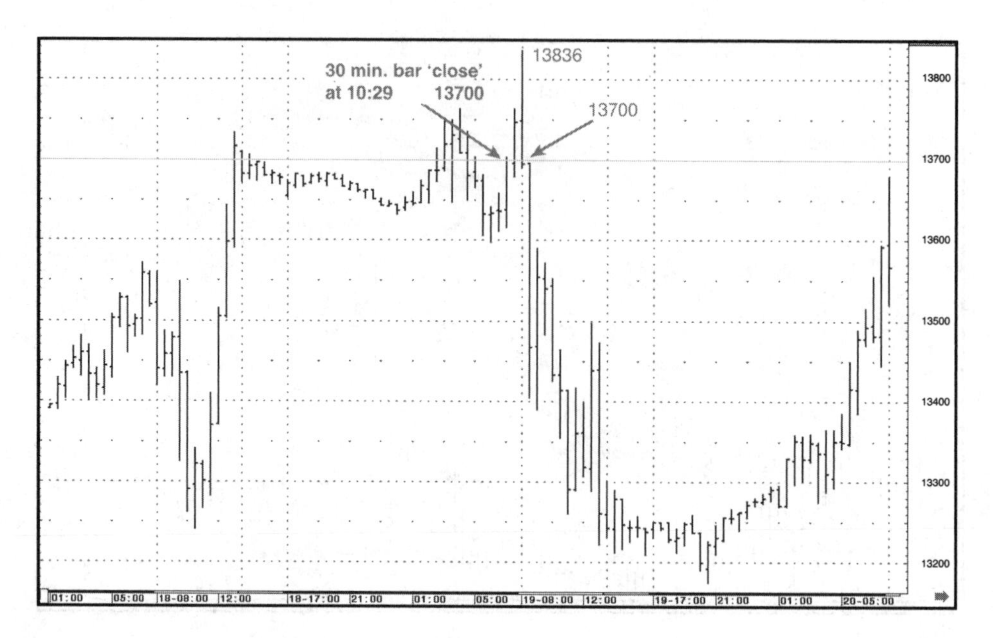

Figure 8.41 June 18 bullish inventory report

Within the following 24 hours, the opportunity arose to make up to $5,000-per-contract profit on the short side, with effectively zero risk after entry. Note that the SNI doesn't tell us when to exit a profitable position. It signals an entry point. You can place your stop close to your entry point, but some alternative method is required to signal your exit. You can utilize a trailing stop. In this example, we saw a reversal bar at the lows with a mini H&S bottoming pattern that signaled the bottom.

The following week, the number was bearish, with a larger-than-expected stock build. Just before the release of the number, the oil market was trading at 13570. (See Figure 8.42.)

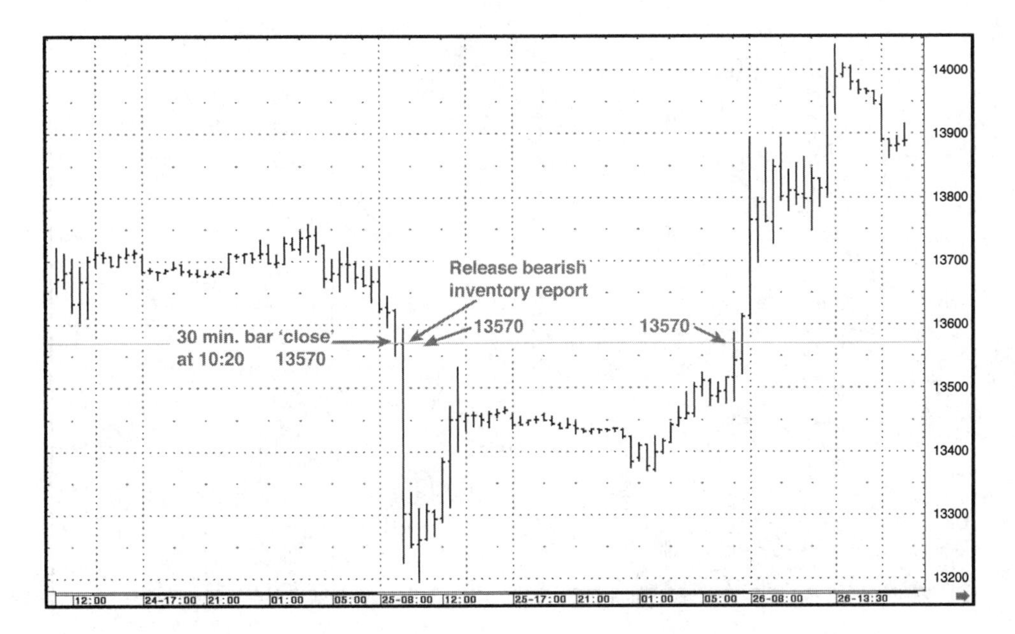

Figure 8.42 June 25 bearish inventory report

After the release of the numbers, the market was initially acting properly (bearishly), and a nimble trader could have gone short by utilizing a trailing stop. The market subsequently bottomed below 13200. But the following day, it was able to trade above the "bearish" number, and this was a bullish sign. Hopefully, if short, a profit was "locked in" via the use of a trailing stop. However, if still short, the minute the market crossed above the 13570 level, all shorts should be immediately covered, and new longs could be entered with a tight stop. The market was now trading above the level of the bearish news, and this is a bullish development according to our fourth rule. Even though this occurred a day later, it was still within a fairly short time period. This is why it's important to note the price level just before the release of significant news (the SNI). SNIs are important numbers and often will act as major support or resistance for days, even weeks into the future.

The SNI works equally well for financial news events. For example, in July 2008, it was anticipated that the European Central Bank would raise interest rates by a quarter-point, but it actually raised rates by a half-point. Just before the announcement, the euro was trading at 15815. Just after the announcement, it acted properly by trading higher, reaching 15853 within an hour. However, that same day, the market crossed below the 15815 level, the price just before the announcement. A sell stop could have been used at just below this number (for example, 15810), based on our second rule. In what turned out to be a zero-risk trade, the market collapsed 200 points, or $2,500 per contract, and never traded much higher. (See Figure 8.43.)

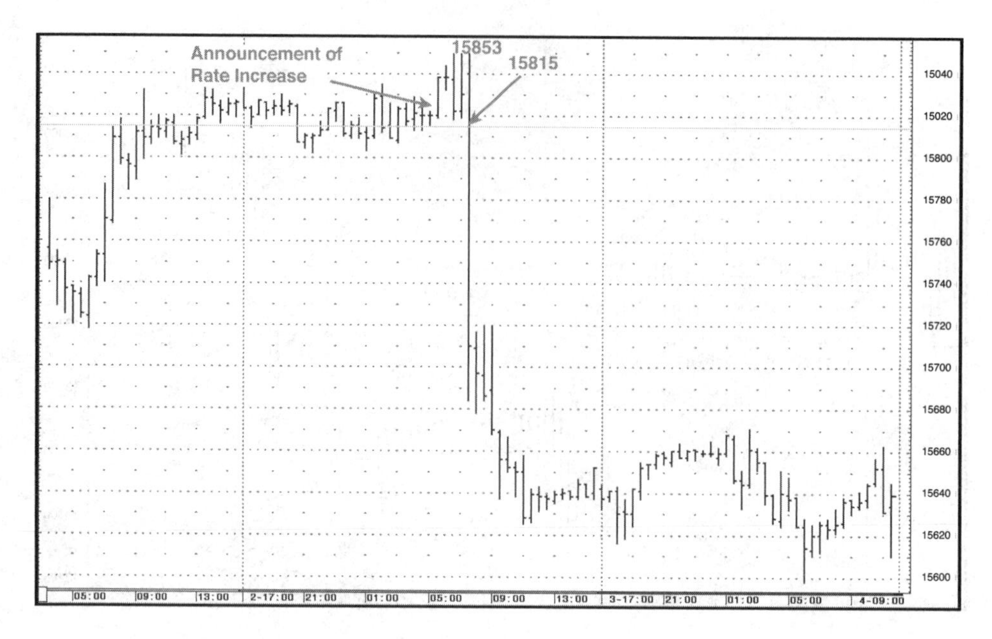

Figure 8.43 July 3, 2008, euro 30-minute chart

I could fill the book with examples similar to these; they occur just about every day. When you know an important report (a crop report, an unemployment report, a Fed announcement, an inventory report, or a stock earnings report) will be released, note where the market is trading just before the release. This level will be your SNI, and you can use it to successfully trade against, usually setting up trading opportunities with high potential reward in relation to the risk. It's all based on the simple premise that is key to successful trading: What matters is not the news but how the market reacts to the news.

Breaking par

"Perfect numbers, like perfect men, are very rare."
—Rene Descartes

In golf, *par* denotes an ideal score for the best golfers, but the generally accepted definition of *par* is merely "average" or "ordinary." Therefore, "above par" has come to mean an above-average or extraordinary event.

In the financial markets, trading "above par"—above the psychologically significant number 100—is considered an important market milestone. If the price of a bond is trading above 100 (for example, at 106), it's trading "above par" and "at a premium." This is a sign of strength. If the same bond falls and subsequently trades down to 94, it would be trading "at a discount" or "under par." Although the number 100 should have no greater significance than any other integer, in the real world, I've discovered that crossing above 100 (the breaking of par) is significant from a trading standpoint. For example, it was a global news event when crude oil first hit $100 per barrel. You can apply this same rule to any big round number, such as 500 or 900; however, those beginning with a 1 and ending in two or more zeros (100, 1,000, and 10,000) are considered the patriarchs.

The loudest cheers ever to ring out from the floor of the New York Stock Exchange resounded on November 14, 1972, when the Dow Jones Industrial Average crossed the 1000 mark for the first time. This was the most important psychological barrier for the Dow to that date. For the previous six years, it had tried and failed to break above "Dow 1000." A few years after 1972, the Dow broke back below 1000 and just kept dropping. During the brutal bear market of 1974, it traded as low as 577. It took eight years for the Dow to cross above 1000 again, but once it was again able to in 1982, it has remained above ever since.

A market breaking above a psychologically significant number creates a trading opportunity. I haven't statistically quantified this, but after making thousands of trades over a wide variety of markets, my experience has been that the market will continue to move higher by another 15% minimum, up to 30%, and, in many cases, by much more. So if a market crosses above 100, odds favor a move to at least 115, and likely 130, before falling back. And to take that to another level, if the price of a stock or commodity crosses above 300, anticipate a move to at least 345 and likely 390.

On April 1, 2004, the price of one share of the Chicago Mercantile Exchange (CME) first crossed 100, closing that session at $100.50 per share. After the first cross of 100, the CME quickly ran to 130 and then 148 before the first meaningful correction. It subsequently has traded as high as 700, and back down to 400, but it never again traded below par until the stock split.

This magical rule of breaking par and continuing upward is one that I've long observed and traded successfully for many years, but it's not my discovery. I first paid attention to this concept after reading *Reminiscences of a Stock Operator*, the semi-autobiographical account of Jesse Livermore written nearly 100 years ago. Livermore writes: "It has been my experience that whenever a stock crosses 100 or 200 or 300 for the first time, it nearly always keeps going up for 30 to 50 points, and after 300 faster than after 100 or 200. It is an old trading principle."

At one point in that book (my absolute top must-read for every trader), Livermore discussed how he waited six weeks without trading for the perfect opportunity to rebuild a trading stake:

> I really began to waver and sweat blood when the stock got up to 90. When it got to 98 I said to myself, "Bethlehem is going through 100, and when it does the roof is going to blow clean off!" I tell you, I saw 100 on the tape when the ticker was only printing 98. So I said to myself, "I can't wait until it gets through 100. I have to get it now. It is as good as gone through par."...I put in an order to buy 500 shares of Bethlehem Steel. The market was then 98. I got 500 shares at 98 to 99. After that she shot right up and closed that night at 115. I bought 500 shares more. The next day Bethlehem Steel was at 145 and I had my stake. But I earned it. Those six weeks of waiting for the right moment were the most strenuous and wearing six weeks I ever put in.

This rule holds equally true for commodities. For example, when sugar first crossed above 1,000 on the monthly chart (10¢ per pound equals 1,000 on the tape) in August 2005, it didn't stop there. It quickly ran above 1100, then above 1200, and then above every *XX*00 until the move was finally over with the February 2006 peak at a price of 1973. (See Figure 8.44.)

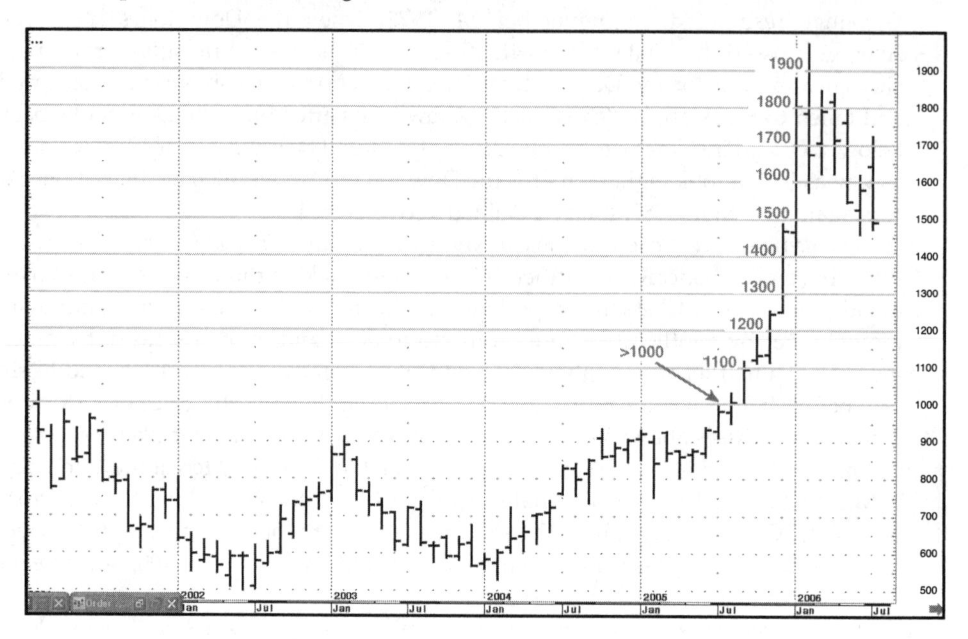

Figure 8.44 2005 monthly sugar

A par case study

In late 2007, the soybean market was in a bull trend. The carryover supplies for 2008 were projected to be very tight, and I was watching the July–November 2008 soybean spread for a possible cross above 100.

July soybeans represent the current crop (the crop that was harvested the previous autumn), and November soybeans represent the "new" crop (the crop that will be harvested the following year). Soybeans are planted in the spring and harvested in the fall. When trading futures, we are certainly dealing with the unknown to an extent, and we knew very little in late 2007 about the November 2008 beans because this contract represented a crop that was not yet planted. Preliminary estimates were available on the acreage farmers would plant in the spring, but these planting intentions would certainly change based on the price of soybeans versus competing crops.

We knew nothing about weather, potential yields, demand, and so on. Anyone buying or shorting November beans was certainly betting on the unknown. We knew more about the "old" July crop because this crop was already harvested. The old crop price had been fluctuating, and would continue to fluctuate, based on demand (for exports, biofuels, livestock feed, and the hundreds of other soy uses) plus differing opinions and future changes in the official supply numbers. July comes near the end of the crop year, and the ultimate price of July soybeans in July is dependent on ending-crop-year supplies being tight or plentiful at this time before the new crop becoming available. This spread historically is volatile because we are dealing with two completely different crop years. Although the overall soybean market might be bullish or bearish, and all the months might move higher or lower together, the different crop years almost always move at different speeds and sometimes in opposite directions.

This was a bullish soybean market, and the old crop (July) had been gaining on the new crop (November) throughout 2007. At one point during the summer, the spread was at "even money" (with the July price equal to the November price), and by Thanksgiving, it was approaching par, or 100. At that time, the July soybeans were trading nearly $1/bushel (100¢ above the November contract). From experience, I believed, as Livermore had taught us, that a break above par would open up a new and potentially profitable trading opportunity. The question was, how to play it? As you read this case study, remember that it is pertinent to all markets, not just the July–November soybean spread. I want to give you a feel for how I approach a potential trade, and this is designed to provide you with a template for analyzing and hopefully successfully trading any market that crosses par.

The first step was background analysis, to find and then analyze what I call analog years of this spread. For example, we can analyze all years the spread broke par while remembering that no two markets act identically.

I knew that this spread had been above par in the past, but not very often. It is a highly unusual event for the July contract to be trading $1 per bushel above the November contract. For the spread to be trading at a $1 difference or higher means something quite unusual is taking place beyond the normal supply-and-demand balance between two consecutive crop years.

Using historical data, I could find only six previous years when the July contract traded at or above 100 more than the following November contract: 1973, 1984, 1989, 1994, 1997, and 2004.

I then examined these analog years to see how the spread acted on a break of 100. For example, look at Figure 8.45, a chart of the July–November 2004 spread.

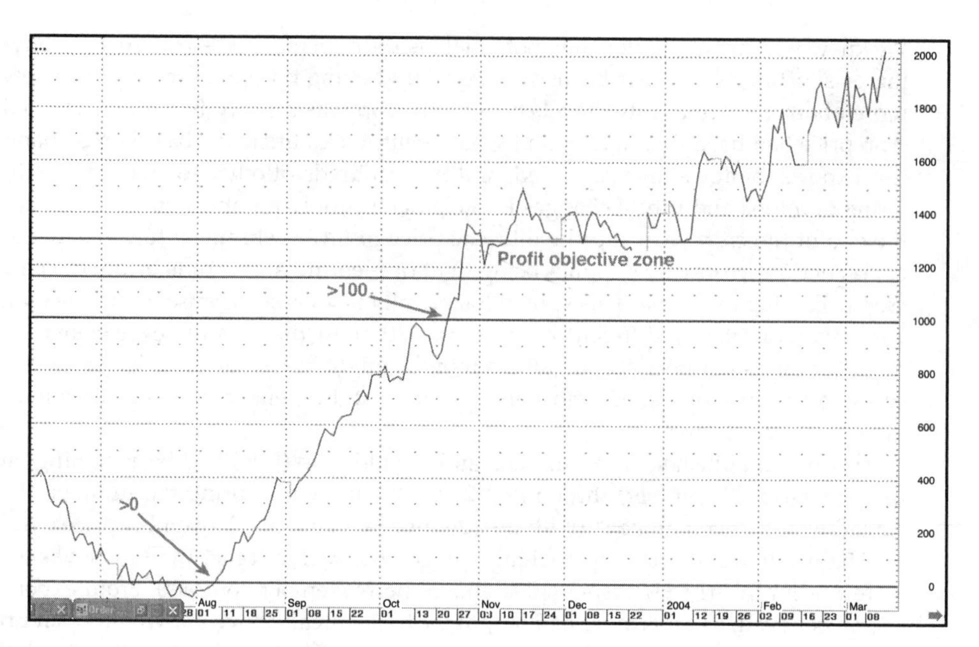

Figure 8.45 July–November 2004 soybean spread

After the spread crossed 100, it never looked back. If you entered the spread on the first cross of 100 (or even on the first close above 100) and risked to a close below, you would never have been in trouble. The minimum profit objective of a 15% to 30% move (or 115 to 130), as outlined in the "profit objective zone," was easily attained. In fact, the spread traded above 200 that year.

After I was armed with this historical knowledge, I was ready to trade the 2007 spread because we knew what to look for when it was trading properly. That year, the spread first broke and closed above 100 on November 29, with the close at a 103 premium for the July contract—a buy signal. However, the next day, it broke and closed under par at 96, indicating that this was a false signal. The proper action at this time was to take the loss of approximately 5¢. (See Figure 8.46.)

The spread remained below par until December 10, when it once again crossed and closed above—a new buy signal. The correct play was to reenter, and this time the profit objective zone was quickly and easily reached and, ultimately, exceeded. However, note that the profit should have been locked in at the first sign of a trend reversal. If it wasn't turned into real cash, the profit eventually evaporated because the spread collapsed after it crossed back under 100 in January. Actually, this theory works both ways. You can play a cross under 100 just as effectively as a cross above: Just reverse the rules and always pay attention to money management.

Livermore's timeless observation that breaking par often results in a quick and significant follow-through is a powerful concept.

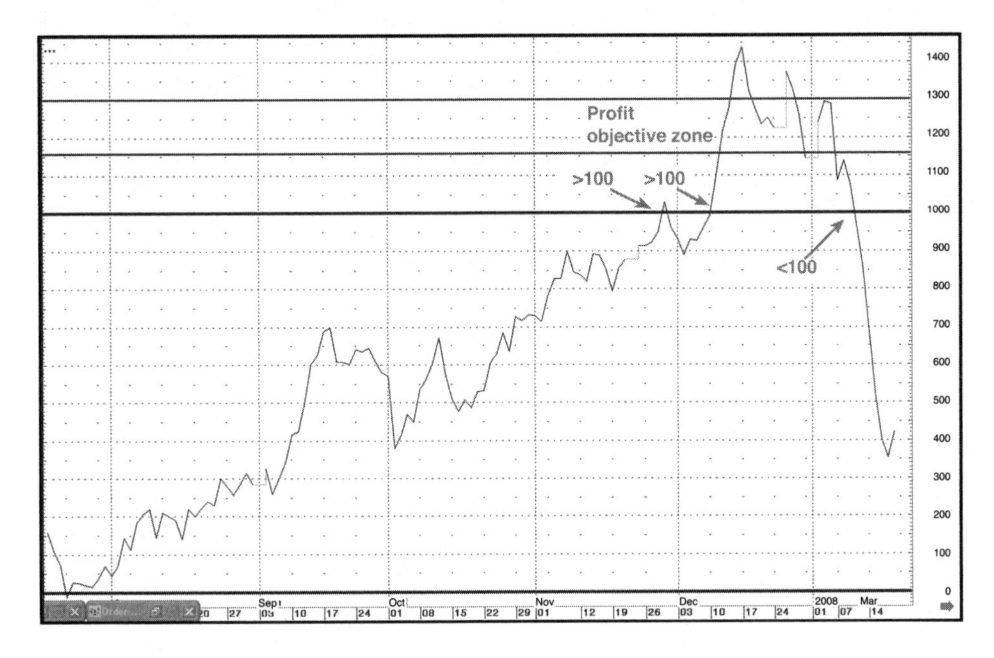

Figure 8.46 July–November 2008 soybean spread

I've given you a lot to work with in this chapter. Check out the patterns and methods and use the ones that suit your personality and risk tolerance. In Chapter 9, you'll get an in-depth look at what I consider one of the most valuable technical tools and a methodology I use daily in my own trading.

9

The Moving Averages Primer

"The future is like a corridor into which we can see only by the light coming from behind."
—Edward Weyer, Jr.

If a holy grail exists for trading, I've not found it. One of the most important lessons I can teach you is this: No single pattern, system, method, or indicator works in all market conditions. The best you can hope for is to find a tool that will place the odds in your favor. If your winning percentage is favorable, and if your average wins are bigger than your average losses, you'll make money. The good news is that excellent technical tools are available that, when used properly, can put the odds in your favor. We discussed many of them in Chapter 8, "The Advanced Trading Course," and I've dedicated this chapter to what I call "the most valuable technical tool" (TMVTT).

As mentioned previously, an old-timer once told me, "If you can correctly identify the trend, you *will* make money." How profound. And it makes sense because if you can correctly identify the trend, the market will likely move your way. Even if your timing is initially off, the trend often will bail you out. One set of technical tools has validity for trend determination, and I have personally found them TMVTT: *moving averages*. I've used them successfully in my own trading in a variety of ways. This chapter discusses the basics: what they are, how they work, and how to use them properly in your own trading.

Bottom pickers versus trend followers

A minority of technical traders are able to pick tops and bottoms with accuracy, and indicators (such as the RSI) and various patterns (such as candlestick "engulfing lines") are designed to help do that. No doubt a trader who can pick tops and bottoms with a degree of success will make the most money; however, I've found that this is very difficult to do. Anyone who trades long enough will be lucky to catch a major top or bottom. I can remember very few trades, over thousands in my career, when I've been lucky enough to catch tops and/or bottoms. I'm not talking about a daily high or low, but a major top or bottom. I'm talking about the contract high or low on the historical charts. Catching one of these is a very lucky and an almost impossible thing to do because in hundreds of trading days every year, there's only one major annual top and only one major annual bottom. Even minor tops and bottoms (daily or weekly highs and lows) are difficult to catch because they're the exception, not the rule.

An old trading adage goes something like this: "Bottom pickers get their hands slapped." As the legendary trader W.D. Gann has taught us, no matter how cheap or how expensive a market might appear, it's never too cheap to sell or too high to buy. As a result, I have found it much easier, and ultimately more profitable, to take a portion out of the middle of a move. This is what moving averages are designed to do. Moving averages are trend-following tools. This means they do not anticipate the market but rather lag it. They are designed to help us determine what the current trend is and when the trend has turned; however, they can tell us these things only after a trend is in place. By definition, this is after the move is already under way. Therefore, it's impossible to pick tops and bottoms using moving averages. However, don't worry about missing the top or the bottom. Too many traders feel that if they haven't picked a top or bottom, it's too late to take a trade. This is one of the primary reasons that the majority of traders never make any money. Gold might have fallen $200 per ounce and already made its low, but after it rallies $30 off the bottom, it doesn't look that cheap to most people anymore. This is because most people have short-term memories, and recent history is the history remembered first. The previous $170 down was a tremendous short sale; anyone looking at a chart could have determined that. Looking back (and hindsight is always 20/20), though, so what if you missed the first $30 of that move? Or what if you were trying to hang on to a long position for the previous $100 down? In that case, I bet you wished you had left that top $30 on the table.

The primary job of a trader is to identify a major trend, and if you can do this with any degree of accuracy, you will make money. So, my advice is not to worry about missing the first part of any move. The next parts can be very profitable, and history has shown that, in most cases, that last part is the most profitable. You should also remember that scores of legendary traders, including Richard Dennis and Paul Tudor Jones, use trend-following techniques, and they have taken hundreds of millions of dollars out of the futures markets.

Moving averages methodologies have been around for more than a century. Richard Donchian is the modern "father of moving averages." Donchian was with the (now-defunct) Shearson in the late 1970s. He developed specific moving averages trading techniques, and for more than 20 years, he successfully managed money using them. They were useful then and are just as useful now. This is because the markets still trend, and as you know already, if you can accurately identify the trend of the market, you will make money.

A moving picture

Any one price is similar to a snapshot in time: It cannot tell us what the trend is. It tells us something, but hardly the whole story. When you take 10 photographs in rapid succession, however, you can get a better picture of the whole story. If the story is the market, you get a better picture of the true trend by looking at the last 10 prices instead of looking at just 1. When you put together a series of 20 blocks of 10 photos each, you have a video that will be infinitely more informative than 1 or 2 photos. This video is analogous to a *moving average line* that you can overlay on a price chart. By observing the direction this line is moving and the strength (or velocity) of the move, you can get a sense of which faction is stronger at the time—the bulls or the bears. *If the bulls are stronger than the bears, the moving average line will appear to move up, and the current price will trade above the moving average and vice versa.* The tough question when using TMVTT is how many prices give the best feel for the trend. If you use too many, the old data can tend to put the true trend out of focus. If you use too few, you cannot really tell what you're looking at.

Remember that when you utilize any trend-following method, you're not trying to forecast when a market move will start or end. Instead, you are using a totally technical approach that relies on a specific type of indicator to tell you what the trend is. Then, by taking a market position in sync with this trend, you attempt to place the odds in your favor. You would also like to have this indicator alert you, with some degree of reliability, when the trend has changed *before* you give back too big a chunk of your paper profits or *before* any unrealized losses become too serious.

Moving averages can indicate when a trend changes. More importantly, they keep you on the "meat" of a major trend, *and this is where the big money is made.* Still, nothing worthwhile is ever easy. In trendless markets, moving averages techniques will generate false signals, and some periods will have strings of smaller losses. Sometimes strings of smaller losses can add up to bigger losses. Be forewarned that drawdown periods will occur, and you must be adequately capitalized to ride them out. Finally, when using moving averages, it is extremely important to never lose your winning qualities of patience and discipline—particularly when the bad strings occur. This is a key to success.

Moving averages come in various sizes. They range from simple, to weighted, to smoothed, to exponential. Traders can use them alone or in combinations as crossovers. They use them in oscillators as moving average convergence and divergence and in bands. The basic underlying assumption is that markets move in a trending fashion more often than they don't. When demand for a particular commodity or a financial asset is stronger than supply, prices (and, therefore, the market) will move in an uptrend. When supply is overwhelming demand at any particular point in time, the market will trend downward.

For example, it's easy for you to tell me the direction of the major trends of the markets in Figure 9.1 and Figure 9.2.

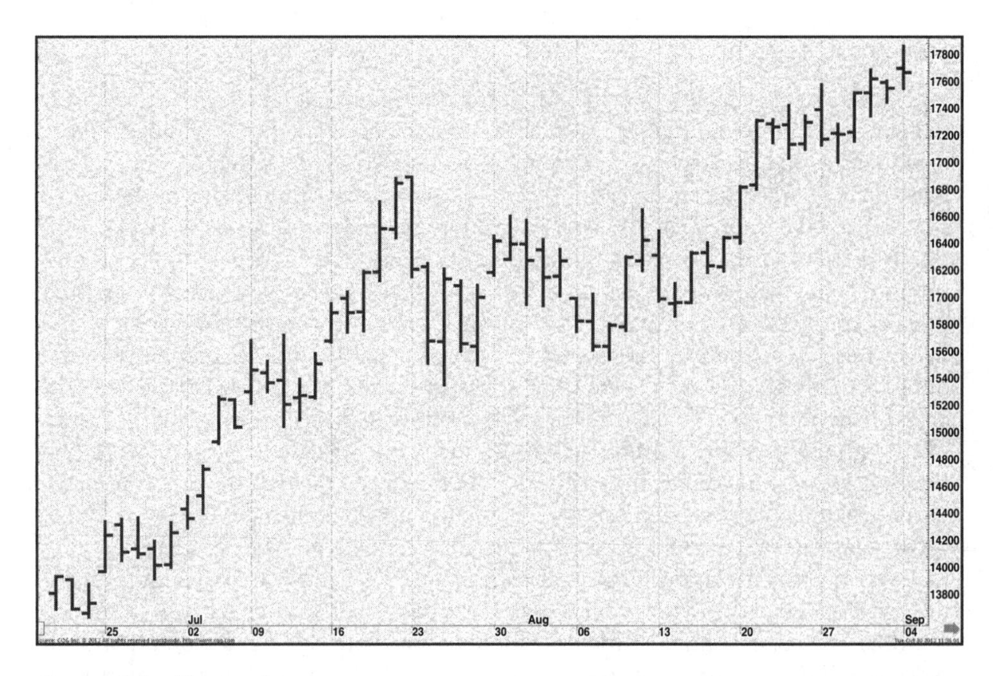

Figure 9.1 Up trend

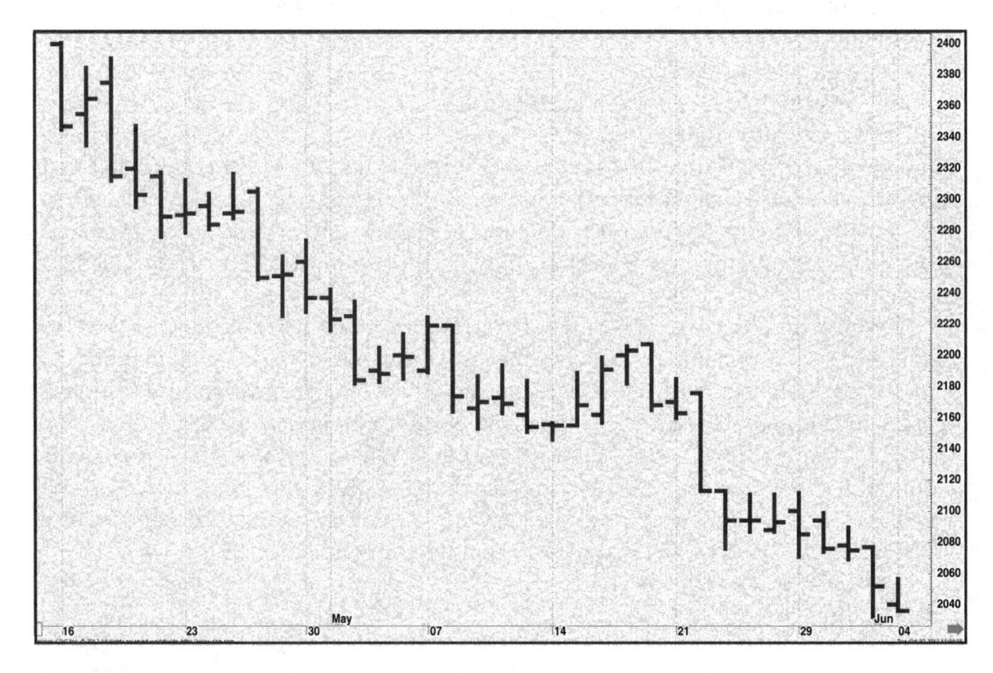

Figure 9.2 Down trend

It's easy to determine trends *after the fact* by looking at a chart. However, it's not easy to determine the trends in the thick of the battle. And the news (the fundamentals) will not help you because the news is often times bullish at the top and bearish at the bottom. Plus, markets do not always trend up or down; they can also move sideways. An erratic up or down period, a trendless market, temporarily wreaks havoc with any trend-following system. You need to use your discipline and patience to persevere in such periods. The good news is that I have found that markets are in up trends or down trends for longer time periods than they are in sideways trends. This is why moving averages methodologies can put the odds in your favor.

The simple moving average

The simplest moving average is simple to construct—and it's called (surprise!) the simple moving average (SMA).

A trader can select any number of days or periods and then use the SMA formula:

$$SMA = (P1 + P2 + P3 + \ldots + PN) / N$$

where P is the price of the commodity being averaged, and N is the number of days (or periods) in the moving average.

The value of an SMA is determined by the values that are being averaged and the time period. For example, a 10-day SMA shows the average price for the past 10 days, a 20-day SMA shows the average price for the past 20 days, and so on. The time period depends on the trader's time horizon—it can be years, months, weeks, days, minutes, or even ticks. You can calculate moving averages based on opens, closes, highs, lows, and even the average of the day's ranges. I recommend using the *close*, or *settlement price*, for each day or interval. On daily charts, it's the most important price of the day since it's the price used to calculate margin calls. If the market closes on the high, or in the high range, most of the short players (unless they shorted right at the high[s]) will have funds transferred *out* of their accounts and placed into the long's accounts. This action makes the shorts a bit weaker and the longs a bit stronger (at least for the next day). The same logic works on shorter-term intervals. Even on a five-minute chart, if a close is on the high of the bar this means that every short during the five-minute interval is on the losing side of that 5 minute price range...at least in the short run.

Let's construct a 5-day SMA of sugar, based on the daily closing prices. Assume that the closes during the past 5 days were 2105, 2110, 2115, 2120, and 2125. The 5-day SMA is 2115. If the market closes at 2155 on the 6th day, it will cause the 5-day SMA to rise to 2125, the average of the past 5 days divided by 5:

$$5SMAday1 = (2105 + 2110 + 2115 + 2120 + 2125) / 5 = 2115$$

$$5SMAday2 = (2110 + 2115 + 2120 + 2125 + 2155) / 5 = 2125$$

In the formula, you always drop the oldest closing price and add the most recent closing price. In this example, when using the 5-day SMA, you always drop the 6th-oldest day. With a 10-day SMA, you drop the 11th-oldest day, and so on. The trend direction is determined by the direction the SMA is moving and by comparing today's settlement price with the moving average. In this simple example, the trend is up because the close on the most recent day—we'll call this day 2 (2155)—is higher than the SMA (2125). On day 1 (the previous day), the close was 2125, and the SMA was 2115, so the trend is up. Even with this limited data, the odds might suggest that we should play from the long side. On day 2, the close was 2155, and the SMA was 2125, so the trend is up, and we stay long. *When the closing price turns down and under the average, a sell signal is generated.*

You can connect each day's value on a chart to produce a line. You can chart this line and overlay it onto a price chart to generate trading signals. A simple trading program would look like this: As long as the line on any particular day is *under* the closing price, the trader would stay long because the SMA has determined that the trend is up. After the line *crosses over* the closing price, the trader would go short because the trend has turned down. If the position is long and the line crosses over the closing price, the trader would reverse the position by selling double the number of contracts owned. The problem with this simple trading program is if you do this every time the line crosses price (especially when using shorter-term averages), you can easily get "whipsawed" (bounced back and forth, with small losses and commissions eating you up). A market can trade in a wild range, moving up and down wildly in the same session, but as I have mentioned before, I believe that the closing price is the most significant.

Incidentally, a physical whipsaw is a saw with a handle at both ends—the kind that was used in the old days by two loggers to cut down trees. Today the best place to find a whipsaw is in an antique shop, but you can picture two guys on either side of a log sawing back and forth. A whipsaw, moving back and forth in alternating motion will help cut a log, but it relentlessly consumes capital when trading.

As a simple rule when trading using daily SMAs, I recommend ignoring intraday movements (which often merely create "noise") and waiting for the *close* to penetrate the SMA to generate a signal. In some markets, it is better to wait for a "two-day close" (two consecutive days of penetrating the moving average at the close) to signal a change in trend and a change in position. However, a problem of waiting for the close is that you take on additional risk since in wide-ranging day, the price at the close could be far above or below the moving average. For example, if you waited for the S&P close on Black Monday 1987 (the day the Dow closed 500 points lower than Black Friday), you were in deep water. This is why good money-management sense says to additionally use an ultimate "down-and-out point" for any position—a physical stop loss. You should do this when using any technical system (or fundamental system, for that matter). Place your stop to create an approximate maximum percentage loss for those abnormal moves. Abnormal moves, although rare, do occur, and you want to *always* avoid that catastrophic loss—the one so big that it renders you unable to continue trading. Option strategies can also help here at times. You can use puts to protect long positions and calls to protect short positions. However, most markets are normal. In normal markets, a general rule of thumb for our first simple trading system is this: On the close, if the market price has fallen *below* the moving average line, a sell signal is generated. On the close, if the market price has risen *above* the moving average line, a buy signal is generated. I've found that most days, when a market closes at an extreme of a day's price range (which often creates the signal), it will follow through in the direction of the close the following day. Sometimes, the violation of the moving average could be a close call. On those days, I would opt to wait one more day instead of risking a false signal. However, you need to know on a daily basis exactly where the average you are following will be coming into the close and use a "stop close only" order to enter a new position or exit an existing one. Alternatively, you can place a market order just before the close.

How many days should you use in your moving average?

The length of the moving average greatly impacts trading activity and, therefore, profitability. Some traders use 5-day moving averages, some 10-day, others use 20-day; I've seen funds use 50- or 100-day, and so on. The length is your decision, depending on the type of trader you are, but length directly determines the sensitivity of any moving average. The length determines how much time a moving average has to respond to a change in price. It is a matter of "lag time." This is a simple but important concept: Shorter moving averages are more sensitive than longer moving averages. A 5-day moving average is more sensitive than a 10-day moving average, and both are more sensitive than a 20-day moving average. The more sensitive a moving average is, the smaller the loss will be on a reversal signal; however, there will be a higher likelihood of a whipsaw (a false reversal signal causing a trader to reverse a trade too soon). A false signal occurs when a minor movement, which ultimately does not change the major trend, is enough to push the moving average in the opposite direction of the settlement price, resulting in a false position change. It is false simply because the trader will subsequently need to reverse once again when the major trend reasserts itself.

It's important to use a moving average that is long enough so that it is not overly sensitive. However, if the moving average is too long, the trader will tend to take too big a loss (or give up too big a portion of unrealized paper profits) before even being aware of a trend change. A longer moving average will keep you in a trade longer, thereby maximizing paper profits, but it can eat into realized profits because it moves too slowly. Like the porridge in the story of the three bears, the moving average cannot be too hot or too cold; it needs to be "just right." The most popular question I'm asked has to do with what is the "right" moving average to use. "Just right" is not always easy to determine and will change with market conditions. Voluminous studies have been done to determine which length is right for which specific market, but I believe that these are useless because market conditions change for all markets. The silver market of the Hunt era is not the same as the silver market of today. Soybeans in a drought market act far differently than in a normal-weather market.

Alternatives to the SMA

You can think of any one price as a snapshot in time. It tells you something about price, but it hardly tells the whole story. Ten photos in rapid succession provide you with a better picture of the story, and 20 blocks of 10 photos each paints an even better picture. If you are looking at a movie composed of 200 snapshots, the last 20 will most likely tell you more about what's probably coming next than the first 20. This is akin to exponential and weighted moving averages. They place more weight on the newest prices, and this can be more valid than the older prices when determining the trend.

Exponential and weighted moving averages

The exponential moving average (EMA) and weighted moving average (WMA) assign a greater weight to more recent events than to events further in the past. The WMA increases the importance of the most recent price by a factor equal to the period used. For example, with a 5-day weighted average, the fifth day is given a factor five times greater than the first. To calculate a 5-day weighted average, multiply day 5 (the most current day) by 5, day 4 by 4, day 3 by 3, day 2 by 2, and the first, or oldest, day by 1, and then divide by 15. The EMA also weights recent events more than distant events, but it smooths out the average for a more consistent result. The smoothing factor (SF) is determined by dividing 2 into the moving average plus 1 of the SMA you want to weight and smooth. For example, if you want to smooth a 5-day SMA, you divide 2 by 6. The result, .33, is the smoothing factor. For a 10-day SMA, the SF is 2 divided by 11 = .18. For a 20-day SMA, the SF is 2 divided by 21 = .096. The SF is a fixed weight applied to the current price, with the balance applied to the most recent moving average value itself. The computer will figure it all for you, but to make it clearer, let's look at a specific example. Let's calculate a 5-day SMA and a 5-day EMA for wheat. Remember, we need at least 5 days of data to produce our starting point for the SMA. Suppose that the closing (settlement) prices for 11 consecutive days of wheat prices are as follows:

Day	Price
1	440
2	446
3	461
4	446
5	463
6	458
7	472
8	470
9	464
10	476
11	481

In hindsight, we can easily see from this data that because the market went up by 41, the trend was up during this 11-day period. However, hindsight is always 20/20, and it's not always easy to know just what the trend actually is while we're in the thick of the battle. This is where moving averages can help.

The SMA is calculated as follows:

Day	Price	Calculation	SMA
1	440		
2	446		
3	461		
4	446		
5	463	(440 + 446 + 461 + 446 + 463) / 5	451.2
6	458	(446 + 461 + 446 + 463 + 458) / 5	454.8
7	472	(461 + 446 + 463 + 458 + 472) / 5	460
8	470	(446 + 463 + 458 + 472 + 470) / 5	461.8
9	464	(463 + 458 + 472 + 470 + 464) / 5	465.4
10	476	(458 + 472 + 470 + 464 + 476) / 5	468
11	481	(472 + 470 + 464 + 476 + 481) / 5	472.6

If you used the 5-day SMA to generate buy or sell signals, starting on day 5, you would have been a buyer at the closing price of 463 (because the price was *above* the SMA). You would have remained long on days 6, 7, and 8. But on day 9, the price fell below the SMA, and you would have sold and reversed (gone short) at the closing price of 464. The result would have produced a marginal trade. Now, you're short at 464 and would have to reverse again on day 10 at 476, for a 12¢ loss. This is a classic whipsaw. You got jerked out of what was a good trade in a definite up trend when one low-ball price (the oldest) is dropped out of the equation.

Now, let's look at how the 5-day EMA performed during the same time period. To calculate the smoothing factor for the 5-day EMA, you divide 2 by 6. Six is used because it is 1 more than 5. 2 / 6 = .33. You multiply this smoothing factor of .33 by today's price and add this to 1 minus the smoothing factor, which is .67, times the EMA:

Day	Price	Calculation	EMA
1	440	Start	440
2	446	[(.33×446) + (.67×440)]	441.98
3	461	[(.33×461) + (.67×441.98)]	448.26
4	449	[(.33×449) + (.67×448.26)]	448.5
5	463	[(.33×463) + (.67×448.5)]	453.29
6	458	[(.33×458) + (.67×453.29)]	454.84
7	472	[(.33×472) + (.67×454.84)]	460.5
8	470	[(.33×470) + (.67×460.5)]	463.64
9	464	[(.33×464) + (.67×463.64)]	463.76
10	476	[(.33×476) + (.67×463.76)]	467.8
11	481	[(.33×481) + (.67×467.8)]	472.15

The results show that the price remained above the EMA during the entire period, even day 9. *Therefore, there's no whipsaw.* The trader would remain long from 446 and still be long on day 11, at 481. Yes, you can still get whipsawed using the EMA in a choppy market, but I've found that many times, WMAs and EMAs are superior moving averages, with fewer whipsaws.

Many traders are using moving averages systems with a percentage band (such as the Bollinger bands) that uses an exponentially smoothed moving average plus a band above this EMA and minus a band below the EMA by the same percentage. A signal occurs whenever the closing price breaks outside the band. Exit occurs when the price recrosses into the band. Some traders prefer to trade within the bands, which is more like top and bottom picking. They sell at the top band and buy at the bottom. The risk point is set at some percentage outside the band. I believe this method has some validity, but because I personally find it difficult to pick tops and bottoms (I'm a trend follower), I leave this to those who are inclined to attempt top and bottom picking.

Also, although it's nice to understand how the moving average is derived, don't stress about the calculations. Almost all the trading software programs on the market today automatically calculate the SMA, WMA, and EMA. If you have access to real-time quotes, the software calculates these averages in real time, based on the last tick, the last bar, the average of a bar, or the close of a bar.

Moving averages are not a panacea, but if used systematically and consistently, they will keep a trader on the right side of the big moves. They are a totally technical approach (because they rely on price only), and it doesn't matter which market you use them on. They work well in bull and bear markets and in both the stock and commodity markets; however, they'll whipsaw a trader in a sideways or trendless market. However, this isn't as big of a disadvantage as it might appear at first because my experience has shown that markets will spend more time in trending modes than in trendless modes. Still, at times, periods with choppy, whipsaw-type markets have lasted many weeks. Sometimes, a seasoned trader can sense that a market is trendless (the time to step to the sidelines), but not always. And if not properly capitalized or disciplined during these periods, a trader can be wiped out or, at the very least, become demoralized and abandon a moving average program. Usually the trader will quit just before the big move starts. Remember that you need to catch the big moves when using a moving average system, or you won't win.

Natural numbers

In my book *The New Commodity Trading Guide: Breakthrough Strategies for Capturing Market Profits*, I introduce a trading methodology that uses moving averages—my "natural number method"—that I continue to use with success. Basically, by using a longer-term moving average (in the case of the natural number method, a 180-period weighted moving average) superimposed on a shorter-term chart (generally 15 to 30 minutes), I see the odds of being on the right side of the prevailing trend increasing. As mentioned before, if we bought every time a market traded above a moving average and sold every time it traded back below, we would be in and out of the market too often during choppy periods, leading to whipsaw activity. So, I started to wonder whether natural numbers could take some of the randomness out of the process.

Natural numbers are round numbers. When you round a number, you "bump it up" or "bump it down" to a nearby cleaner number. My definition of a "master natural number" is a number that ends in two or more zeros. The classic master natural number is par (Livermore's favorite), or 100, with other master natural numbers being 200, 300, and so forth. However, any number that ends in one or more zeros—meaning a multiple of 10—is what I term a *natural number.*

Humans generally view natural numbers as significant. If your car odometer is rolling over to 10,000 or 100,000, don't you want to see it happen? If you have kids in the car and the odometer hits 49,999, you'll probably make an announcement to your passengers so that they can see the rollover to 50,000, right? Businesses and individuals go to extra effort to get a phone number such as 555-7000 or a post office box like 3000 because round numbers are typically easy to remember. Recall how people around the globe celebrated the new millennium at the beginning of the year 2000? Even though the event wouldn't really occur until the end of that year (the beginning of 2001), the rollover to 2000 was a really big deal; I don't remember New Year's 2001 as having the same pizzazz.

In the universe of numbers, natural numbers are rarer than their common siblings and therefore hold a special significance for people. People make markets, and any student of the markets has probably observed that volumes generally increase at natural numbers. A number of years ago, I hypothesized that natural numbers would act as significant support or resistance points. After extensive testing, I determined that natural numbers possessed statistically greater odds of being important support and resistance levels than random numbers. I then used that information to develop the trading methodology that I outlined in another book. (For a full explanation of my natural number method, see *The New Commodity Trading Guide.*) The point I want to make here is that moving averages remain, in my opinion, TMVTT, and using them in conjunction with natural numbers is one means of averting a significant percentage of whipsaws, and this leads to a smoother profit curve.

In Chapter 10, "GK's Pivot Indicator," I introduce a simpler technical trading methodology I personally use—one I've not disclosed previously—and that you might also wish to consider.

10

GK's Pivot Indicator

"I have the 'thing' worked out—the trick or the surprise; the *pivotal* fact. Then I just start somewhere and let the story work itself out."
—Lee Child, Author, *Jack Reacher*

When it comes to making money trading commodities, there's no holy grail—no single methodology that's correct. There are numerous paths to profitability, and plenty more lead to loss. You'll need to identify a method that fits your personality. You might feel more comfortable using a longer-term time horizon, but this path has higher risks with the higher rewards. You might be short-term oriented and consider day trading with zero "overnight" risk but lower average rewards. What I present in this chapter is a fairly simple *setup* and *trigger* that I believe will enhance your trading performance. It's not the total answer (reread the risk disclaimer in the beginning of this book since it applies), and this method requires monitoring and active management. It can be utilized for longer and/or shorter term horizons. I use it, and perhaps it could help you too.

I call this my "pivot indicator," and if you have an interest in using it in your trading, I suggest that you first "paper trade" it. Review various market scenarios and hypothetically test it on various charts until you're totally comfortable with how it works—the good, the bad, and the ugly. Personally, I use it in conjunction with other indicators, such as volume, my natural number method, and chart patterns.

As mentioned previously, my primary goal is to determine the trends of the markets I trade. I believe if you are able to accurately determine the trend of any market, then you will, over time, make money. Just as it's easier to paddle downstream than up, and it takes less effort to walk with the wind than into it, it's generally more profitable to trade with a trend than against it. The best tool I've found for determining a trend with a degree of accuracy is the moving average. My pivot indicator uses a simple moving average with a buffer and a trigger. It gives you an entry point into a trade and a risk point. It does *not* provide you with a profit objective; that is the primary component you'll need to determine. However, if a trade is working, where to take the profit is the kind of problem you want to have.

I sourced all the charts in this chapter using real market data on a CQG, Inc., platform; all rights reserved worldwide.

Generating the buy signal

The process of generating the buy signal begins with calculating the 10-day simple moving average (SMA). The SMA is calculated based on the settlement (closing price). Calculate it and then draw it on a daily chart.

Why the 10-day SMA? It's a dynamic number I've found useful over a diversified portfolio of uncorrelated markets. Other similar periods will work just as well, but for this methodology, a very short term (such as 5 day) is too sensitive, and a longer term (50 day or greater) lags too much. So, here I use the 10-day SMA for the purpose of setting up trades in the direction of the major trend.

Entering a new pivot trade from the long side requires three steps:

1. Setup bar
2. Buffered entry price
3. Triggered entry

1. Setup bar

Watch the daily bar chart for a day the market *closes above* the 10-day SMA. If the market *closes* above the average, that day's market activity creates the *setup bar*.

A day that the market merely *trades* above the 10-day SMA *does not* qualify as a setup bar day because the market could subsequently trade back under the 10-day SMA line that day prior to the bar's close. A true setup is created only on a daily *close* above the line.

2. Buffered entry price

Once we've determined our setup bar, the next step is to calculate our market entry price. Our entry for a buy will be triggered by a subsequent market move above the *high* of the setup bar. In other words, entry will take place only on a "momentum move" (that is, the market has to subsequently trade above the high of the setup day). My experience is that *buffering* the entry price works better than just entering on a very small move above the high of the setup bar. In other words, entry does not take place on a move of just a tick or two above the high price since this increases the odds for a false signal.

To determine the *buffered* entry price, you take the high price of the setup bar, multiply it by .05%, and add that to the high price. The resulting number is the *buffered order entry price.*

3. Triggered entry

If the buffered entry price is hit (via the 'buy stop' we entered above the market at the buffered order entry price), you are now into the market on the long side at your triggered entry price. The next step is to immediately place your risk point, or sell stop. Your initial stop is a tick (or two) under the low of the previous day. At the market's close on your entry day, the stop can be adjusted (raised) to just a tick (or two) under the low of the entry day.

For example, in the soybean chart shown in Figure 10.1, the high of the setup bar day was \$14.52. $\$14.52 \times .05 = 7.26$¢. $1452 + 7.26 = 1459.26$. Since the soybean contract has a minimum tick size of a quarter penny, the closest buffered order entry price is \$14.59 and a 1/4 (or 14592). Note that the market remained above the 10-day SMA, with the buffered order entry price hit the third day after the setup bar day. (If the market had subsequently closed under the 10-day SMA *without* triggering the buffered order entry, this potential buy signal setup would have been negated. Actually, in the case of a close under the 10-day SMA, a new setup bar with a potential sell signal would be set up.) However, the buy *was* triggered. So to determine the risk point, note that the previous day's low was \$14.31; therefore, the sell stop would initially be placed just under that price by a tick or two, at \$14.30 1/2 (or 14304). In this example, the low of the entry day was \$14.35, so after the close, the stop could have been adjusted upward by about 4¢. Note that the market continued to move up to \$16.80 after the buy signal, for a potential \$2.21 profit—or over \$11,000 profit potential per contract traded. (Each penny move in a 5,000-bushel soybeans contract is equivalent to a \$50 profit or loss per 1¢ move.) While the odds of any one trader picking the top is slim to nonexistent, you can see that in this trade there was an excellent opportunity to realize a profit point along the way without taking undue risk. (Later in this discussion, we'll review various methods to determine a profitable exit point.)

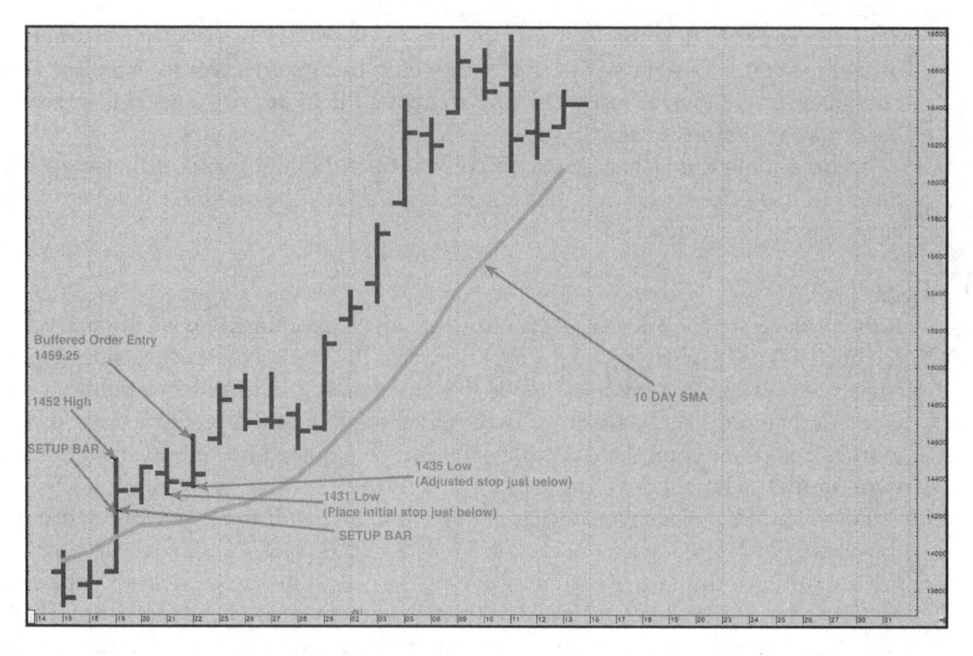

Figure 10.1 Pivotal buy signal

Generating the sell signal

The process of generating the sell signal begins the same way as generating the buy signal—by calculating the 10-day SMA. The SMA is calculated based on the settlement (closing price). When determined, draw it on a daily chart.

Entering a new pivot trade from the short side requires three steps:

1. Setup bar
2. Buffered entry price
3. Triggered entry

1. Setup bar

Watch the daily bar chart for a day the market *closes below* the 10-day SMA. If the market *closes* below the average, that day's market activity creates the *setup bar*. Note a day that the market merely *trades* below the 10-day SMA *does not* qualify as a setup bar day because the market could subsequently trade back above the 10-day SMA line that day prior to the bar's close. A true setup bar is created only on a daily *close* below the line.

2. Buffered entry price

Once you've determined your setup bar, the next step is to calculate your market entry price. Your entry for a sale will be triggered by a subsequent market move below the *low* of the setup bar. In other words, entry will take place only on a "momentum move" (that is, the market has to subsequently trade below the low of the setup day). My experience is that *buffering* the entry price works better than just entering on a small move below the low of the setup bar. In other words, entry does not take place on a move of just a tick or two below the low price since this increases the odds for a false signal.

To determine the *buffered* entry price, you take the low price of the setup bar, multiply by .05%, and subtract from the low price. This number is your *buffered order entry price*.

3. Triggered entry

If your buffered entry price is hit (via the "sell stop" we entered below the market at the buffered order entry price), you are now into the market on the short side at your triggered entry price. The next step is to immediately place your risk point, our buy stop. Your initial stop is a tick or two above the high of the previous day. At the market's close on your entry day, the stop can be adjusted (lowered) to just a tick or two above the high of the entry day.

For example, in the coffee market chart shown in Figure 10.2, the low price of the setup bar day was \$1.35/pound. \$1.35 × .05 = .0675¢. In market terms, 13500 – 68 = 13432. Since the coffee contract has a minimum tick size of a .05, your closest buffered order entry price is (in market terms) 13430 (or \$1.3430/pound). Note that in this example, the buffered order entry price was hit the day immediately following the setup bar day. (If the market had subsequently closed above the 10-day SMA *without* triggering the buffered order entry, this sell signal setup would have been negated. Actually, in the case of a close above the 10-day SMA, a new setup bar with a potential buy signal would be set up.) However, the sell was triggered. So, to determine the risk point, note that the previous day's high was 13940; therefore, your stop would initially be placed just above that price by a tick or two, at 13950. In this example, the high of the entry day was 13685, so *after* the close, the stop could have been adjusted downward by about 2.5¢ (or 250 points). Note that the market continued to move lower, to just under \$1.20/pound (12000), for a potential profit of 14¢, or over \$5,000 potential per contract traded (because each penny move (a 100 point move) in a 37,500-pound coffee contract is equivalent to a \$375 profit or loss). While the odds of any one trader picking the bottom is slim to nonexistent, you can see that there was the potential to pick up a nice profit somewhere along the way without taking undue risk.

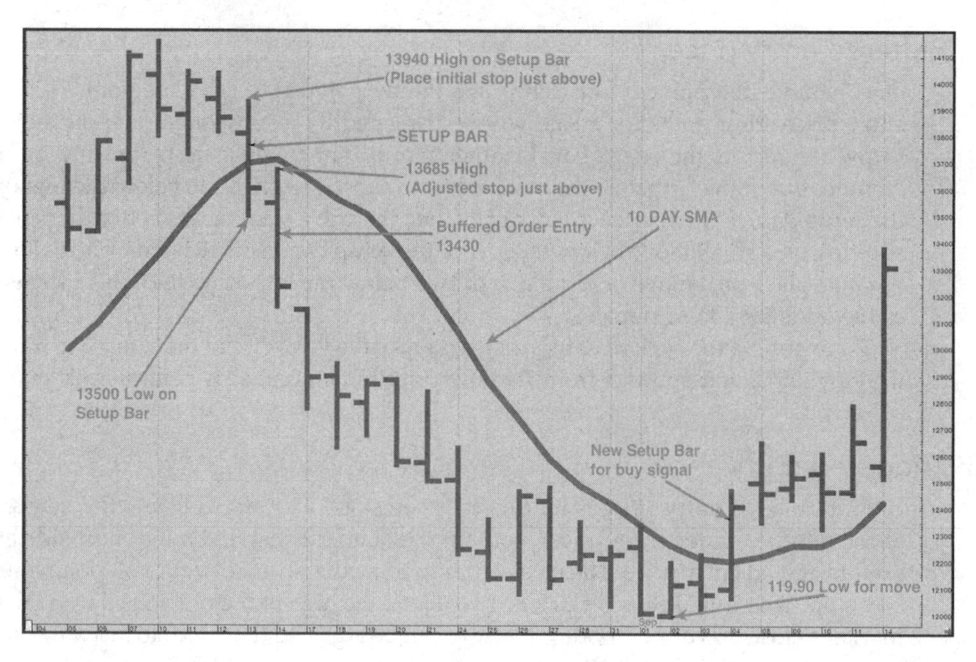

Figure 10.2 Pivotal sell signal

The pivot indicator method in practice

My experience using the pivot indicator process is that it works in aggregate, regardless of market or time frame. It certainly does not work on every signal, but it has built-in risk control. The risk per trade is limited to just above the high or below the low of the previous day, so you can determine the potential risk to a fairly close degree. The beauty is that during a major move, the profits are allowed to run. I could show you "cherry-picked" moves that ran long and hard, with awesome profit potential. However, let's look at what I would consider a typical period by looking at a six-month period for a soybean contract I picked at random (see Figure 10.3).

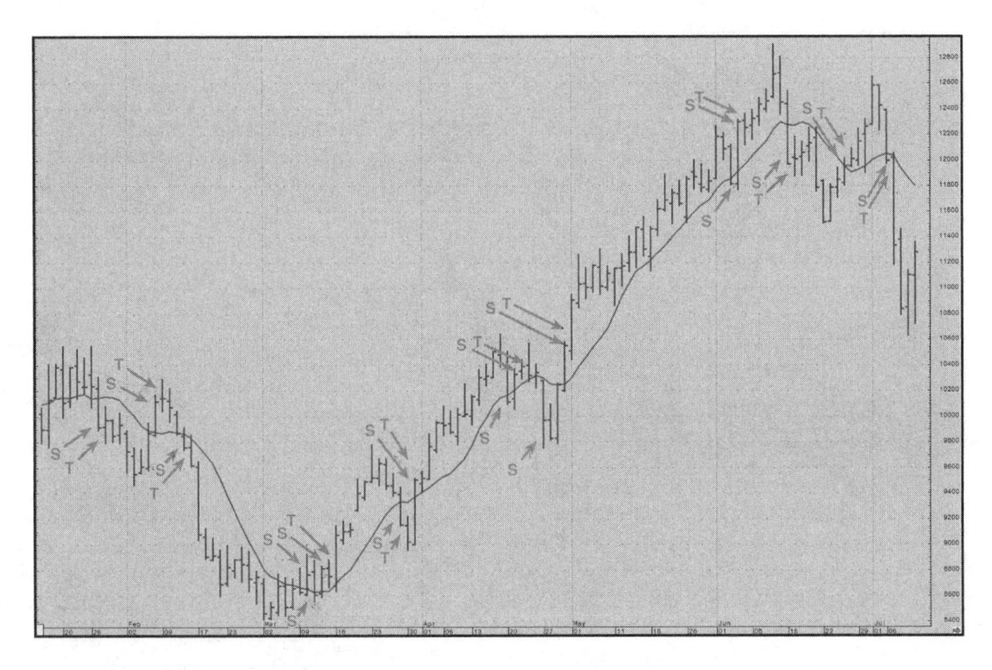

Figure 10.3 Typical signals

In Figure 10.3, the setups are indicated with an *S*, and if the buffered entry price was triggered for a buy or sell signal, this is indicated with a *T*. During this fairly typical six-month period, note that there are 17 setups but only 12 triggered entries. There are two reasons a setup does not lead to an entry. The first is that the market just grazed the setup high or low and the buffer kept you out of trouble. The other is that there is no follow-through after a setup and therefore no signal. If you magnify a typical signal, it will look as shown in Figure 10.4. In fact, a setup that is not triggered would lead to what I call a "reverse pivot."

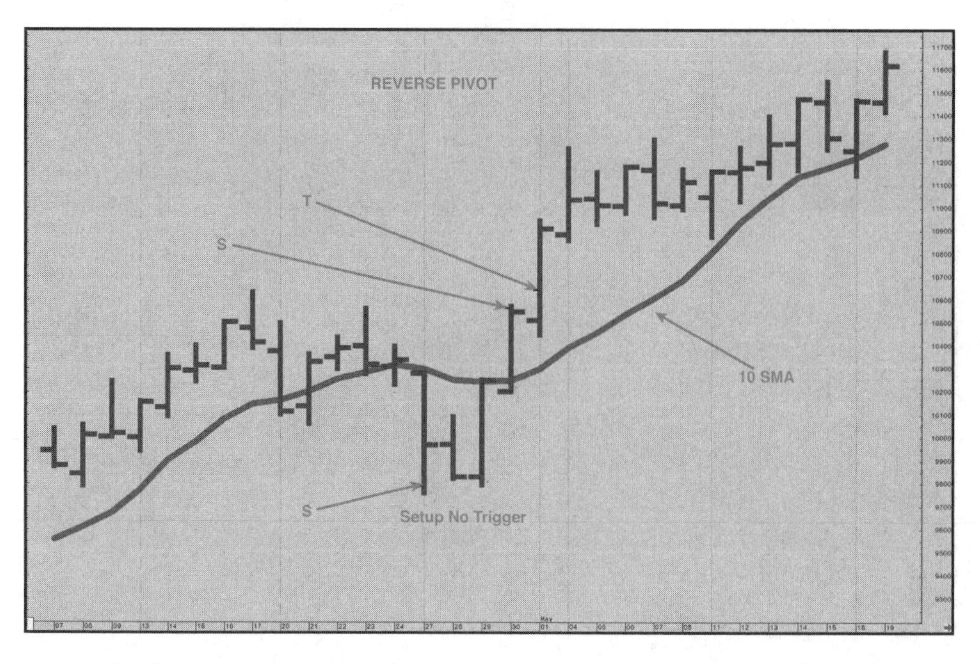

Figure 10.4 A reverse pivot

A reverse pivot occurs when a setup that is not triggered leads to a confirmed signal in the opposite trend direction. My experience has been that reverse pivots more often than not lead to powerful signals with above-average reward-to-risk ratios.

Look back at Figure 10.3. Of the 12 signals, there are 7 buy signals and 5 sell signals. Since we can see, in retrospect, that the market was in an up trend for a greater percentage of the time, this is what we would have expected. Of the 12 signals, 5 were false, most likely leading to the stop loss being hit. The average risk was approximately 20¢ ($1,000 for a soybean contract). The potential profit on the 7 profitable signals averaged $1.05 ($5,025 for a soybean contract). The potential reward to risk was about 5 to 1. In practice, it is impossible to pick tops and/or bottoms, and therefore it is fairly impossible to reap the maximum potential profit. However, you can see that the pivot indicator method can generate signals that provide you with that potential. Recall that if you are correct on a trend, you should make money. If your major problem is the timing of when to cash in on a profitable trade, that is the kind of problem you want to have, is it not?

So, when the pivot indicator method has identified a profitable trade, there are some methods you can employ to determine when to take a profit. The key lies in letting the market tell you the best time to exit. Let me share with you a couple of techniques I've found useful. The first involves using the concepts presented in Chapter 8, "The Advanced Trading Course," specifically using time-tested chart patterns. For example, the bottom in Figure 10.5 was formed with a head-and-shoulders (H&S) bottom. The pivot indicator method for this signal triggered a buy just above the neckline. You certainly could use the H&S measuring rule to determine a minimum profit objective and then either accept the profit or use a tight trailing stop to assure some profit and maximize the signal.

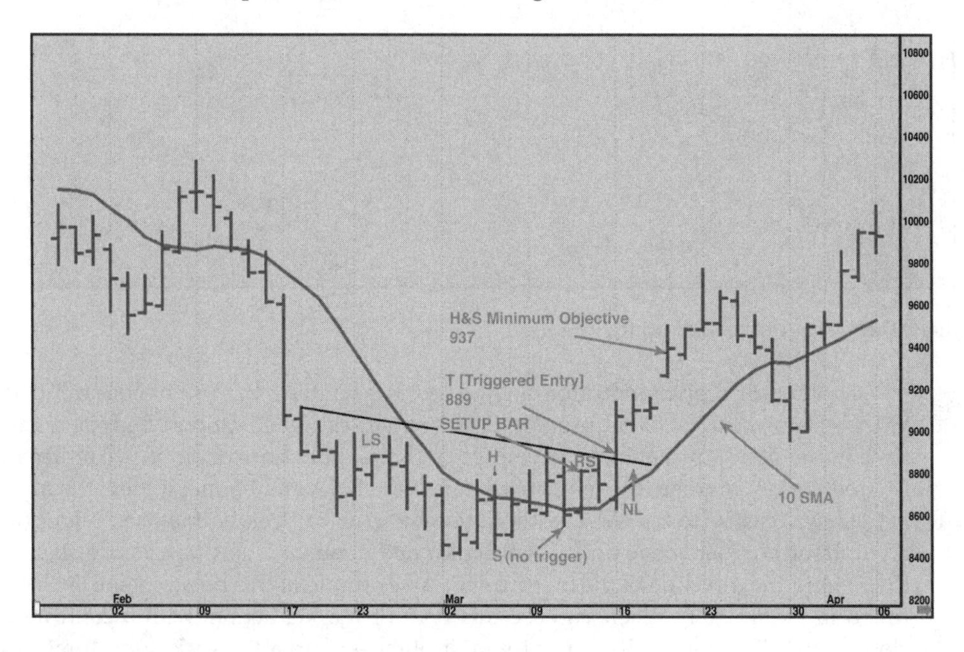

Figure 10.5 Profit objective using chart patterns

Another method I've found useful is to fully utilize what I refer to in Chapter 9, "The Moving Averages Primer," as "the most valuable technical tool" (TMVTT): moving averages. To do this, you simply wait for a close under the 10-day SMA (technically a setup bar in the reverse direction) to exit. This would keep you on the meat of the up trend during one of the profitable signals from the soybean chart in Figure 10.3, for a gross profit of $5,850 per contract, as indicated in Figure 10.6.

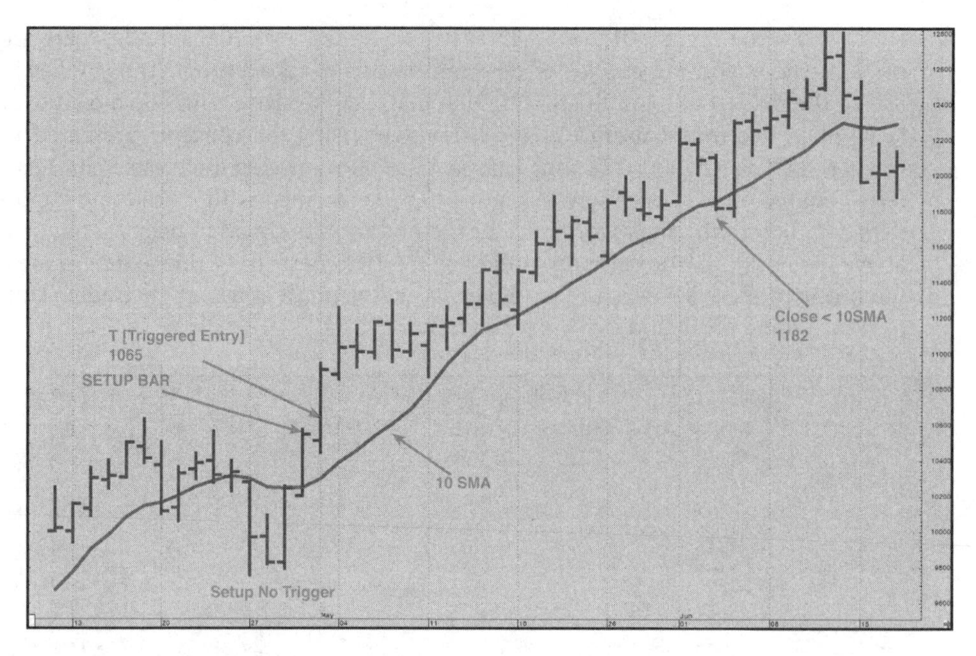

Figure 10.6 Profit objective using SMA

Another useful pivot indicator method tool is one I term the "pivot bounce." The SMA is a powerful tool that provides a strong indication of support and/or resistance in the marketplace. In reviewing your charts, note how often, in a confirmed up trend or down trend, the market will touch the SMA and bounce. Often, the market will trade close to the SMA, without touching, or will gently trade just under (in an up trend) or just above (in a down trend) and "bounce," closing above or below the SMA in the direction of the major trend. An example of this phenomenon is illustrated in Figure 10.7. When you see this type of market action, with a confirmed close in the direction of the major trend, it often sets up a low-risk opportunity to pyramid a trade that's working. The risk point would be just below the pivot bounce day (or just above it, in a down trend).

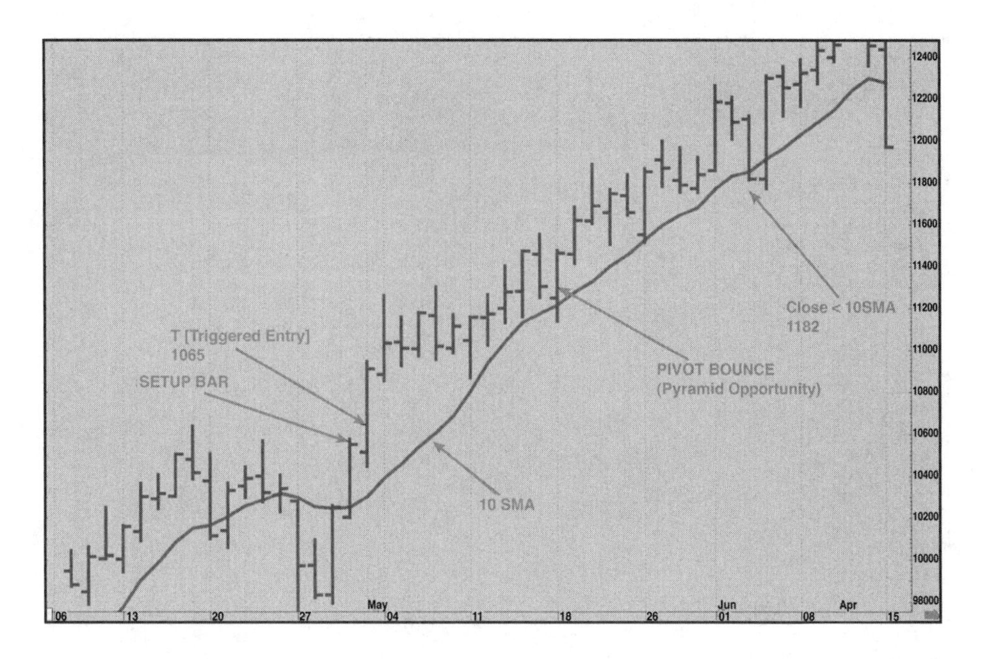

Figure 10.7 Pivot bounce pyramid

In addition, there is no rule that constricts you to only trade this on a daily time frame. If you are a short-term trader, the pivot indicator method works just as well on a shorter-term time frame. An illustration of this is Figure 10.8, which shows a corn chart as a 30-minute bar chart (with each vertical line representing 30 minutes of trade, compared to a full day, as in the prior charts).

Note that the setup bar, buffered entry price, and triggered entry work exactly the same, with the difference being that a shorter time frame typically results in reduced risk (and reduced profit) per trade signal. Just use the time frame that suits your personality.

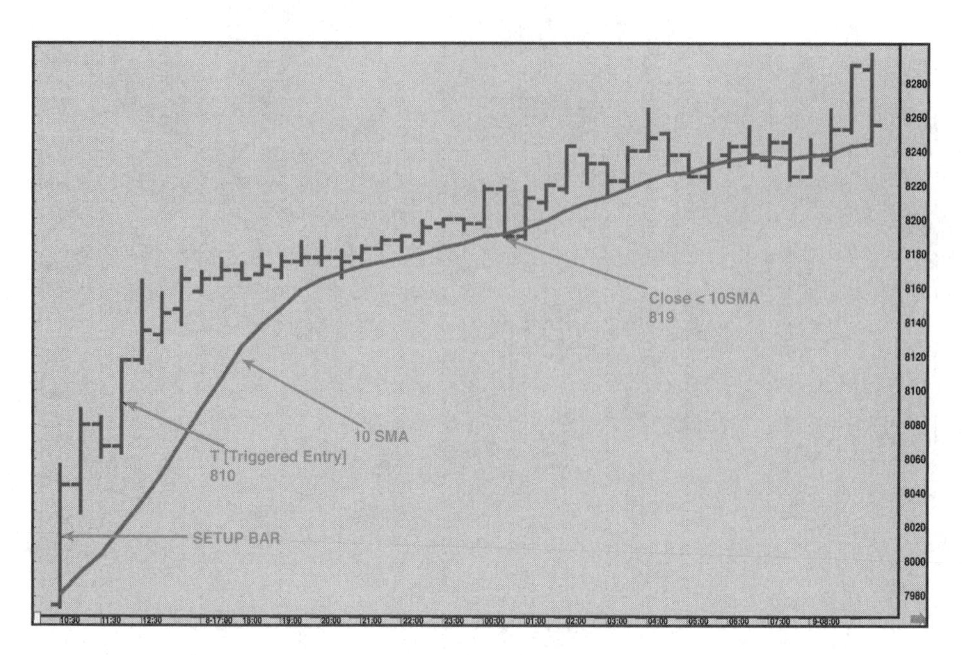

Figure 10.8 Shorter-term trading using the pivot indicator method

Diversification

When trading using my pivot indicator method, I recommend diversifying into a minimum of three unrelated markets. These markets should be liquid to allow for stop orders with minimal slippage. Although this rule is not written in stone, and I also believe that you can make money using this methodology trading just one or two markets, this generally requires greater patience, particularly if you start at the wrong time. The idea is that the greater the diversification, the greater the chance of catching a major move *somewhere*. At any point in time, one market might be in a major up trend and one might be in a major down trend, with a third trendless. The pivot indicator method works because the major moves will be profitable enough to offset the inevitable smaller losses inherent in those choppy market situations. The odds of catching major moves increase with the number of markets traded. One caveat: *They should be unrelated markets.*

Although the Swiss franc and the euro can move in opposite directions at times, they generally move in the same direction (albeit at different speeds) in relation to the dollar. Soybeans and soybean oil can move in opposite directions (and they sometimes have, in the short run), but because they are related products, they generally move in the same direction (albeit at different speeds).

In picking the optimal markets to trade, I personally like those that traditionally have the tendency for more dramatic moves (instead of the slower movers) because the more volatile markets will have moves large enough to overcome the inevitable trendless periods when you consider the inherent costs of commissions and slippage. For example, I generally prefer corn to oats because of corn's greater volatility. I like markets with good volume and major commercial participation (for example, the grains and the energies). The commercial interests and hedge funds have deeper pockets and tend to support their positions longer. Consider trading one currency because currencies have a tendency to trend nicely. Any of the major currencies (the euro, the British pound, the Australian or Canadian dollar, and the Japanese yen) works well. I also prefer to trade a grain, and I personally prefer soybeans (technically not a grain, but an oilseed) and corn because they both tend to trend nicely and possess sufficient volatility. Finally, I recommend that you consider rounding off your portfolio with a metal (my personal preference is gold) and a financial, such as a stock index or an interest-rate product.

The pivot indicator method is dynamic, and it works over time if used systematically on a variety of unrelated markets or any single market. However, my experience has been that thin markets, such as lumber and orange juice, place the odds against us at the start because the fills are often disappointing.

At times, stops will *just* be hit, and sometimes they will *just* be missed. I've found that these "justs" (just getting stopped, just missing a profit) appear to even out over time. It's all a function of the "market gods" and is not within our control.

11

And Finally

"This is the fifth book I've written, which isn't bad for a guy who's only read two."
—George Burns

So, you've stayed with this to the final chapter. I've shared a lot with you, and you now feel ready to go. However, statistics on winners and losers tell us that the majority are missing the essential elements for success. People often think they have the keys to success before they begin trading. After all, the research is fundamentally sound or the trading system looks to be a sure winner (on paper). The majority of traders embark on their journey confidently, so why do so many fail?

Trading is exciting, but it is also extremely difficult. In this final chapter, my goal is to steer you to focus on your inner self and the ability to concentrate totally on the task at hand. This chapter is a treatise on discipline, one of the essential qualities for success. This, in turn, relates to money management, a critical subset of discipline. I could have alternatively titled this chapter "The Psychology of Trading" or "Trading Consistently," but it all really boils down to one thing: your state of mind. For a successful trader, the mental game is as important as all the other trading rules combined! As Danny Ozark, former Phillies manager, once said, "Half this game is ninety percent mental."

Determining your motive

In the first chapter of this book, we discussed what it takes to become a successful trader. Have you personally analyzed your true motives? I know you want to make money. We all do. But your motives should go well beyond that.

Hedgers use the markets for business reasons—to manage the risks inherent in the commodity or financial markets associated with their businesses. Speculators should be in it for the same reason—to enhance bottom-line profitability. Still, many folks are trading for another reason: the thrill, the excitement, and the adrenaline rush. These people, and I think the numbers are significant, are looking for the same rush as a horse better or a crap shooter. Although it's not impossible to make money as a Vegas gambler, and some do, most don't. So, your question to yourself should be "What are my real motives?" Only you can answer this question, but if your real motive is action, and if you require instant gratification, you will fail. Your state of mind will prompt you to trade without regard to conditions, and the conditions must favor your actions, or you will fail.

So, what should your motives be? Not to just make money—that's not enough. You most likely are a competitive person, one who enjoys playing games and solving puzzles. You should strive to act in a disciplined, consistent, and unemotional manner. In this way you will trade when the conditions favor your trade. This is not a guarantee of profitability, but at least will place you on the right track.

Overcoming the six hurdles to trading success

Prior to each trade, you need a well-thought-out plan for that trade. The plan will include expectations for a positive outcome, but it needs to have a built-in contingency for an unexpected (unprofitable) outcome. You need to act in a confident and unhesitating manner.

Your plan must overcome the six hurdles to successful trading:

1. Trading for the thrill of it
2. Trading for revenge
3. Lacking money management
4. Lacking a well-defined trading plan
5. Being unable to pull the trigger
6. Being unable to admit you're wrong

The following sections discuss ways to overcome these hurdles.

1. Condition yourself to be unemotional

Once you determine your true motives for trading, you will be better able to positively condition your state of mind. If you are trading for the thrill of the game, you might trade when the conditions favor your methods, but you will also trade when they don't. When you trade emotionally, you overtrade because that is an inevitable outcome of thrill trading. You overstay your welcome on trades that aren't going your way, and this invites disaster. It might work for a time, but there will come another time when thrill trading will wipe you out. Then there are people who trade for the adrenaline rush but are subconsciously uncomfortable with risk. If you are one of these people, you tend to undertrade or place your stops too close, and this isn't a recipe for success either. If you cannot condition yourself to assume the risk of a leveraged market, place your hard-earned money in Treasury bills (or gold coins) and go home.

2. Avoid revenge trading

Has this ever happened to you? You were stopped out for a loss, a bigger loss than you had originally anticipated. Perhaps it was a bad fill beyond your stop due to some unexpected news. It's early in the trading day, and you feel you can make it back. Plus, you just cannot go home today with a large loss. The market owes you your money back, it will pay you back, and it will do it today! Have you ever had this feeling? I have, and let me tell you that when I'm out for revenge, 9 times out of 10 it leads to a bigger loss. The reason is that there's an unstable state of mind. Trading angry inevitably leads to bad decisions. When you get this feeling, force yourself to take a step back and relax. Walk away from the screen, maybe do some pushups or other exercise. The market will be there tomorrow, and there are always opportunities. This isn't the time to compound a problem; it's the time for your essential quality of patience to take over.

Too many people let a loss affect their psychology on the next trade. I'm not saying it is always easy to be unemotional; emotion is a human trait. But, you must condition yourself to remain in control, and if you feel you are out for revenge, force yourself to step aside for a time.

3. Preserve your capital

When you have little to no money management program in place, it is impossible to preserve your stake. Unless you condition yourself to risk only a small percentage of your account on any one trade, that one trade that looks perfect will inevitably come along, and you'll trade it too heavily. After all, the trade "looks so right," "everything is falling into place," and before you know it, you're dipping into the till once again.

Let me share a secret with you: They all look so right. I wouldn't enter a trade unless it looked good, but there is no way to know in advance which trade is going to be the big winner. If you knew this, then these would be the only ones you'd take. I've found that most years only a few trades make my year , and it is usually not the trades I thought would be the big winners. If I had no money management plan in place, I would be long gone before ever capturing those major moves. You must preserve your capital, and this means taking small and consistent hits on the many inevitable losers. The goal is to still be in the game when those mega-trades finally do materialize.

4. Ensure that your trading plan is well defined

Nobody enters a position expecting a loss; however, even the top traders experience numerous losses. If the best lose, why would you be any different? A well-defined plan defines success and failure both. Ask yourself, "Why are you buying gold?" If the answer is something like "Because it just broke above the 10-day moving average" or "Because inflation is heating up, and in the long run gold is sensitive to inflation," you have not defined your plan. You have reasons you entered but no clear exit strategy. You are trading on hope, and this is not a recipe for success.

You must define your loss point *before* you enter a trade, and if you are not prepared mentally to lose, you'll never win. It is essential to realize that you'll lose countless battles in the trading war, or the war will never be won. You should have a profit goal. Profit goals can be flexible, but stop loss points shouldn't be. You can have contingency plans when your profit objective is reached. The plan might be nothing more than something like this: "I am risking $500 per contract on this trade; my technical profit objective is $1,200. If the market moves $500 my way, I will move my stop up to an approximate break even. If it moves $900 my way, I will move the stop up to approximately a $400 profit. If it reaches my technical objective, I will watch closely for signs of failure. If the market shows these signs, I will sell at the market. However, if it moves through, I will tighten my stop to just under the previous low." This plan might or might not work, but at least it is a plan, and without a plan, you're ultimately doomed to failure.

5. Act without hesitation (if you have a good reason to do so)

What if you are indecisive? Consider this quote from Lee Iacocca, when he was bringing Chrysler back from the dead in the early 1980s: "So what do we do? Anything. Something. So long as we just don't sit there. If we screw it up, start over. Try something else. If we wait until we've satisfied all the uncertainties, it may be too late."

And don't forget John Steinbeck: "The best laid plans of mice and men. . ." When you paper trade, you always take the loss or the profit. In the heat of the battle, it is not as easy to pull the trigger. Too many times, even good traders do not take the loss when the planned risk point is reached. It is human nature not to be able to admit you are wrong, and it is seductive to wait just a bit longer or take just a bit more risk, hoping the market will turn back your way. In the great majority of cases, this will only exacerbate the pain. How do you overcome this shortcoming? Very simple: Place a physical stop loss order the moment you enter the trade, and then just let the "market gods" determine your fate. You won't be stopped out of the best trades. Taking profits when the time presents itself, although not as critical, can be just as important. I always have a mental profit objective in mind. It's not so bad to watch the market when it reaches the profit objective because the best markets many times exceed your minimum profit objective. However, if the market appears to hesitate as you near the goal line, cash in. Just do it because, many times, the market will not give you a second chance. And whenever I am unsure, I just move my stop very tight and make sure I lock in a good portion of the profit. The majority of times, I give up something, but sometimes I'm able to squeeze out quite a bit more. Stops are valuable tools that give you an edge—so use them!

6. Condition Yourself to Be Humble

Having an ego is not a trait of a successful trader. With apologies to Vince Lombardi, I must say that winning is not everything, and it certainly is not the only thing. I once had a client with an S&P day-trading system, one who made money on four out of five trades. The problem was that the fifth losing trade more than offset the four winners. Yet, until he ran out of money, he kept trading it for small profits because it felt good. I've had numerous clients try to pick tops and bottoms, but this is an almost impossible task because every major move has just one top and just one bottom. Who cares whether any one particular trade makes money, or whether you have more winners than losers? The name of this game is not how many winners you have but making money at the finish. The ultimate triumph is consistently having winning months. And in a winning month, my experience has been that you most likely have accepted losers throughout that month. Most people have trouble admitting they are wrong, which is why they lose money in futures trading. In my own case, over the years, my biggest losses have come in those markets in which I have had a strong opinion. I have at times fought the market, taking too much risk, and voiding my money management principals. At times, I have been forced out of a market just before the turn in my favor. In other words, in this instances, I may have been right in my opinion, but my timing has been off. (A margin clerk, however, doesn't care if you are ultimately right.) Other times, some new news I was unaware of would surface to demonstrate why I was wrong and the market was right. It is better to let the market tell you what it is saying than to try to dictate, because there is no doubt who's going to win that argument.

Most people take profits too soon because taking profits is psychologically pleasant. I always have profit objectives for my trades, but they're not written in stone. After all, there is only one top in every bull and only one bottom in every bear. I am not arrogant enough to assume that I am the one who can pick those tops and bottoms. Can you? A better plan is to see how the market acts when it does reach your profit goal. Many times it goes much further, so if the market wants to keep going, why not let it? Forget about being right on any particular trade and focus on making money!

Developing the winning touch

You see, the traits that lead to success in trading are different from those you have learned during your lifetime—those that lead to success in everyday life. You've been taught that perseverance will ultimately lead to triumph, but in trading you need to lose repeatedly to win. It takes conditioning to train your mind to act in a manner contrary to what works outside trading. In life, it is generally a recipe for disaster to act impulsively; it is better to sit back and reflect on your situation. In trading, however, you must condition yourself to act, perhaps not impulsively, but quickly without hesitation and unemotionally to cut a loss (or take a profit). After you condition your state of mind, you have control over your trading emotions. You have greater confidence when taking losses and entering new positions because you know your trading plan will prosper over time. Condition discipline, one of the essential qualities for trading success. Know you are going to have losing streaks. If your series of losing trades is a result of a lack of planning, and the margin clerk forces you out of the market, it's difficult to bounce back. You lose confidence in your ability to recoup. On the other hand, if you know you followed your disciplined program of cutting losses according to a well-defined plan, you can't be devastated because you followed your plan and know that over time it will work for you.

How can you trade in control, relaxed, unemotionally, and with confidence? The simple answer is to develop a consistent money management strategy with a positive outcome. Time and time again, I've heard from winning traders that a mediocre system with good money management triumphs over a superior system with poor money management. Money management is the vital element required for success, yet few traders concentrate on it.

So, what's the best money management strategy? I think a beginning trader is looking for the holy grail, but as you know, I've not found it. In my own trading, I strive to risk a maximum of 5% (in most cases much less) of available equity on any one trade. However, I realize that slippage and extraordinary events could potentially raise that number for any one particular losing trade. If you keep your loss per trade to 5% maximum, it takes 20 losing trades in a row to get wiped out. With a reasonable trading program, the risk of total ruin under these parameters is small. Of course, you must stick to the parameters you create, and this is where conditioning comes into play.

After I've defined my normal risk, I also define my normal reward. I personally am shooting for at least a two-to-one reward-to-risk ratio, and in most cases better than that. Of course, many trades result in a smaller profit, or smaller loss, and because I try to never let a decent profit turn into a loss, I seem to have many scratch trades (small profit, small loss, break even).

Let's analyze the ramifications of this simple system. Suppose that you had a very small trading account of $10,000. (With the leverage inherent in the futures, you should start with more, but let's use this number to keep it simple and assume that you're trading less volatile markets.) You could have seven losing trades at $500 each and three winning trades at $1,500 each (three-to-one), and you would still be a winner:

$7 \times (\$500) + 3 \times \$1{,}500 = \$1{,}000$

Think about this: You are *wrong* 70% of the time and still come out a winner! This is the beauty of a good money management program. Sure, there will be times when you project a loss of $500, a bad crop report is released, and that loss turns into $750. However, my experience has been that these extraordinary events seem to even out over time. At some point down the road, there will be a favorable unemployment report, the market will gap in your favor, and you will reap an additional $300 per contract profit over and above your original objective. Let's term this the "Even Steven effect." (I don't know why the good and the bad even out; it is one of the mysteries of nature.)

Finally, you must continually adjust your position size, based on market volatility. A small account should concentrate on less volatile markets, so the risk can be adjusted to suit the account size. A quick and simple way to evaluate volatility is to obtain a list of margin requirements by market. The clearing firm has, to a major extent, determined the volatility levels for you because margin requirements are adjusted based on volatility. Although there are always exceptions due to market inefficiencies, my general rule is that the initial margin for one position should not exceed 15% of your total excess equity available for trading. If you have a $100,000 cash account and the margin for soybeans is $1,250, a suggested maximum position size would be 12 contracts. But if the projected risk in this case is $500 per contract, you would be risking $6,000 with 12 contracts, which is 6% of total equity. Therefore, you should pare down your position size by a few contracts if you want to stick within the 5% rule. If the perceived risk as determined by your system is $750 per contract, then only six contracts should be traded for this position. If you always adjust your position size to volatility, then even in the bad times, you will have capital left to stay in the game. The name of the game is to avoid catastrophic risk of ruin.

If you don't feel right, you won't trade right

Rodney Dangerfield once complained, "It's been a rough day. I got up this morning, put on a shirt, and a button fell off. I picked up my briefcase, and the handle came off. I'm afraid to go to the bathroom." If this is the way your day starts out, don't trade.

You must follow a well-thought-out money management plan, but another important factor is your state of mind and your health.

Hundreds of thousands—perhaps millions—of traders who have a loser's state of mind are potentially on the other side of your trade. They might not realize it, but their actions in the marketplace attest to this fact. This will tilt the markets your way if you can modify your behavior to act in a positive manner. If you do this correctly, trading will be enjoyable and not fraught with the anxiety so many face. Research your trading plan, develop good money management techniques, condition your mind for success, only trade when you feel healthy, and you will succeed!

Jesse's secret

I've tried to spare you the market axioms that sound terrific in theory but really don't help you much in practice. ("Buy low and sell high," for example.) There is, however, one secret to making the big money that I've saved for last. It is simply this: Maximize the big move. This principle takes a long time to learn, and many traders never get it. The truth is that you won't have many trades that turn into big movers. The big movers are rare. For me, it's just one or two trades that make a big year. Capitalizing on only two or three major trading campaigns could mean a lifetime of difference for you!

When I first started on the floor of the Grain Exchange, I'd see this one member, a relatively young man at the time, who'd show up every so often. He'd appear maybe once a week, joke with some of the traders, check the markets, and at times place a few orders. He'd disappear for weeks or months at times. Over time, I got to know him better and learned he lived a happy life. The reason we wouldn't see him for months was because travel was his passion, and he could well afford to pursue his passion. He was independently wealthy, and it wasn't inherited money; he came from modest means. His story centered on the "Russian grain steal" markets of 1973–1974. He was working for a living back then and trading on the side. I don't know exactly how much money he finally took out of the markets, but judging by his lifestyle, I believe it was substantial. He started with a modest sum and made his big money in the soybean market. He was fortunate to be on the right side of one of the biggest soybean moves in history. He was smart enough to have a vision, had the guts to pyramid his position, and was disciplined enough to stand firm until the market told him the move was over. (This was a market where soybeans ran from less than $4 per bushel to nearly $13). Bottom line: In less than two years, this man was able to change his life dramatically for the better. What he did is rare, almost impossible, but he is living proof that it is possible.

Think about how tough it must have been to do what he did, to constantly avoid the temptation to cash in on what must have been huge paper profits during the move. Human nature would have urged him to "book the profit" every time the market rallied to new highs. After all, you can always "get back in" and reestablish a position on the next correction, right? Taking profits is pleasurable behavior and the easiest road to follow. After a big run, when the correction does materialize, a trader can pat himself on the back for cashing out. Profitability is enhanced every time you book a profit and are then able to buy back cheaper. After all, there's another market axiom that sounds great in theory: "You never go broke taking a profit."

The truth is, you never get rich that way, either. The major glitch in "taking profits" has to do with the corrections. Although the corrections will come, they don't always occur on schedule or from the level where you decided to exit. This man, unlike most, had the discipline to forgo "normal" profits and hold out for "life-changing" profits. How did he do this? I believe he had a vision. He had to believe prices could do what others could never envision. At that time, how could anyone have envisioned "beans in the teens?"

A vision is the key, but this man also must have had the patience to hang in there until the trend absolutely changed direction. This isn't easy to do, and it's not always easy to see. He had to have the courage to hang on during vicious shakeouts. (Take a look at a chart of the soybeans market at that time; like all the other major moves, this one had sharp and deep shakeouts even while the major trend continued north.) He must have had the guts to pyramid his position for maximum profitability, and this isn't all that easy. It takes "smart guts." If he had been too timid, he never could have achieved life-changing profitability. If he had been too bold, he would have overtraded and become undermargined, unable to hold his position.

Jesse Livermore, the legendary trader of the 1920s, made and lost mega-fortunes countless times over his trading career. This was a man who made more than $15 million in the crash of 1929, a mega-fortune at the time. Unfortunately, he also must have possessed a fatal flaw, because he somehow lost his multi-fortunes. Jesse was a compulsive gambler, and at the end of his life, he died penniless. He was found dead in the early 1940s with a self-inflicted bullet wound through his head. Apparently, he did not follow his own advice in his writings. He cautioned traders to always lock away for retirement, unavailable for trading, half of any big profit. Years before his death, Livermore told us in *Reminiscences of a Stock Operator* (a semi-autobiographical account of his trading career up to 1923), that he actually did this (put half his profits in an irrevocable trust for his wife and son). I guess he must have taken out the key and turned it at a weak moment. Still, he had the amazing ability to take millions out of the markets, starting with relatively modest sums. This wasn't a one-time fluke, either; he made millions numerous times throughout his career. The high point was his huge short position in 1929, which he covered at the lows on the day of the famous crash.

What was Jesse's secret to make the big money? He shared it in the book. In today's world, we have computerized trading and financial futures, but the basics of trading and winning haven't changed, and human nature hasn't changed. In the 1920s, stocks were traded like commodities are today: highly leveraged on small margin. Early in his career, Jesse suffered from the same malady most of us have. Unlike most, however, he was able to unlock the secret. In *Reminiscences,* Jesse relates the tale of old Mr. Partridge:

> You find very few who can truthfully say that Wall Street doesn't owe them money. Well, there was one old chap who wasn't like the others. To begin with, he was a much older man. He never volunteered advice and never bragged of his winnings....Time and again I heard him say, "Well, this is a bull market, you know!" as though he were giving you a priceless talisman...and, of course, I didn't get his meaning...."But I couldn't think of selling that stock," Mr. Partridge would say. "Why not?" I would ask. "Why this is a bull market. My dear boy, if I sold that stock now, I would lose my position, and then where would I be? And when you are as old as I am, and you have been through as many booms and panics as I have, you'll know that to lose your position is something nobody can afford—not even John D. Rockefeller. I hope that stock reacts and that you will be able to repurchase your line at a substantial concession, sir. But I myself can only trade in accordance with the experience of many years. I paid a high price for it, and I don't feel like throwing away another tuition fee."

Jesse then goes on to say:

> The more I learned, the more I realized how wise that old chap was. He had evidently suffered from the same defect in his young days and knew his own weakness. I think it was a long step forward in my trading education when I realized at last that when old Mr. Partridge kept on telling the other customers, "Well you know this is a bull market," he really meant to tell them that the big money is not in the individual fluctuations, but in the main movements—that is not in reading the tape, but in sizing up the entire market and its trend.
>
> After spending many years in Wall Street and after making and losing millions of dollars, I want to tell you this: It was never my thinking that made the big money for me. It was always my sitting. Got that? My sitting tight! You always find lots of early bulls in bull markets and early bears in bear markets. I have known many men who were right at exactly the right time and began buying or selling when prices were at the very level that should show the greatest profit. And their experience invariably matched

> mine—that is, they made no real money out of it. Men who can be both right and sit tight are uncommon. I found it one of the hardest things to learn. But it is only after a speculator has firmly grasped this that he can make big money.
>
> It is literally true that millions come easier to a trader after he knows how to trade than hundreds did in the days of his ignorance.
>
> (Reprinted from Edwin Lefevre, *Reminiscences of a Stock Operator*, Traders' Library Publications 1993, by permission of John Wiley & Sons, Inc.)

I've had certain clients make big scores in the markets, but it's rare. I've been fortunate enough to do the same at times, but not as often as I should have. When I go back and look at my broker statements, I see the same pattern for my "'best-of-the-best" trades. A position entered into generally before it was the popular play. A position held for a greater period of time than most of my trades, held through major shakeouts or sharp short covering rallies. A position pyramided (but not always the largest positions). Substantial money can be made with a fairly modest position, if the timing is right and held for a good portion of a move.

To achieve success, you have to resist your human weaknesses. Human nature prompts us to take premature profits because it's pleasurable. The major moves, the ones you want to maximize, are the hardest to hold. Your technical tools can help here. Moving averages will help to keep you on the trend; actually, any tool that helps you determine the trend and maximize profits while cutting losses in a systematic manner is better than thinking too much. Technical tools can provide you with the discipline to stay with moves you otherwise would cash in on prematurely. The big moves are always available, but most of us never see the forest for the trees.

Looking at recent charts, again I see numerous markets that have trended for big moves. Major moves take place every year and in both directions, but most of us see these moves only in hindsight. What's exciting is that they continue to develop, and there is probably one starting soon that could provide you with success beyond your wildest dreams. You'll need discipline, guts, and courage, and you'll need to take the road less traveled. It's not easy, but the opportunities are there.

Comments or questions?

I invite you to email me at gkleinman1@mac.com with questions or comments as I'm interested in hearing about your experiences.

I hope you'll be able to use the concepts presented in this book to your benefit, and of course, I wish you an enormously successful trading experience.

Good luck and good trading!

Appendix

25 Trading Secrets of the Pros

"History doesn't repeat itself, but it does rhyme."
—Mark Twain

When I've done well in the markets, it has usually been because I acted in a certain manner. When I've done poorly, it usually has been because I didn't. The "secrets" presented here are partially from experience (the "school of hard knocks") but also originally gleaned from reading the masters. Two masters of the past come to mind first—Jesse Livermore and W.D. Gann. Their heyday was the 1920s; however, for me, they both still live through their writings. A trader can learn more from their failures than their triumphs. The same mistakes made 50 and 100 years ago continue to be made by traders every day. Technology might change, but human nature never does. I thank these two men. Many of the "secrets" discussed here, although written in my words, come from them.

If you disregard what's presented here, you likely will become lost in the financial desert, dying of thirst. (Perhaps that's a bit strong, but trust me, this is good stuff!)

Secret 1: The trend is your friend!

Don't buck the trend. The way to make the really big money is to determine the major trend and then follow it. If the market will not go your way, you must go its way. When you are in a bear market and the major trend is down, the plan should be to wait for rallies and sell short, not try to pick the bottom. In a major bear market, you can miss the bottom several times on the way down and end up losing all your money. The same applies (in reverse) during a major bull market. Always go with the tide—never buck it. Let me repeat this, because it is important: It is easier to walk with the wind than against it, it is easier to swim with the tide than against it, and the big money is made by going with the trend, not against it.

As Livermore told us, in a major bear market, it is safer to sell when the market is down 50 points from the top than when it is down just 10. The reason is, at down 50, all support is gone, and those who bought the breaks have lost all hope, are demoralized, and, in a leveraged market, are at the point where they all try to exit the same small door at the same time. The result, at times, can be an unexpected avalanche. I can give you many examples of markets that have trended long and far, made some people rich, and wiped out many others. You might have heard about the poor soul who lost his farm. I can almost guarantee that guy was bull-headed and fought the trend until he finally ran out of money.

How do you stick with the trend and not fight it? It isn't all that easy. That's why most people don't make money in futures. You need to have a strong will. When you can determine the trend of the market, don't change your mind until the tape shows the change. In any major move there will, of course, be corrective moves against the trend. Some news will develop that will cause a sharp correction, but it will be followed by a move right back in the direction of the major trend. If you listen to this news, you will be tempted to liquidate prematurely. Avoid the temptation and listen to no one—listen only to the market. One way to do this is to never set a fixed price in your mind as a profit objective. The majority of people do this, and there's no good reason for it—it's a bad habit based on hope. Do not set a fixed time to liquidate either. This is the way the amateurs do it. They buy silver at $35 because their broker told them it's going to $50. Well, it gets to $39.97, turns and heads south again, and they're still holding, looking for $50, watching and waiting as their unrealized profits melt. I've seen it, and this is just plain bull-headedness.

I've seen the opposite, too. The market closes at $35.95, looks strong, and is fundamentally and technically sound. The amateur has his good-until-canceled order sitting to sell at $36, because this is his price. The market gaps up and fills him at $36.15, and his broker is pleased to report he sold better at this price. However, this is a form of top picking, and who is smarter than the market? The market probably gapped up above $36 because the buying interest was able to overwhelm the sellers. I've seen many cases like this one, in which the open was sharply higher but still turned out to be the low of the day. In other words, it was the kind of market that never looked back until it hit $50. This is all a version of bucking the trend—something I do not recommend. Conditions do change, and you must learn to change your mind when they do. A wise man changes his mind; a fool never does. Just be sure that if you change your position, it is based on sound reasoning.

Secret 2: When a market is cheap or a market is expensive, there probably is a good reason

This secret goes hand in hand with "the trend is your friend." Livermore told us that he always made money selling short low-priced markets, which are the public's favorite and in which a large long interest had developed. Alternatively, he cashed in on expensive markets when everyone was bailing out because the public thought the market was high enough for a healthy reaction. The public was selling soybeans short at $6 per bushel in 1973 because this was an all-time high and into resistance.

Who could have guessed that soybeans weren't even halfway to what would be new record highs—close to $13? Always remember that it is not the price that's important, it's the market action.

Secret 3: The best trades are the hardest to do

You need to have guts, and you need to be aggressive on entry. You need to quickly cut your losses when the market is not acting right. The news always sounds the most bullish at the top and appears to be the most hopeless at the bottom. This is why the technical tone of the market is so important. If the news is good but the market has stopped going up, ask yourself why and then heed the call. Bottoms can be the most confusing. The accumulation phase, where the smart money is accumulating a position, can be marked by reactions, crosscurrents, shakeouts, and false reversals. After the bottom is in place, many traders look for the next break to be a buyer. After all, the market has been so weak so long that the odds favor at least one more break, right? But it never comes. The smart money won't let it. The smart money's objective after the bottom is in place is to move the market up to the next level. The best time to buy can feel very uncomfortable. However, the train has already left the station, and you need to have the courage to hop on for the ride.

Secret 4: Have a plan before you trade and then work it

If you have a plan and follow it, you will have the ability to avoid the emotionalism that is the enemy of any trader. You must try to stay calm during the heat of a session and remain focused. To do this, you have to be totally organized prior to the opening bell. Your daily mission, should you decide to accept it, is to make money each day or, barring that, at least not to lose much. In normal markets, you should take normal profits. In unusual markets (that occur rarely), you need to shoot for abnormal profits. This is one of the keys to success. The next is that you must always limit losses on trades that are not going according to plan! This takes willpower and is as essential a quality as having plenty of money. In fact, it's more important than having lots of money. Money is not to hold on with; that's for the sheep, and you don't want to be sheared. If big risks are required, don't take that trade. Wait for an opportunity where you can place a tighter stop. Livermore's method of trading was to look for opportunities where he could enter close to his risk point. In that way, his risk per trade was small in relation to the profit potential.

If you do not have the willpower to take the loss when your risk point is hit during the trading session, then you absolutely must use stop loss orders to maintain your discipline. Simply place your stop at the same time you place the trade. You probably have heard stories about the traders or the computers "running the stops," but I assure you that in the good trades, the majority of the time you will not be stopped out. You will be stopped out of the bad ones, and that's a good thing.

Personally, I have a trading plan laid out the night before. I generally know what I will do if the market acts the way I anticipate it should and, just as importantly, what I'll do if it doesn't. It is a guide, of course, not written in stone, and it is flexible. However, if a market is not acting "right" according to my plan, I know it is time to take action—either to take the profit if available, or cut the loss if not. Generally, I've found that when I try to fudge the plan, I get my head handed to me. This doesn't always happen (and this is why it's hard to follow plans many times), but it happens enough to know that, in the heat of the battle, the plan is smarter than I am.

Secret 5: Be aggressive

Be aggressive when taking profits or cutting losses (if there's a good reason to do so). A good trader acts without hesitation. When something is not right, she liquidates early to save cash and worry. Never think too much. Just do it! And don't limit your price—go at the market! Many times, a market gives you one optimal opportunity to act and that's it—so go with it. As Gann said, "The way to benefit through intuition is to act immediately."

Secret 6: No regrets

When you liquidate a trade based on sound reasoning, never regret your decision. Just go on, and if it was a mistake to get out, all you can do is learn from it. We all make mistakes. Don't beat yourself up, or you will lose your perspective and become too cautious in the future.

Secret 7: Money management is the key

You do not necessarily need to have a high win-to-loss ratio, but your average win must be higher than your average loss if you want to succeed. To do this, there must be (at least some) "big hits." You have to maximize some trades. You need these big wins to offset the numerous (and hopefully small) losses that are inevitable. I've found that being able to cut losses early, by even a small incremental amount per trade, like $100, can make a major difference to the bottom line. This takes decisiveness, so be decisive if the trade is not acting right. Waiting for a few more ticks is generally not a recipe for success. And one more point here: It is generally bad practice to cancel or extend a stop loss order. My experience has been that the majority of times canceling a stop is the wrong thing to do. It's okay to cancel a profit-taking order at times, but the sooner a loss is stopped, the better. When you get out of a bad position quickly and with a minimum of trauma, not only is your capital base maintained but your judgment improves. Without a well-defined risk point, there's no judgment. The term for that is hope, and you should never trade on hope alone.

Secret 8: Success comes easier when you specialize

Every market has its own personality. Some markets tend to make tops and bottoms with a fast run up and reverse (called an inverted V top, or the opposite, a V bottom). Some have rounding tops and bottoms, some double tops and bottoms, and some top and bottom with a long consolidation. You can read a market better when you become familiar with its idiosyncrasies. Familiarity comes from concentration and experience. If a market does not fit with your nature, find another one. When certain markets don't seem to work for you, leave them alone and stick with the ones that favor you. There are plenty of markets are out there.

Secret 9: Patience pays

As Gann once said, "People are in too big a hurry to get rich, and as a result, they go broke." Don't try to get rich in a few months. Don't try to catch all the fluctuations. Market movements of importance require weeks or even months to get ready. A few days (or longer) after a big move gets under way, there's generally plenty of time to buy or sell. At times, a man or woman with nerve, knowledge, and a bit of luck can turn a small amount of money into a fortune. However, this cannot be done continually. The very best trades come along only rarely. You need the patience to wait for the right trades. When they come, you need the patience not to be overanxious and get in too soon or overtrade. When you do get in and the market starts to move your way, you must have the patience to hold on tight until there's sufficient cause for closing out the trade. Remember that every act, either opening or closing a trade, must have a sound basis. Never trade for the thrill of it. If you cannot see a definite trade, use your essential quality of patience and wait!

After you are out of the market with a big profit, you don't need to be in too big a hurry to get back in. The best opportunities might be just around the corner, but they're not there every day. You need the patience to wait. Big account balances lead to the temptation to play for less-than-desirable trades. If you made a good profit, then look at it this way: You can now afford to wait a few weeks or months for the next big move.

Secret 10: Guts are as important as patience and more important than money

Some traders are too bold, and as a result, they overtrade. Others have trouble pulling the trigger, and this is a weakness that must be corrected. You must train yourself to trade in such a way that there is no hope and no fear. When you enter or exit a position, do it decisively and without emotion. You need the guts to press hard when you are right. And guts are particularly important after a tough losing streak. I've witnessed traders who still had money left after suffering a string of losses, and when the best opportunity of the year came along (one they identified), they didn't have the guts to act. In cases like this, guts are more valuable than money.

Secret 11: The "tape" (quotes) will trick you

Gann once said that it's impossible for a man who stands over "the ticker" every day to identify a big move before it starts. The tape will fool you every day while accumulation is taking place (and it takes time to accumulate or distribute a large position). Gann actually felt that the tape (today we call it the *quote screen*) was there to fool traders. "The tape moves in mysterious ways, the multitude to deceive" is the way he put it. Prices can look the weakest or strongest at the strongest or weakest times. Watching quotes all day causes you to change your mind constantly. Trade too often, and this increases your percentage of being wrong. If you get in wrong, the quotes tend to keep you in wrong longer than you should be because every tick your way renews your hopes. If you get in right and you watch the screen too closely, there will come a minor move against you that will shake you out. This move, in the long run, means nothing, and as a result, you will lose a good position.

Secret 12: Be skeptical

Another way to put this is that it pays to be a contrarian. To be successful, you need to be a student of human nature and do the opposite of the general public. Sell on your first clues of weakness; don't wait until everyone is bailing out. If you're day trading the S&P, this rule could apply to moves of 15 minutes. If you're swing trading, this rule could apply to a move lasting 3 days. It certainly applies to moves lasting weeks or months. And be wary of tips. The tip-giver might be well intentioned, but tips invariably influence you in the wrong direction. Remember that the market doesn't beat you—you beat yourself. Following tips and not the market is just another sign of human weakness.

Secret 13: Be time cognizant

It's important to know how much time a move has taken to get where it is. The longer a market moves in one direction, the greater the velocity of the buying or selling in the final stage of the move. In many cases, the most significant portion of a major move takes place in the final 48 hours, and you'll want to be there for that!

While we're on the subject of time, watch the volume after a market has made a long-term move. Volume tends to run higher than normal at the end of a move because this is the "distribution zone," where the smart money is unloading their position to a public who is frenzied by the news.

Actually, it's important to know what "zone" the market is in. Market phases tend to act in a similar manner. Many times, at the bottom, a market can rally on small volume. This indicates that there really isn't much for sale at the price. The bottom can follow a period of panicky conditions, pessimism, and apathy. Even the prior bulls start to sound more cautious, and say it could get worse before it gets better. It seems nobody is interested in buying. This is the time to watch your moving averages closely. If they flash a buy signal, then immediately cover shorts and start to buy. Tops are the opposite of bottoms. It seems nobody notices that the market is saturated, yet the market might stop going up. After the first break from the top, many times there will be a low-volume "failure test of the high." When the market fails at a lower high, if you are not out already, this could be your last best chance to liquidate.

As a general rule, the big money is made in the last stage of a bull market, when prices are feverishly active. The big profits on the short side are made in the last stage of a bear market, when everyone wants to sell, and it seems no one wants to be a buyer.

As Gann told us, "It is always darkest before the dawn and brightest at noon just before the sun starts to recede."

Secret 14: Watch the reaction to "the news"

Remember, it's not the news but how the market reacts to the news that's important. Certainly it's the news that sets the public perception, but you must be alert for divergences between the news and market action. It all has to do with expectation versus reality. Look for the divergence between what's happening and what people think is supposed to happen. When the big turn comes, the general public will always be looking the wrong way. Use GK's Significant News Indicator (discussed in Chapter 8, "The Advanced Trading Course"), and be aware of the following ways to analyze reactions to news (or even a lack of news):

- If bad news is announced and the market starts to sell off in large volume, it's a good bet the market's going lower.
- If the market doesn't react much to good news, it's probably been discounted.
- Moves of importance invariably tend to begin before there is news to justify the initial price move. When the move is under way, the emerging fundamentals slowly come to light. A big rally (decline) on "no news" is almost always bullish (bearish).
- It is generally not good practice to buy after a lot of bullish news or sell after an extremely bearish report because both good and bad news are often already discounted in price. Of course, you should always consider whether the trend is down or up when the news is made known. A well-established trend generally continues, regardless of the news. Consider this "breaking news" from 2003: "March 18: BAGHDAD (AP)—Iraq's leadership on Tuesday rejected the U.S. ultimatum that Saddam Hussein and his sons leave Iraq or face war, and the United Nations pulled its weapons inspection staff out of the country as battle appeared inevitable." Today, few remember that on that day, world oil prices collapsed by 10% (before the Iraq war had even started) because the market had already discounted the worst outcome.
- When unexpected news occurs (news that the market has not had time to prepare for), and the market opens in a wide range, or gaps lower or higher, sell out your longs or cover your shorts and wait. Watch the market for 30 minutes to an hour. If the market opened sharply lower with heavy selling and was not able to trade much lower than that, it's into support and can be bought at the market with a tight risk point. Watch the market closely at this point. Note the tone of the rally. If it's small and the market is able to again fall under the levels made when the bad news came out (or above the good), it is safe to assume that the market is going lower (higher).

Secret 15: Never trade when you're sick, worried, or tired

Good health is essential to success. If you don't feel well, close out your positions and start over again when you do. Rest is equally essential to success. It is a good idea to close out all your trades periodically, get entirely out of the market, and go on vacation. The market will still be there when you return; trust me. I've heard from some of the most successful traders that they trade their best right after a vacation. If you stick to something too long without rest, your judgment becomes warped. Traders who are continually in the market day in and day out lose their perspective and ultimately lose.

Secret 16: Overtrading: your greatest enemy

Gann called overtrading the "greatest evil." He thought it was the cause of more losses than anything else, and who am I to disagree with one of the masters? The average novice trader really doesn't have a clue about how much money is needed to be successful, and he invariably buys (or shorts) more than prudence dictates. He might be right in his basic analysis, but because he takes too big a position, he's forced to liquidate when the margin clerk calls. When he's liquidating, so are the other novices, and that's when the smart money moves in.

Secret 17: Keep a cool head during blow-offs

Markets tend to top out in the same way. When close to the end of a major move, markets can turn wild. Volume is huge, activity is feverish and erratic, and the imagination of most traders blossoms. If you've had the vision to ride the trend to this point, your payday has come; however, in extreme markets, men and women of reason lose all sense of proportion. They start to believe the propaganda that the world will literally run out of this or that, but it never happens. The Hunts ran silver from $5 an ounce to more than $50. They felt it would go up forever, but they forgot that at some price, Grandma's silver candlesticks come out of the cupboard and into the smelter. The richest men in the world (at that time) lost all sense of reason and proportion and lost $2 billion in the process. The history of the world has shown that there has never been a time when there was a great demand for anything that a supply in excess of demand didn't develop.

Extreme markets are not the time to pyramid—they signify the beginning of the end. All good things come to an end, and your mission is to jump before the big bump. At some point, "the herd" will want to exit by the same door at the same time—and you want to make sure you've already left the room. When everyone wants to sell and all buying support disappears, profits can run into losses fast. In the stock market crash of 1987, profits made in the first 10 months of the year were wiped out in 2 days, and this was repeated in the dot-com mania in early 2000 and once again during the financial collapse of 2008.

How do you turn your paper profits into cash during a runaway market? In blow-off markets, the corrections are generally short and sweet. The market is feverish, and everyone is bullish. (The bears have already thrown in the towel.) The public is buying madly. Weeks might go by without a major correction. You'll hear of fortunes being made, and if you are fortunate enough to be on the move, your paper profits will grow geometrically. The end might be near, but in fact, nobody can see the forest for the trees. Only about 10% of those with big paper profits ever cash in near the top.

Here's a rule I follow: In this type of market, it does not pay to take a loss amounting to more than two consecutive days' fluctuations. If the market goes against you more than two days, it's likely to go more. Plus, be alert for a day when the market opens off dramatically, without news to account for the break. It might rally weakly, but when the rally fails, this is your sign of the end. The market has reached the saturation point, where it's run out of buyers; supply has finally overwhelmed demand. Also, watch for a failure test of the high. Many times, after the first break, the market has a secondary rally that fails under the high. If you failed to get out on the first break, this could be your last good chance.

Secret 18: Never let a good profit turn into a loss

If you have a decent profit in any position and you are absolutely sure it is going to grow larger, at the very least, place a physical stop where (in the worst case) you'll break even. If the market is any good, your stop won't be hit. Should the market continue to move favorably, keep moving your stop to lock in at least some profit. The objective is always to protect your principal in every way possible, and when you are fortunate enough to start accumulating paper profits, lock them in.

Secret 19: When in doubt, get out

If the market is not acting right according to your plan, get out! If the market has not started to move in your favor within a reasonable amount of time, get out! Your judgment deteriorates the longer you hang on to a losing position, and at extremes, you will do the wrong thing. One of the old timers once said something like this, "I am prudent enough not to stand in the middle of the railroad tracks while I try to decide if the headlight I think I see is a freight train or an illusion."

Secret 20: Spread your risks by diversification

Distribute your risk among a variety of trades and markets. One way to achieve this is to divide your capital and never risk more than a maximum of 5% on any one trade. One good profit often totally erases four or five small losers. On the other hand, if you take big losses and small profits, you have no chance of success. I also suggest concentrating on active, liquid markets—those that allow you to enter and exit when you want to with a minimum of slippage.

Secret 21: Pyramid the correct way

Big money is made by pyramiding a good position in a trending market. You have an excellent opportunity to use leverage with your unrealized profits to create a larger position than would otherwise be possible. Pyramiding takes both courage and self-control. The "weak hands" seldom make the big money, primarily because they do not have the guts to pyramid and maximize the opportunities they're right about (or they do not have the smarts to do it right).

There is a right way to pyramid, and there's a wrong way to pyramid.

The masters suggest that you never "reverse pyramid" (that is, add a greater number of contracts than your initial position while the market moves your way). Your first risk should be your greatest risk. It is generally better to decrease the size of your position throughout the ride, not increase it. In this way, you have the opportunity to increase your profitability without dramatically increasing your risk.

Let's look at a hypothetical example. If you start out with a purchase of 10 cocoa contracts at 1300, the correct way to add to this position is 5 contracts at 1350, 3 at 1400, 2 at 1450, and 1 every additional 50 points up indefinitely until the move is over. You would follow this position up with a trailing stop loss. In this way, your last trade or two shows a loss, but all the others show big profits. The point here is that by pyramiding with the larger position underneath for longs or above for shorts, your average price is always better than the market. When trading this way, a correction is more likely to show bottom-line profitability.

Two additional (and useful) pyramiding rules:

- Never try to pyramid after a long advance or decline. The odds are against you. I did this in soybeans during the floods of 1993. I started to be a buyer at just the right time and close to the lows, but I got too bullish at the top, added too many contracts, and never made any money out of that one. The time to begin a pyramid is when the trend first turns up or down after a long move. Your technical indicators can help you here.

- It is always safer to pyramid after a market moves out of accumulation or distribution—in other words, a breakout from consolidation (see the next secret). The more time that passes prior to the breakout, the greater the move you can expect.

Secret 22: Watch for breakouts from consolidation

I've already discussed this in depth, but it's powerful and cannot be overemphasized. You need to know what kind of market you are in. In a consolidating market, you can make money by scalping small moves back and forth. However, you won't make big money in this kind of market, and you never should attempt to pyramid in this kind of market. Big profits are made in the runs between accumulation and distribution. I've found that you can make more money by waiting until a commodity plainly declares its trend than by getting in before the move starts. Too many traders are fixated on picking the top or bottom, and as a result, they miss the big picture. What difference does it make if you buy 10, 20, or 30 ticks off the lows, as long as you make money? Get the idea of price out of your head and concentrate on market action. Just forget about picking tops and bottoms, wait for the breakout.

The longer the consolidation, the better. When a market has remained in a narrow range for a long time, a breakout out of that range becomes more significant. The market is telling you that a major shift in the supply and demand fundamentals is taking place. If it has taken a long time to form, there is more fuel available for the coming move, and this is the best type of market to play to the hilt!

Secret 23: Go with the relative strength

I'm not referring to the RSI (relative strength index) here. What I mean is that it is important that you follow the trend of each market and always buy the strong one and sell the weak one. This is especially important for related markets. Silver and gold are both precious metals and generally move in the same direction; however, they move at different speeds. In early 1987, silver started to run, and in a short time, it ran up almost $6 per ounce, representing profits of close to $30,000 per contract. We had clients who did not want to "chase the market" after silver made its first $1 run-up, but they had no hesitation buying gold. It was, after all, "cheap" in relation to silver and would have to catch up eventually, right? Gold did run up, about $60 per ounce, or $6,000 per contract. Not too bad, but you would have made five times more by buying the strong one instead of the weak one. Moves of this nature don't come along very often.

If hogs are going up and cattle are heading down, you should sell the cattle if your trend indicators tell you to do so. It doesn't matter that they're both meat products; the markets are telling you fewer people are eating beef—at least now. When I first started in the business, I remember a time when bellies (delisted in 2012), which usually traded at a 10¢ to 20¢ premium to the hogs, were trading at the same price as hogs. Everyone at Merrill Lynch said this was a slam-dunk—you just had to make money spreading bellies and hogs. (Buy the bellies and sell the hogs.) This made perfect sense. The logic was sound: How could a finished product ever sell for less than the raw material? We all piled on this one, and you probably can guess what happened. The bellies continued to head south and the hogs north until the bellies were selling at a $5 discount to the hogs. This was a loss of $2,000 per spread at the time in a "no-risk" trade (and, of course, we overtraded this one because it "couldn't lose").

The point is that you need to judge a market by its own signs; always sell the weak one and buy the strong one.

Secret 24: Limit moves are important indicators of support and resistance

When a market is bid limit up or offered limit down (for those markets that still have limits, such as cattle or corn), this is a level where you could be unable to buy or sell. There is more demand at the limit-up price than available supply or vice versa. The market "should" continue in the direction of the limit move. On corrections, it should find support above the limit-up price (or below, if a limit-down move). Watch for this. If a market again trades under the limit bid price or above the limit offered, go with the flow. These are trades that possess reasonable risk, because they indicate the previous support or resistance is now absent. If anyone can now buy a market where it previously was unable to be bought (or sell where you previously couldn't) this is a major sign of weakness or strength.

Here's one example from my memory: The day before the high price was hit in the big bull corn market of 1996, a trader was unable to buy corn. It was not only limit bid, but there were more than 30 million bushels wanted, with no sellers at the limit price. A few days later, the market crossed under the limit bid price, and anyone could buy as much as he wanted. After it crossed that price, the market never saw the light of day. It started on a bear trend, one that lasted for six months and didn't end until prices were $1.50 per bushel lower.

Secret 25: Never average a loss

We'll conclude with this one because it is so critical. I've talked to stock investors who've had great success averaging down. When a stock they liked got cheaper, they bought more. When the longer-term trend turned back up, they made out like bandits. A leveraged market is different, however. Averaging a loss might work four times out of five, but that fifth time will wipe you out. It's a very bad habit to get into.

Look at it this way: If you make a trade and it starts to go against you, then you're wrong—at least temporarily. Why buy or sell more to average the loss? When it's getting worse day by day, why potentially compound the problem? Stop the loss early, before it is eternally too large; don't make it worse.

Gann thought that if you could avoid three weaknesses—overtrading, failing to place a stop loss, and what he called the "fatal" mistake, averaging a loss—then you would be a success. Excellent advice.

Index

A

accumulation, 97
advantages of options, 47- 49
agricultural products, 21
agriculturals, 78, 83-102
AIG, 126
algorithms, 117-118
  effect of, 118
  volatility, 119-125
aluminum, 31, 105
analysis
  charts, 129
    breakouts from consolidation, 137, 140-144
    H&S patterns, 170, 175
    Japanese candlestick, 166
    P&F, 165
    patterns, 144-149, 154-155
    resistance/support levels, 136-137
    trend channels, 134-135
    trendlines, 130, 134
    volume, 156
  Elliot wave, 163-164
  fundamental, 76-77
  OI, 156-159
  options, 49
    advantages/disadvantages, 47
    changes in price, 55
    converting, 46
    exercising, 55, 57
    hedging, 59-61
    overview of, 45-46, 49
    prices, 51-53
    quotes, 48
    ratios, 69-70
    rules, 71-74
    selling, 57-59
    stock indexes, 61
    strategies, 61-66
    strike price, 48
    styles, 48
    time, 50
    time decay, 50
    types, 47
    volatility, 54
  RSI, 159-160
  SNI, 177-186
  spreads as forecasting tools, 167-170
  stochastic, 162
  technical, 76-77, 128
  trading success
    aggression, 232
    averaging losses, 240
    breakouts, 238
    discipline, 233
    diversification, 237
    doubt, 237
    emotions, 236
    good health, 236
    intuition, 231
    limit moves, 239
    money management, 232
    overtrading, 236
    patience, 233
    plans, 231-232
    prices, 230
    profits, 237
    pyramiding, 237-238
    quotes, 233
    reaction to news, 235
    regrets, 232
    RSI, 239
    skepticism, 234
    specialization, 232
    time, 234
    trends, 229-230
  trends, 129
apex, 149
Arabica coffee, 100
Argentina
  grains, 84
  oilseeds, 83
asked price, 41. *See* also offers
associated daily price limits, 25
at the money, 53

Australia, softs, 100
averages
  losses, 240
  moving
    alternatives to SMAs, 199
    EMA, 200-202
    length of time, 199
    overview of, 193, 195
    SMA, 197
    WMA, 200-202

B

backgrounding, 96
backspreads, 70, 73
bailouts, government, 126
bakery products, 85. *See* also grains
banks, metals, 104
Barusch, Bernard, 122
basis gains/losses, futures, 39
basis risk, futures, 36-37
beans, 83. *See also* agriculturals
bear spreads, 110
Bear Stearns, 126
beef, 21. *See also* meats
beginning stocks, 85
bids, 41. *See also* prices
bonds, treasury, 79
boom markets, 11
bottom pickers, 193
boxes, 146
Brazil
  oil, 82
  oilseeds, 83
  softs, 100
  technical analysis, 128
breakaway gaps, 152
breakfast commodities, 99
breaking above psychologically significant numbers, 187
breakouts, 238
breakouts from consolidation, 137-144
Brent Crude Oil, 80, 83
Bretton Woods agreement, 102
brokers, futures, 34
bubbles, 123-124
buffered entry prices, 207, 209
bull spreads, 110
Bush, George W., 118
bust markets, 11
buying
  algorithms, 117-118
    effect of, 118
    volatility, 119-125
  chart analysis, 129
    breakouts from consolidation, 137-144
    patterns, 144-155
    resistance/support levels, 136-137
    trend channels, 134-135
    trendlines, 130, 134
    volume, 156
  covering, 27
  Elliot wave analysis, 163-164
  futures
    contracts, 22
    order placements, 41-43
  H&S patterns, 170, 175
  intermarket spreads, 111-114
  intramarket spreads, 110-111
  Japanese candlestick charts, 166
  OI analysis, 156-159
  options, 49
    advantages/disadvantages, 47
    changes in price, 55
    converting, 46
    exercising, 55-57
    hedging, 59, 61
    overview of, 45-46, 49
    prices, 51-53
    quotes, 48
    ratios, 69-70
    rules, 71-74
    selling, 57-59
    stock indexes, 61
    strategies, 61-66
    strike price, 48
    styles, 48
    time, 50
    time decay, 50
    types, 47
    volatility, 54
  P&F charts, 165
  pivot indicators, 206
  RSI, 159-160
  stochastic, 162
  technical analysis, 128
  trends, 129

C

calendar spreads, 66
California Gold Rush, 123
calls
  margins, 29
  options, 46-47, 49
  vertical call spreads, 65
Canada
  grains, 84
  metals, 104
  oilseeds, 84

cancel/replace orders, 42
canola, 84
capital, preserving, 221
capitulation, 124
cash settlements, 33
cattle, feeder, 96. *See also* meats
Cattle on Feed Report, 98-99
Cattle Inventory Report, 99
central banks, metals, 104
channels, trends, 134-135
charts, 129
  breakouts from consolidation, 137, 140-144
  H&S patterns, 170, 175
  Japanese candlestick, 166
  P&F, 165
  patterns, 144-149, 154-155
  resistance/support levels, 136-137
  trend channels, 134-135
  trendlines, 130, 134
  volume, 156
Chicago Board of Trade, 5
Chicago Mercantile Exchange. *See* CME
chicken, 96. *See also* meats
China
  grains, 84
  metals, 102, 104
  oil, 82
  oilseeds, 83
  softs, 100
clearing fees, 117
closing prices, SMAs, 198
CME (Chicago Mercantile Exchange), 48
  financial futures, 79
  Live Cattle contracts, 96
cocoa, 21, 99
  ICO, 101
coffee, 21, 99-100
COMEX, 24
  selling short, 27
commissions, futures, 34
commodities
  breakfast, 99
  continuing education, 107-109
  demand, 124, 126
  futures. *See* futures
  leverage, 28-31
  options, 45. *See also* options
  order placement, 41-43
  overview of, 21
common gaps, 152
consolidation, 146
  breakouts from, 137, 140-144, 238
consumer tastes, meats, 98
consumption, oil, 82
contango, 167
continuation patterns, 146
continuing education, 107, 109
contracts
  futures
    basis gains/losses, 39
    basis risk, 36-37
    brokers/commissions, 34
    delivery months, 31-33
    hedgers/speculators, 34-36, 40
    long hedges, 38-39
    margins, 28-31
    order placement, 41-43
    price determinants, 40
    selling short, 27
    short hedges, 37-38
  markets, 22-26
  OI analysis, 156-159
contrary opinion theory, 109
copper, 31, 104
  selling short, 27
  trades, 24
corn, 21, 84. *See also* grains
  margins, 30
  prices, 98
  size of futures contracts, 23
Corzine, John, 17
costs
  feeder, 98
  of options, 46
cotton, 99
covered option writing, 64
covering, 27
crashes, 11, 123-124
crop yields, 102
crossovers, moving averages, 195
crushers, 85
Cuba, softs, 100
currencies, financial futures, 78-80
cycles, Elliot wave analysis, 163-164

D

daily price limits, 25
Daily Slaughter Levels report, 99
danger points, 8
dates, prompt, 31
decay, time, 50
deliverable stocks of grain, 86
delivery
  futures, 22, 31-33
  selling short, 27
demand, commodities, 124-126. *See also* supply and demand
determinants, prices, 40

development
  of methodologies, 15
  of trader's sense, 8
disadvantages
  options, 47
  selling, 49
discipline, 7, 12
  trading success, 233
diversification, 237
  pivot indicators, 216-217
double tops/bottoms patterns, 144
doubt, 237
down trends, 197. *See also* trends
Dystant, Ralph, 162

E

economic activity, metals, 106
education, continuing, 107-109
effectiveness of technical analysis, 128
electronic trading, 117-118
  effect of, 118
  volatility, 119-125
Elliot, Ralph, 163
Elliot wave analysis, 163-164
EMA (exponential moving average), 200-202
emotions, 220, 236
  trading success, 232
ending carryover stocks, 86
energies, 78, 80-83
Enron, 118
errors, futures, 24
European Central Bank, technical analysis, 128
exchanges
  energies, 83
  futures, contracts/markets, 22-26
exercising options, 55-57
exhaustion gaps, 154
exotic orders, 43
expiration of contracts, selling short, 27
exponential moving average. *See* EMA
Export Inspections, 86
Export Sales, 86
exports
  grains, 86
  meats, 98

F

Fannie Mae, 126
feed prices, 98
feeder cattle, 96. *See also* meats
feeder costs, 98
financial futures, 78-80
flag patterns, 146
flows, money, 125
fluctuations, 24
Fooled by Randomness, 11
forecasting tools, spreads, 167-170
foreign currencies, financial futures, 80
formulas, stochastics, 162
France, metals, 102
full-sized futures contracts, 22
fundamental analysis, 76-77, 128
  charts, 129
    breakouts from consolidation, 137, 140-144
    patterns, 144-149, 154-155
    resistance/support levels, 136-137
    trend channels, 134-135
    trendlines, 130, 134
    volume, 156
  trends, 129
futures, 21
  basis gains/losses, 39
  basis risk, 36-37
  brokers/commissions, 34
  contracts, 22-26
    delivery months, 31-33
    margins, 28-31
  delivery months, 31-33
  financial futures, 78-80
  groups
    agriculturals, 83-102
    energies, 80-83
    metals, 102-107
  hedgers/speculators, 34-36, 40
  leverage, 28-31
  long hedges, 38-39
  markets, 22-26
  order placement, 41-43
  price determinants, 40
  selling short, 26-28
  short, selling, 26-28
  short hedges, 37-38

G

gains, basis, 39
Gann, W. D., 7-8, 122, 233, 240
gaps, 152-155
gasoline, 82. *See also* oil
General Motors, 126
generating
  buy signals, 206
  sell signals, 208-209
Germany, metals, 102
goals, 8
gold, 23. *See also* metals
  California Gold Rush, 123
Governments
  bailouts, 126
  policies, grains, 86

grades, future contracts, 23
grains, intermarket spreads, 111. *See also* agriculturals
Great Britain, metals, 102
Great Depression, 123
groups
  agricultural futures, 83-102
  energy futures, 80-83
  financial futures, 78-80
  metal futures, 102-107

H

H&S (head and shoulders) patterns, 170, 175
health, 9, 236
hedging
  futures, 34-36, 40
  long hedges, 38-39
  options, 59-61, 74
  short hedges, 37-38
hesitation
  avoiding, 222
  trading success, 232
history, resistance/support levels, 136
hogs, 97. *See also* meats
Hogs and Pigs Report, 99
humility, 222

I

ICE (InterContinental Exchange), 100
ICO (International Cocoa Organization), 101
IMF (International Monetary Fund), 102
imports, grains, 85
in-the-money
  avoiding, 71
  options, 51
indexes
  RSI, 124, 159-160, 239
  stocks, options, 61
India
  grains, 84
  metals, 102-104
  oil, 82
  softs, 100
indicators, 12
  analysis, 159. *See also* analysis
  charts, 129
    breakouts from consolidation, 137, 140-144
    H&S patterns, 170, 175
    Japanese candlestick, 166
    P&F, 165
    patterns, 144-149, 154-155
    resistance/support levels, 136-137
    trend channels, 134-135
    trendlines, 130, 134
    volume, 156
  moving averages
    alternatives to SMAs, 199
    EMA, 200-202
    length of time, 199
    overview of, 193, 195
    SMA, 197
    WMA, 200-202
  pivot, 205, 210-215
    buy signals, 206
    diversification, 216-217
    sell signals, 208-209
  RSI, 159. *See also* RSI
  SIN, 235
  SNI, 177-186
  stochastics, 162
inflation, metals, 104-106
initial margins, 29-31
insurance, options, 45. *See also* options
InterContinental Exchange. *See* ICE
interest rates, financial futures, 78-80
intermarket spreads, 111-112, 114
International Cocoa Organization. *See* ICO
International Coffee Organization, 102
International Monetary Fund. *See* IMF
intramarket spreads, 110-111
intrinsic value, options, 51
intuition, trading success, 231
inventory
  long hedges, 38-39
  short hedges, 37-38
Iraq, oil, 82
Italy, metals, 102

J–K–L

Japan
  candlestick charts, 166
  metals, 102
  oil, 82
  softs, 100

knowledge, 8-9
Kuwait, oil, 82

Lane, George, 162
lead, 31, 104-105
Lehman Brothers, 126
length of time, moving averages, 199
leverage, 28-31
limits
  moves, 239
  orders, 41
  variable, 26

liquidation, 97
  delivery months, 33
  margin calls, 29
Livermore, Jesse, 8, 187, 226
LME (London Metal Exchange), 31
  overview of, 104
  stocks, 106
long hedges, futures, 38-39
long positions, OI analysis, 156-159
losses, 7, 18-19
  acceptance of risk, 12
  averaging, 240
  basis, 39
  management, 14
  margins, 29

M

Mackay, Charles, 122
macro trends, 124
Madoff, Bernie, 17
maintenance margins, 29
management
  losses, 14
  money, 12, 221
  trading success, 232
manias, 123-124
margins, 28-31
  initial, 29
  long hedges, 38-39
  maintenance, 29
  profits
  requirements, 26
market-if-touched (MIT) orders, 43
markets
  analysis. *See* analysis
  crashes, 123-124
  fundamental analysis, 76-77
  futures
    agriculturals, 83-102
    energies, 80-83
    financial futures, 78-80
    groups, 78
    metals, 102-107
  orders, 41
  performance
    aggression, 232
    averaging losses, 240
    breakouts, 238
    discipline, 233
    diversification, 237
    doubt, 237
    emotions, 236
    good health, 236
    intuition, 231
    limit moves, 239
    money management, 232
    overtrading, 236
    patience, 233
    plans, 231-232
    prices, 230
    profits, 237
    pyramiding, 237-238
    quotes, 233
    reaction to news, 235
    regrets, 232
    RSI, 239
    skepticism, 234
    specialization, 232
    time, 234
    trends, 229-230
  patterns, 7
  predictions, 11
  technical analysis, 76-77
  weather, 87
measuring gaps, 153
meats, 96-98. *See also* agriculturals
Memoirs of Extraordinary Popular Delusions and the Madness of Crowds, 122
Merrill Lynch, 33
metals, 78, 102-107
methodologies, 12
  development of, 15
  futures contracts, 22
  natural numbers, 203
  updating, 122
MF Global, 17
million British thermal units. *See* MMBtu
mini futures contracts, 23
minimum fluctuations, 24
minimum moves, 24
mining strikes, 106
Minneapolis Grain Exchange, 85
MIT (market-if-touched) orders, 43
MMBtu (million British thermal units), 83
money
  flows, 125
  management, 12, 221
  trading success, 232
months, delivery (futures), 31-33
motives, determining, 219
movements, prices, 6
moves, minimum, 24
moving averages
  alternatives to SMAs, 199
  EMA, 200-202
  length of time, 199
  overview of, 193, 195
  SMA, 197
  WMA, 200-202

N

NASDAQ, financial futures, 79
natural numbers, 203
nerve, 9
Netherlands, metals, 102
New Commodity Trading Guide, The: Breakthrough Strategies for Capturing Market Profits, 117, 203-204
New Haven railroad, 118
New York Board of Trade (NYBOT), 116
news, SNI, 177-186
nickel, 31, 105
Nigeria, oil, 82
Nixon, Richard M., 102
normal time decay, 51
Northern Hard Spring Wheat, 85
notice days, 32
novice traders, losses, 18-19
NYBOT (New York Board of Trade), 116

O

oats, 84. *See also* grains
observations, 6
OCO (one cancels the other), 43
offers, 41. *See also* prices
offsets, 22
  delivery months, 31
OI (open interest) analysis, 156-159
oil, 82. *See also* energies
oilseeds, 83. *See also* agriculturals
one cancels the other. *See* OCO
OPEC (Organization of Petroleum Exporting Countries), 82
open interest. *See* OI
opinions, 109
options
  advantages/disadvantages, 47
  buying, 49
  changes in price, 55
  converting, 46
  exercising, 55-57
  hedging, 59-61
  overview of, 45-46, 49
  prices, 51-53
  quotes, 48
  ratios, 69-70
  rules, 71-74
  selling, 49, 57, 59
  stock indexes, 61
  strategies, 61-66
  strike price, 48
  styles, 48
  time, 50
  time decay, 50
  types, 47
  volatility, 54
orange juice, 21, 99
orders
  exotic, 43
  limit, 41
  placement, futures, 41-34
  market, 41
  MIT, 43
  stop, 42
oscillators
  RSI, 159. *See also* RSI
  stochastics, 162
OTC (over-the-counter) options, 48
out-of-the-money
  avoiding, 71
  options, 51
over-the-counter. *See* OTC
overtraders, 31
overtrading, 236

P

P&F (point and figure) charts, 165
palladium, 103, 105
palm oil, 84
panics, 5, 123-124
paper trades, pivot indicators, 205, 210-215
  buy signals, 206
  diversification, 216-217
  sell signals, 208-209
patience, 7-8
  trading success, 233
patterns
  charts, 144-149, 154-155
    continuation, 146
    double tops/bottoms, 144
    gaps, 152-155
    rounding tops/bottoms, 146
    triangle, 149
  markets, 7
pennant patterns, 146
performance, 220-228
  aggression, 232
  averaging losses, 240
  breakouts, 238
  discipline, 233
  diversification, 237
  doubt, 237
  emotions, 236
  good health, 236
  intuition, 231
  limit moves, 239
  money management, 232
  overtrading, 236
  patience, 233

plans, 231-232
prices, 230
profits, 237
pyramiding, 237-238
quotes, 233
reaction to news, 235
regrets, 232
RSI, 239
skepticism, 234
specialization, 232
time, 234
trends, 229-230
personal goals, 8
Peru, metals, 104
pit traders, 117, 122
pivot indicators, 205, 210-215
buying, 206
diversification, 216-217
selling, 208-209
placement of orders, futures, 41-43
plans
trading, 221
trading success, 231-232
platinum, 103-104
plunge, 31
point and figure. *See* P&F charts
Ponzi schemes, 17
pork, 21. *See also* meats
precious metals, 102. *See also* metals
predictions
markets, 11
OI analysis, 157. *See also* analysis
spreads, 167, 169-170
premiums, 51-53
changes in, 55
options, 46
volatility, 54
preserving capital, 221
prices
buffered entry, 207, 209
corn, 98
currencies, 80
daily limits, 25
determinants, 40
fluctuations, 24
futures contracts, 23
movements, 6
OI analysis, 157
options, 45, 51-53. *See also* options
changes in, 55
volatility, 54
P&F charts, 165
resistance/support levels, 136
selling short, 26-28
settlement
alternatives to SMAs, 199
SMAs, 197
strike price options, 48
trading success, 230
triggered entry, 207
production
grains, 85
metals, 106
profits, 237
margins, long hedges, 38-39
strategies, 11-15
prompt dates, 31
protein, oilseeds, 84. *See also* oilseeds
put options, 46-49
vertical put spreads, 65
pyramiding, 237-238
pivot bounce, 215

Q–R

quality of futures contracts, 23
quantities, future contracts, 22
quotes
futures contracts, 23
options, 48
trading success, 233

ratios, 69
spreads, 70
stocks-to-usage, 101
reaction to news, trading success, 235
rectangle patterns, 146
Relative Strength Index (RSI), 124
Reminiscences of a Stock Operator, 187, 226, 228
requirements
margins, 31
markets, 26
resistance, 239
levels, 136
rest, health and, 9
revenge trading, 221
reverse ratio spreads, 70
rewards, risk, 31
rice, 21
right to exercise (options), 46
risk, 7
acceptance of, 12
basis, futures, 36-37
diversification, 237
loss strategies, 14
options, 46, 49
rewards, 31
spreads, 110. *See also* spreads
Rockefeller, John D., 227
rounding tops/bottoms patterns, 146

RSI (Relative Strength Index), 124, 159-160, 239
rules, 13
  breakouts from consolidation, trading, 143-144
  daily price limits, 25
  gaps, trading, 155
  H&S patterns, trading, 175
  OI, trading, 158-159
  options, 71-74
  SMAs, 198
  SNI, trading, 177, 180
Russia
  grains, 84
  metals, 102-103
  oil, 82

S

S&P 500 Index, financial futures, 79
Saudi Arabia, oil, 82
screens
  quotes, 233
  trading, 121
seasonality, 87, 97
selling
  algorithms, 117-118
    effect of, 118
    volatility, 119-125
  chart analysis, 129
    breakouts from consolidation, 137, 140-144
    patterns, 144-149, 154-155
    resistance/support levels, 136-137
    trend channels, 134-135
    trendlines, 130, 134
    volume, 156
  Elliot wave analysis, 163-164
  futures contracts, 22
  H&S patterns, 170, 175
  intermarket spreads, 111-114
  intramarket spreads, 110-111
  Japanese candlestick charts, 166
  OI analysis, 156-159
  options, 49, 57, 59
    advantages/disadvantages, 47-49
    changes in prices, 55
    converting, 46
    exercising, 55-57
    hedging, 59-61
    overview of, 45-46, 49
    prices, 51-53
    quotes, 48
    ratios, 69-70
    rules, 71-74
    stock indexes, 61
    strategies, 61-66
    strike price, 48
    styles, 48
    time, 50
    time decay, 50
    types, 47
    volatility, 54
  P&F charts, 165
  pivot indicators, 208-209
  RSI, 159-160
  short, 26-28
  stochastics, 162
  technical analysis, effectiveness of, 128
  trends, 129
sessions, variable limits, 26
settlement prices
  alternatives to SMAs, 199
  SMAs, 197
settlements, cash, 33
setup bars, 206, 208
SF (smoothing factor), 200
short, selling, 26-28
  delivery months, 33
short hedges, futures, 37-38
short positions, 5-6
  OI analysis, 156-159
signals
  buy, 206
  sell, 208-209
significant news indicator. *See* SNI
silver, 23. *See also* metals
simple moving average. *See* SMA
SIN, 235
size of futures contracts, 23
skepticism, trading success, 234
skills, 7
  health and rest, 9
  knowledge, 8-9
  motives, determining, 219
  nerve, 9
  patience, 8
  success
    aggression, 232
    averaging losses, 240
    breakouts, 238
    discipline, 233
    diversification, 237
    doubt, 237
    emotions, 236
    good health, 236
    intuition, 231
    limit moves, 239
    money management, 232
    overtrading, 236
    patience, 233

plans, 231-232
prices, 230
profits, 237
pyramiding, 237-238
quotes, 233
reaction to news, 235
regrets, 232
RSI, 239
skepticism, 234
specialization, 232
time, 234
trends, 229-230
slippage, 32
SMA (simple moving average), 197
alternatives to, 199
buy signals, 206
sell signals, 208-209
smoothing factor (SF), 200
SNI (significant news indicator), 177-186
Soft Red Wheat, 84
softs, 99. *See also* agriculturals
Soros, George, 80, 125
South Africa, metals, 103
soybeans, 21. *See also* agriculturals
specialization, trading success, 232
specifications, futures contracts, 36-37
speculators, futures, 34-36, 40
speed
acceleration, 121
methodologies, updating, 122
spreads, 110
as forecasting tools, 167-170
calendar, 66
intermarket, 111-112, 114
intramarket, 110-111
options, 65
ratios, 70
vertical
calls, 65
puts, 65
Spring Wheat contracts, 85
statistics, fundamental, 76
stochastics, 162
stocks
beginning, 85
ending carryover, 86
indexes
financial futures, 78-80
options, 61
LME, 106
stocks-to-usage ratios, 101
stop orders, 42
straddles, 73. *See also* spreads
buying, 66-67
selling, 67
strangles, 73
buying, 68
selling, 68
strategies, 7
futures, 21
basis gains/losses, 39
basis risk, 36-37
brokers/commissions, 34
delivery months, 31-33
hedgers/speculators, 34-36, 40
leverage, 28-31
long hedges, 38-39
markets, 22-26
order placement, 41-43
price determinants, 40
selling short, 26-28
short hedges, 37-38
options, 61, 63-66
success, 11-15
trading
plans, 221
success, 231-232
strike prices, options, 48
strikes, mining, 106
styles of options, 48
substitution effect, 98
success
skills for
health and rest, 9
knowledge, 8-9
nerve, 9
patience, 8
strategies, 11-15
trading, 220-228
aggression, 232
averaging losses, 240
breakouts, 238
discipline, 233
diversification, 237
doubt, 237
emotions, 236
good health, 236
intuition, 231
limit moves, 239
money management, 232
overtrading, 236
patience, 233
plans, 231-232
prices, 230
profits, 237
pyramiding, 237-238
quotes, 233
reaction to news, 235
regrets, 232
RSI, 239
skepticism, 234

specialization, 232
time, 234
trends, 229-230
sugar, 21, 99-100
supply and demand
fundamental analysis, 76-77
grains, 85
resistance/supply levels, 136
support, 239
levels, 136
switches, 110. *See also* spreads
Switzerland, metals, 102

T

Taleb, Nassim, 11
technical analysis, 76-77
effectiveness of, 128
Technical Analysis of Stock Trends, 131, 170
Thailand, softs, 100
theories
contrary opinion, 109
Elliot wave analysis, 163-164
time
algorithms, effect on volatility, 120
decay, options, 50
methodologies, updating, 122
moving averages, 199
options, 50
trading success, 234
value, 51
tin, 31, 105
TOCOM (Tokyo Commodity Exchange), 103
tools
charts, 129
breakouts from consolidation, 137, 140-144
patterns, 144-149, 154-155
resistance/support levels, 136-137
trend channels, 134-135
trendlines, 130, 134
volume, 156
Elliot wave analysis, 163-164
forecasting, spreads as, 167-170
H&S patterns, 170, 175
Japanese candlestick charts, 166
moving averages
alternatives to SMAs, 199
EMA, 200-202
length of time, 199
overview of, 193-195
SMA, 197
WMA, 200-202
OI analysis, 156-159
P&F charts, 165
RSI, 159-160
stochastics, 162
technical analysis, effectiveness of, 128
trends, 129
total demand, grains, 86
total supply, grains, 85
trader's sense, 8
traders, losses, 18-19
trading
algorithms, 117-118
effect of, 118
volatility, 119-125
chart analysis, 129
breakouts from consolidation, 137, 140-144
patterns, 144-149, 154-155
resistance/support levels, 136-137
trend channels, 134-135
trendlines, 130, 134
volume, 156
copper, 24
currencies, 80
Elliot wave analysis, 163-164
fundamental analysis, 76-77
futures, 21
basis gains/losses, 39
basis risk, 36-37
brokers/commissions, 34
delivery months, 31-33
hedgers/speculators, 34-36, 40
leverage, 28-31
long hedges, 38-39
markets, 22-26
order placement, 41-43
price determinants, 40
selling short, 26-28
short hedges, 37-38
H&S patterns, 170, 175
Japanese candlestick charts, 166
losses, 7
OI analysis, 156-159
options, 49, 71-74
P&F charts, 165
pivot indicators, 205-215
buy signals, 206
diversification, 216-217
sell signals, 208-209
plans, 221
revenge, 221
RSI, 159-160
stochastics, 162
success, 220-228
aggression, 232
averaging losses, 240
breakouts, 238
discipline, 233
diversification, 237

doubt, 237
emotions, 236
good health, 236
intuition, 231
limit moves, 239
money management, 232
overtrading, 236
patience, 233
plans, 231-232
prices, 230
profits, 237
pyramiding, 237-238
quotes, 233
reaction to news, 235
regrets, 232
RSI, 239
skepticism, 234
specialization, 232
time, 234
trends, 229-230
technical analysis, 76-77, 128
trends, 129
variable limits, 26
trading discipline, 12
trailing stops, 42
treasury bonds, futures, 79
trendlines, 130, 134
trends, 118, 129
channels, 134-135
Elliot wave analysis, 163-164
followers, 193
macro, 124
moving averages, 195
OI analysis, 157
trading success, 229-230
triangle patterns, 149
triggered entry prices, 207, 209
triple witching hour, 46
troy ounces, 23
trust, 117
types
of margins, 29
of options, 47
of spreads, 110

U–V

U.S. Bank, 17
Ukraine, grains, 84
United States
grains, 84
meats, 96
metals, 102
oil, 82
oilseeds, 83
softs, 100
units, futures contracts, 23
updating methodologies, 122

values
fluctuations, 24
long hedges, 38-39
short hedges, 37-38
technical analysis, 128
time, 51
variable limits, 26
vegetable oil, 84
vertical call spreads, 65
vertical put spreads, 65
Voice from the Tomb, 88-92
volatility
algorithms, 119-125
options, 54
risk rewards, 31
volume, 156

W–X–Y–Z

wars, effect on metals markets, 106
Wasendorf, Russell, Sr., 17
weather
grains, 86
meats, 98
weighted moving average. *See* WMA
wheat, 21. *See also* grains
whipsaws, 202
White Wheat, 85
Wilder, Welles, 159
WMA (weighted moving average), 200-202
writing, options, 57-59
covered option writing, 64
rations, 69
WTI (West Texas Intermediate) Crude Oil contract, 81

yields, crops, 102

zinc, 31, 104-105